Digital Insurance

Also by Bernardo Nicoletti

MOBILE BANKING

LEAN PROCUREMENT

CLOUD COMPUTING AND FINANCIAL SERVICES

THE METHODOLOGY OF LEAN AND DIGITIZE

SERVIZI AZIENDALI PRE E POST VENDITA

LA METODOLOGIA DEL LEAN & DIGITIZE

GLI STRUMENTI DEL LEAN & DIGITIZE

ASSISTENZA TECNICA E QUALITÀ TOTALE: Come migliorare la soddisfazione dei clienti e la redditività delle imprese di assistenza tecnica

MANAGEMENT PER L'EDILIZIA

LA GESTIONE DELLA QUALITÀ

I CIRCOLI DI QUALITÀ

CASI DI ORGANIZZAZIONE E MANAGEMENT (*with Franco Fontana and Marco Lacchini*)

STRATEGIA AZIENDALE E SVILUPPO TECNOLOGICO (*with Giorgio Eminente*)

L'IMPRESA MONDIALE: NUOVE STRATEGIE DI PRODUZIONE (*with Michael J. Baker, Kristian Moller and Stephen T. Parkinson*)

Digital Insurance

Business Innovation in the Post-Crisis Era

Bernardo Nicoletti
Università degli Studi di Roma Tor Vergata, Rome, Italy

palgrave
macmillan

First published 2016 by
PALGRAVE MACMILLAN

Palgrave Macmillan in the UK is an imprint of Macmillan Publishers Limited, registered in England, company number 785998, of Houndmills, Basingstoke, Hampshire RG21 6XS.

Palgrave Macmillan in the US is a division of St Martin's Press LLC, 175 Fifth Avenue, New York, NY 10010.

Palgrave Macmillan is the global academic imprint of the above companies and has companies and representatives throughout the world.

Palgrave® and Macmillan® are registered trademarks in the United States, the United Kingdom, Europe and other countries.

ISBN: 978–1–137–55326–3

This book is printed on paper suitable for recycling and made from fully managed and sustained forest sources. Logging, pulping and manufacturing processes are expected to conform to the environmental regulations of the country of origin.

A catalogue record for this book is available from the British Library.

Library of Congress Cataloging-in-Publication Data

Nicoletti, Bernardo.
Digital insurance : business innovation in the post-crisis era / Bernardo Nicoletti.
pages cm
ISBN 978–1–137–55326–3 (hardback)
1. Financial services industry – Technological innovations. 2. Insurance. I. Title.

HG173.N53 2015
368.00285—dc23 2015029079.

To my family, for all the time I stole to write books

Contents

List of Figures

List of Tables

List of Abbreviations

ABI	Associazione Bancaria Italiana
ACH	automated clearing house
AML	anti money laundering
AOF	ancillary own fund
API	application programming interface
APM	application performance management
Apps	applications (normally on smartphones)
ATM	automated teller machine
B2B	business to business
B2C	business to consumer
BI	business intelligence
BOF	basic own funds
BPaaS	business process as a service
BPM	business process management
BPO	business process outsourcing (also business process optimization)
BPR	business process re-engineering
BYOD	bring your own device
C2B	customer to business
CA	controlling authority
CapEx	capital expense
CAPTCHA	completely automated public turing test to tell computers and humans apart
CAS	claims administration system
CDR	call detail record
CEIOPS	Committee of European Insurance and Occupational Pensions Supervisors
CEO	chief executive officer
CFO	chief financial officer
CI	credential issuer
CIO	chief information officer
CLID	caller line identification
COR	cost of revenue
CRC	customer relationship center
CRM	customer relationship management (sometimes credit risk management)

CSA	cloud security alliance
CSF	critical success factors
CSR	customer service representative
CTI	computer telephony integration/interface
CTQ	critical to quality
DDD	data driven decision
DDoS	distributed denial of service
DLP	data loss protection
DM	direct mail
DMTF	distributed management task force
DW	data warehouse
EA	enterprise architecture
EBS	economic balance sheet
ECM	enterprise content management
ECMS	enterprise content management systems
EDI	electronic data interchange
EEA	European Economic Area
EIM	enterprise information management
EIOPA	European Insurance and Occupational Pensions Authority
EN 9000	European Norms for ISO 9000
ERP	enterprise resource planning
ETSI	European Telecommunications Standards Institute
EU	European Union
FAQ	frequently asked questions
FASB	Financial Accounting Standards Board
FI	financial institutions
GRC	governance, risk, compliance
GSM	general global system for mobile communication
HMO	health management organization
HP	Hewlett Packard
HPC	high performance computing
HTTP	hypertext transfer protocol
IaaS	infrastructure as a service
ICAAP	internal capital adequacy assessment process
ICP	integrated command platforms or Internet content provider
ICT	information and communications technology
ID	identification data
IECR	internal economic capital requirement
IFRS	international financial reporting standard
IM	instant messaging
IP	Internet protocol

IPR	intellectual property rights
IRM	information rights management
ITIL	information technology infrastructure library
ITSS	information technology services standard
ITU	International Telecommunication Union
IVR	interactive voice response
IxD	interaction design
KPI	key performance indicator
KYC	know your customer
LAN	local area network
M&A	mergers and acquisitions
MBPP	mobile bill presentment and payment
MCR	minimum capital requirement
MDM	master data management
MIB	man in the browser
MII	major industry identifier
MIM	man in the middle
MMS	multimedia messaging service
MNO	mobile network operator
MPOS	mobile point of sale
MPP	mobile proximity payment
MRP	mobile remote payment
NAIC	National Association of Insurance Commissioners
NCA	national competent authority
NGO	non governmental organization
NIST	National Institute of Standards and Technology
NLP	natural language processing
OCR	optical character recognition
OEM	original equipment manufacturer
OpEx	operating expense
ORSA	own risk and solvency assessment
OTP	one time password
OTT	over the top
P&C	property and casualty
PaaS	platform as a service
PAS	policy administration system
PAT	production acceptance testing
PC	personal computer
PCI DSS	payment card industry data security standard
PDA	personal digital assistant
PDCA	plan do check act

PFM	personal finance management
POS	point of sale
PPC	pay per click
PPIP	prudent person investment principles
PPO	preferred provider organization
PSE (EU)	payment services directive
PSP	payment service provider
QIS	quantitative impact studies
QoS	quality of service
QR	quick response
R&D	research and development
RBC	risk based capital
RDC	remote deposit capture or remote desktop customer
RFC	request for change
RFID	radio frequency identification
RM	relationship manager
ROE	return on equity
ROI	return on the investment
RPO	recovery point objective
RTO	recovery time objective
RTS	report to supervisors
S&T	science and technology
S2S	service to sale
SaaS	software as a service
SCR	solvency capital requirement
SDM	secure domain manager
SEI	strategic emerging industry
SEO	search engine optimization
SFCR	solvency and financial condition report
SIM	subscriber identity module
SLA	service level agreement
SME	small and medium enterprises or subject matter experts
SMI	solvency modernization initiative
SMS	short message service
SOA	service oriented architecture
SOX	Sarbanes-Oxley Act
SRP	supervisory review process
SSN	social security number
STP	straight through processing
TAM	technology acceptance model
TCMS	transactional content management system

TCO	total cost of ownership
Telco	telecommunication organization
TLS	transport layer security
TSM	trusted service manager
UCM	unified content management
UN	United Nations Organization
UPC	universal product code
UT	usability testing
UX	user experience
VIP	very important person
VM	virtual machine
VoC	voice of the customer
VoIP	voice over Internet protocol
VSC	virtual support center
WAP	wireless application protocol
WEP	wireless encryption protocol
XML	extensible markup language

Introduction

The world has been in a financial crisis for a long time. It started in 2008, but it is still unclear when it will be completely over. In this situation, financial institutions need to

- improve their financial ratios in a drastic way;
- take strong actions to improve their positions in the markets; and
- become better at coping with the market dynamics and changing socioeconomic factors.

This means they must increase their revenues and reduce their costs.

This book provides arguments in support of the following thesis: insurance companies must become more agile and flexible in the conduct of their business in order to increase revenues and decrease costs. This means that insurance companies need to become more agile, leaner, and more automated. The adoption of new paradigms, new processes, and technological components can lead to the achievement of more revenues, cost efficiency and control, an increased pace of innovation, and especially business agility. Better methods and more effective solutions can help, if used in the right way. An important opportunity in this direction is to move toward digital insurance. Digital insurance means that an insurance company uses all available solutions to make the processes and services of the company lean, to automate them, and to deploy excellent functions for selling/buying products and delivering services in a multichannel approach.

Digital insurance is one of the most interesting trends today, not only in the customer domain but also in business organizations. It can have a heavy impact, from a personal, social, and business point of view. Insurance companies have traditionally been cautious in innovating. Yet the world is changing. A McKinsey report underlines that financial institutions are increasingly aware of the need for innovation in products, processes, organizations, and business models.[1]

Insurance companies should consider digital insurance not with a passive attitude but with a proactive posture. Digital insurance has the ability to transform the business of insurance companies and their relationships with their customers.

Insurance is experiencing the entry of other organizations into the market. As matter of fact, there are potentially several new entrants (such as Google[2]), but also other services organizations, such as banks, telecommunication organizations, merchants, and others are potentially interested in entering this market.

This means that the market available to be defended or conquered is open for the time being. The initial entrants will own it, as online banking has demonstrated, unless the incumbents act promptly.

Insurance companies should innovate fast

One of the industries that needs to push fast in innovation is insurance. Banks are continuing to change.[3] Insurance companies need to catch up after a long period in which their innovation has been rather limited. With innovation, insurance companies can aim to

- grow market share through the execution of a strategic approach;
- gain competitive advantages by improving and consolidating processes; and
- create an integrated approach to deliver higher-quality service, more reliable information, and lower costs.

Insurance companies can innovate in several ways, but in all the sectors:

- products
- processes
- organizations
- business models

In terms of products, the more extensive use of information and communication technologies makes possible new types of services. For example, even if still limited, reinsurance is growing in importance, thanks to the possibility of communicating easily with people all over the world.

In terms of processes, insurance companies are more and more active in using new channels, like call centers, the Web, social networks, and mobile devices. These channels can bring substantial reduction in costs and hence potentially on the prices of products. However, at the same time these channels make it possible for the customer to switch insurance companies more easily and especially to compare prices and conditions, either with a personal search or through the so-called comparators. Information and communication technologies (ICT) are becoming more and more important, similar to what has happened for the banks.[4] As a consequence, processes are being automated at an increasing speed. The increasing use of digital channels also makes it easier to sell in distant markets. Compliance and regulations are becoming more and more relevant. Of course, this requires greater expertise in risk and compliance management.

In terms of organizations, insurance companies are reducing their sales and services through their agencies in favor of more direct digital connections with the customers. At the same time, they are finding it more and more important to be active in marketing, also through digital media.

In terms of business models, the most dramatic change has been in no longer selling insurance only through the traditional channels of agencies and brokers. Insurance companies are increasingly selling in two different ways:

- Selling can be direct to the customers, through digital channels. This takes place initially for more standard products, like motor insurance. It is now spreading more and more to other property and casualty (P&C), life, and health products.
- Selling can also be conducted through banks, in what is called bancassurance, and other merchants, such as travel and transportation companies. These channels have been available for many years, but they are now expanding, especially for life and travel insurance.

These innovations could have drastic changes in the medium to long term.

Insurance companies need to be leaner. Consequently, the application of lean thinking is spreading. Lean processes should rely on digitization. The best approach is the one of Lean and Digitize.[5]

Digital tends to permeate all the sectors in the new models of insurance companies. It is becoming essential in marketing and is important in operations. It is also becoming more and more important in risk management. Big data analysis can help in a substantial way.

Competition is increasing, thanks to digitization, which makes easier to sell in distant markets and through comparison of prices and conditions especially for some standard products, like motor insurance. The result is that there is a strong pressure on cost reduction. ICT expenses and investments are growing, and as a result finance scrutinizes closely any expense or investment. Procurement can help. Digital insurance pushes the use of new technologies, such as cloud computing.[6]

This book analyzes digital insurance. It begins by reviewing the transformation of financial institutions. Then, it moves to an in-depth discussion of the opportunities available, thanks to new solutions. The book deals with the management of digital insurance and its risks, but also the remediation and especially the management of the change. It concludes with a glimpse into the future.

The book deals with all the aspects of the management, the functions, the processes, the solutions, and the structural points of view of digital insurance.

Digital insurance is a disruptive and systemic innovation. Such an innovation helps create new opportunities.[7] It eventually goes on to disrupt existing markets and value networks (over a few years or decades) by displacing earlier models. A disruptive innovation improves a product or a service in ways that the market does not expect, typically, first, by a design aimed at a different set of customers in a new market and, later, by lowering prices in the existing markets and changing the business world and possibly also social models. When cars were first introduced, for example, they were like a carriage with an engine instead of horses. In time, cars have proved to be a quite different product. The design and specification changes over time have increasingly multiplied. The result of that innovation was not only to replace the horses but also to arrive at a different organization of economics, the city, and society. The consequences of this innovation were "destructive" of the previous models.

Digital insurance is also a systemic innovation.[8] It is a set of interconnected innovations, in which each is dependent on the other, with innovation both in the components of the system and in the ways that they interact. To clarify the systemic nature of digital insurance, it is sufficient to examine the strict connections between mobile, cloud computing, big data analytics, and so on.

With digital insurance, something analogous is also occurring with regard to financial services. Take, for example, policy comparators. They are not just a replacement for the agency with a personal computer or a smartphone or similar devices for selecting and subscribing to a policy. They are substantially different. Through this solution, it is possible to communicate promotions, launch marketing messages, specify the value of the expenditure incurred up to that time, and so on.

At the same time, digital insurance tends to blur the distinction between insurance companies, telecommunication organizations, merchants, and especially intermediaries. New business models will emerge causing deep changes in the insurance companies or even in the concept of insurance. For instance, the insurance market is becoming open to new types of organizations and entering new markets, as is increasing possible, for instance, in the Euro zone.

This book describes how digital insurance can help transform insurance companies in terms of new products, new processes, new organizations, and new business models. This book moves from a vision of the future insurance company to a possible strategy to implement it. Practitioners should select tactical ways to progress in such strategies. An excellent approach to moving in this direction is Lean and Digitize which allows users to improve processes and at the same time automate them.[9,10]

1
Innovation in Insurance

Introduction

The focus of this chapter is on innovation in the digital insurance context.

This chapter starts by discussing innovation and innovation modes in general. The following sections apply the general concept of innovation to the specific case of insurance companies. We call such transformation digital insurance. Digital insurance refers to the provision and operations of insurance and connected financial services with the help of digital solutions. The scope of the services may include transactions to make insurance or personal investments, administer policies, and access customized information.

The main challenge standing in the way of innovation in the financial services industry, in general and in insurance companies in particular, is the conservative nature of many such institutions. The less they change, the better, their executives feel. Consequently, mainly outsiders have introduced innovations:

- A small financial institution in the Netherlands pushed for online banking. It became a global leader in internet banking: ING Direct.
- An outdated post office launched a prepaid card in Italy and became a leader in that market with almost 12 million cards: Poste Italiane.
- A telecom operator launched a person-to-person (P2P) money-transfer service using mobile phones. It became a market leader in Kenya: Safaricom.

Insurance companies for several reasons, including Solvency II regulation, will need additional equity. These requirements imply substantial cuts in operating costs to free needed funds.

It is time for insurance companies to take the lead in innovation and make their processes leaner and digitized. It is possible to do this profitably in almost all the financial sectors, including in insurance companies. Most of insurance companies have been static for a long time. It is now time to change under the push of four disruptive factors: urbanization, technology, demographics, and globalization.[1] The requirements are clear:

- There is a need for new product innovation. Since insurance companies essentially manage information, this should be relatively easy and not very expensive.
- There is a need for agility, for instance, in inquiries and especially in processing the claims from the customers. Speed is the name of the game. If a customer needs a policy or should make a claim, he/she would like to submit and get them immediately. Risks should be managed, but with the right balance between customer satisfaction and loss avoidance.
- There is a need for continuous and secure operations. This should be pursued by moving to a multichannel strategy based on lean agencies, online insurance, or entirely digital insurance. Security is at a premium. It should not delay the speed of the operations. Digitization can help quite a bit. In this case, a middle office can provide support in taking the burden off the front office.
- There is a need to slim the back office. This should be reduced and possibly outsourced or offshored.

Innovation

Definitions

The importance of innovation for organizational success can be traced back to Joseph Schumpeter. He defined innovation in the following way:[2]

> changes of the combinations of the factors of production as cannot be effected by infinitesimal steps or variations in the margin. They consist primarily in changes in the methods of production and transportation, or in the production of a new article, or in the opening up of new markets or of new sources of material.

This definition of innovation has stood the test of time. Ideas like entrepreneurship and similar (highlighted in this chapter) have emerged in more recent times, yet the essence of innovation remains the same.

Peter Drucker, almost 50 years later, generalized what Schumpeter had written, defining innovation as[3]

> the means by which the entrepreneur either creates new wealth-producing resources or endows existing resources with enhanced potential for creating wealth.

Over time, innovation management has changed.[4] It is interesting to examine the basics and the evolution of innovation management and how it is possible to apply them to digital insurance.

Invention and innovation

Innovation is the only way to obtain competitive advantages. Lean management and information and communication technologies (ICT) can provide a powerful impetus to innovate by supporting the business strategy with solutions for improving processes and digitizing applications.

Not innovating can be dangerous, since there is the maxim "evolve or die" synthesized in the sentence attributed to Charles Darwin:[5]

> It is not the strongest of the species nor the most intelligent who will survive but those who can best manage change.

"The Dinosaurs" were strong, but they have disappeared. In contrast, the human species thanks to their adaptability, have survived and expanded. This statement is true for animal species as well as for organizations. They need to innovate. Organizations need to strive to add value to their customers and to the organizations themselves, eliminate waste, and drive competitive advantages.

Before proceeding, it seems important to define some words. In the *Oxford English Dictionary*, invention is defined as the means for creating or devising something new. Invention is also regarded as devising new ways of attaining given ends.

An invention must satisfy the following conditions:

- It results in something new.
- It involves some inventive (new) step.
- It is useful.

Innovation is different. The *Oxford English Dictionary* defines innovation as the means for introducing something new. Innovation can be said to be the introduction of a new product or service, process, organization, or business model into the marketplace.

The National Innovation Initiative (NII) of the United States defines innovation as the intersection of invention and insight, leading to the creation of social and economic value.[6]

Innovation is important. Frank Gens, VP and IT adviser at IDC states that[7]

> The industry's drastic and disruptive shift to its 3rd Platform for innovation and growth (built on cloud, mobile, social, and big data solutions) will accelerate: Spending on these technologies and solutions – growing at 13 percent – will account for one-third of all industry revenue and 100 percent of growth.

The main differences between invention and innovation are synthesized in Table 1.1.

Innovation models

Innovation should be approached in a holistic way. To meet this challenge, it is possible to refer to the combination of the Chandler model

Table 1.1 Differences between innovation and invention

Invention	Innovation
Transforms money into ideas	Transforms ideas into money
The creation of a new product, service, or process	The introduction of a new product, service, or process, or organization, or business model
May not be commercialized	Results in commercialization
Inventions can be either autonomous or induced	Innovation is usually induced
Invention may be for non-economic or economic motives	Innovation is usually for economic motives
Normally performed in a research and development (R&D) center	Activities and applications spread across the organization
Normally does not bring changes in the organization	Normally brings organization changes either directly or indirectly
Precedes innovation	Can follow invention
Invention = Innovation – commercial exploitation	Innovation = Invention + commercial exploitation

of connecting strategy and structure,[8] and the Leavitt diamond model,[9] by considering four connected variables:

- structure (organization)
- processes
- technology
- persons

An example of this approach, applied to digital strategy, is shown in Figure 1.1.

Innovation and financial services

The current economic crisis is still affecting Europe. There is a need to come out of this situation as soon as possible, particularly in order to increase the employment of the younger generations. The most effective way to this is through innovation. It is important to analyze in more depth how it is possible to innovate.

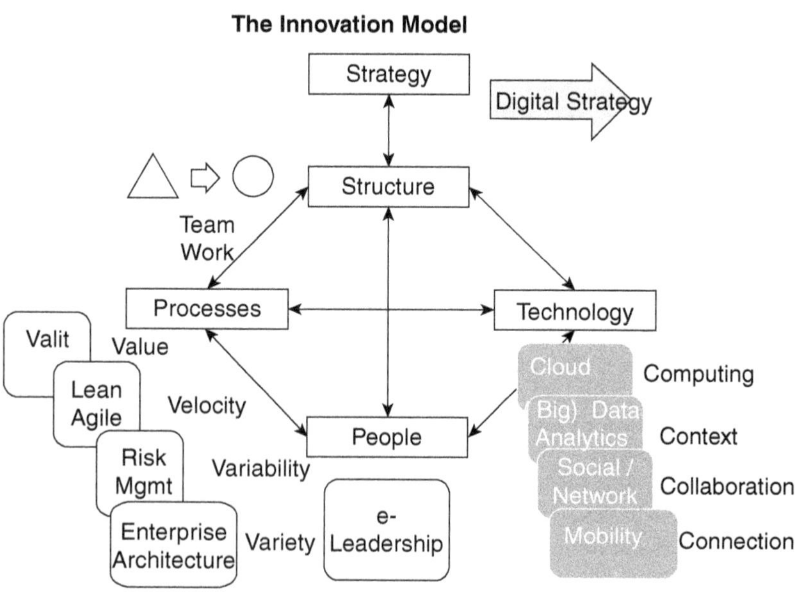

Figure 1.1 A model for an integrated innovation strategy

Classifications of innovation

Innovations can be of several types:

- open and closed
- incremental and radical
    - incremental – sustaining
    - evolutionary
    - radical, altering, disruptive (see Figure 1.2)
- modular and architectural
- generic and epochal
- technovation/technological
- spontaneous/autonomous and induced
- individual, systematic, systemic, semantic

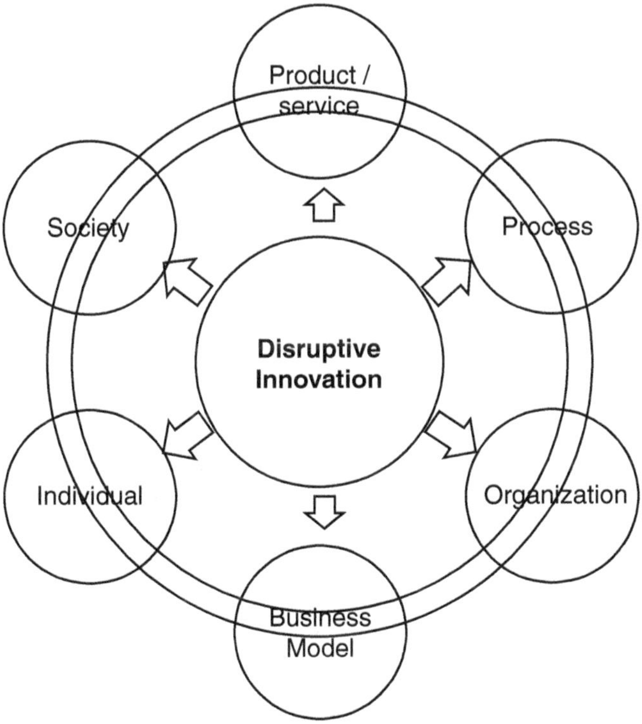

Figure 1.2 The impact of disruptive innovation

These types can be combined in different ways (see, for instance, Figure 1.3).

The components of innovation can be:

- a hardware component, consisting of material or physical aspects of the innovation
- a software component, consisting of an information and decision base that is needed to use the innovation
- an evaluation component that is useful for assessing the decisions related to the adoption of the innovation

Innovation levels

The innovation process needs support at three levels (see Figure 1.4):

- At the macro level, that is, at the national level, innovation directly depends upon the national government's policies and support.

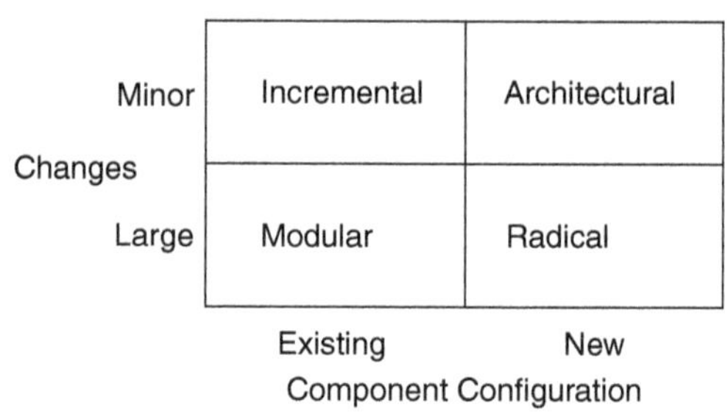

Figure 1.3 Classification of innovations

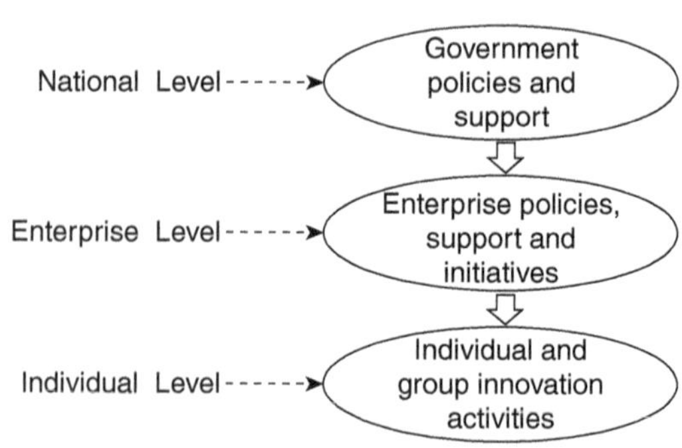

Figure 1.4 Levels of support for innovation

- At the enterprise level, innovation depends upon top management's support and commitment.
- At the bottom level, that is, the individual level, organizations should create multifunctional teams and encourage individuals involved in the innovation process.

Types of innovation from the point of view of the motivation ("why")

From the point of view of the motivation, there are three types of innovation:

- customer-driven
- technology-driven
- design-driven

In customer-driven innovation, the change is born out of the specific needs or requirements of the customers. It can help resolve some urgent needs for which customers require solutions.

In the second case, innovation is driven by technology. The initial push to make changes is driven by the existence of new technologies.

The third case is more complex. Design-driven innovation is obtained through the introduction of products and services that have a radical new meaning.[10] They might provide a completely new reason for customers to buy the products. The typical example is the iPhone. Customers did not ask for it. The technology was available for a long time and used in different ways. Steve Jobs launched an entirely different product that created a completely new and huge market.

There are not many examples of design-driven innovation in the case of financial innovation. Most of them are connected with using big data analysis to create mass individual insurance products.

Of the three types of innovation, the customer-driven type normally requires less investment than the other two. The greatest rewards can come from design-driven innovation. There will be more and more of these innovations in the future.

Types of innovation based on the content ("What")

From a practical point of view, innovation can be in the area of:

- products (or services)
- processes
- organizations
- business models

All these types of innovation are important. There are innovations that can encompass all the points on the list. For example, Mobile Digital Insurance is:

- a product innovation, since it can be offered as a completely different service
- a process innovation, since the interaction with the customer is completely different with respect to the traditional agency holding the relationships with the customer
- an organization innovation, since it determines drastic changes in the organization of the insurance companies, for example, the need to create a middle office
- a business model innovation, since it creates the basis for alliances or partnerships between insurance companies and telecom operators or other types of merchants

Types of innovation based on the process ("How")

Linear innovation models. Another classification of innovation processes is based on "how" innovation is done. Models of this type are linear or waterfall innovation process models. Under this latter model, a product or service concept is frozen at an early stage so as to minimize risk.

In this model, the innovation process in the enterprises involves a series of sequential phases/steps arranged in such a manner that the preceding phase must be cleared before moving to the next/succeeding phase (see Figure 1.5). The project must pass through tollgates with

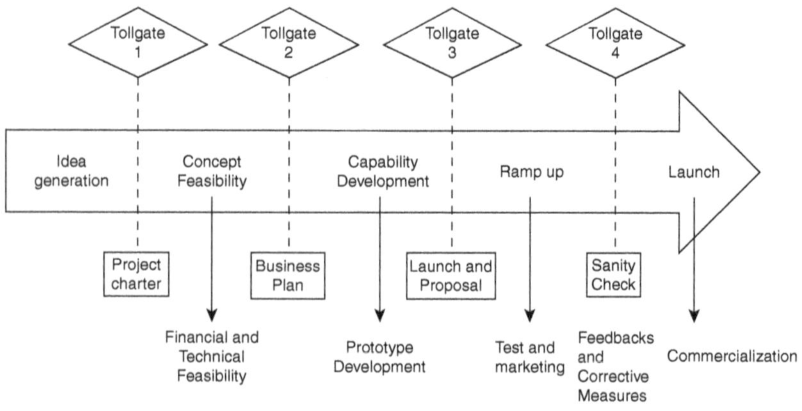

Figure 1.5 Linear innovation process

the permission of a gatekeeper, before moving to the next/succeeding phase. The criteria for passing through each toll gate and the person or committee at each toll gate (gatekeeper) are defined beforehand.

The gatekeeper examines whether the stated objectives for the preceding phase have been properly met or not, and whether the desired development has taken place at the preceding phase or not.

This model is generally followed for incremental innovation. It is linear in the sense that the innovation process is sequentially controlled and directed from the beginning toward set targets/goals. These models are also safe and suitable for a first-time beginner.

Linear models work well only when:

- the time required to innovate is shorter than the rate of change in the environment and;
- a strong emphasis is placed on quality, reliability, security, and safety requirements

Weaknesses and limitations of the linear innovation process models are:

- Low gatekeeper knowledge may lead to poor judgments, delayed evaluation, or rejection of good projects.
- It is a slow and serial process, as it is a stage-by-stage approach, and is thus time consuming.
- The concept might be frozen too early. Innovation needs/market requirements may undergo change subsequently at later stages.
- It is focused on control through toll gates, not on the customer.
- It requires a long review preparation time.
- It might have narrow criteria for evaluation, which may be rigid.
- It is more focused on attaining target/maturity, and less focused on learning.

Agile or innovation models

Cyclic or agile innovation models can be an alternative to linear models. Such models are cyclical in the sense that they are driven by the product improvement cycle. This cycle often begins with the customer's needs, which keep changing. An enterprise may be working on several new product developments simultaneously. Thus, at the same time there might be products at different points in the cycles of innovation. Readers who are interested in analyzing these models can refer to the literature.[11]

Hybrid innovation model

The best approach is normally a mix of the linear and the cyclic innovation models. An example is the Lean and Digitize innovation model. It can be described as the 7D's (Define, Discover, Design, Develop, Digitize, Deploy, and Diffusion) (see Figure 1.6).[12] It is essential to apply this method and its tools through strong partnership between the sectors of the organization involved, and the quality and support organizations (such as ICT, Finance, or Operations). Stakeholders from all parties need to align in, set up, and staff the improvement project team. Perhaps more importantly, the organization must treat the initial application of the Lean and Digitize innovation method as the beginning of an iterative cycle that generates continuous improvement and leads to a change in the culture of the organization toward Lean thinking. A "problem" or "challenge" should not trigger process improvement efforts. Rather, it should be a substantial and ongoing part of the organizational culture.

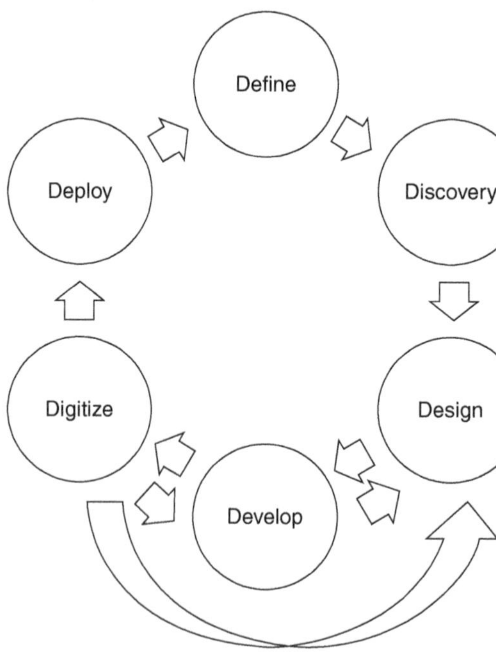

Figure 1.6 The Lean and Digitize innovation model (7 D's)

Digital insurance

Digital insurance refers to the provision and operations of insurance and connected financial services with the help of digital solutions. The scope of the services may include transactions to make insurance or personal investments, administer policies and claims, and access customized information.

This book uses the term "insurance companies," including all the different types of financial services involved in insurance activities of all types, be them retail, corporate, and so on.

The status of insurance companies

Customers, especially younger ones, are less and less satisfied with insurance companies. This point emerges, for example, from the survey "World Insurance Report 2015," which regularly investigates customer experience in the field of insurance in a number of aspects.[13] Insurance companies should constantly strive to find innovative ways to be closer to their customers, trying to respond in a robust and concrete way to their diverse needs. This commitment, however, seems to have little effect in many situations.

This negative trend embraces all insurance sectors without distinction in this area: ranging from policies for insuring motors and house roofs to health or life insurance.

The customers who are less happy are the so-called Generation Y or Millennials. This category refers to the customer segment with ages between 18 and 34 years. These digital natives operate mainly via the Web, social media, and online and mobile channels. This segment is important. This population represents a great challenge for all insurance companies in terms of the renewal of products, processes, platforms, and people. Generation Y represents a quarter to a third of the world's population. Moreover, it represents an important part of the future market due to the young ages of the customers in this segment. For these reasons, this group appears to be a vital target for every insurance company.

The "World Insurance Report 2015" provides interesting insight in terms of geography. The deterioration on the level of satisfaction was observed, especially in more developed countries such as North America and the Asia Pacific regions, where Generation Y is rather large due to the higher birth rate.

In such a situation, it is essential that insurance companies move rapidly to innovate by using a digital approach. This strategy is what this book calls digital insurance.

Some insurance companies are investing in information and communication systems migration. They have also significantly upgraded web technologies and created innovation and testing centers. Insurance companies increasingly realize that to succeed with digital initiatives, they must adopt the habits and culture of digital natives. For example, they must connect to Internet comparators (which allow customers to compare offers from different companies). They should pursue lean and agile management, or host virtual meetings to foster intensive digital collaboration using social networks.

There should be no slowing in the pace of innovation. In the next few years, digital sales have the potential to account for a large percentage of new revenues in the most progressive geographies and customer segments. These innovations will certainly be drastic among insurance companies in Scandinavia, the United Kingdom, the United States, and Western Europe. Companies in these countries will have a substantial inflow revenue in most products coming from digital sales, whether online or mobile. Insurance companies in other parts of the world very likely will trail these improvements, although there might be exceptions. As has happened in the case of mobile payments, Western countries sometimes are trailing innovations such as Safaricom in Kenya. Hence, insurance companies in emerging countries will also very likely raise significant new inflow revenue through digital insurance.

Among insurance products, motor and travel insurances first and life insurance second, as well as insurance services to small and medium enterprises, are expected to see a substantial inflow of revenue coming from digital by 2020.[14]

These forecasts are different for different markets. In Southern Europe, for example, less than one-third of revenue is forecast to be from sales strongly influenced by the digital world by 2018, but in Scandinavia that figure is 62 percent. In other areas, the forecast for digitally disrupted revenue ranges from 29 percent in Eastern Europe to 42 percent in the United States and 51 percent in Western Europe.[15]

Certainly, digital sales disruption in life insurance and pensions (30%) and mortgages (20%) is forecast to emerge less rapidly due to long product maturity, customer preference for in-person advice, and the slow development of online refinancing. Although these forecasts may take longer to materialize, the digital transformation is at an inflection point. Insurance companies have just a few years to adapt. It is vital that companies appreciate the magnitude of the opportunity and the gravity of the threat. That is just the first step in formulating a winning digital strategy. Digital will touch every aspect of insurance operations, from product development to risk management and especially channel management. Successful strategies need to be based on:

- a clear understanding of how digital insurance creates value
- detailed perspectives on what would add value to the customers and the market dynamics
- careful prioritization by management among several potential digital initiatives

Meanwhile, new entrants are moving into the broader financial services sector in many markets. In Italy, for instance, the Direct Line direct insurance company has captured almost 25 percent growth in assets in a few years since its launch, and it has become the tenth company in the market for value of the premium in motor insurance.[16] In response, incumbent insurance companies must also use digital to innovate and remain profitable.

Challenges for financial institutions

Today, insurance companies face several challenges. They can be summarized as the six C's:

- culture
  - acting customer-centric
  - balancing the interests of the stakeholders and the organization
  - being lean, automated, and agile
- customers
  - empowered and demanding
  - complex and confused
  - sometimes malicious
- competition
  - more and more aggressive
  - global
- computers
  - innovation based on new technology
  - customers always connected to networks
  - communication available through new devices, such as mobile ones
- compliance
  - more fraud
  - need for security

  - increasing legislation and regulation
  - governance, risk, and compliance (GRC) management
- costs
  - huge push for improving the return on equity
  - better procurement, for example with more outsourcing

To overcome these challenges and ensure the future of the organization, it is necessary to accelerate changes.

A worthwhile approach to facilitating change should be based on leaning and digitizing.[17] Adding value to customers, process improvement, reduction of cycle times, and waste cutting require knowing the processes and being able to measure them. In theory, making improvements in processes should be relatively easy in an insurance environment, since insurance companies are often inefficient, and they do not have physical products with complex supply chains, but essentially manage information.

Strategic choices for insurance companies in the digital age

A January 2015 article in *McKinsey Quarterly* by Henk Broeders and Somesh Khanna described strategic choices for retail banking in the digital age.[18] A similar approach can be taken for insurance companies. Traditionally, insurance companies have lagged with respect to banking in terms of innovation.

A strong expansion of life insurance has recently characterized retail insurance companies, bringing an increase of more than 20 percent in the managed assets. Digital insurance will be the recipe for the near future in support of a potential additional increase in the volume of the activities. This will include innovation in direct sales and the broader transformation of existing applications in systems enabled by digital technologies. This book calls such an innovation digital insurance.

The urgency of acting is acute. Insurance companies have three to five years at most to become digitally proficient. If they fail to take action, they risk declining in a way similar to laggards in other industries or becoming irrelevant due to new entrants.

The word "digital" in the term "digital insurance" should be considered with caution. This word does not mean only to implement excellent ICT systems in insurance companies. Rather, in order to reap all the benefits of digitization, it is essential to approach innovation from a holistic point of view. There is a need to redo completely the branding, the processes, the organization, and even the products or the business models. It is certainly necessary to define a multichannel policy.

Digital insurance can be defined quite broadly as a product, process, organization, or business model that is perceived as new by the customers. It requires some significant changes on the part of adopters, and is often embodied in or enabled by ICT.

Digital insurance should have the following elements:[19]

- It should deliver a customized but consistent experience to customers across all channels and points of interaction.
- It should be underpinned by analytics and digitization.
- It should reflect a change in the branding and the operating model, namely products and services, processes, organization, culture, skills, and ICT platforms, and possibly even business models.
- It should have the objective of delivering demonstrable and sustainable value to customers and the insurance company stakeholders.

Revenues and profits will migrate more and more toward insurance companies that successfully transform into digital insurance. These companies will develop new channels in an integrated way, automate processes, create new products, improve regulatory compliance, transform the experiences of their customers, and innovate key components of the value chain. Customers, financial markets, intermediaries, and even in some cases regulators will penalize companies that resist digital innovation. Similar to what happened for retail banking, digital laggards among insurance companies might see their net profit eroded in double digits percentages, while winners may improve substantially the bottom line. A 2014 survey by Accenture, among 141 insurance companies in 21 countries, found that 75 percent of the top managers believe that digital will transform radically the world of insurance in the next five years. The survey found that:[20]

- Thirty-nine percent of managers think that digitization will reduce margins.
- Fifty-nine percent are afraid that in the distribution of insurance products, there will be competitors such as Google or Facebook.
- Eighty-four percent think that digitization is changing the expectations of customers.

A big challenge for the insurance industry: innovation

The insurance industry is on the brink of major innovations. This is important since there is strong evidence in favor of the hypothesis that insurance development contributes to economic growth. Mario

Greco, CEO of the global insurance company Generali, stated during the 2015 annual company assembly: "The challenge we need to win is the innovation."[21]

From a practical point of view innovation can be in:

- products (or services)
- processes
- organization
- business models

To get a 360-degree view of innovation, it is necessary to consider two other aspects:

- the innovation in people
- the projects to implement innovation

All these aspects are important. There are innovations that can cover the full list. The remaining parts of this book will analyze them in detail. Digital insurance can be:

- a product innovation, since it can be offered as a completely different service
- a process innovation, since the interactions with the prospects and the customers can be completely different with respect to the traditional agencies dealing with the customers
- an organization innovation, since digital insurance requires drastic changes in the organization of the companies. For example, it might require to create a middle office This office should take care of the relationships between the customers (or the front office) and the back office of the insurance companies
- a business model innovation, since it creates the basis for alliance or partnerships between different financial and nonfinancial institutions, such as banks, in order to be able to offer bancassurance

In fact, there are different aspects of this type of innovation that must be considered. Take, for example, the role of the intermediaries. In the past, most of the insurance products were sold through either brokers or agencies. Digital insurance was introduced in order to sell directly to the customer through the new media: telephone and the Web. The problem is that the Web allows new forms of selling. A powerful feature is the possibility of comparing practically, in real time, offers from different sellers. In this way, what was born as a direct channel becomes once again indirect, this time with virtual intermediaries, the comparators, who are also called aggregators.

This change in the organizations has other consequences.

Pricing becomes an extremely important aspect. Therefore, the position on the search screens of a comparator is extremely important. Normally, this is done according to pricing. Pricing for insurance products needs to become much more sophisticated. For instance, with respect to the annual or semiannual payment of premiums, a certain number of insurance companies have introduced a monthly payment. This leads to more accounting and control work, but this approach has become acceptable thanks to the automation of the back office.

Other companies have launched insurance payments by consumers that is based on the use of the object insured, such as a car. This is possible thanks to so-called black boxes, which are devices that allow the use of the insured infrastructure or machine, for instance a car, to be measured, practically in real time.

The use of comparators has become relevant for the information and communication departments of the insurance companies. Now the companies are required to interface a large potential number of external partners in a situation in which there is very seldom a standard interface. Moreover, the number of quotations tends to become extremely large with respect to the real sales, with a large number of false positives. There is a huge impact on the use of ICT resources.

Application usability also becomes important, since the insurance company is in a direct relationship with the customer. If the automatic response of a company to the request for a quote is not fast enough, the prospect might simply purchase the insurance product offered by a competitor.

Advertising is also very important. For instance, by using social networking it is possible to detect signals that somebody is either buying a new item, be it a car or a home or something similar, or is in search of a convenient insurance company.

Relationships with the customer also become important. It is necessary to take into account that there might be several ways of interacting with the customer, whether by phone or through chats, e-mail, social networks, and so on. The different channels should be seamless and consistent.

New products. Thanks to the type of innovation described, there are many opportunities for insurance companies. Customers have a strong interest in seeing insurance companies develop innovative products that include new characteristics (for instance, coverage) and are deployed close to the source of their needs. Therefore, insurance companies need to add value for their customers by addressing these expectations and operating much more effectively, efficiently, and especially economically. This standing is not easy for incumbent insurance companies due to their legacy products, processes, systems, and organizations. They will need to take actions on these challenges.

For example, a significant number of applications in insurance will use the connected sensors and devices that are part of the so-called Internet of Things (or Internet of Everything, as Cisco calls it). The Internet of Things (IoT) is a scenario in which objects, animals, or people are provided with unique identifiers and the ability to transfer data over a Internet network without requiring human-to-human or human-to-computer interaction.

With IoT, the insurance companies will be able to collect new data sets and assess risk in completely different ways from the methods used today. This has the potential to radically reshape product propositions and reduce the size of global risk pools. Property and casualty insurance is likely to get the biggest long-run impact from this digital insurance-disruption as it moves from actuarial risk assessment using statistical techniques to structural risk modeling based on real-time observations, such as the use of the cars and potentially the driving speed of their insureds. Similar changes are likely to take place over time in health and life insurance. Insurance companies that seize these opportunities can become leaders in the market. Those that do not could slowly decline, and possibly disappear, from the market.

Garth reports some examples of product innovations for motor insurance:[22]

- accident forgiveness, which keeps rates from going up because of an accident
- safe driving bonus, which rewards customers with up to 5% of their premiums back for every six months of accident-free driving
- new car replacement, which replaces a car if an insured has an accident during the first three years of owning a new car
- recover care, which pays for assistance with cooking, cleaning, shopping, transportation, and yard work if the insured is injured in a car accident
- lifetime car repair warranty; which reduces costs by using authorized repair shops to guarantee all repairs
- disappearing deductible, which rewards good driving with a reduction in the collision deductible by $150 and which continues to provide reductions of $50 for each year of an insured's good driving record

New processes. Insurance companies need to rethink completely their customer engagement processes. Customers' overall digital experience with insurance companies lags that of other industries. This is true especially when it comes to "moments of truth" such as paying claims. As customers continue to integrate digital experiences into their lives, they expect these experiences, as well as their relationships with insurance companies, to become more direct, simple, secure, seamless, and effective.

This process innovation requires, for instance, very effective contact centers in order to assure the management of the quality and nonquality (such as long responses to claims, incorrect assessments by appraisers, and so on) of the services provided. To make the contact center effective, it is useful to set up a middle office. This is the part of a financial institution's operations that provides the link between the revenue-generating front office and the administrative back office (see Figure 1.7). For instance, transactions executed by the front office staff (be they telephone operators or virtual agents on the Web or something similar) may be processed by the middle office before being completed by the back office.

Insurance companies have four ways of using digital capabilities to create value for their customers and good business for themselves from the process point of view:

- Digital solutions increase an insurance company's connectivity – not just with customers but also with agencies, brokers, employees, and merchants. This extends from online interactivity and the issuing of policy to mobile functions. There are also possibilities for pushing insurance company brands in social media. It is estimated that 80 percent of the global customers use multiple channels to search and buy services.[23] Seventy-seven percent would like their insurance companies to be always available on the Web.

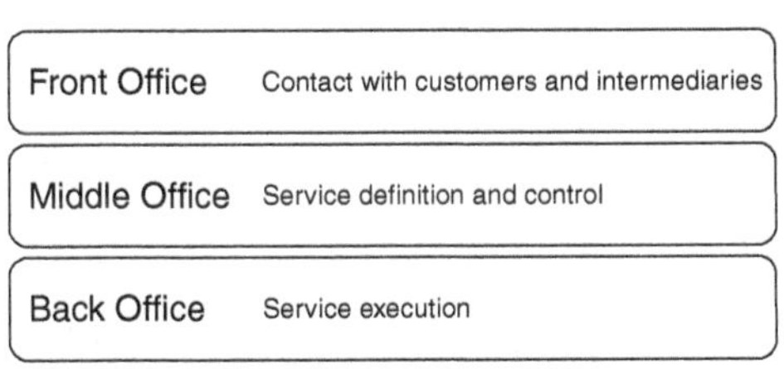

Figure 1.7 The role of the middle office

- Digital processes based on big data analytics can be used to extend and refine decision-making processes. Such analytics are being deployed by the most innovative insurance companies in many areas, including sales, product design, pricing and underwriting, and the design of truly effective and delightful customer experiences.
- Digital creates value by enabling straight-through processing, that is, automating and digitizing a number of repetitive, low-value, and low-risk processes but also making possible innovative and complex analysis, decision making, and operational tasks. Process apps, for example, boost productivity and facilitate regulatory compliance, while imaging and straight-through processing lead to better content management and more efficient workflows.
- Digitization is a means of fostering innovation with new innovative processes, such as social marketing and crowdsourcing, and "digitally centered" business processes, including networking with other businesses.

Insurance companies' management can use all or some of these ways of creating value through digital insurance. Developing a digital agenda and driving a digitally centered process transformation is a complex task. It requires an unusually high level of coordination of cross-company initiatives spanning prioritization, resource allocation, and collaboration in execution. Furthermore, most insurance companies are only in the early stages of developing the capabilities and culture of digitally native organizations, which include several elements:

- Design-driven innovation. Customer experiences should be compelling and highly differentiated, combining customization, speed, and ease of use for all processes, including applying and getting approved for a coverage, opening and understanding how to make full use of an insurance policy, and reconciling payments. To make this leap in the delivery of customer experiences, insurance companies need to act quickly to acquire deep capabilities in user experience and customer interfaces and satisfaction.
- Customization, leveraging data, and advanced analytics. Most data collected by companies still go unused. Yet there is significant value in applying advanced analytics to create better processes, for instance cross-selling and upselling. This can be achieved by making data usable in real time, such as at the point of contact (be it at an agency, a call center, or online), and combining the data with analytical tools to generate insights provided by risk management and/or marketing.

- Rapid experimentation and lean and agile management. Insurance companies need to learn to rapidly acquire or match high-value initiatives for customers, while showing tolerance of failures in trials. Insurance companies often struggle with this trialling and testing culture. In addition, they need to move from a waterfall project management approach in which there are several months between releases to agile management, with weekly sprints. However, the companies should use this agile model whenever it fits the purpose and not necessarily always.
- Use of the Internet of Things. Insurance companies might benefit greatly from the IoT, the machine-to-machine interconnections, such as the black boxes in the infrastructure (for example in motor vehicles) to monitor the use of an insured object.

Esurance

Esurance Insurance Services, Inc. is an American auto insurance provider. The company is a wholly owned subsidiary of Allstate. It sells car insurance direct to customers online and over the phone. It is a good example of innovation in insurance. The company expanded its online services by offering self-service claims.[24] Esurance's solution provides a revolutionary claims experience through processes characterized by reflexive, conditional questioning, real-time triaging, assignment, and scheduling repairs.

New organizations. Digitization needs to go hand in hand with changes in the organization. It introduces big changes especially in channels. The expectation is that, similarly to what is happening with a reduction in branches for retail banks, there will be some substantial reductions in the number of agencies for insurance companies in the near future. Some channels, such as the banks, will become more important. Insurance companies need to define a clear strategy for multichannel, in a situation in which there is not much experience in the field.

Across the value chain – from operations and ICT to marketing and sales to product development and finance – the data and technology required to realize the digital insurance in an insurance company often are already available.

Certain functions such as ICT, risks, procurement, and compliance will become more and more relevant. Very likely, insurance companies will not be able to man these functions only with internal staff but will need to hire from other companies or outsource some functions (especially in ICT, in terms of software packages acquisition, application development, maintenance and testing, and, additionally, the running of the systems will be increasingly outsourced to third parties). As a matter of fact, some insurance companies have hired managers from the banking sector as well as telecommunication industries in order to introduce this change of culture.

Similarly, marketing needs to change in some drastic ways and move to a digital mindset. One of the biggest difficulties will be in changing branding, promotion, and advertising. There is the need to manage all the channels in a consistent and integrated way. The term for this activity is "omnichannel." It refers to

- "Zero drop rate" channel integration. The customer should be able to move seamlessly among different channels. This means, for instance, that the customer should be able to retrieve a previously saved application process or have a follow-up with an agent without having to re-enter and retype data. This highlights the importance of real-time information and the consistency of data across channels.
- Optimization of a cross-channel user experience by building on individual channel strengths. Each channel is different. The way the customer engages with, for instance, mobile is different from his/her interactions at an agency, over the phone, or even online. All channels should offer similar functions or allow the customers a way to access the same information, while taking into account the characteristics of the specific channel. Customer experience in an individual channel should be designed to the strengths of that channel. For example, an insured person might want a timely alert of the expiration of his/her policy on the mobile and have the ability to act on an information connected with a claim, he or she, but is likely to prefer online and physical channels for in-depth communication or consultancy.
- Mutually reinforcing channels (for example, a live video chat with an agent from within a mobile app or an automated kiosk inside an agency or on a conversation with a broker). Customers often use concurrent channels at the same time, such as looking at an online screen while talking to a customer service attendant on the phone.

Intrasurance

Intrasurance is a Dutch full-service broker and third-party administrator, as well as a technology company. It is an excellent example of a highly technology-intensive insurance service provider.[25] It is achieving levels of efficiency that are much higher than the single-digit percent improvement used in some consultancy model. This is possible thanks to a fully digitized business and the maximum use of digital solutions in both the front and back offices. Its services and product model are very customer oriented. Intrasurance uses digital solutions highly effectively to empower, advise, and support its customers. It develops and distributes products based on a continuous analysis of customer and competitor behavior. A necessary corollary of this fully digital model is that half of Intrasurance's staff are technology professionals: ICT is truly a core capability of this company.

Genialloyd

Genialloyd is an Italian direct insurance company. It belongs to the Allianz Group. Genialloyd revised its website, adapting it to display on more devices.[26] This new version was designed also with a view of home insurance, the settlement of which is regulated by the Italian insurance regulator Ivass. The website has various characteristics, including that it can automatically adapt to all devices: mobile, tablet, or desktop.

Genialloyd, as prescribed by the Italian Supervisory Authority, provides the customer area, where each insured may manage his/her position and retrieve all the information he/she needs, autonomously, for quotations and policies. It is also possible to use the system in mobility. The homepage, in addition to the Super Fast Quote service, allows the possibility of a customer's receiving a quote on compulsory car insurance by simply providing his/her car plate number and date of birth. There is also a contact area with real-time update of the level of service performance of the telephone support.

New business models. More and more, insurance companies need to consider changing their business models. They should consider possible ecosystems suitable to the current (or near future) environment. In this model, multiple players collaborate. Insurance companies will need to agree or extend, for instance, partnerships with solution providers that can supply and service networked devices. More stringent partnerships would be also useful with banks, which can represent another relevant channel. Additionally, insurance companies need to set up broader partnerships to secure direct access to customers and valuable information. The rising importance of ecosystems brings the risk that new players will enter the insurance industry at different points of the value chain. New players could also take control of these ecosystems – potentially leveraging far more detailed customer insights than the ones available to the incumbent insurance companies. The long-term result could be lower returns for insurance companies if they lose control of the relationships with the customer. Big data analytics, described in a later chapter, can really help in this respect.

To defend their markets, insurance companies must aggressively build new business models that focus on meeting customers' delight with their digital experiences. They should apply the capabilities of new solutions to improve the ways in which they assess risk and operate their businesses. The biggest winners in the market will be insurance companies with the foresight to identify new, effective innovations that may not be necessarily ready for immediate utilization (for instance, in marketing), but could have a significant long-term impact on the industry.

Digital insurance companies are looking to different business models. Some years ago the prevailing model was bancassurance: the liaising with banks. Fifty-nine percent of the managers surveyed by Accenture envision new competitors such as Amazon and especially Google.[27] These companies, after some proofs of concept in the United States, are ready to launch their services worldwide. The major concern among the current insurance companies is the danger of disintermediation by the big players on the Web. The latter ones enjoy a strong position with Web users. Therefore, many leaders in the insurance field are evaluating the possibility of growing in digital insurance through partnerships with the Web majors or through the acquisition of innovative firms. For this type of operation, the main targets are ICT companies, policies comparators, and firms specializing in big data analytics.

Insurance companies could embrace two potential strategies. They could become:

- digital transformers, that is, companies very digitalized with strong e-competencies (they could represent around 22% of the potential global market)[28]
- followers, very limited in terms of knowledge of the customers (albeit possibly second in the market with a certain innovation in order to reduce their risks)

Accenture surveyed the possible postures of a large number of insurance companies and discovered the following:[29]

- Eighty-two percent plan to make acquisitions to improve their competitive position.
- Forty-three percent are planning to acquire start-ups or innovative digital enterprises.

- Sixty-one percent are evaluating new noninsurance products to improve their offering, in order to reinforce relationships with their customers.
- Seventy-two percent have entered into or are planning new distribution agreements with technological companies.

Insurance companies started to sell mainly through agency and brokers channels. Later, many insurance companies started to set up contact centers to market and sell insurance products and services. Increasingly, insurance companies sell their products directly through contact centers or websites or mobile apps, managed either directly by the insurance company or by the so-called outsourcers or comparators. Comparators or aggregators are a sort of "virtual brokers." They are third parties that use a web application that draws together syndicated contents from various insurance companies' online sources and displays them in a single location for the user's convenience. In less than a decade, insurance comparators have become the dominant distribution channel for auto insurance in several important markets. In 2013, customers in the United Kingdom bought more than 60 percent of their auto insurance policies online.[30] Most of them buy through comparators rather than from the companies' websites. Apart from comparators, another important channel, especially for life insurance products, are the banks, through the so-called bancassurance. Another target for bancassurance is to sell property and casualty insurance products not only in connection with mortgages or credit products as they have mainly done until now.

Consider another example: the automotive and insurance industries are colliding. How and where a car is driven is the best predictor of the incidence and severity of accidents. Cars are rapidly becoming computers on wheels for other reasons (such as security, simplification of use, and so on). It is interesting for motor insurers to acquire lower-risk drivers as customers and keep them loyal. The new business model could be an ecosystem with alliances among insurance companies, network providers, and original equipment manufacturers or OEM's.[31] Players should begin to position themselves today.

Projects. Insurance companies need to pursue these innovations through innovation projects. This is not easy, since traditionally insurance companies have relied on conservation rather than on innovation. The innovation discussed in this chapter might require an infusion of new blood into the management of insurance companies. A later chapter presents a method for running digital insurance projects.

Digital insurance as a new model for financial institutions

Financial services need to innovate. The current economic and financial crisis is a powerful accelerator in this respect. In this regard, the crisis is welcome since it is finally forcing financial services to change after having been mainly static and conservative for a long time.

The model of the services also needs to change in a drastic way. This is a threat, but it is also a great opportunity. Consequently, there will be significant changes in the share of the markets of the players in insurance services.

There are two possible paths to take in order to meet these challenges. One possibility is to reduce working capital through the sale of assets. Several insurance companies have embraced this path. It does not seem that there is much more to squeeze, however. An alternative is to cut the ratio of operating costs to operating income (the so-called cost-income ratio, a simple indicator of efficiency).

This is a correct diagnosis, but it is not the recipe for success. It is important to analyze what insurance companies could do to try to achieve the objective of cutting costs. Digital insurance is one of the most interesting solutions. Digital customers tend to be valuable customers. At one extreme, they are rich and young. At the other extreme, they are poor and uninsured. Both these sectors are interested in innovative insurance companies' products and services.

To be a viable competitor today, an insurance company has to offer a robust digital insurance service.

Marketing analysis is becoming very important. As digital insurance moves out of its infancy, insurance companies need to develop their service offerings to meet customer expectations and accelerate growth. Reaching maturity in digital insurance will require focusing on several dimensions:[32]

- satisfying customers with improved functions
- enhancing solutions and adding new useful functions
- protecting customers with better security
- being effective, efficient, economical, and compliant

Although these dimensions are interrelated, each of them encompasses its own set of complexities and challenges. Later chapters will discuss each of these items in detail. The following section defines the environment on which to implement all these aspects.

Satisfying customers with an improved experience

Pleasing customers today is not easy. The bar is set very high for insurance companies. In fact, pleasing customers is not enough. It is important to delight customers ahead of the competition. Especially in the case of Web and mobile applications, customers have become used to the kind of experience that is possible when interacting with the likes of Google or Amazon. This is what they want from their insurance companies. Customers expect a consistent level of service, security, and simplicity across all insurance company's channels, including mobile, online, in person at the agency, on the phone, or at a kiosk.

Yet this kind of experience is insufficient, as insurance companies must also be continuously accessible. They must deliver services faster and more effectively than before. The proliferation of mobile applications has created the expectation that features and functions will improve continuously and that they will be provided free or cheaply. If customers do not see new features or multiple application updates during a single year, they may be inclined to seek other institutions for a different or more satisfying and advanced experience.

Delighting customers will also require new servicing procedures. Insurance companies personnel at call centers, service centers, and branches need to understand mobile features, functions, and devices so that they can support remotely their customers effectively. Training employees so that they can encourage customers to use the new effective and low-cost mobile services – as well as help them troubleshoot – is essential in increasing the adoption rates for the new solutions.

Insurance companies in the West are well on their way to making the most of digital strategies in their business. A survey commissioned by Infosys to Forrester Consulting found that for many companies, there is a lack of focus on the customer experience to make a success of digital insurance initiatives.[33]

The study reported recognition among insurance companies that digital insurance can play a major role in their growth (47%) and drive a unified customer experience (44%). In more detail, the survey found that:

- Forty-four percent identify digital self-service as a key priority for improving customer experience and thus driving revenue growth.
- Twenty-nine percent believe that big data analytics is having a positive financial impact on the business, primarily through reduced risk in underwriting.

- Over one-fifth identify IoT as a catalyst for creating positive financial impact on bill payment, policy administration, and agent management.
- Twenty-five percent acknowledge the role of digital marketing in attracting new customers.

The study reported that, when exploring the challenges and obstacles that organizations face around leveraging digital for customer portals, 60 percent of insurance companies highlighted that they confront obstacles in the poor quality of customer insights. The result is that some insurance companies could be making wrong choices about their digital investments. The report also revealed that:

- Nearly two thirds (65%) of the more than 200 ICT and business managers surveyed said that their digital solutions portfolio is the result of an as-needed/ad hoc procurement approach.
- Fifty percent said that the lack of a digital innovation strategy prevents delivery of digital marketing initiatives to support growth.
- The biggest obstacle to making digital solutions effective (reported by 24%) is the lack of the right skilled people.

The survey recommends that insurance organizations:

- forge cross-company relationships to develop and support digital insurance
- leverage big data analytics to create high-value contextual experience
- choose carefully what and to whom to outsource with the objective to accelerate the speed of digital time to value

Tokio Marine & Nichido Fire Insurance Company Co., Ltd (TMNF)

TMNF has introduced multiple products developed in partnership with the telecommunication firm NTT Docomo.[34] Their experience demonstrates how an insurance company can apply learning from successive digital product introductions and deliver increasing sophistication of features to meet ever-widening customer needs. It also underlines the importance of different business models with partnership with technological companies.

The product set of TMNF extends from one-time, event-type insurance to medical coverage that offers almost continuous interaction with the user. An algorithm uses various data in order to develop suggestions concerning healthy lifestyle options for the insureds on a daily basis.

> The traditional insurance purchasing process presents insurance companies with a number of challenges. TMNF has been able through various product implementations to deliver increasing levels of benefits to its customers, to the company, and to the Japanese community.

Protecting customers with better security

Insurance companies have to balance the pace at which they introduce new and innovative features with the need to keep transactions and data secure. Therefore, insurance companies are forced to apply the same level of rigor and scrutiny to digital insurance as they do to their other intermediaries, be they agencies, brokers, merchants, or other financial services.

Application software that is currently available for digital insurance is in its infancy. It is not easy to ensure the same level of security enjoyed by other channels. Hackers are flocking to these new media as they become more and more common. Therefore, insurance companies need to strengthen preventive and monitoring strategies to mitigate emerging threats and improve customer trust.

Other key servicing procedures on which to concentrate attention are fraud and anti-money laundering efforts. The mobile channel might be more challenging in this respect. How insurance companies monitor for fraud that is possibly generated through mobile or person-to-person payments may not be materially different from how they police other fraudulent behavior. Certainly, the digital media facilitate frauds, in terms of speed and volume. Insurance companies need to monitor these behavior patterns carefully. More advices on this aspect are included on later chapters.

Consider, for instance, what happens if a customer's phone is stolen. Does the customer call the financial services institutions first or the telecom organization? Anticipating these kinds of situations and preparing appropriate remediation are critical for insurance companies that offer digital insurance.

Effective and compliant insurance companies

More and more customers of the largest insurance companies are using digital insurance. Nevertheless, only a fraction use a digital platform that supports the end-to-end processes (with the possible exception of some direct insurance companies). When those numbers are included in the financial institution's profit-and-loss statement, they still represent a relatively small percentage of the overall business.

It is not easy to compute the costs/benefits of digital insurance. However, the value of digital insurance is widely recognized. Consider the simple act of getting a policy issued. Compared to an in-agency transaction, where the cost of the infrastructure, salaries, and so forth is clear, the cost of the same transaction via a digital platform is several magnitudes less.

As the volume of digital insurance transactions grows, the financial benefits will become more visible and substantial. It will then be possible to evaluate more easily the benefits for the insurance company of the new model.

It is in the best interest of insurance companies to move customers swiftly from traditional to digital channels. Marketing campaigns can increase customer awareness in the form of scripts and training for agencies and contact center employees, brochures, e-mails, social networks, and advertisements. It is also interesting for insurance companies to use newer approaches, such as QR codes that lead to videos demonstrating how to use a digital application or a social network.

Insurance companies need to move quickly with newer and better digital insurance options in the face of growing competition from many corners, including start-ups and smaller insurance companies. Because their size makes them more agile, it is easier to use mobile and digital services to entice private customers and start-ups to encourage them to switch insurance companies. A superior digital service can be bundled with something else to convince customers to change institutions altogether. This could enable smaller players to make money on premiums and other traditional streams of insurance revenues.

Enhanced solutions

Among the immediate challenges for insurance companies to address is how to integrate and make transparent services and systems so that the right information gets to the right people, at the right time and place, from the right application, and on any channel.

The volume of data to which insurance companies have access is growing drastically due to the expansion of online commerce, mobile devices, IoT, and regulatory requirements regarding data storage and reporting. Mobile devices can capture much more information than a traditional transaction does. If users allow it, a mobile device can show, among other things:

- where they are
- what they are doing

- which kind of device they are using
- what kind of search they have done
- what links they have clicked
- what their browsing behavior on other sites was
- pictures of some objects connected with the transaction
- how many times the users visited a transaction page before taking action
- which other insurance companies they have perused (in the case of comparators)

All this is in addition to the other information the insurance company has obtained about its customers through traditional channels.

Normally all these data do not reside in one place. Insurance companies are not usually able to synthesize the data in such a way that will give them immediate insight into, for instance, what are the urgent needs of their customers. The ability to do so is complicated by the need to ensure that the security of the data is not compromised and that all the necessary safeguards are in place to be compliant (especially with data privacy) and provide customers with the confidence to use the new channels.

What insurance companies require is an architecture for aggregating data and analyzing them in real time so that the companies can anticipate their customers' needs and satisfy them. They also need the ability to make changes to their applications quickly, easily, and in a cost-effective way. This requires strong and effective big data analytics capabilities and flexible applications.

Quicker turnaround times are driven by insurance companies' need to compete in the face of innovation. The claim request whereby the customer can take a picture of the incident via a smartphone or tablet is one example. Once a company introduces such a feature, other insurance companies need to respond with similar solutions or risk falling behind.

The ability to respond immediately requires an insurance company to have a forward-looking view of where it wants to be in the future. Its architecture should have this flexibility, as should its component base. An example would be the mobile devices themselves. Some insurance companies have separate solutions for every device: Windows, BlackBerry, iOS, Android, and so forth. Each time a new device is introduced or the operating system is updated, a new solution has to be developed and thoroughly tested. Each time new features are added, each type of device has to be upgraded individually. Each time, it is necessary to do a thorough test. In contrast, a component-based, future-proof architecture is a single platform that is consistent across the full range of available devices. This component-based architecture:

- reduces complexity development and testing costs
- shortens time to market
- gives insurance companies more control over the process
- ensures less exposure from a data and security perspective

There are other solutions and business decisions for insurance companies to consider:

- how to evaluate new and untried vendors
- how to anticipate and react to new regulations
- whether to build, buy, or collaborate with other vendors in the smart commerce ecosystem
- how to automate regression testing

While insurance companies have a number of key advantages and capabilities, they may still need to join forces with other partners in order to compete effectively. For example, some of the more cautious insurance companies make use of access to mobile payment services provided by others or white-labeled from others. The more ambitious companies may decide to develop their mobile solutions, and may do this in partnership with another financial or technology organization to improve time to market.

The bottom line is that insurance companies need an innovative set of people, products, processes, and platforms to operate a digital insurance offering that is compelling to customers, competitive in the market, and capable of delivering a return on investment.

The 4 P's in insurance

The insurance industry is on the brink of a major technology-driven innovation, according to "Evolution and Revolution: How Insurance Companies Stay Relevant in a Digital Future," a report by the Boston Consulting Group and Morgan Stanley Research.[35]

This is certainly true, but innovations need to be managed properly and certainly not left only in the hands of the ICT gurus.

In any innovation, it is essential to consider four different aspects, the 4P's:

- people
- products
- processes
- platforms

This is true in general. An example is the case of digital insurance, in which the company is directly responsible to the insured, without involving an intermediary, with the possible exception of a comparator/ broker. It is also called primary insurance.

Often managers believe that to move or to launch a direct insurance means only to develop a platform to manage the channel to interact directly with the insured, such as a phone or web or mobile platform. Certainly, a platform is needed and it might be rather complex, but it is not enough: it is necessary to redesign the product and introduce or review the processes and the people.

The platform

From the point of view of the platform, direct insurance involves the possibility of producing quickly a quotation with appropriate pricing. From the point of view of the customer, buying insurance directly means that he/she will receive the benefits of paying less with a more comfortable transaction, thanks to the reduced distribution costs that the insurance company can enjoy and the possibility for the customer to do the transaction when he/she wants.

From the point of view of insurance companies, it is essential to have a way to "know your customer" (KyC). The KyC is fundamental from several points of view: risks, compliance, but also marketing and finance. More and more it is possible to use big data analytics to support KyC. This is the process of examining large data sets containing a variety of data types to uncover hidden patterns, unknown correlations, market trends, customer preferences, possible risks, and other useful business and market information.

The ideal is also to consider, in the big data analytics, data coming from outside the insurance company, such as those available from the comparators, search engines or in social networks. With this, we mean a website or an online service that facilitates communication among a community of people with a common interest. They use the website or other technologies to communicate with each other and share information, resources, and so on. The social network can also be an extremely important channel for promoting and advertising insurance products.

Due to the distributed nature of digital insurance, the best platform for distributing them is the so-called "cloud computing." In the definition of the National Institute of Standards & Technology (US) (NIST), cloud computing is a model for enabling ubiquitous, convenient, on-demand network access to a shared pool of configurable computing resources (for example, networks, servers, storage, applications, and services) that can be rapidly provisioned and released with minimal management effort or service provider interaction.

The processes

Processes change drastically in moving from the traditional insurance model to the direct insurance one.

There will be much more communication with the insureds. This will require a contact center that is very effective. To make this contact center effective, it is normally useful to have a middle office. This is the sector of a financial institution's operations that provides the link between the revenue-generating front office and the administrative back office

Also, the payments from the insureds become more complex. Traditionally, the financial transactions were in charge of the agencies. Payments can be done in several ways:

- credit cards
- debit cards
- prepaid cards
- money orders
- direct debit

Also ICT processes will change. For instance, testing will become much more important, since access could be done via different devices and channels. These channels are not controlled by insurance companies, since they are in the hands of their customers or prospects. They would change over time, for instance, with the new release of browsers. Hence, testing becomes an almost continuous activity for the insurance companies.

Geico

Geico is an American insurance company that has been in business for more than 70 years. It is ranked among the top five US auto insurers, and is a leader in online quoting/selling. Geico expanded customer interaction by connecting the company's website with Facebook, allowing customers to tell their stories, including product reviews and cost savings, and thus exchanging relevant customer recommendations.[36]

The people

The most important aspect in innovating insurance companies is to build a strong relationship with the customers. In the past models, agencies mainly managed the relationships with the customers. Now the interaction with the customers is mediated through the Web or mobile or phones or the comparators. The change will involve people, whether they are employees, contractors, or agencies. In fact, the number of agencies will diminish drastically. The surviving intermediaries will need to change. The customers will do most of the routine transactions. The intermediaries will need to provide added value. They must become consultants rather than clerks. There will be the need for massive retraining and requalification programs.

There is a need for a new professionalism. For instance, marketing will change deeply, moving from traditional to new media, such as the Web or mobile.

Drastic changes will take place also in the ICT departments, and the importance of ICT will increase. There will be the need for many more architects, project leaders, developers, testers, and vendor managers (the latter ones due to the increased use of external vendors). New skills will be necessary. For instance, there will be a need for data scientists. A "data scientist" is an employee or business intelligence (BI) consultant who excels at analyzing data, particularly large amounts of data, to help an insurance company to gain a competitive edge.

The most important task for the digital designers and marketers will be to assure consistency in the four P's mentioned above, and consistency with the branding of the insurance company. This may seem an easy task, but it is not. Think, for instance, about the need to be consistent in a multichannel environment. This will require being excellent in omnichannel. This is a multichannel approach to sales, and in general in the relationships with the customer, that seeks to provide the customer a seamless experience, whether the customer is interacting with the insurance company online from a desktop or mobile device, by telephone or in a brick-and-mortar agency.

Certain basic characteristics are necessary for staff people in insurance companies who are involved in digital insurance, in order to make it successful. They must be:

- Strongly aspirational. They should set up a challenging and consistent digital insurance vision, including steps such as getting a board-level digital sponsor and creating a digital-specific budget;
- Willing and able to acquire new capabilities. They should hire staff, especially at the management level, with the skills needed for digital transformation rather than only considering experience in the insurance industry. The best people in digital product management of user-experience design may not currently work in insurance. It is necessary to search in adjacent business and hire them. It is particularly important that they have the capabilities, the potential, and the willingness to learn all their life long.
- Willing to challenge everything. They should not accept the status quo. Digital insurance leaders must aggressively challenge all aspects of their business – both front office as well as middle office and back office systems and processes;
- Fast, agile, and fact driven. They should move to a cycle of continuous proposition iteration and improvement, adopting methods such as agile management and trial-and-error approaches (the so-called "trystorm" environment) supported by big data analytics, in order to increase the speed and success of the transformation efforts:
- Able to follow the money. They should invest in digital across the value chain, choosing the investments that create the most value. They should never forget to move forward one step at a time.
- Obsessed with the customer. This obsession with improving customer experience and learning from every customer interaction is the basic of any digital transformation. This is also the case for insurance companies. This must extend to all channels: customers expect the same frictionless experience in agencies as they do online or on calls.
- Able to carefully select and cultivate talents. They should nurture digital talents, providing them their own environment and tools, taking care to make their job interesting.
- Capable of setting up small, cross-functional teams that work together through rapid testing and continuous improvement programs.

Developing these capabilities is a crucial and critical part of the digital transformation. These capabilities must become the seed to changing the culture of the organization. That requires adopting a mindset similar to that found in successful digital enterprises when it comes to everything from establishing a challenging and coherent digital vision to acquiring new data capabilities and adopting a test-and-learn approach with rapid iterations.

Becoming aware of the need for change is the first challenge that management in insurance companies faces. The next challenge is to take the lead in the development and execution of a holistic change program that simultaneously addresses the products, the people, the processes, the organization, the platform, and the business models.

Some basic decisions to make are the following:

- Disruptive innovations can be the best option when an insurance company has little to lose in a geographic area or product segment. Defensive strategies can be a better option for incumbents to avoid cannibalization and margin erosion – at least for a time.
- Some new attackers can be thwarted, but cooperation in certain areas can make sense. This could be the best way to access new customers or to offer innovative capabilities to existing customers more rapidly.
- A portfolio of digital initiatives can reduce risk through diversification, but genuine game changers require time, money, and leadership drive. Sometimes insurance companies seed multiple ventures and then double down on scaling up those that deliver impact.
- Integrating digital operations can quickly provide insurance company customers with multichannel capabilities. In some cases, it might make sense to set up a completely separate entity active in digital insurance.
- A business-led digital transformation can be very successful, particularly if the top management directs the digital agenda.
- Sometimes digital transformation will lead an insurance company to shuffle the businesses in its portfolio through deal making.

The scope of these changes demonstrates that digitization requires a difficult and complex roadmap, to be clearly defined and agreed upon with all the stakeholders. Capturing the opportunities it provides will require investments, painstaking planning, and coordinated decision-making that involves the entire insurance company and in many cases its intermediaries, like the agents. Digitization is rewriting the rules of how insurance companies compete. Incumbents that fail to anticipate this risk will damage franchises that were built over generations. If management is able to manage the multiple strategic challenges posed by the digital insurance model, they will position their insurance company in such a way that it will be able to compete effectively, with economic efficiency, and be ready for growth.

Some customer expectations might be that they wish to be able to do the following:

- see online in real time the status of their contracts and receive alerts when a policy expires
- accept apps that record the behavior of the driver in the vehicles, registering bad driving, with a discount on the premiums possibly based on such behavior
- signal in real time using their smartphones an accident and mark the damage by touching the screen and inserting Band-Aids where they had some damage
- record fitness and nutrition, which could help in reducing the price of health policies

Vitality

Vitality, part of the South African group Discovery, submits to their customers a voluntary agreement to sign for digital control of their habits in terms of eating and sports activity.[37] They reward a healthy lifestyle with a lower price on their health insurance policies.

Conclusions

In concluding this chapter, it is interesting to analyze the possible strategies for insurance companies in approaching digital insurance.

Michael Porter has described a category scheme consisting of three general types of strategies that are used commonly by businesses to achieve and maintain competitive advantage.[38] These three generic strategies are defined along two dimensions: strategic scope and strategic strength. Strategic scope is a demand-side dimension, and it looks at the size and composition of the market a business intends to target. Strategic strength is a supply-side dimension and looks at the strength or core competency of the company. Porter identified two competencies that he felt were most important: product differentiation and product cost (efficiency).

Porter reduces the possible best strategies to three. They are:

- cost leadership
- differentiation and
- market segmentation (or focus)

Market segmentation is narrow in scope, while both cost leadership and differentiation are relatively broad in market scope.

Insurance companies can launch the digital insurance following one or more of these strategies:

- The cost leadership requires a basic product with no frills. The low price might be the free availability of a certain number of optional services or an increase in the interest rate for the savings of customers who use only digital insurance for their life insurance.
- A differentiation strategy requires the development of unique capabilities to be delivered with a very high quality. They could be, for instance, Snap-On, that is, the possibility of taking a picture of an accident using smartphones and then sending them to the insurance company through their app to support their claims.
- The segmentation strategy requires the development of digital insurance models for customers in certain niches of a market, for instance small and medium-size businesses.

The low-cost strategy does not work in the long term. Moreover, it normally requires a large share of the market, which would be unlikely for new entrants. In the medium term, the winning strategy is a segmentation strategy. The ideal is a segment of one, in other words, completely customize to one customer the digital insurance products. This can be achieved without spending a significant amount of money by using digital insurance.

Big data analytics is the answer. It is necessary to use big data analytics to develop a one-customer insight, by analyzing his/her behavior, looking at social networks, and, whenever it is cost justified, making direct contact (either with phone calls or e-mails). In other words, the objective is what can be called "mass private insurance": private insurance for the masses. This is similar to the "family banker." In this case, the customer would get a fully digitized "family insurer." This requires the use of the Lean and Digitize method, which is presented in the following chapters. In other words, it is necessary to strip down the processes of digital insurance as much as possible and at the same time to use all the automation possible in the lean processes.

Mass private insurance is excellent because it allows for the creation of an ecosystem around digital insurance, along with the participation of intermediaries, telecom companies, financial institutions (such as banks), and merchants (such as travel or logistics companies). It would enable personalized advertising or customized loyalty points.

The next chapters concentrate on the solutions that can be offered via digital insurance.

2
The Management of Digital Insurance

Introduction

Marketing and economics are two important aspects in the implementation, launch, and upgrade of digital insurance. In order to examine these aspects, it is important to consider the characteristics of potential customers and to take a multigenerational view in the implementation of digital insurance.

Marketing, benefits, and associated costs change according to the characteristics of the customers and the digital insurance functionality. Once the benefits and the costs are defined, it will be possible to consider the return on investment (ROI) and to detail the actions necessary to make digital insurance a success in the specific situation.

This is the subject of this chapter.

A digital insurance model

Digital insurance refers to the provision and use of insurance and connected financial services with the help of digital solutions. The scope of the solutions may include transactions to purchase insurance or personal investments, administer policies and claims, and access customized information.

Digital insurance includes a wide range of services. These services may be categorized from a conceptual point of view as following: informational, accounting, brokerage, and support:[1,2,3]:

- Informational services refer to nontransaction-based services of an informational nature. This application may be divided into categories: 1. Quotations, 2. Policy, 3. Market information.

- Accounting services refer to activities that involve monetary transactions. Such transactions may involve an external account, for instance, when a customer is paying for a premium, or an internal account, for example, when a prospect is subscribing to an insurance policy. Standardized insurance policies, such as a motor or travel insurance policy, may be purchased online. This service could be particularly attractive in time-critical situations. For instance, if a customer has to set out on an urgent, unplanned journey, he/she may need to subscribe to a travel insurance policy at the very last minute.
- Brokerage services refers to intermediary services related to the policies. They could be variations or versioning. Brokerage, too, may be divided into two categories in order to differentiate between services that are essential to operate an insurance policy and services that are essential to administer that account.
- Support services refers to activities that are undertaken by an account holder to maintain his or her account. This may involve activities like access administration and policy copy requests.

mBank

mBank S.A. is one of the biggest financial institutions in Poland. The organization provides services to different groups of customers, ranging from young people, micro-entrepreneurs, and affluent clients to the biggest corporations. mBank introduced a complete digital transformation of insurance delivery to retail and small and medium enterprises in Poland[4]. It launched a model in which banking customers are offered a broad lineup of insurance products in a fully digital, ultramodern process, and in a channel of their own choice.

Digital insurance: the voice of the customer

In the past, insurance companies have interpreted the potential use of digital insurance as rather limited. Initially, digital insurance was implemented through exchanges of short message service (SMS) messages. Most of the time, they were simple exchanges of information: from the customer to the insurance company and vice versa, for instance, to provide a quotation. In the case of tablets, initially some insurance companies have been advising customers simply to use the mobile browser to access the online insurance.

Great benefits can come from a digital insurance that makes use of the real competitive features of digital solutions. For instance, using mobile to interact with the insurance company provides the possibility of using the apps everywhere and any time, since, for the individual, the mobile is even more important than his/her wallet. Another distinctive feature of digital insurance is the integration of more than one service and function. For instance, in the case of mobile digital insurance, it is possible to use picture taking and processing, voice processing, biometrics, optical character recognition (OCR), contactless features, and so on.

The main benefits of digital insurance are the following:

- In traditional insurance, there is a separation of different functions: quotations are a different function with respect to policies and payments, underwriting is different from reinsurance, and so on. With digital insurance, this separation does not make sense. Customers can now use their devices to manage end-to-end their policies. They can use their equipment as payment devices and to do any other insurance or financial transaction.
- The applications can work as many quotations as the customer wants, since the policies become virtual policies.
- At the same time, the mobile devices have also communication capabilities. The customers can communicate with the contact centers via voice, chats, or SMS's, and video.
- The customer can buy tickets for railways, flights, and so on. He/she can use the device as an access/check-in control system and at the same time buy insurance on the trip he/she is starting.

In an innovation, it is important to listen to the Voice of the Customer (VoC). The Dutch Group ING surveyed 11,000 customers in 12 countries to understand better their needs and desires of financial services.[5] The results show that customers appreciate very much the possibility of managing with their mobile their relationships with a financial service, mainly because in this way they can get faster services. Customers also welcome the agility of the service.

In this survey, customers of financial services also mentioned that they use social networks (Facebook and Twitter) to follow the activities of their institutions. They look for a channel in which they can communicate with these institutions without having to wait to visit an agency and interact with an insurance company representative. Social media account holders like to receive tips on how to insure, save, or invest in the best possible ways.

Customers expect more and more direct interactions with the insurance company through digital insurance with targeted services such as:

- alert systems to inform them that a policy needs to be renewed
- interactive features for direct connection with the contact center of the insurance company
- advice on how to manage their life or health insurance
- the ability to use social networks as a channel of relationships with other insureds and with the company
- quick and effective ways to report a claim and get reimbursed

Digital insurance has also a social value. It is available to the disabled or to people with limited mobility. This is an important aspect due to the aging population.

Corporate digital insurance

Digital insurance was developed as a concept for customers, in support of the retail side of insurance companies' operations, as a solution for private customers. It can be extended to corporate and professional/businesses. One of the trends in the use of information and communication systems and telecommunication is the so-called information and communication technology (ICT) consumerization[6]. The meaning of this term is that innovations are initially launched in consumer markets and later they move to the business market. This is contrary to what happened in the past, when ICT innovations were mainly launched first for businesses and later moved to the consumer market. A clear example is the computer. Initially, the mainframes were targeted only to businesses that could afford their costs and were able to use them. Only later was the personal computer launched for the consumer market.

There are several examples of ICT consumerization. A typical example is the smartphone. On day one, the iPhone was targeted to consumers. Only later, mainly with the BlackBerry, businesses started to use smartphones. This is now happening with tablets. Another interesting case is cloud computing. Almost all consumers have their private e-mail accounts or similar applications in the cloud. They access the applications from remote servers, yet they do not know where the applications and their data are located. They access their applications through the Internet. Most of the time, customers do not pay for the applications. When they are charged, they pay on the basis of their use of the resources (an example is storage with Dropbox). Now, businesses are moving their applications to the cloud, and they are finding benefits from the use of a similar model.

A similar trend is occurring with digital insurance. It was essentially born for the consumer market, where it is enjoying growing success. More and more insurance companies are starting to customize digital insurance for corporations and small and medium-size enterprises (SMEs).

The requirements for corporate digital insurance are different than for individuals. In most cases, the business requirements are more stringent. Businesses, for instance, require much more security. The amount of money involved in business transactions tends to be much higher for businesses than for individuals.

Some applications are specific to the business world. Some examples are:

- management of multiple (and possibly linked) policies
- large payments and claims
- the authorization workflow, since in most cases more than one manager must be involved in authorizing the purchase or renewal of a new policy

As a matter of fact, digital insurance is an excellent solution for business clients also. The biggest benefit of corporate digital insurance is that it offers the possibility of using it everywhere and at any time, for example, for policy presentments and payments.

The future will see interesting developments in this direction. More and more Enterprise Resource Planning systems (ERP) are being redesigned to be used also from mobile devices, for example, the Infor 10 ERP Enterprise[7]. It has interesting features in terms of mobile access also in connection with insurance. There are apps built on ERP platforms that provide business managers the ability to approve pending transactions, release wire transfers in order to pay premiums, and view past transactions, among other functions. The new generation of corporate digital insurance apps has more transactional capabilities, as well as informational ones, such as the capability to view all their policies in one go, be they linked or not. This trend will spearhead the widespread adoption of corporate digital insurance as more organizations take advantage of these capabilities.

Not only are ERP's moving to mobile, but there are also interesting expansions to ERP, for instance, in support of procurement. A mobile function that is becoming popular with business customers is the ability to manage commercial accounts and expenses via mobile. At the same time, it provides program administrators with the ability, for instance, to review transactions, before or after they are approved. It can also feature an electronic workflow that includes online routing and receipt imaging. Recent developments of the Ariba and Bravo Systems are exactly in the direction of the networked economy. They are similar to what comparators are for individual customers. These applications are more and more used to integrate with digital insurance. These approaches are great ways to move to an agile corporation that is lean and digitized.

The requirements of corporate customers

The biggest concern with digital insurance is security. Treasurers and business executives might like the convenience of accessing online the insurance accounts in their daily activities. Given the sensitive nature of corporate data, every precaution must be taken to protect their data and transactions.

Businesses are increasingly accepting the policy of Bring Your Own Device (BYOD) for their employees.[8] This policy entails that the employees can use their own devices to access business applications. In this situation, it makes sense to extend to the Web in a secure way the functions traditionally available on the office desktop, since very likely many employees will use their own smartphones or laptops rather than desktops.

It may only be a matter of time before there is a "mobile revolution" in the business space that is similar to what is happening in consumer insurance. Corporate digital insurance needs to increase the quality and amount of actionable information and transactions provided to the employees. In this way, insurance companies can not only retain these important customers but also improve their satisfaction and increase the potential of cross-selling or upselling a large number of insurance services.

Drivers for corporate digital insurance

In order to succeed in the launch of a corporate digital insurance initiative, it is important to understand the critical success factors for such a move. This section attempts to describe the most important of them.

Customer satisfaction levels dropped during the financial crisis, and they have remained low. The role of finance departments has thus become strategic and global. Insurance offerings need to evolve quickly to address these new demands. Finance departments need easy access to a real-time or near real-time consolidated global view of their insurance positions, especially from a risk and compliance perspective. They require more analytical tools in order to perform their responsibilities effectively. Many insurance companies are addressing these needs through next-generation corporate online portals, peer-to-peer connections, and mobile offerings that provide fast access and exchange of information and eliminate delays resulting from time spent outside the office.

Corporate digital insurance helps eliminate delays in processing, and therefore results in accelerated fee-generating activities for the insurance companies.

In addition to accelerating the receipt of fee revenues, corporate digital insurance in itself has the potential to create new and interesting streams of revenue for insurance companies, especially in the mid-market.

Small and medium-size enterprises

Small and medium-size enterprises (SME) represent the bulk of the economy sector in many countries all over the world, but especially in Southern Europe and in emerging countries.

Not all insurance companies have paid enough attention to this mid-market. From the risk point of view, especially large insurance companies have regarded SMEs with suspicion since their rate of delinquency tended to be higher than in corporate companies or in individuals.

Small insurance companies are devoting more attention to this part of the market. They were not always able to compete with larger insurance companies in other parts of the market. In order to be able to attack the market of larger corporations, they needed to procure the resources, the expertise, and the geographical coverage that large companies demand.

From the customer's point of view, small insurance companies can have an interesting mid-market share since they can offer SMEs a highly personalized service and make possible an excellent customer experience.

It is not surprising that in many cases, small and medium-size insurance companies have pioneered digital insurance for SMEs. Throughout the industry, applications designed for SMEs are few. Industry analysts attribute the lack of specific ICT systems for the mid-market to many factors:

- Businesses' adoption of digital solutions is slower.
- The needs of the mid-market are very diverse.
- Even defining the category is a challenge for SMEs, where entrepreneurs mix personal and business matters.

It may be hard for insurance companies to come up with a one-size-fits-all product for their business customers. Some insurance companies will rebrand for the SMEs their retail platforms with minor tweaks, such as changing the logo. This is not sufficient. Unlike individuals, business customers potentially:

- have more users
- need more complex products
- need entitlements, added security measures, and more robust audit trails
- manage often multiple business accounts alongside their personal accounts
- require policy statements, including up to several years of transactions

However, they are a rich and growing market.

Online-only insurance companies

A certain number of online-only insurance companies have been launched recently. Their characteristic is to offer the full set of insurance products on the mobile (including smartphones and tablets) or on the Web.

History repeats itself. One of the first online banking companies, ING Direct, was similarly launched initially as an online banking company only. Later, it started to open branches in certain countries.

The initial launches of some mobile-only insurance companies have been successful: in a short time, there have been a relatively large number of new customers.

Until now, there has not been a standard model for online-only insurance companies, even if some common features are emerging. Online-only insurance companies' concept and ease-of-use get good responses from younger, tech-savvy, and not rich customers. Any user of the Web, and especially of mobile, might come to like it. It is very important that the apps, websites, and various features be simple and easy to navigate and understand.

Normally, mobile-only insurance companies have an online back-up accessible via the Internet for emergency.

The value of digital insurance

For a successful innovation, it is necessary the introduction in the organization of a culture, a method, and a set of tools to improve the value of the products and processes.[9] Digital insurance can be an important factor for innovation in insurance if it becomes a source of value in different dimensions.

The first dimension:

- customers looking for the possibility of buying insurance anywhere, any time, and on any device
- insurance companies looking for new models to promote insurance
- merchants, such as travel and logistics companies operators, in search of new categories of value-added services for their customers

The second dimension:

- agencies and brokers searching for sources of process optimization and improvement of customer service
- public administrations looking for sources of cost reduction, improved services to citizens, and ways to fight tax evasion
- the community at large seeking to improve the life, health, and economics of their constituencies

The following sections examine each one of these stakeholders' interests.

The value for the customers

The value of digital insurance for the customer depends on the ability of the operators (be they insurance companies, agencies, promoters, or brokers) to take advantage of all the possible functionality of digital insurance. Services should be:

- faster, for instance, by reducing the time spent queuing in the agencies or on the phone with a contact center
- more convenient than other channels, such as providing an opportunity to renew or suspend insurance without having to go to the agency
- more accessible, for example, by encouraging the purchase of a last-minute promotion at any time and any or specific places
- cheaper, because use of the services would require less effort and cost.

Digital insurance can enable two categories of services:

- Services related to insurance. Digital insurance can help improve the quotation, payments, administration, renewal, suspension, and claims, such as, for example:
  - buying a travel policy while waiting in line to start a journey
  - controlling savings with big data analytics from a unit-linked insurance
  - receiving and using digital discount coupons, for instance, for health checkups
  - using the phone as a loyalty card and accumulating points automatically
  - sharing with friends opinions on companies or services/products
- Services not closely related to insurance. An NFC mobile phone can become a corporate badge or an ID card, or become a self-scanning tool in stores. The NFC mobile application can help the customer, for instance, to buy insurance on his/her flight on a kiosk.

The value for insurance companies

For insurance companies, digital insurance represents an opportunity to improve services, reduce costs, grow the use of paperless communication, attack new markets, and improve profitability.

It is important for insurance companies to consider the value that digital insurance can bring in terms of the relationship with the customer. The potential entry of the so-called over-the-top (OTT) operators (for instance, Google, which has already applied for insurance services in several states in the United States[10]) could put at risk the quality – in terms of confidence and stability– of the relationship with customers. Past experiences with OTTs clearly show how these entities monopolize the relationship with the end users. They do not show friendly behaviors. They have put in place aggressive and often disruptive strategies against the business models of the incumbents, sometimes relegating them to service providers with low added value.

The value for the intermediaries

The intermediaries – such as agencies, brokers, promoters, banks, travel operators, telecom operators, even OTTs, and so on – are a category of actors pivotal to the spread of digital insurance.

On the one hand, the propensity of intermediaries to invest in digital systems by developing applications or by changing the technology and processes in the agency, and to pay potential costs, depends on a clear understanding of their benefits. On the other hand, many of the benefits for the customers depend on the ability of the intermediaries to transform this innovation into better services and/or lower prices and especially more revenues. Proper awareness of the value of digital insurance for the intermediaries is therefore a decisive factor for both the diffusion of services and the full potential of benefits to all stakeholders.

In the case of digital insurance, there are four major potential sources of value for intermediaries, which need to move more and more from payment recipients to insurance consultant for their customers:

- There is a reduction in the costs of cash management for the payment of policies. This includes the costs for counting cash, possible errors, and the risks of losses, theft, and robbery. The cost of handling cash or checks varies from 0.5 percent to 15 percent of sales.
- The digitization of processes and documents is possible, from the management of the quotations and the policies to the management of tickets for accessing the service. The savings for the intermediaries come out of less paper handling and more security in the operations.
- The shorter time for purchasing a service in an agency allows intermediaries to reduce the overall time of service, the risk of lost sales, and/or operating costs incurred in guaranteeing a given service time. The reduction of the time of payments compared to cash and traditional cards could range from 5–30 seconds, with an impact on the performance of service more than proportional to the increase in the rate of adoption. The final benefit would be a reduction in the costs (estimated at 1 percent to 2 percent), thanks to a reduction in the number of agents.
- The spatial and temporal ubiquity is the possibility of selling an insurance anywhere and at any time, thus creating a channel of purchase/payment, which in certain cases might create unique customer experiences or be less expensive for the customers and for intermediaries adopting the solution.

Many intermediaries – with some notable exceptions – unfortunately tend to resist or at best be passive with respect to digital insurances. They try to hang on to the existing way of selling insurance. They have not developed a specific analysis or a quantification of impacts on their processes. They expect that customers predominantly do not adopt this innovation. Unfortunately for them, this is very unlikely over time and dangerous for their business.

The value for the ICT companies

The ICT companies, be they system integrators, telecommunication companies, outsourcers, or similar entities (such as the internal ICT departments of the insurance companies), are experiencing a progressive reduction in revenues due to the increased competition and, in the case of telecommunication companies, a switch to flat rates, reduction in the use of SMS, and so on. Therefore, they have a big interest in finding new sources of revenue that will open up new business. Digital insurance is a great opportunity for these organizations to provide better products, services, and processes. The prerequisite is to be ready to innovate in the products and services.

The value for the public administration

The public sector charges and collects various transactions: taxes, fees, and fines. Digital insurance can help to reduce the costs of such collection, but especially control that they are properly paid. For example, the public administration, thanks to digital insurance, can start checking the payment of compulsory insurance (as in the case of motor insurance in some countries) or medical prescriptions (as in the case of health insurance) using either a contactless Point of Sales terminal (POS) or in remote.

The value for the community

Digital insurance can have (and it now has in a certain number of countries around the world) a social value. This is a critical success factor. Insurance companies, customers, and community (the 3 C's) are distinct but closely related stakeholders.

Digital insurance and mobile payments have the potential to expand financial access to uninsured or underinsured persons by reducing transaction costs and increasing the accessibility of financial products and services.[11]

Critical success factors for digital insurance

Once the VoC is collected, the next step is to define the measures of success: the critical success factors (CSF). It is interesting to analyze a model developed in the past for evaluating the acceptance of new solutions (Technology Acceptance Model, TAM).[12] A number of recent studies have adopted this model to study the acceptance of the Internet and mobile-related technologies, such as mobile payments, digital insurance, and m-commerce.[13,14,15,16] The evaluation of TAM is based on the premise that the fundamental determinants of the adoption and use of new solutions are:

- The perceived usefulness (PU), which is the degree to which people think that using a particular system will enhance their actions. The measures of PU include performance increase, productivity increase, effectiveness, overall usefulness, time saving, and increased task performance.
- The perceived ease of use (PEOU), which is the degree to which a person believes that using a particular system requires little effort. The measures for PEOU include ease of control, ease of use, simplicity, clarity, and flexibility of use. This has a significant and direct effect on the intention of insured or uninsured people to adopt digital insurance services.

These two beliefs create a favorable disposition or intention toward the use of a technology and consequently affect its use.

As a matter of fact, there are other factors to take into account when considering digital insurance with respect to the basic TAM. Despite the unique benefits of digital insurance, overcoming trust issues is for instance a major challenge to the adoption of any digital insurance.

A more complete model for TAM should include (see Figure 2.2)[17,18]

- behavioral intentions (BI), which is the propensity to adopt a new solution
- perceived economic factor (PEF), which has a significant and direct effect on the intention of customers, but especially prospects such as uninsureds or under-insureds, to adopt digital insurance services
- perceived usefulness (PU), which has a significant and direct effect on the intention of the customer to adopt digital insurance services. It is determined by the level of convenience (CON) and affordability (AFF) derived from digital insurance services
- perceived trust (PT), which has a significant and direct effect on the intention of un/insureds to adopt digital insurance services
- age and gender of un/insureds, which affects their perceived ease of use of digital insurance services
- digital operator (MNO) characteristics
- non quality of the service provided (NQ)

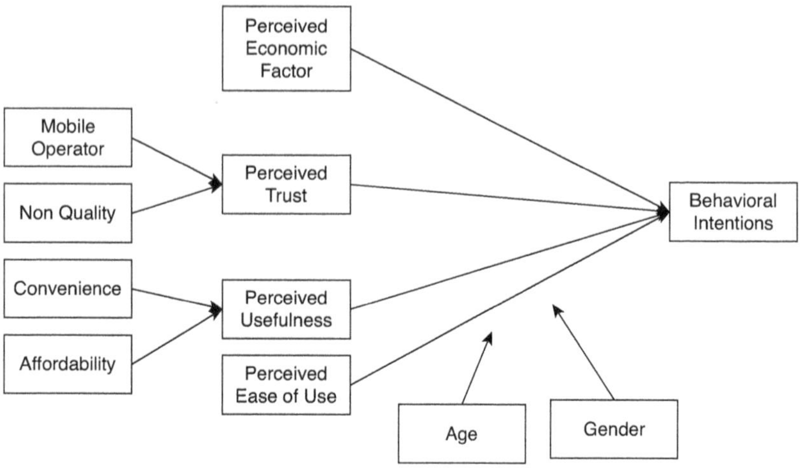

Figure 2.1 Technology acceptance model

Different models for digital insurance

Accenture has presented four different models for insurance companies in adopting digital insurance:[19]

- The channel-enabler model is chosen by insurance companies with growth- and sales-oriented strategies. These companies wish to enhance their customer relationships with personalized products and services. This model focuses on enabling existing channels and business models by the use of digital insurance. Insurance companies adopting this model will not realize as much value as those that focus on new digital channels and business models. This model is used by many companies, especially in Europe. Agents remain one of the key channels for these insurance companies, estimated in 2015 to account for 32 percent of businesses in Europe, a percentage that drops only marginally to 30 percent by 2016.
- The tailor-made model suits insurance companies that focus on the customer relationship. Their business strategy tends to focus on improving profitability and customer retention. Companies following this model aim at becoming real and full digital insurance companies. Such companies seek competitive differentiation using digital solutions to offer personalized products and services using

digital solutions such as online or mobile access to their services, or mass customized personal insurance.

- The online model is adopted by insurance companies that are reducing the importance of existing agency and branch networks by offering a greater range of direct online services. Agencies and branches are focused on providing consultancy and niche services to certain market segments. Like the tailor-made model, this model suits insurance companies whose business strategies are focused on customer retention and bottom-line optimization, but who prefer simple customer relationships.
- The hybrid model attracts insurance companies that see digital insurance as offering them the opportunity for complementing their existing business with a new digital business. They effectively create two businesses. This model suits companies with a high focus on growth and sales, but a desire for an adaptive customer relationship. Insurance companies adopting this model will use digital solutions both to enable existing channels and create new ones, thus maximizing value.

Multigenerational view of digital insurance

It is important to consider the different models for insurance companies in strategizing their approach to digital insurance. It is also interesting to consider a dynamic approach, by analyzing a possible multigenerational model as the ideal roadmap to full digital insurance. The model should define a progression from communicating information to the customers, through enabling transactions, to finally interacting with customers around their insurance potential requirements as part of their lifestyle management, and engaging in noninsurance activities.

Several analysts have introduced models that consider the possible life cycle of financial services. Tower Group has introduced one of the most successful model.[20] It essentially would consider the following generations in the case of digital insurance:

informational

- transaction history
- SMS alerts
- agency location finder

transactional

- premium installments payments

interactive
- transaction verification
- actionable alerts
- personal insurance management
- personal lifestyle management
- mass marketing

orchestrative
- opt-in preference management: marketing alerts, offers, and loyalty offers (such as offering discounts for purchasing insurance for more cars in the family)
- location- and context-aware service
- cross-channel process management
- claims capture

Beyond the generations in the Tower Group model, there are some further generations:

social
- social media integration
- exchange of information, and especially of experiences among insureds
- comparison of lifestyles among friends or acquaintances
- gamification
- voice recognition

multienterprises
- partnerships with intermediaries, other financial services, and merchants
- targeted marketing
- advanced insurance products and services (such as unit-linked insurance policies)
- colocation marketing (for instance, merchant-funded rewards)

In the future, very likely there will be additional generations. Insurance companies need to reinvent continuously the possibilities of additional services, increased access, functional bandwidth, process optimization, and how those factors will bring value for their customers.

Marketing digital insurance

The marketing of digital insurance is substantially different from traditional marketing.[21,22] The following sections will examine some of the peculiarities of digital insurance marketing.

Different types of customers in digital insurance

The rapid adoption of digital insurance is transforming the marketing of insurance companies. These changes introduce new ways in which customers do insurance activities and interact with insurance companies. In this context, it is imperative to differentiate among categories of customers based on what they consider a priority, such application's performance, functionality, price, and so on.

Ericsson ConsumerLab produced a report that identifies six different categories of customers of smartphones. Each category attaches different priorities to the services offered by telecom operators.[23] It was based on qualitative interviews conducted in Sweden. It is possible to use a similar approach to evaluate the possible categories of customers of digital insurance.

The key factors influence the customer experience and the relationship that customers have with their insurance companies: functions, quality, cost, and experience. The quality of the functionality offered is one of the most important factors that have an impact on the loyalty to an institution. As a result, the security, simplicity, and range of functionality offered are essential for the insurance company in building a lasting relationship with their customers, assure a great customer experience, and attract new prospects.

Experience is the name of the game in customer relationships as well as in other services. The value of services is a decisive factor for many customers. Digital insurance that meets the insurance services needs of the customer is important. It is not sufficient to ensure the loyalty of the customers. There are other factors that can significantly improve the experience of the customer and hence generate his/her loyalty. TAM, described in a previous section of this chapter, can help in this endeavor.

Many customers perceive their relationship with their insurance company as distant and unfamiliar. Especially, the good customers without claims are upset with insurance companies that "steal" money from them without giving back anything (except, of course, in the case of claims). Yet the majority of customers do not experience a negative relationship with digital insurance. However, with digital insurance they may miss having a personal touch and the human relationship with an agent or an insurance company employee. Insurance companies may appear too focused on technology. It is therefore essential to improve the relationship between the customer and the insurance company. Programs that reward loyalty and personalized offers can help very much in this regard. This approach makes customers feel more involved, and thus increases their levels of satisfaction.

Based on these factors, and similar to the Ericsson ConsumerLab survey, it is possible to identify six categories of customers of digital insurance:

- Performance seekers consider the fundamental quality of the functionality and services offered by the insurance company and the connection. They think that they can do everything through a connected device if proper functionality is available.
- Smartphonatics are customers for whom the smartphone is not only a communication tool but an object that represents a lifestyle and a status symbol. To please these customers, the insurance company must make available more and surprising functionality in digital insurance.
- VIPs are those customers who consider essential the direct interaction with the representatives of the insurance company. They love to feel like privileged customers through receiving personalized services and promotions offered to meet their needs.
- The cost cutters give priority to the pricing of the insurance products and services offered. They are looking for cheap deals and reward insurance companies that do not surprise them with unexpected additional costs. On the contrary, insurance companies should entice these customers with some unexpected reduction in the premiums or some additional free services.
- The curious novices are those customers who are entering the world of digital insurance. They are gradually discovering the potential of the new channels. For this category, the priority is the relationship with the insurance company, from which they expect technical support and friendly advice. The performance of the network, the functionality, the usability of the application, and possibly handholding in using the digital insurance features by the contact center, are other key elements that affect the relationship between the insurance company and this category of customers.
- The control seekers attempt to avoid unpleasant surprises with policies by monitoring the use of digital insurance constantly.

Marketing mix of digital insurance

The marketing mix is a business tool used by marketing professionals to define policies and strategies. The marketing mix is often crucial when determining a product's or a brand's offering. It is often synonymous with the four P's: price, product, promotion, and place:[24]

- Product is an item that satisfies what a customer demands or that resolves his/her need. It is a tangible good or an intangible service, or a mix of the two.

- Price is the amount of money a customer pays for the product and the way in which he/she pays.
- Promotion is all of the methods of communication that an insurance company may use to provide information to different parties about its products and services. Promotion comprises elements such as advertising, public relations, personal selling, and sales promotions.
- Place (or distribution) refers to providing the product at a place that is convenient for customers to access and use.

In the marketing of services, the four P's have been expanded with three additional P's to address the different nature of services:[25]

- Physical evidence is the elements within the selling point – the storefront, the uniforms that employees wear, the signboards, the website, the advertisement, and so on.
- People are the employees or the contractors of the organization with whom customers come into contact.
- Processes, which along with the systems within the organization affect its marketing and operational processes.

It is interesting to analyze what, in the case of digital insurance, these seven P's become:

- In terms of Products, digital insurance allows the insurance company to mix in an excellent way the different services: policies, payments, coverages, and so on, to combine with different media, as in taking pictures of checks or of the driver's license when the customer applies for a new policy.
- In terms of Price, digital insurance can bring a substantial reduction of the total cost of the service. Apart from the reduction in commission fees to the intermediaries, digital insurance does not require that a customer goes to an agency or an ATM. This opportunity reduces the costs for the customer in substantial ways. Digital insurance can be accessed everywhere. In most cases, access does not require additional costs. Many insurance companies do not charge for downloading the app or for most of the transactions. Normally, the insurance company is willing to share its cost reduction with its customers through, for instance, a decrease of the premium. In adopting these approaches to pricing, insurance companies need to protect their relationships with their intermediaries.
- In terms of Promotion, digital insurance allows, for instance, the insurance company to send personalized promotions, based on

location (for instance, an airport), thanks to the Global Positioning System function in the mobile.
- In terms of Place (distribution), digital insurance can be accessed from anyplace, from any device, and at any time.

Digital insurance also changes and improves on the additional three P's. Unfortunately, many insurance companies do not devote much time and effort to these important aspects:

- The Physical evidence underlines the importance of the branding and the usability of the access and simplicity in the use of the digital insurance applications. This aspect is, for instance, critical for mobile digital insurance due to the smaller size of many smartphone screens.
- The People are important essentially in terms of the customer relationships center. The mobile phone helps in this regard since it is a tool that was born for communication and possibly video communication.
- The Processes are extremely important. They must change, for instance, with respect to the traditional agency channel. They need to provide an excellent experience to the customers.

How to market digital insurance

Insurance companies should market digital insurance with a multichannel approach. They should communicate to prospective customers and educate existing customers on the benefits of digital insurance. This marketing should be aimed also at intermediaries, contact center, online and mobile channels. It should highlight multiple areas of the digital insurance features, such as policy issuing and renewals, claims opening and processing, and so on. The approach should show how digital insurance is an excellent extension of what customers already do at agencies, making it much more convenient. For instance, it would be possible to use a video on the Web or on the mobile to show customers how they could use their devices to get a quotation. Additionally, icons could redirect customers to pages on the insurance company's website, where they can either compare policies or sign up for additional services.

To promote the website or the mobile app, the insurance company should leverage a variety of different advertising initiatives, such as commercials that show the functionality and products available in digital insurance.

Digital insurance continues to grow. However, customer education is still a challenge for many insurance companies. Therefore, leveraging other channels such as video, online ads, and comparators to promote digital insurance is an interesting way for insurance companies to attract new customers and retain existing users.

Mobile and web marketing in digital insurance

Marketing basically means thinking about people's needs and adjusting to those needs in order to provide the customer a sense of satisfaction and an excellent user experience. Mobile and web marketing strategies can be tailored to these digital insurance objectives.

Web marketing is definitely more than just a theoretical expression. It is a brand new, different way to approach the customer.[26] The starting point is the same as that in traditional marketing: an analysis of the target customer's needs.

Organizations can advertise their products on television or in newspapers. They are introducing interruptions in whatever the reader/watcher is doing to deliver the organizations' messages. Customers are passively suffering violence: the break in the middle of a movie or their reading.

In web marketing, the world can be upside down. The potential customer is not passive anymore. If he/she has a need, he/she can look for it on a search engine. With a well-designed site, the customer will be able to find the functionality he/she needs through the search engine on the insurance company or a comparator site. Once it is found, he/she will enter the insurance company page. Then, he/she can browse, looking for more detailed information on the product/service that he/she is seeking, such as coverage, pricing, and so on. The customers can then ask, chat, or send messages to get more information.

Mobile marketing is the newest agency of web marketing.[27] It uses the same principles of the classic web marketing. It should be adjusted to a very different medium: mobile.

The revolution between the old marketing and the new web marketing lies in the role of the customer, who is not the prey anymore, but rather the predator.

Insurance companies should, for example, run banner ads in the smartphone app store that feature scrolling animation to promote their mobile services. Additionally, the insurance company can use YouTube masthead ads.

Social networks/media in the marketing of digital insurance

A certain number of insurance companies use social networks such as Facebook or Twitter in digital insurance. They are useful tools to promote many different services and the insurance business. They fit especially into small/medium-size insurance companies that want to improve their customer base by reaching more potential customers or to larger insurance companies that want to expand in other markets or launch new products.

Social networks can help insurance companies improve the customer experience with digital insurance. These platforms are perfect for having fun, getting updates on news, being part of a virtual group, and doing many other activities. Yet few insurance companies are using them.

A possible useful social media tool for marketing digital insurance would be for example Foursquare or similar sites, which are location-based social networks. It allows a person's friends to know where that person is at a particular moment.

Thanks to a specific application, a person can check in at a public place (such as a merchant location), and then his/her friends will know immediately, through the same social network, the location where that person is. If the person's friends want to and if they are not too far away, they can contact that person. Applications like Foursquare can reduce the distance between the social network and the real world.

Foursquare might be not the perfect solution for combining mobile web marketing and digital insurance. Nevertheless, location-based social networking is excellent for combining digital insurance and real, everyday life.

A potential scenario for using a location-sensitive social network in combination with digital insurance could run this way:

- An insurance company provides a list (an online map would suit best) of agencies or intermediaries to its digital insurance customers.
- The institution and the agents have already agreed to make available a certain discount to customers who check in there.
- The digital insurance customer is motivated to choose a specific agency (included on the map) for consultancy and advice, and eventually purchase through it his/her insurance products/services, enjoy the product/service, and, finally share his/her experience online with a comment attached. Other friends, who are customers of the same insurance company and therefore are part of the same digital insurance platform, can read on the experience of their friends and can plan to consider similar products and services in the near future or whenever there is the need at the same agency.

Each party would win in this approach:

- The customer using digital insurance would save money and get better insurance. He/she could choose among a wide range of opportunities always at his/her disposal online.

- The insurance company would attract more potential customers, and it would increase their loyalty and their purchase of insurance products and services.
- The intermediary would get free advertising for their business, which would draw more customers.

Different intermediaries connected with digital insurance could compete with each other, for instance, by proposing and promoting different types of discounts or consultative services included in the policy.

The difference between this potential digital insurance website and what other websites do (like Groupon) lies in the way in which the discounts are promoted. Traditional discount sites mainly use e-mails to let customers know about the discounts. Digital insurance, using geolocalization, can be much more social and effective.

The economics of digital insurance

To evaluate a business case for digital insurance or some of its enhancements, it is useful to compute its return on the investment (ROI). To this end, it is necessary to evaluate the possible benefits and the costs.

Benefits

Improvements through a shift to digital insurance would come mainly in these areas:[28]

- The ability to mine the digital data that consumers leave on the Web, social media, and apps, as well as even health-monitoring wearables, could help insurance companies better target customers, price and underwrite policies more accurately, and manage claims more effectively.
- The digitization of existing insurance processes (allowing quotations to go straight through processing, for example, and rapid product configuration) can yield strong improvements to operating profit margins.
- There is the possibility of connecting with existing customers to better upsell, cross-sell, and retain valuable customers.
- The opportunity exists to sell products and services to uninsureds and underinsureds.

The key drivers of the profitability of digital insurance, considered as a new business line, are the average transaction numbers and the average float value.

The benefits connected with digital insurance are different according to the level of functionality offered. A previous section in this chapter refers to the modified Tower Group multigenerational model for digital insurance. From one generation to the next, the benefits are additional to that specific stage, and they overlap among generations.

Informational stage

- Improving customer satisfaction. According to Fiserv data (compiled from interviews with several financial services companies ranging from $2B to $28B in assets[29]), a good rule of thumb is to assume that the potential exists for 20 percent of all transactions to migrate to digital insurance over the course of a year, allowing the insurance company to reduce costs. In the case of advanced digital financial services for Italian financial services companies, there was a 32 percent improvement in the image of the financial services companies and in customer satisfaction.[30]
- A Forrester consumer survey backs up the notion that digital insurance, for instance the mobile channel, can reduce service costs.[31] American users of mobile financial services mentioned that mobile has changed their use of other channels. Forty-three percent said they had made fewer phone calls to their financial institution's contact center since adopting digital solutions. More than one-third (35 percent) said they visited agencies less often than they did before adopting digital solutions. Forrester set up a model of a bank with 500,000 retail customers. The model bank could achieve a savings of more than $150,000 per year by the reduced traffic in the branches and call centers.

Transactional stage

- Digital insurance customers are less likely to leave. In the Forrester study mentioned above, the attrition rate for all mobile financial services customers was 40 percent lower than that of other financial services users. This customer survey also reinforced the idea that digital financial services increase customer retention. This increased customer stickiness can result in recurring revenue for insurance companies. Forrester analysts project that a financial institution with 500,000 retail customers could get more than $450,000 in annual revenues from reduced attrition among their customers.[32]

- Digital insurance customers are more profitable. Customers using mobile financial services were 46 percent more profitable than online banking customers.[33]
- Digital insurance generates activity.

Interactive stage

- Digital insurance at the interactive stage further reduces channel costs. Digital insurance enables the migration of customers from high-cost offline channels, such as call centers and intermediaries, to lower cost, higher convenience digital channels. To project savings, insurance companies must first know the average transaction costs of each insurance product channel and determine how the expenses are offset by diversion to the digital channel.

Orchestrative stage

- Digital insurance tends to generate more transactions. Its use encourages value-generating activities such as travel insurance at the start of a journey. Thanks to the simplified access to digital insurance services, customers increase their average transaction numbers and the average transaction value.
- Payments, like bill payments, also increase customer loyalty in measurable ways. Once friends, family members, roommates, and merchants use digital insurance, they can stop writing and mailing paper checks. Transaction volumes can increase with a network effect.

Social stage

- Digital insurance helps in expanding the customer base. It can attract new customers by positioning the institution as innovative, in sync with the pace of today's households and the need for customers to save time and make transactions on the go.
- Social networks are excellent ways to capture customer behavior and status data. By connecting digital insurance with social networks and using an advanced big data analytics model, it would be possible to personalize services to a specific customer.

Multienterprise stage

- Digital insurance can provide merchant-funded offers.
- Digital insurance service provides a way to promote services through the mobile channel. It can help cross-sell other insurance products

and services. Forrester's survey found that 18 percent of financial services users say they are more likely to buy more products from the financial institution by using digital channels.[34]

- Digital insurance similar to other financial services could be 32 percent more profitable overall and 46 percent more profitable than online customers.[35]

Other benefits

Digital insurance is a great opportunity that allows additional benefits with respect to the ones already mentioned. According to a Javelin report, since 2010 customers of insurance companies have reduced their visits to agencies by 10 percentage points.[36] Financial services institutions should push more and more on transactions payments through the Web and mobile devices. This can be obtained also by providing alerts, suggestions, or opportunities, and so on.

Digital insurance can help reduce costs. As the number of digital insurance companies grows, customers' visits to agencies will decrease. In the future, they will not be more than 30 percent of the contacts between the customers and the insurance companies. Digital insurance accesses will rise by the same amount. This brings substantial cost reductions, from $4.25 per an agency visit to $ 0.10 for a mobile access.[37]

This means a drastic reduction in the number of agencies and their different role and positioning. If customers use agencies only for obtaining insurance advice and consultancy, as has been experienced in other financial services companies, there is no reason for agencies to be on the streets. It will therefore be possible to move to the upper floors of buildings or even to remote locations and to connect via videophones or simply phones.

Digital insurance can do much more for insurance companies. They need to customize their relationship with each customer. Insurance companies who move in this direction will gain big competitive advantages from these steps. It is essential to move from mass insurance to personalized insurance. To do this, insurance companies need to understand the needs of each customer and how to satisfy (and indeed delight) them.

Insurance companies cannot afford the costs that they incur today in personalized insurance. There will be a need to reduce the costs of mass personal insurance. The two words "mass" and "personal" may appear conflicting. Modern solutions can make them compatible. Technology can help. Big data analytics solutions can help in this respect. Big data analytics is an advanced way to deal with data, whether they are varied (structured or unstructured) or very large in volume. It especially offers the possibility of increasing the velocity in accessing data. A later chapter goes into detail on this aspect.

Costs

The main operational costs for insurance companies come from buildings, call center and back office staff, software, and hardware maintenance/operations, the cost of communications, and material used to promote the use of digital insurance (if they are used).

Major areas of fixed costs derive from the acquisition and development of software and hardware, and the establishment or the growth of a call center or a back office. Opportunities to lease the software, the hardware, or the resources from a vendor that provides the service on a per-transaction basis are beginning to emerge.

Marketing is a semi-variable cost. In some senses, it is closer to a fixed cost since it is difficult to tie it to the numbers of policies either activated or active. Since digital insurance is a new concept for most insurance company customers and since, for instance, life insurance is itself a new concept for some people, successful implementation requires significant expenditure on marketing and education. Customers need to feel that they can trust the company as well as understand how to use the new services.

The costs of acquiring a new account derives mainly from:

- the cost of getting and processing the software
- the commissions paid to the distribution channel
- the employee or the outsourcing costs
- the cost of calls if a customer relationships center is required

The higher the cost of acquiring new customers to digital insurance, the larger the number of transactions necessary to reach a reasonable payback period per account.

Compliance is also a big (and increasing) driver of costs since digital insurance might increase the amount of documentation collected as well as the information to be stored and reported. On the other side, better compliance might improve also the availability of reliable information to manage the companies.

Return on investment

Although companies adopting digital insurance recognize the importance of riding the digitization wave in order to keep up with trends, stay current, and connect with customers, they are not only in it for those abstract reasons. As well-run, successful businesses, these companies want and expect a significant return on the investments they are making in digital insurance.

Indeed, digital insurance could boost their premium income by 8 percent, compared with 4 percent for digital followers. They also target a 2.3 point combined ratio improvement, compared with only 1.4 point of cost of revenue (COR) improvement for digital followers.[38]

However, even companies adopting digital insurance are far from what could be achieved through digitization in terms of value generation, as outlined in an Accenture report.[39] This suggests the possibility of a combined ratio improvement of 4 to 7 percentage points over a three-year period.

One might argue that the Accenture report, based on delivered projects for insurance companies, might be conservative compared to what can be achieved. Actually, a certain number of insurance companies have already achieved and improved on these values.

This digital value generation gap is huge, as aggregate global insurance companies are probably underestimating the potential of digital insurance's impact on profitability by $15 billion to $30 billion.[40]

Based on the experience of a certain number of insurance companies, a thoughtful digitization program can deliver up to 65 percent in cost reduction and a 90 percent reduction in turnaround time on key insurance processes, and improve conversion rates by more than 20 percent[41].

Successful digital insurance investments (by way of customer impact, cost, and adoption) have very high Return on Investment (ROI). The performance of less-successful implementations could potentially be smaller (possibly even with negative ROIs) when adoption is very low. Therefore, it is important to approach digital insurance by taking into account its challenges and remediate to them.

ROI does not depend solely on the product. Rather, it depends on its design, its launch, its performance, its functionality, and, not least, its marketing.

Digital insurance should improve the economics mainly by lowering operating costs and, to a lesser extent, also by applying analytics techniques to risk selection, pricing, and fraud detection loss ratios. Lowering distribution costs comes as a third opportunity in terms of value.

All of these approaches make sense and are clear value generation opportunities for insurance companies. There are additional actions that could further improve the profitability of digital insurance:[42]

- increasing the efficiency of cross-channel transformation, and particularly the speed and efficiency of transforming digital leads and quotations, as there are still huge differences in transformation rates among insurance companies, which can significantly impact acquisition costs
- optimizing customer processing channels, both by improving customer experience and reducing costs of servicing, and leveraging new service channels options like social media and remote video communication and support
- improving customer retention, one of the highest benefits in terms of value generation given the continued growth of the switching economy

Consumers in the United States suffered during the rollout of Healthcare.gov and the state health insurance exchanges. They could not get online. Once online, the information was hard to understand. For consumers accustomed to easy shopping on the Web, choosing a health insurance plan online was an exercise in frustration[43].

This situation highlights how important it is for insurance companies – not only health insurance companies but also property and casualty and, increasingly, life insurance companies – to master digital. Insurance marketing is already massive. Insurance companies spend more than $6 billion a year on marketing in the United States. Geico alone spends more on marketing than McDonald's or Coca Cola.[44] Even so, while retailers and cable companies moved their businesses online years ago, many insurance companies, struggling with legacy technology and outmoded organizational structures, are playing catch-up.

Swot analysis

Swot analysis is one of the most interesting analyses to evaluate the status and the perspectives of a company, a product or a service. It is a structured planning method used to evaluate:[45]

- strengths: characteristics of the business or initiative that provide an advantage over others
- weaknesses: characteristics that place the object of the analysis at a disadvantage relative to others
- opportunities: elements that the business or initiative could exploit to its advantage
- threats: elements in the environment that could cause trouble for the business or initiative

The identification of Swots is important since the analysis can provide support in planning for achieving the insurance company's objectives. Users of Swot analysis need to ask and answer questions that generate meaningful information for each category (strengths, weaknesses, opportunities, and threats) to make the analysis useful and use it to find their competitive advantages.

In the case of digital insurance, such analysis can help in understanding the feasibility of reaching the objectives of the initiative and finding the competitive advantages of the insurance company. Digital insurance is characterized by (see Table 2.1) the following Swot:

- The strengths of digital insurance are clear. The customer can access his/her insurance company from everywhere, always, with any channel, and with the level of privacy that the customer prefers.
- The weaknesses are clear. The digital connection might not be available or be of low quality. The situation is improving, but certainly, it is still a problem in a certain number of areas.
- The opportunities for digital insurance are great. Young people are an interesting part of the market, not only because they are digital natives but also because they represent the future. If the insurance company can make them faithful customers, the duration of the relationships is potentially very long. Most digital insurance customers are valuable customers: rich, young, and interested in profitable insurance company products and services. These services are saving institutions money. As the number of users of digital insurance has grown, agency visits have decreased considerably. Javelin Strategy Research released a report entitled "Leveraging an Omnichannel Approach by Mobile Banking: Fight for $1.5 B in Mobile Banking Insurance Profits."[46] The same could apply also to digital insurance. The evidence is growing that the rising customer adoption of digital technologies alters the agency-based distribution model in the financial services.[47]
- The threats are similarly rather powerful. Devices and data can be lost or stolen, and in the case of the loss of a mobile device, with it will go even the possibility of contacting immediately the support that would block any further transaction. Latency might be a problem, especially if the insurance company has not designed the application well and does not operate it properly. The integration with the rest of the insurance operations (other channels, other applications, and so on) might be challenging and not always easy to implement.

Table 2.1 Swot analysis for digital insurance

Strengths	**Weaknesses**
Established brands	Limited frequency of consumer interaction
Expertise in pricing and risk management	Legacy ICT systems, operational complexity
Detailed understanding of claims patterns and processing	Lagging other industries in the "digital" consumer experience – especially in claims processing
Large existing consumer base	Channel conflicts
Ownership of face-to-face distribution	Network coverage and accessibility
High degree of customer trust	Size of the screen in the case of the mobile
Accessible everywhere	Multiple OS, devices, networks
No need of a human intermediary, but possibility to interact through the network to purchase or get servicing	
Opportunities	**Threats**
Development of new flexible products – meeting unmet customer needs	Risk of adjacent entrants into insurance
Increased cross-selling potential	Possibility of disruptive models – for instance, crowd insurance
Possibility to manage new emerging risk types – for instance, cyber risk	Industry is not used to work as a ecosystem or with many other partners
Step change in operational efficiency	Smaller risk pools given to telematics
Improve service offers to customers	To be a late adopter of technology
Possibility to reach interesting markets: • Young people • Uninsured • Underinsured	Loss or stealing of the customer device
	Latency
	Complexity of integration

Source: Adapted by the author from the Morgan Stanley document: Insurance and Technology, Evolution or Revolution in a Digital World, 8 September 2014.

Overall, this is the Swot of digital insurance. The actions are clear: enhance your strengths and reduce your weaknesses, chase the opportunities and minimize the threats.

The reward might be very high. The results might be well worth the efforts. The recommendations are:

- have a clear vision of where you want to go and the target customers
- perform a comprehensive and detailed Swot analysis for your target market
- set detailed achievable goals and objectives
- proceed cautiously: one step at a time. You can eat an elephant, but only in bites

Challenges

Apart from the Swot analysis, there are many challenges that need to be overcome when launching digital insurance. This chapter lists some of them. They should not prevent a further diffusion of digital insurance. Certainly, they do require appropriate remediation to reduce their probability of occurrence and their impact, and at the same time improve the alert process.

Integration. A relevant challenge with digital insurance is the integration with the remaining insurance systems of the company and channels. Integration is necessary. Interestingly enough, this is a technological problem mimicking the organization problem. For the latter, one of the solutions (as in Genialloyd in the case of Allianz) is a complete separation with respect to the traditional financial institution. This is not possible in the case of information and telecommunication applications. Insurance companies need to integrate digital insurance applications with the hundreds of other applications of the insurance company (core insurance, financial systems, risk management, reporting and compliance applications, content management, customer relationship systems, and so on). The launch of digital insurance on a public cloud might solve some of these challenges and allow a quicker launch in the market. Not all insurance companies are yet willing to take this route. One of the reasons is that the mergers and acquisitions during the last years in the insurance world have brought to an average increase in the size of the companies. This has pushed many insurance companies to do insourcing rather than outsourcing.

Handset operability. One challenge with digital insurance is that there are many operating systems, handsets, and network operators. None of them is under an insurance company's control. Potentially, an insurance company would like to allow access to digital insurance from any device, any time, and anywhere. This requires, for instance, the ability to cater to different operating systems like iOS, Android, Windows, Palm, BlackBerry, and so on.

Similarly, there are a large number of different mobile phone devices. Another big challenge for insurance companies is to offer digital insurance solutions on any type of devices. Some of these devices support Java ME, and others support SIM Application Toolkit, a WAP browser, or only SMS.

Some similar challenges would apply to the network in case the insurance company desires that the same solution should work in more than one country or with all the operators.

There is a challenge of interoperability between digital insurance applications due to a perceived lack of common technology for digital insurance. In practice, it is too early in the service life cycle for interoperability to be addressed within an individual country. Some insurance interfaces are defined, and for instance money movements between insurance companies follow the IS0–8583 standard. As digital insurance matures, money movements between service providers should naturally adopt the same standards as in the financial services world. Similarly for interfaces there are the standards like ISO/IEC JTC 1/SC 35.[48]

Mobility, risk, and change. In approaching mobility in the organizations, it is essential to balance improvements and the risks connected with their uses.

In the past years, there has been a path of revolutionary transformation in digital insurance. More change will come in the near future. There are radical innovations that the growth of wireless technologies, combined with the cloud and the ability to manage large amounts of data, is allowing insurance companies to deploy widely. Cloud computing is making it much easier to use different channels to connect to the applications and data of an organization.[49] Therefore, it is important to analyze the challenges and the remediations that decision-makers should embrace to continue and enhance this growth and innovation.

The reasons why customers now use digital and mobile devices are several: lower costs, ease of use, and mostly demand from customers and businesses.

In the case of corporations and even more frequently in Small and Medium Enterprises (SME), users tend to prefer to use their own mobiles, tablets, and laptops rather than the one supplied by the organization. This is the so-called Bring Your Own Device (BYOD) approach.

According to a Novarica survey of 86 insurance company CIOs, support for BYOD for tablets and smartphones is widespread and expanding among both large and midsize insurance companies, while support for BYOD laptops lags behind.[50] Supporting BYOD is rapidly becoming a standard cost of doing business for insurance companies. While it does involve managing security challenges, insurance companies need to plan for a short-term future in which BYOD plays a bigger role, also taking into account that this might be a similar problems of their customers using their own devices.

BYOD policies certainly have raised the risk to organizations with regard to internal threats. The primary challenge is the ability to manage the risks associated with mobile access to corporate data and applications, while securing respect for the organization's policies.

It is important to balance anything personal with the proprietary and regulated world of corporate data and applications. Even if an organization uses tools to manage the devices, it still has limitations and issues to overcome. One relevant issue is dealing with a difficult user base. The users may be concerned that the organization can spy on them and monitor their every move. Some regulations in particular countries make it difficult to use such monitoring and management systems.

The situation today is that:

- malicious threats to mobile devices are increasing
- user carelessness is widespread
- customers demand less expensive ways to use services, content, and data

All these are challenges for ICT, security, and compliance leadership in adapting and continuously innovating in this area. Digital insurance is moving faster than most departments can keep up with it.

It is very important to define and enforce policies. Risk, legal, and compliance departments should contribute to define policies, which would include:

- acceptable use
- access to personal and sensitive data and to social networking
- cellular networks
- mobile devices
- data governance
- employee agreements

Risk management. The possible concerns about digital insurance are real, if not in the real world, then certainly in the mind of a certain number of customers and managers. It is useful to define how to approach these issues in a rational way. Risk management helps. The approach should be based on the so-called three P's[51]: be predictive, proactive, and prescriptive.

Enterprise risk management is a process intended to identify potential events that may affect the organization's performance. Its aim is helping managing threats within the limit of an acceptable risk and to provide reasonable assurance regarding the achievement of corporate objectives. It should be a continuous process, pervasive, and repetitive, that has an impact on the entire organization, where it should be used throughout the organization in its individual assets, in each line of business, and in any organizational unit.

The phases of a project for risk management are:[52]

1. identification of the value for the customer; define targets to reach
2. risk identification: identify the risks within the organization
3. risk evaluation: determine the probability, impact, and ability to be able to get early warning of the realization of risks
4. risk setup: locate the internal/external sources needed for the measurement and risk identification of the key risk indicators (KRIs)
5. risk monitoring: organize a structured model of reporting that allows an insurance company to monitor the evolution of the risks and highlight in a timely way the increased likelihood, impacts, and alerts for each risk
6. risk response: take action when a risk arises, in terms of remediation, reduction, reinsurance, or even acceptance

Skills and experiences

Another challenge connected with digital insurance is the lack of skills available in the market to design, develop, test, deploy, and maintain digital insurance and its security. The use of excellent consultants and organizations is strongly recommended.

Remediation

There are many ways of remediating the challenges mentioned previously in this chapter. The following chapter on Governance deals with the remediation of security challenges.

Once the digital insurance application is launched, the most important remediation is provided by excellent support. This can be done in the ways detailed in the next sections.

User support

Migration support

Insurance companies expect to see the consistent adoption of digital insurance, at least in the medium-long term, once they make digital insurance available to their customer base. Help-desk requests must be minimal, as a verification of the usability of the application.

However, the customer might need help. Thus, it is essential to provide a functional and technical support that also includes the possibility of chatting, talking, or exchanging messages with the help desk. Talking would be best, since other modes might lead to misunderstanding or require too much keying. On the other side insurance companies desire to use less expensive ways of communication.

Another possibility is to provide for a "steward of the technology." This is a proven approach, for example, in air transport, in which organizations have begun to implement self-check-in kiosks in airports as an alternative to physical or online check-in. If left alone in front of an unfamiliar machine, a passenger may prefer to get in line rather than try to check in with a machine. But if, for the start-up phase, the organization makes available attendants who invite the passenger to try the do-it-yourself kiosk, and assist the passenger for the first two or three times, the passenger may then go directly to the automatic kiosk the next time. Similarly, insurance companies may have to provide services (via online or telephone, human or with avatars [the virtual person performing help desk in a web application]) that are well structured to accompany their customers in the move to digital insurance.

This migration to digital insurance opens up an interesting scenario in which the agency is no longer considered as a place in which any insurance transaction is done. The agency should thus take on a higher and specialized profile. It becomes a possible reference point and a focus, even in the customer's mind. This requires a complete reorganization of human resources: the front-line employees should devote more of their time to managing more complex tasks with high added value, for which the agencies continue to remain a reference point. The fact that most of the agencies might not be a legal part of the company might complicate the task. However, it must be done anyway to ensure the survival of the agencies.

Call centers

All systems are targeted to a high quality; however, sometimes there may be issues of non-quality. In this respect, a study from IBM shows the importance of customer relationships.[53] The survey shows that 66 percent of managers indicate customer relationships as the third most important key source of sustained economic value.

One of the ways that organizations use to interface with customers is through call centers. Call centers are changing due to several factors. The way in which they are changing is important, but the way in which their names are changing due to their evolving roles is also interesting.

A call center is typically defined as an operations center that interfaces with customers in a variety of ways, from technical and administrative support, billing, and provisioning, to technical support and more.

Over the last several years, the design and organization of call centers has changed drastically. There are many reasons for this, such as the fact that organizations have high costs of maintaining the technology and the personnel required by a call center.

There are several current trends for the call center:

- There is an increase in the scale and scope of call center operations. Customers' expectations for high-quality service from call centers have risen. Important competitive advantages in today's marketplace are service quality, convenience, speed, accuracy, and value.
- Multichannel communication centers are used in which several new channels provide a wide variety of services to customers. For example, phones, Web, e-mails, web chats, and social networks are all used to maximize opportunities for increasing customer contact.
- Call center operations are also being outsourced to remote locations. Advanced telecommunications systems have enabled organizations (for instance, financial services [as Bank of America, BNP Paribas, American Express, and so on or Telecom Operators such as BT, Vodafone, Telecom Italia, and so on]) to outsource their customer support centers to offshore locations (for instance, India, the Philippines, or North African countries).

In light of these changes, it is interesting to see how call centers have changed in substance and in their names:

- Initially organizations used the term "call centers." The idea was to provide the customers a place where they could "call" somebody to describe the issues and get advice on how to resolve them. It was indeed a passive way for a company to view the relationship with the customer.

- Later, call centers started to be called contact centers. This name reflects one important aspect of the call center: they are an important contact point between the organization and the customer. This name emphasized the way the organization "saw" the call center as the frontier of the organization.
- The next step was to change the name to call center in customer service. This denomination introduced the concept of service. It was still very much an internal view of the relationship and indicated a passive approach toward the customer.
- Call centers are being asked to perform more and more nontraditional tasks with the same resource allocations. While the more traditional roles of call centers (such as collections and customer support) are still important, current trends suggest that more strategic roles (such as building the customer relationship and selling company products and services) have become more prevalent. The call center started to be named customer care. The idea is that it is important to care for the customers.
- In some cases, call centers are called customer support centers. The idea is that customers need support in their activities, which implies that it is necessary to improve the centers' user friendliness.
- A better name for customer care would be customer relationships center (CRC). This term underlines the fact that the call center is one of the most important points for customer relationships management. It must be a place for adding value to the customers and to the organization. The name CRC is important. It underlines the fact that the interaction with a call center is an important "experience" for the customer. The underlying idea is that the organization provides more an experience than just information on a product or a service.

Over time, the call center has become more and more an active part of the organization. It is an extremely important point at which it is possible to move from being a passive call center to an active service-to-sale (S2S) point. Call centers are indeed a key contact point with customers. In other words, the moment at which a relationship is taking place with the customer can and should be used as an important moment for selling additional services and products.

Live chats

Chats in digital insurance are essentially text messaging with an insurance company associate. However, the live chat is still not widely used to interact with customers in most of the large insurance companies. Nevertheless, given customers' rising dependency on digital insurance and increasing usage of text messages, live chats address these two trends and present a win-win scenario for insurance companies and their customers.[54]

Chats benefit everyone. They are less formal than an e-mail and less time consuming than live phone calls. For insurance companies, live chats allow customer service agents to address multiple inquiries all at once. If the chat feature is offered after the log-in phase, insurance companies can offer a much more personalized experience. It is possible to display customer information, account history, and past customer service interactions for the associate to see. As a result, these sessions are likely to be shorter and more effective. A live chat can help in reducing or eliminating the waiting and time in line inside an agency.

As with every other form of communication, customer live chats are another channel for pushing on S2S. The associates interfacing via the live chat provide assistance. They also use the opportunity of the contact with the customer to offer other insurance services.

Furthermore, insurance companies may consider improving live chats by connecting them to their secure customer-messaging platforms if they offer one. The secure messaging platform can assist the live chat feature by continuing the conversation even after the chat has ended. Follow-up for service evaluation, for example, can play a major role in enhancing the customer service experience. Chats can allow also screen sharing so that agents can show customers how to navigate the mobile apps and sites. The next stage of the evolution of live chat will be live video chats.

New online-only insurance company start-ups have the most to gain from providing a web or mobile chat service. Organizations such as Genialloyd, Genertel, Direct Line, and so on are positioned to act as catalysts for the adoption of mobile chats.

In perspective, avatars, or virtual agents, can perform some basic chatting activities in support of digital insurance.

Fraud

The biggest challenge with digital insurance is fraud. Particularly dangerous are employee frauds, even if external users of digital insurance can also do them. People have always attempted and carried out fraud in insurance. The danger of digital insurance is that frauds can be bigger and faster, thanks to the underlying technology.

Fraud is the risk that affects the accuracy of the accounting records apart from the loss of assets and threat to reputation. Frauds result in misstatements of assets and expenses in financial statements. Major frauds also endanger the ability of an organization to continue its operations. Many control policies and procedures should protect against fraud.

Components of a fraud

The most common frauds consist of three acts:[55]

- Theft of assets. Because of its liquidity, the most desirable asset to a thief is currency. Most organizations implement controls to make the theft of currency difficult to commit and conceal. Therefore, most frauds involve stealing other assets such as checks, inventory, equipment, or even information.
- Conversion of assets. When a criminal steals an asset other than currency, usually the asset itself is not valuable to the criminal. So the criminal attempts to convert the asset into currency.
- Concealment of the theft. A thief who has an ongoing relationship with an organization, such as an employee or business intermediary, attempts to conceal the theft. This either prevents or delays recognition or prevents identification of the thief. Concealment provides additional opportunities to steal and can lead to an ongoing fraud.

A more comprehensive list of common frauds is in Table 2.2.

Table 2.2 Most common frauds

Type of fraud	Examples
Theft of cash	False or overstated claims Stealing checks, cash receipts, petty cash Altering insurance investments Forgery Using company accounts to pay personal bills
Billing fraud	Sending fictitious or overstated invoices and intercepting the resulting payments Lapping of accounts receivable
Sourcing fraud	Paying excessive prices to get kickbacks from suppliers Purchases from nonexistent suppliers Fixing competitive bids
Kiting of funds	Using cash transfers between accounts to conceal a shortage of cash
Misuse of company resources	Using company payment cards or purchase orders for personal purchases Using company equipment for personal purposes Unauthorized sale of assets or trading
Payroll crimes	Cashing unused paychecks Overstating hours worked Issuing paychecks to fictitious employees or consultants

Source: Adapted by the author from W. Steve Albrecht, Gerald W. Wernz, Timothy L. Williams, *Fraud Bringing Light to the Dark Side of Business*. Burr Ridge, IL: Irwin Professional Publishing, 1995, 13.

The fraud triangle

In order to fight fraud, it is important to analyze it in detail. There is a model that is rather useful, and it is described in the next few pages.[56] It can be represented in the form of a triangle with the three aspects of a fraud: pressure, opportunity, and rationalization.

- Pressure. Usually individuals commit fraud as a result of some form of pressure. Most often the pressure is financial: the fraudster wants to get the money for personal purposes.
- Opportunity. A person who commits fraud must be in a position that provides an opportunity. Sometimes the person has custody of an asset or has authority to initiate transactions in an asset. In the case of claims, the person will overstate the damages possibly with the support of some third parties.
- Rationalization. The other factor is rationalization. Individuals who perceive themselves as honest may engage in criminal behavior because they rationalize their actions. They convince themselves that they are justified in committing the fraud.

A good system of control should be able to limit the opportunities for fraud to be committed. It is therefore important that there be a proper segregation of duties. This would mean examination of a claim, normally using an appraiser, definition of the value to be paid to the insured, separating custody, record keeping, the authorizing of transactions, payments. Thus, if a person commits a fraud, the company possibly can discover it. However, even good systems are limited by the possibilities of collusion, or management can override or if there is sloppiness of controls.

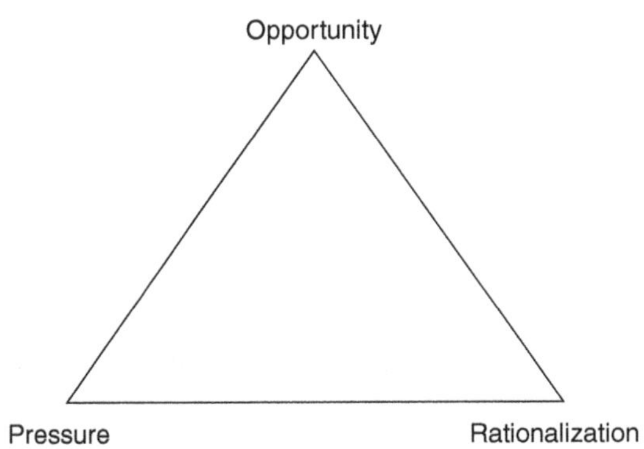

Figure 2.2 The triangle of fraud

Source: Krause et al. (1999), op. cit.

Whenever a fraud occurs, the three aspects of the fraud triangle are present. The person must:

- feel pressure from some sources to commit the crime
- have an opportunity
- be able to rationalize his/her behavior

Just as recognizing the elements in the fraud triangle can aid in preventing fraud, so can the knowledge of the components of any fraud can provide a way of detecting them and possibly prevent them.

Fraud detection

Each of the previous acts provides an opportunity for detecting fraud. Accountants may see one when performing their routine duties, or auditors may suspect fraud while conducting an audit. The actions for what may be detected include:[57]

- Reconciliation, periodically reconciling asset records with assets on hand. If records indicate that assets are missing, the auditor or the accountant should alert HR and/or the management at least one level higher than the employee responsible for the claims or the assets, or the police, in the case of suspected external fraudster;
- Conversion, which occurs when a thief converts a stolen asset into currency. Many forms of asset conversion are not easy to detect from within the organization.
- The concealment of a theft. To conceal a theft, the fraudster must do some fake action such as, for instance, keeping the recorded assets equal to the actual assets on hand or in the case of false claims get the support of a third party or of the appraiser. Because assets have been stolen, the fraudster must make a fraudulent credit entry to an asset account in order to delay the discovery of the fraud.

Many organizations also have a security officer, whose responsibility includes maintaining adequate security and integrity.

Security

Security is one of the major challenges since in digital insurance the insurance company does not have control of all the components of the digital insurance, such as the network and especially the devices. It is important to manage security also since many customers have concerns about it. It must be addressed and remediated as much as possible.

Penetration testing is a great way to test the robustness of the security in web and mobile applications. The chapter on Governance deals in detail with security.

Conclusions

This chapter stresses the fact that strategy, marketing, economics, and challenges are very important in digital insurance. Insurance companies should take into account several points in connection with each one of these aspects.

Insurance companies need to understand the economic impact on the entire customer relationship. Digital insurance is still in its early maturity. Insurance companies should consider it as a fully fledged approach to the business and to the market, with a dedicated, passionate support structure. It is important to define an effective vision, strategy, and plan.

Marketing is important in digital insurance, since it allows, for instance, insurance companies to up-sell and cross-sell insurance and other financial or nonfinancial services. It offers the potential for reaching new and unexplored markets, like underinsureds, uninsureds, immigrants, and so on. These are the potential next generation of insurance customers, who otherwise may not ever become customers of an insurance company.

It is important to orchestrate lifestyle management, such as branding, preferences, content, social relationships, and information.

Measurement matters. The most advanced insurance companies in digital insurance generally have the best sense of the effect of their approach on customer behavior. Measuring outcomes is essential to the development of an impactful initiative. This would avoid the risks of considering digital insurance only as cost generation or applying pressure to provide revenues from digital insurance pricing and activities.

Insurance companies can be successful at marketing, technology or functionally strong or process-oriented. The more successful institutions in digital insurance are those that are strong in all these aspects. Leaders in digital insurance should continually monitor and leverage the evolution of digital solutions.

Top management support and staff engagement are widely mentioned as critical in this as in many other initiatives that insurance companies can take.

On the other side, digital insurance has many opportunities and challenges. It can provide many excellent opportunities to increase the value to all stakeholders, get more customers, sell more services, and optimize costs. Digital channels are particularly effective for facilitating the ways in which customers and insurance companies interact and transact.

To close this chapter on a positive note, the outstanding characteristic of digital insurance is that it is virtual and not physical. It allows its use and launch in many markets at the same time. In a united Europe or other similar regions, this is important and can be done in a matter of months. This will bring great and large economies of scale. The challenge here is that the insurance companies need to design one solution for many countries, languages, cultures, economies, types of customers, diverse risks, compliance, and so on. Globalization helps, but insurance companies need to retain control. Digital solutions can help in customizing products, processes, organizations, and business models.

Finally, digital insurance is one of the best examples of how to digitize and become lean in an insurance environment. With the economic crisis continuing, this is a great opportunity to become more agile, hence effective, efficient, economical, and ethical. This is the subject of the chapter on Governance of digital insurance.

3
The Digital Insurance Basic Solutions

Introduction

The insurance industry is evolving. Customers are informed and demanding. The entire organization and the Information and communication technology (ICT) departments need to establish a stronger customer orientation, build deeper relationships with their internal and external clients, deliver products to market faster, and be prepared to partner.

New regulations, dynamic capital markets, and mergers and acquisitions are growing.[1] Insurance companies face stiffer competition for good customers from traditional and nontraditional players using new solutions. These factors can lower earned premiums and reduce resources available to serve customers.

To maximize earned premiums, some successful insurance companies optimize their distribution network and connect wherever possible directly with the customer, while maintaining the old distribution network. This approach helps enable and motivate a diverse channel and reduce time to market.

In order to reduce operating costs, successful insurance companies pursue integration and the streamlining of processes. This can help eliminate waste and get the right information to the right persons at the right time.

To run better, an insurance company must deliver superior customer service by better connecting with its customers. This approach helps ensure that a company does not lose hard-won customers to a more appealing competitor. Insurance companies need to take into account that more and more customers will be able to change their insurance company more easily. To succeed, insurance companies must provide "customer delights" in the user experience and not just financial services.

Focusing on customer delight enables the insurance company to:

- increase customer focus in a multichannel environment, delivering the right products to the right customers by using the right channel and the correct pricing
- reduce operational costs by streamlining core insurance processes across major lines of business
- manage enterprise-wide risk and compliance using real-time insights, while supporting jointly risk and finance decisions. This integration under one unified landscape offers competitive advantages for controlling costs and managing change and risk. It improves data quality and enables quantitative and qualitative integration across systems, accounting principles, and risk approaches. With this level of integration in place, insurance companies can effectively adopt additional valuation principles, risk model approaches, or other analytic applications as needed

The ability to understand what might delight customers and not only satisfy their basic needs and at the same time provide a quick response with the right products delivered through the right channels earns customer loyalty and enhances operational efficiency. To reach these objectives it is essential to use sound information and communication solutions to delight the customer.

This chapter analyzes in detail some of the basic solutions of the insurance information and communication systems that are able to meet the basic challenges which the introduction of digital insurance requires.[2] Later chapters present more advanced and effective solutions.

Enterprise architecture

Enterprise architecture (EA) is a well-defined practice for conducting enterprise analysis, design, planning, and implementation using a holistic approach at all times for the successful development and execution of strategy.

Successful EA requires a strong vision in business and solutions that enables insurance companies to fulfill their medium and long-term strategy while coping with immediate, tactical initiatives. EA is a continuous process at the heart of the enterprise.

Technology alone will not drive an organization to EA and data maturity. Technology is an enabler, but EA requires strong stakeholder awareness and buy-in, ownership, and understanding of the business domain and processes. Insurance solutions should be built using a modular architecture that simplifies changing and extending the system's functions during the maintenance phase.

The best way to start with digital insurance is to define the enterprise architecture for a specific company. In doing so, it is important to consider reference models possibly using a component approach.[3] Figure 3.1 provides a component reference model for insurance companies. The

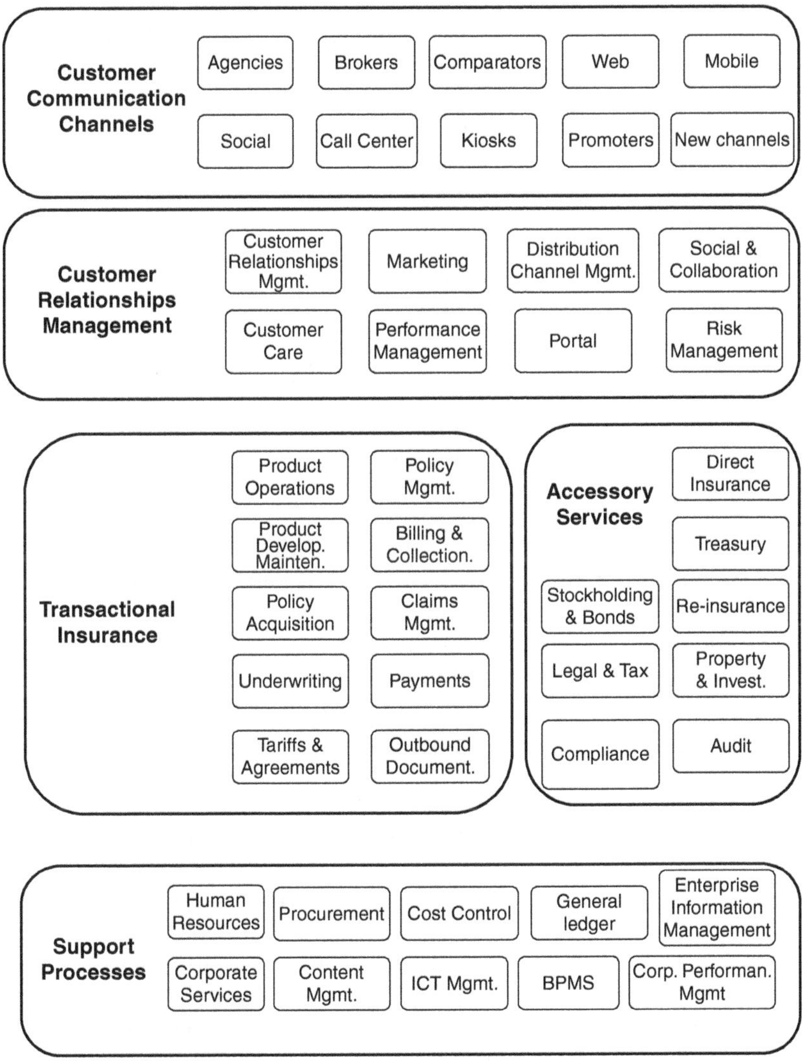

Figure 3.1 Component reference model

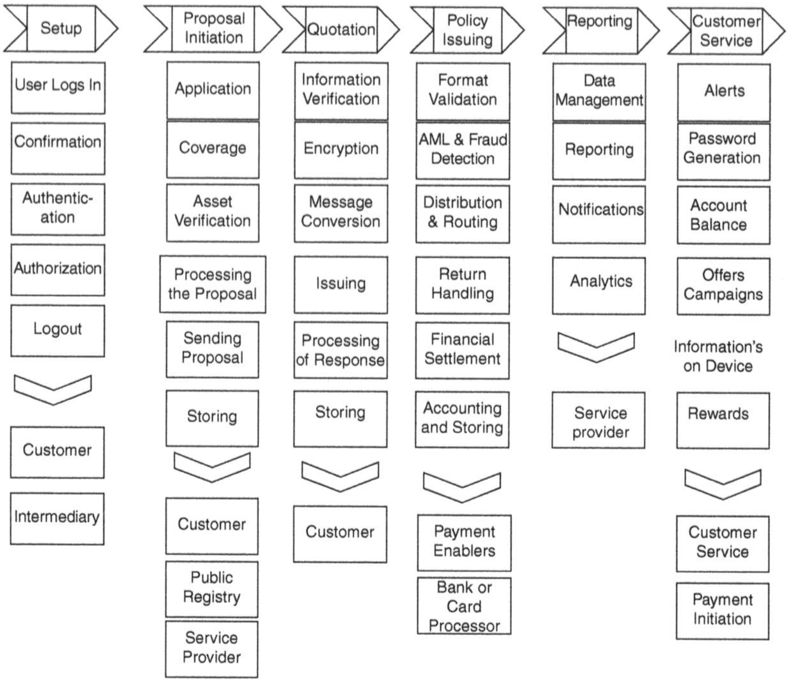

Figure 3.2 Example of reference model for policy management

solution suite constitutes a comprehensive environment for digital insurance solutions. A more detailed model can be found in the literature.[4,5,6]

It is possible to dive into the component reference model. An example might be the policy management process. An example of such a model is described at a very high level in Figure 3.2.

Processes in an insurance company

One approach to analyzing the myriad of transactions, systems, processing, procedures, interfaces, and databases in a digital solution is to classify them into a limited number of logical processes. The definition of each process stems from the activity included within that process.

Each individual process in a digital insurance solution encompasses related logical steps (activities) that must be completed in an insurance operation, regardless of the configuration of the system or the organizational structure of the company.

The main processes within an insurance company are:

- the policy and insurance contract management module, including the functions to support the sales agents and intermediaries to do their jobs effectively, efficiently, and economically
- claims and loss reward regulations management and reporting
- reserve calculations, recalculations, and reporting
- reinsurance and coinsurance
- treasury
- investments
- Human Resources (HR) and payroll
- procurement

There are also two supporting processes:

- Accounting and financial reporting or back office, unlike the other processes, usually does not support directly customer transactions but provides information to the various levels of management, investors, and regulatory bodies.
- Innovation manages the transformation of the insurance company, especially in terms of products and services.

Each process has seven characteristics:

- activities, subprocesses, or functions
- workflow or sequence of activities
- transaction postings that record an event
- documents that substantiate the transactions performed
- databases or files used for storage or further processing
- interfaces that exchange data with other internal processes or external entities
- resources to perform the activities

An activity is a major processing task or an element of an insurance information and communication system that processes logically related transactions. Although each insurance company's activity is unique, every company must perform the activities identified within each process. Every activity involved in processing transactions, including management supervision, control, and review, can be identified within the eight plus two processes listed above.

This process concept focuses attention on the flow of data through the system rather than on the effect of transactions on specific accounts.

This focus emphasizes the interrelations of the various processes and reveals the impact of a single event on many elements of an insurance information and communication system.[7]

In addition to processing transactions, some of the processes usually exercise control over the insurance company's assets. For example, the treasury process is responsible for cash and cash equivalents and the investment process is responsible for securities and nonsecurities investments.

This description of insurance processes is not intended to typify normal organizational structures. Insurance companies frequently establish separate organizational units or outsource activities relative to a particular process or subprocess. However, the activities performed, not the departments performing them, determine the processes to which they belong.

The following sections analyze the previous processes according to the classical macro process structure in a company:

- demand to order, which covers from the customer inquiry to getting an order
- order to remittance, which covers from the order to its fulfillment and the payment
- procure to pay, which covers the procurement cycle
- record to report, which covers the administrate and management control activities

Particular attention is dedicated to the second macro-process due to its relevance in terms of resources required.

Demand to order

To satisfy highly variable and dynamic customer demand, insurance companies need to understand and anticipate customer needs. They also need to create and propose offers that are personalized, easy to consume, and consistent across indirect and direct channels.

Insurance companies should benchmark and model service levels similar to the ones provided in other industries. Customers expect the same (or better) user experience from their insurance companies as they have with their banks, retailers, or consumer-products companies.

Customers or prospects need to understand their insurance policies and the risks they have to secure. They want simple, high-quality products and services – and an insurance company they can trust, which is responsive and reliable.

Customers also want to contact their insurance company through the channels of their choice via quick and simple interactions – anytime, anywhere, and on any device.

They expect real-time responses to help them solve their issues through excellent, personalized experience. They also expect insurance companies to have a true 360-degree view and the ability to recommend products and services personalized to their individual needs.

Customer engagement intelligence, customer relationship management, and sales force optimization, including incentive and commission management, are major areas of improvement for insurance companies. They must also manage policies across lines of business to gain a 360-degree view of the customer base. There is the need for systems that provide end-to-end solutions for:

- marketing, which helps companies gain a real-time, 360-degree understanding of the target customers, enabling effective responses to the customer requirements, better visibility, and full support for campaigns, offers, and product processes, including characteristics, eligibility, and pricing
- a product and proposal management process, which provides a streamlined quotation management processes and flexible maintenance of existing and new products. This process should also provide product tools to create and deliver personalized offerings to customers and support multiple lines of business in a single solution
- channel management, which involves establishing consistency and enabling flexible, intuitive interactions that anticipate customer needs in a uniform way across channels
- sales, which consists of streamlining operations by giving customers access to information and processes on any channel to delight customers
- sales force optimization, or supporting sales professionals, be they employees or intermediaries, to acquire, grow, and retain profitable customers, accelerate buying decisions, and identify opportunities for improving sales effectiveness and efficiency

Insurance is becoming a commodity for a growing number of individuals and corporations. This is a danger for insurance companies in their efforts to create and sustain competitive advantages. The remediation to this situation is that insurance companies must act fast in bringing mass customized products to the target prospects and customers.

Typical functions of the demand-to-order process include proposals, quotations, and rating. Quotation and rating transactions are the foundation of the policy administration systems that support the issuing, variation, and processing of the policies. Details such as administrative and technical descriptions of the coverage or additional insureds needed for complete policy processing are required information for the quotation of a policy. With the arrival in the insurance market of comparators, which allow prospects to immediately compare offers from different companies, the demand-to-order process has become more complex. It starts with an anonymous proposal, which is stored for a limited period of time, and is accessible from the prospect. If the proposal is accepted, the proposal is transformed in a formal quotation, which the insurance company must respect for a defined period of time. During this period, the customer can accept it or not. If the quotation is accepted, the customer must provide supporting documentation and pay the premium (or part of it depending on the insurance product). At the end of this contracting phase, the quotation becomes a valid policy or contract.

Critical source documents in the demand-to-order process are policy applications. Data that are used in this process reside in the quotation master database, the prospect database, the sales force (mainly agents) database, the product catalogue, and the pricing database, any of which may be used for management information reporting. The quotations and their different versions need to be kept in the quotation master database for a certain period of time, normally defined by the company policy or by regulations.

The premium process involves many functional departments: sales, production, underwriting, policy services, billing, and intermediaries.

Murray Group Insurance Services, Inc.

The Murray Group Insurance Services, Inc. is a family-owned independent insurance agency in Albany, New York. It is the cliché agency: a single location on a main street in a midsize town, with a long history of writing predominately personal insurance policies.[8] They have been marketing their agency online for several years. Currently inbound, unsolicited new business revenue from Internet-related sources makes up about 15 percent of overall production and it is growing. The company tracks return on investment (ROI) on all online marketing activities and has produced a positive ROI every single year.

Order to remittance

To compete, insurance companies must streamline operations and deliver relevant products and services to the target markets in a timely manner. They need to ensure a favorable experience during the policy-management and claims processes and stay vigilant and transparent to possible risks and frauds.

The claims process is not only an insurance company's largest cost and loss but also a defining moment of truth for the customers. It can influence customers' loyalty and their decisions to stay with a company or move on and tell all of their friends why they are leaving rather than promoting the company.

Insurance companies must have transparency into risk also to the portfolio ceded to reinsurance and coinsurance and manage their portfolio in real time.

With customer expectations constantly on the rise, many insurance companies now view customer service, billing, and payments as sales and marketing tools rather than simply operations or financial processes. Insurance companies need to use efficient billing and payments as one way to meet customer expectations across all distribution channels and establish a customer-centric approach.

There is the need for solutions that provide a series of competitive end-to-end solutions to streamline insurance operations while delivering products to market quickly:

The reference architecture is composed of the following processes:

- policy management process to streamline relationships with the customers
- broker and commission management to help manage the relationships with intermediaries, particularly from the point of view of the commissions at all levels, be they for the agency owners, the employees of the agency, or the employees of the call center, or similar
- billing and payments to realize greater cost efficiency through integrated, customer-centric billing and receipts across all products and lines of business
- claims to help reduce loss-adjustment expenses and increase customer loyalty and retention through an integrated, complete claims process
- services to build lasting customer loyalty by orchestrating consistent customer experiences, assuring that every type of contact builds on previous engagements to create a meaningful interaction. As a matter of fact, services should become part of the sales processes (the so-called service to sales (S2S) approach) since they can exploit the relationships with the customer
- fraud management to help insurance companies optimize their combined ratio by identifying frauds and avoiding payments on incorrect or fraudulent claim requests

- legal support to the litigation process, in addition to also being a service offered to the customer with a premium
- reinsurance and coinsurance processes to administer reinsurance and coinsurance contracts and facilitate recovery through transparency into treaty and facultative management. They help companies expand the amount of business ceded to reinsurance and coinsurance and manage their exposures

Due to the importance and peculiarities of these processes, the following sections go into more detail on some of them.

Policy processes

An insurance company collects much of its initial data and generates the bulk of its revenues during the policy process. Typical activities of the policy processing workflow are premium processing, collections, master database maintenance, and accounting preparation.

These activities are relatively independent from each other. The policy administration systems support the issuing, variation, and processing of the policies. Details such as administrative and technical descriptions of the coverage or additional insureds' information needed for complete proposal processing are required postings for the quotation of a policy. Subsequent acceptance of the policy would, however, require entry of all the additional fields, both from an administrative and a technical point of view, necessary for the policy management process to take place.

Premium collection and master database maintenance are byproducts of the policy issuing and processing components of the premium process. Changes to the master database are reflected as policy-level transactions that in turn affect accounting preparation and posting.

Critical source documents in the policy process are insurance policies, premium notices, and reinsurance and coinsurance treaties and agreements.

Data connected with the policy processes reside in the policy or contract master database, the customer database, the sales force (mainly agents and brokers) database, the product catalogue, the pricing database, the policy statistical database, the commission rate tables, the application database, the technical accounting database, and so on. Policy processes data of primary interest to many insurance departments are policy, endorsement, and billing transactions, as well as premium data transmitted to the treasury process, the reserve-reporting process, the general ledger, the statistical database, any of which may be used for supporting management information reporting.

The policy processes involve many functional departments: production, underwriting, policy services, billing, and intermediaries or direct accounting. By viewing policy-writing transactions in terms of processes, the artificial barriers created by organizational infrastructures should not hide tracking or accounting for the flow of funds through the company and its intermediaries.

Losses, reserves, reinsurance, and coinsurance processes

The processes of demand to order also include the loss and loss-adjustment expense, reserve-reporting, reinsurance, and coinsurance processes.

Providing quality service is a key concern of insurance company management. The activities performed in the loss and the loss-adjustment process fulfill the insurer's obligations under the insurance contract. Company reputation and continued financial well-being depend on insureds' and claimants' satisfaction with the loss-adjustment process. Indemnity payments represent the insurance company's greatest expense, thus justifying extensive monitoring, control, and auditing.

In addition to providing good service, holding reserves for the final payment of losses is critical to the insurance company's profitability and indeed survival. Insurance companies must also maintain reserves to comply with statutory and regulatory accounting requirements.

The loss and loss-adjustment expense process consists of operations necessary to record, accumulate, and evaluate loss and loss-adjustment expense reserves and payments. Its typical activities include the initial reporting of claims, processing of claims, payment of claims, receiving cash for salvage, subrogation, refunds, and reinsurance or coinsurance payments, and establishing loss and loss expense reserves. The critical source documents in this process are the notifications of loss, claim jacket databases, claim coverage forms, proofs of loss, payment authorization forms, claim offset and correction memos, and reinsurance worksheets. The most important databases involved in the loss and loss expense process include the claim registers (with both the accident events and the damages tables) for:

- reported claims, the policy master database, and the claim master database, as well as the policy terms, coverage information, and possible reinsurance/coinsurance from the claim master database
- interface with the policy processes, and cash disbursements and cash receipts from claim offsets interface with the treasury process. In addition, the process produces the accounting for loss and loss expense items.

Reserve processes

The reserve process consists of steps for establishing liabilities for the insurance company. Typical activities in this process are the identification of reserve-requirements, the selection of acceptable raw data, the selection of the approved method of determining liability, and the calculation of reserves. Source documents are less critical in the reserve processes. Inputs may come from loss factor tables; loss-adjustment expense factor tables; other expense records; schedules of taxes, licenses, and fees, and pro rata factors used in unearned premium calculations. The databases for the reserve processes are the claim history and the premium history master databases. Interfaces between the reserve processes and the premium, loss and loss expense, payroll, and procurement expense processes provide data for the reserves. In some companies, the reserve processes also produce general ledger postings and information for management control.

Reinsurance and coinsurance processes

The reinsurance and coinsurance processes have several functions, of which the principal one is to enhance the insurer's financial stability. The two terms can be distinguished in the following way:

- Reinsurance occurs when an underwriter (or insured) wishes to share some of the policy's liability with another underwriter. While the original underwriter writes the policy for the full amount of the transaction, it purchases reinsurance for claims arising from a certain amount from another underwriter or more underwriters.
- Coinsurance occurs when two or more title insurance underwriters proportionally insure a given transaction via separate title policies. The amount of risk is shared in proportion to their policy amount. It is possible for one underwriter to carry more of the liability than the other and therefore share in a higher percentage of the liability and, of course, of the premium.

The volume and nature of reinsurance and coinsurance activities vary widely among companies, depending on the types of insurance coverage offered, the nature, and size of risks underwritten, the management strategy, the size and global presence of the company, and in the case of reinsurance, whether it is inward or outward. Although occasional reinsurance activity can be processed within the premium, loss and loss expense, reserve, and financial reporting processes, the essential functions of the reinsurance and coinsurance processes are the management of the relationships with the other insurance companies. This means, in the case of reinsurance, paying the premium due for reinsurance ceded, taking into account the commissions, processing reinsurance recoveries for claims, and reporting reinsurance.

Critical source documents in these processes include contracts or treaties, bordereaux, notices of losses, and periodic reports.

The process principal databases are the premium, the loss, and the history master databases. The reinsurance process's major interfaces are cash payments or receipts to or from the treasury process, inward or outward reinsurance to or from the revenue process, inward or outward reinsurance to or from the reserve process, and reinsurance postings to the financial reporting compliances, and risk processes. There should be also interfaces to the compliance ICT applications and to the claims administration system.

The applications able to manage these processes should be multicurrency and multicompliance if the two companies are in different nations. Normally, the language used for the communication is English.

Outbound communications

All these systems will produce communication with the customers and reporting. This content needs to be stored, printed (either physically or logical as electronic files), and delivered to the different parties.

Traditionally statements, bordereaux, and other communications have been provided in paper format. More and more they are being issued in a digital format. In such a case, customers should be able to see their statements online for at least a reasonable number of days (normally at least 90 days).

Social networks lend themselves to several innovative services such as real-time assistance (especially on Twitter), contests and promotions, some insurance transactions (for instance, donations), or the opening of insurance accounts for specific projects.[9] In some cases, statements must be produced in more than one language, currencies, and media.

Other functions

In many countries, there are interesting examples of digital insurance services that extend well beyond the current account as, for example,

- applications for management of pension plans (ICBC)
- proposals for insurance policies (BNP Paribas)

- information services on museums and exhibitions or news (Deutsche Bank)
- searches for retail estate for sale (ING Direct)
- donations for environmental sustainability (La Caixa)

Record to report processes

In addition to the premium, loss and loss-adjustment expense, reserve-reporting, and reinsurance and coinsurance processes, insurance information and communication solutions also include the record to report processes.

The objective of these processes is to enable finance executives to walk a fine line: balancing sound stewardship and value creation, and enabling entrepreneurship, while exercising caution and taking into account the big picture, with the possibility of zooming in on the details, if necessary.

Cost pressures and the need for finance to support the growth of the organization are other drivers for organizing finance processes. CEOs look to get far more for less from their finance functions. There is a heavy focus on investing in streamlined scalable architecture that can support in a flexible way the growth or the reduction of the business. Finance is under pressure to show it can be a better business partner, adding more value while also responding to compliance requirements.

With software solutions for finance, insurance companies can optimize compliance efforts and manage risks, meet financial objectives, create sustainable value, and deliver superior service at lower cost.

To align performance with strategy, executives use solutions to adjust plans and allocate resources for rapid market change. They define and cascade strategy, model cost drivers, improve financial forecasting, and analyze and report large amounts of data.

With cross-functional insight, managers can streamline budgeting processes, capture growth opportunities, short-circuit predicted variances against key performance indicators, and create a customized business process to achieve targets. The intended result is increased profitability and a closer match of tactics with organizational vision.

Information and communication systems help insurance companies cope with risk management, balanced investments, and compliance with this set of end-to-end solutions:

- Financial planning and analysis manage financial and operational performance to gain insight into costing, improved financial planning, more accurate forecasting, and management control.

- Accounting and financial close should be able to run accounting and financial close quickly (within a few days of the end of the period), accurately and in compliance, and at a lower cost.
- Governance, risk, and compliance activities help the insurance company monitor key risk indicators and compliance effectiveness, business processes, and ICT solutions to align risks with compliance strategy and financial objectives.
- Solvency management helps ensure compliance with Solvency II and other regulations through analytics with increased data quality and transparency.

Traditionally, insurance companies have invested in real estate or bonds or shares. Their management requires specific solutions that are not described in this book.

Treasury and investment processes

The treasury process coordinates the receipt and application of funds. Its activities typically include banking services and analysis, cash management and disbursement, and stock issuance and retirement.

Treasury includes in particular cash and asset management to achieve compliance and enable transparency on one platform for the entire asset, investment accounting, and risk management business. The investment process is not entirely a back office operation. Actually, some investments are connected (in some cases even individually) to the policies, as for example in the unit-linked policies.

The critical source documents are cash, stock certificates, and letters of credit, debt certificates, and interest and dividend payments.

Databases may include a master registrar of the shareholders, a listing of commercial paper holders and investors' interest and dividend schedules, loan compliance checklists, records of loans to affiliates and other financial institutions, account balances for cash, money market and commercial paper accounts, long-term debt subsidiary accounts, shareholder subsidiary accounts, and intercompany accounts.

The treasury process generates daily reports for cash management and interfaces with the investment, premium, loss and loss-adjustment expense, payroll, taxes, and procurement expenditure processes to transfer funds for company operations and with the financial reporting process to produce accounting and management reports.

The investment process uses the funds generated in the company operations for income producing but also for hedging coverage in order to get protection from external events. The essential activities in the process are the authorization of investment transactions, the processing of principal and income, the hedging process, and the safekeeping of securities.

Source documents for the investment process include buy-sell advice, buy-sell confirmations, safekeeping receipts, mortgage and loan service reports, and payments and drafts. These documents generate the main databases, the investment master database, and the investment safekeeping records. Interface with the treasury process accounts for funds expended and received in investment activities, and with the financial and management reporting process, produces accounting and management reports.

Management reporting

In addition to the processes presented in these sections, insurance information and communication systems also incorporate financial reporting and management control processes. The financial reporting process of an insurance company normally does not deal with transactions as other processes do. It retrieves accounting and operating information from other processes and analyzes, evaluates, summarizes, reconciles, adjusts, and reclassifies the information so that it can be reported to regulatory bodies, to the management and other interested parties outside the company.

The information and communication system needs to take into account also the support to the budgeting process that underlies the major planning and control processes for an insurance company.

Budgeting is the important process of preparing a detailed statement of financial results that are expected for a given time period. It includes also the process of monitoring the financial results and computing variances. The program and the actuals are done per responsibility centers (for instance departments) or for products or for initiatives.

Payroll and human resources (HR)

The payroll process encompasses the activities involved in paying employees and accounting for that expenditure. Activities of the payroll process include hiring, attendance and time reporting, payroll accounting, payroll adjustments, travel and living expenses, and personnel tax reports. Critical source documents are personnel action notices, time sheets, and special payment authorizations. The employee master database constitutes the primary database for the payroll process, although it may also draw on a current-hours database and a tax table and deductions database. Output of the payroll process includes pay slips, payroll registers and related reports, required government and regulatory forms, general ledger postings, budget reports, and tax documentation to pass to the employees or send to the internal revenue services.

The HR system is also used to support employee management. It contains data on the appraisal process, information on the resume and capabilities of the persons in the company, education and training history, and any personnel information necessary for the management of employees.

Procure-to-pay

The procure-to-pay (P2P) process supports the acquisition of goods and services needed in the company's operations.

The main components are the following:

- Supply base management applications help procurement organizations solicit and manage vendor information, risk, and performance. They can include financial performance data, social sentiment analysis, news, and public information, such as export filings. Internally generated data, such as audit records and performance statistics, round out the information managed in the P2P process.
- e-Sourcing applications help organizations solicit and evaluate information (request for information – RFI) and proposals (request for proposal – RFP). E-sourcing supports bidding where the outcome should normally be a long-term agreement. This generally does not include prices or requests for quotes (operational sourcing or request for quotations – RFQ), which are activities that are more commonly supported in a peer-to-peer (P2P) solution. Some solutions enable large-scale, complex bid events with thousands of line items and awards spanning multiple vendors.
- Contract management solutions help organizations document and manage supply agreements and orders.
- Automated spend analysis is used in procurement and sourcing to quantify spend by vendor, category, and purchased item, and to identify opportunities for cost reduction and vendor consolidation.

Important sourcing documents are requests for acquisition, information, proposals and quotations, purchase orders, acceptance documentation, vendor invoices, debit/credit memos, payment requests, and expense sheets.

Databases used in the procurement process include a vendor master database (which includes a vendor rating), an open and paid expense database and marketplace (if used in the company), a noncurrent asset inventory ledger, and contract documentation.

Third-party information on vendors can be pulled in via web services, Rich Site Summary (RSS) feeds, or manual input. The process output includes documentation with the vendors, cash disbursements, general ledger postings, and cost accounting and budget reports.

Supporting systems

Enterprise portal and apps

Portal solutions began with the mission of making life easier for the insurance sales force. For a number of years, solutions in this space were referred to as agency portals. Insurance companies invested in them to reduce the difficulty in the initial stages of the insurance sales process.

Many portal offerings have expanded their scope to serve a wide range of stakeholders, from prospects to policyholders to intermediaries and vendors.[10] Data exchange and translation continue to be core capabilities. Some offerings also include work management and collaboration tools, which allow insurance companies to front-end multiple legacy systems with a single platform.

The portal need to provide a certain number of important features:[11]

- home page
- login/security for the reserved area
- content management
- customization
- search capability
- collaboration and social
- proactivity
- dynamic characteristics
- responsiveness
- ease of use
- attractiveness
- extensibility/embedded applications
- scalability
- administration tools
- contact and help

Portals can also be sophisticated from a technological point of view.[12] Traditional portal content, business applications, and analytics should be easily aggregated. Portal content should be available also for smartphones and tablets empowering the mobile users. Internal or external style designers help the company implement branding in a consistent fashion.

Customers today do not want only products and services. They want a different experience, based on a new global perspective. People talk about "experience economy". This view requires a certain number of features. Products are no longer enough: service is mandatory. Holistic value drives business. Innovation is important via breakthrough solutions. Companies must define a new world of opportunities for the customers. Innovation is about connecting people, disciplines, ideas, cultures, and so on. The design of products and service should have an empathetic design[13]. Finally, a Lean and Digitize approach is particularly important.

It is important to design a portal or an app in such a way as to provide customers with an "experience" on the Web or on a smartphone.[14] This is not easy since the customer is not in the premises of an insurance company agency. There is no contact person to provide the service. There are just the customer and his/her device. Certainly, devices are becoming more and more function rich. Phones, for instance, are more and more mobile computers rather than just phone handsets. These capabilities should be used to provide a rich and delightful experience to the customer. In the case of financial services, it must be a "peace of mind experience."

Certainly, at the bottom, the customer is interested in an experience connected with a secure transaction. Security is paramount in the customer relationship with an insurance company. Therefore, in developing digital insurance it is essential to give priority to security for the customer and the insurance company. It is necessary to take all possible actions to ensure that the person who is connecting is indeed the customer accessing his/her account. It is essential also to provide a secure connection, which very likely means an encrypted transmission.

It is necessary to ensure, at the maximum level, privacy in a transaction. In this respect, digital insurance is at a premium since when a customer or a prospect uses his/her device, it does not disclose his/her business to a human representative of the insurance company. The customer wants to be reassured that nobody will access his/her data and transactions. Security and privacy are non-negotiable characteristics in digital insurance. They are never enough.

Following the example of Steve Jobs, simplicity of operation is extremely important. The requirement mentioned by Jobs: "I want a computer with just one button" translates in this case into: "I want to do the transaction with one click." It is possible to accept two clicks, for instance, to be sure that the customer did not make an error in keying the data in the transaction. But no more than two clicks should be needed. Similarly, messages or instructions should be extremely clear.

However, the customer might need help. It is essential to provide a help function that also includes the possibility of chatting or talking or exchanging messages with a help desk. Talking is preferred, since other modes might lead to misunderstanding or require too much keying. The insurance company might wish to use less expensive ways of communication.

A satisfying experience would mean also the possibility of performing more than simple transactions such as getting a quotation or having a policy issued. Customers should be able to perform payments, renewal, suspensions, claims, and so on.

The design of the applications should be beautiful. It is important to improve their usability and ergonomics. The transactions should be compliant with standards (where applicable), and take into account the branding and characteristic of the insurance company.

Celent conducted a survey exploring customer self-service in life insurance by asking 17 questions related to the current use of and future plans for websites and mobile devices. The survey asked about current customer service volumes, availability of customer-focused websites and mobile apps, website and mobile app functions, and future plans regarding both channels.[15]

Some results of this survey are as follows. The primary reason life insurance companies implement customer self-service is to make agents happy, with a secondary reason of improving efficiency. Life insurance companies cited meeting policyholder demands as the third most important reason, tied with improving quality. Surprisingly, improving customer service and retaining customers are near the bottom.

Business data warehouse

During all business activities, insurance companies create large amounts of data. The analysis and interpretation of this data is very important for preserving and enhancing the competitive edge of an insurance company. The data warehouse and the business intelligence (BI) unit need to provide tools and functions that enable insurance companies to optimize processes and react quickly in line with market needs.

The data warehouse needs to integrate, transform, and consolidate relevant business information from operational applications and external data sources. The BI needs to provide a high-performance infrastructure that helps evaluate and interpret this data. In this way, decision-makers should be able to make well-grounded decisions and identify target-orientated activities on the basis of the analyzed data.

The characteristics of the data warehouse and BI are:[16]

- the data modeling, data extraction, further processing of data, and the administration of the data warehouse management processes, for instance, for deduping the data
- the integration, transformation, consolidation, cleanup, and storage of data from all sources, as well as the retrieval of data for analysis, interpretation, and further processing
- the provision of on-line analytical processing (OLAP), which is a set of software techniques for interactive and fast analysis of large amounts of data. It makes it possible to analyze such data with rather complex functions and services, as well as to provide services for BI-integrated planning and analysis process design
- the availability of generic tools and services to support the insurance company in developing BI objects and processes, supplying data in the system landscape, performing tests and tracings, and monitoring BI in the insurance company system environment and ecosystem
- the basis of an open architecture able, for instance, to extract data from various sources or to evaluate these data using various front-end tools

The Ergo Group

To manage more effectively and productively their marketing campaigns, the Ergo Group, one of the major insurance groups in Europe, has decided to integrate information for life and property and casualty (P&C) portfolios.[17] Ergo started from its own system supporting Customer relationship management and insurance transposed instances. It implemented a solution that is based on three major components: customer relationship management (CRM) operational database, and business intelligence.

The CRM component, customized for the insurance companies, provides a comprehensive view of the customer/prospect both in terms of products acquired and potential sales. It also supports Ergo in managing its marketing campaigns and optimizing the services offered by the contact center.

The registry is the central point of reference for the CRM to assure the quality of personal data in terms of standardization and of deduplication. Looking ahead, this component may become the master registry system for all portfolios of the Ergo Group companies, if compliant with data privacy.

The component of business intelligence, with the modules of data mining, supports marketing activities by identifying clearly the variables that affect good customer management and optimizing the process of identifying the target of campaigns. Finally, the application provides KPIs and reporting on specific characteristics and dynamics of the Ergo Group portfolio.

Business process management and integration

All organizations face the challenge of managing processes that are complex, inefficient and costly in terms of time, resources required, and productivity. A process orchestration software can help insurance companies improve the management of those processes. They can be of different types: simple workflows or integrated processes that span applications and organizational boundaries, or perform other functions, such as the following:

- Analysis of processes is needed to identify potential bottlenecks and gain transparency into processes through powerful monitoring and analytical capabilities. The advanced applications have also some simulation capability to perform "what-if" analysis.
- Collaborative model processes enable ICT departments to provide a shared environment for the codesigning of new processes and the adaptation of existing ones – based on the user-friendly business process model and notation standard (BPMN). It is also possible to use collaborative decision-making tools, to help distributed teams of process experts collaboratively and simultaneously design process models.
- Execution of what was modeled to help companies efficiently manage process models from an initial high-level definition, to the specification of all technical implementation details, right through to process deployment and execution.
- Business functions can be reused from service-enabled applications to get the benefits of service-oriented architecture (SOA), which is based on the interaction between loosely coupled services that function independently.
- User-friendly interfaces provide business users intuitive access to applications and information through various channels, including mobile phones and tablets.

To fully exploit the business process design, the ICT systems should provide the tools for process integration, enabling insurance companies to reliably exchange information across distributed business applications on the basis of these tools, which need to include features such as the following:

- Standards-based, high-performance enterprise services bus (ESB) in order to reliably exchange information across distributed applications through a mediation layer, rather than costly point-to-point connections. The ESB can reduce the connection between applications and databases in a substantial way, thanks to the fact that once you connect an application to the ESB, any other application connected to the ESB can communicate with it.

- Packaged adapters or connectors or web services are used for application integration. They can implement business-to-business (B2B) requirements and allow the company to migrate from the traditional electronic data interchange (EDI) systems to industry standards, partnering exchange mechanisms, or leveraging secure http:// for direct interactions over the Internet. The objective is to let companies integrate and network with trading partners, customers, and vendors, allowing electronic data exchange with any business partner regardless of their technical capability. Insurance companies should be able to connect by using these tools with any trading partner by joining the network once and linking with pre-built business partner profiles. The full-service solution eliminates the need for costly point-to-point integration.
- Business Rules Management Systems (BRMS) is a software system used to define, deploy, execute, monitor, and maintain the variety and complexity of decision logic that is used by the applications supporting the insurance company. This logic is referred to as business rules, which include policies, requirements, and conditional statements. They are used to determine the tactical actions that need to take place in the applications and systems to complete an activity. The BRMS are important since they allow the updating of policy rules and coverages to be delegated directly to the user departments rather than to the ICT professionals.

Intranets and extranets in insurance companies

Digital insurance is certainly important from an innovation point of view, since it supports new products, new processes, new organizations, and even new business models. However, it is possible to use digital insurance also to improve the internal effectiveness, efficiency, economics, and ethics (compliance) of the insurance company itself.

Intranet and extranet applications are a particular case in this respect. Insurance companies have used intranets for a long time, mainly to improve internal communication and collaboration. Intranets are aimed at internal employees of the insurance company. Extranets connect with partners. In the case of insurance, extranets are particularly important since they allow connections to be made with agencies, brokers, and other types of intermediaries. From this point onward, this section will discuss intranets, which will also include extranets.

It is interesting to analyze where a digital insurance approach would be able to replace or complement intranet applications. A recent study by ABI Lab and the School of Management of the Politecnico di Milano, Milan, Italy, has pointed out and demonstrated how, in Italy, corporate intranets are evolving in the direction of mobility.[18] One-third of Italian financial institutions are planning to increase investments in intranets. More than half will keep their budget unchanged. Only a few financial institutions will reduce investments in intranets.

Corporate intranets are already widely used by financial institutions for internal communication (80% of the institutions analyzed), compliance (54%), customer service (60%), financial transactions (50%) and credit (46%), and the management of human resources (60%). According to the Politecnico di Milano survey, in 2014 over 50 percent of the sample financial institutions' intranets assumed more strategic roles, further developing support for all of these functions. Fifty-six percent of the financial institutions will combine them with commercial functions. This is a particular aspect that will become more and more relevant in time. Insurance companies' customers are using more and more mobile devices and functions. It makes sense, therefore, for these companies also to use more digital solutions (such as mobile) for internal employees to liaise with external customers and partners. A BYOD (Bring Your Own Devices) approach, where an employee uses his/her personal device rather than the company-owned one, pushes in this direction.

Digital solutions will also support more and more "mobility" in the workplace. This is certainly true for insurance companies' salespersons and agents. It will become more and more relevant as well for other functions in insurance companies, whether they be in relationships with the customers or not.

The Politecnico di Milano survey confirms the industry's attention toward mobility: more than 80 percent of the financial institutions surveyed intended to increase the accessibility to the corporate intranet from any device, location, and at any time. The proportion of financial institutions that aimed to improve integration with the social and collaborative business environments increased from 14 percent to 36 percent. The percentage that will integrate the intranet with personal devices is expected to move from 7 percent to 14 percent.

Financial services are also extending mobility to other internal functions, such as procurement, and to the extranets: the networks that support relationships with intermediaries and vendors. This is particularly interesting, since some insurance companies are focusing more and more on their core businesses. As a consequence, relationships with third parties are becoming more and more important.

> AXA
>
> AXA equips its sales force with state-of-the-art tablets in France.[19] As part of its digital strategy, AXA, in 2012, initiated the i-Nov project, aimed at providing its sales force with tablets and Salesforce.com's cloud solution. These sales tools cover all business lines. It enables the immediate underwriting of contracts via a mobile device using digital signatures. AXA's initiative demonstrates how mobile solutions and cloud computing can be integrated with product underwriting in a single, easy-to-use tool, thus enhancing the productivity of the sales force.

Management of the digital insurance infrastructure

Due to the nature of insurance companies, the requirements of the digital insurance infrastructure are particularly high in the following areas, examined in more detail in the following pages:

- Implementation of new applications and bug fixing – The deployment of any change in the digital environment requires special attention.
- Multicontext – There is more and more a large diversity in the environments, platforms, applications, and access devices which need to be properly managed;
- Integration – Usually, insurance companies run large numbers of different applications. The technical integration of the core applications with these applications through middleware needs to be ensured.
- Scalability, workload management and performance – Due to the business dynamics in insurance companies, system load may vary greatly over time, resulting in the need for a highly scalable and flexible digital insurance infrastructure.
- Operations and monitoring – Many operational tasks that are needed to optimally support the application workload are typically performed at the infrastructure level when critical applications are run. However, they must not interfere with them.
- Business continuity and disaster recovery – Applications need to be kept available 24*7 to ensure that company operations are up and running, and available to customers, employees, and partners. This is particularly relevant if the insurance companies use single global instances and are direct to consumer. Hence, there is the need to properly archive the information in such a way as to support abnormal events.

- Security – Protection of the customer, the company, and other sensitive data is vital to all kinds of businesses and must be ensured at all times.

The following paragraphs go into more detail on these processes.

Implementation of new applications or bug fixing

When implementing applications or bug fixing for insurance, requirements on the infrastructure should be analyzed carefully. If necessary, the architecture should be determined based on the reference architecture. For example, the insurance company needs to select the application server platform. The company needs to define an integrated environment for the production, pre-production, training, development, and test systems in order to assure quality to the customers and the other parties.

Particularly important are the user acceptance testing (UAT), and the production acceptance testing (PAT). The latter is done very seldom, but it is of the utmost importance. In direct insurance, the applications go directly to the consumers. The customers cannot accept flaws or bad performance in the use of the insurance company's systems.

Integration

Application integration is a key part of the digital insurance strategy for every business. Typically, insurance companies run many different applications and have a need for seamless integration. Solutions must be open and should be integrated with other applications.

Using open standards for the technical integration of applications is an important design aspect of system infrastructure. Service-oriented architecture (SOA), an architectural concept in which business functions are supported by application modules called "services" that foster flexible application integration, is having a major impact on the standardization of integration. It is also promoting the alignment of ICT and business processes.

Scalability, workload management and performance

Core applications often play a central role within the digital insurance landscape of insurance companies. The more an application is used, the more important it becomes to process transactions and fulfill reporting requests with superior, predictable, and reliable performance. This requires scalability and workload management in order to respect the service level agreements (SLA) with the business.

Operations and monitoring

To successfully run an application for insurance, it is necessary for the operators and system administrators to perform different tasks. An important aspect of reducing operational costs and ensuring the quality and reproducibility of operations is automation. End-to-end monitoring is the basis for performance optimization. Integration of an application process management with infrastructure management enables common infrastructure scenarios like system provisioning, cloning, copying, and refreshing. This leads to environments that are as agile as required by the business.

In the fields of digital insurance, application performance management (APM) is the monitoring and management of performance and availability of software applications. APM strives to detect and diagnose application performance problems to maintain an expected level of service. APM is the translation of digital insurance metrics into value for organizations.

Multicontext capability

The multicontext capability is a requirement for solutions that enable insurance companies to run one single code base of their application for as many different users as possible. These users of digital insurance services may vary by language, nationality, knowledge level, functional role, or by the devices they are using to connect to the system. The latter case is particularly relevant in the case of direct insurance which liaises directly with the consumers and hence cannot dictate the devices or network used by them.

Business continuity and disaster recovery

Traditionally, large companies had more stringent business continuity requirements compared to small companies in most industry sectors – like banks, for example, in which the continuous availability of business services became essential many years ago. With the rise of the Internet and the demand for round-the-clock availability, the landscape of the industry has changed drastically. Customers are used to services provided around the clock. Insurance company customers, for instance, expect that they can access insurance services from their devices at any time. In general, the more applications can be accessed directly by the customer, the more relevant business continuity becomes. Examples are direct insurance, customer relationship management, customer servicing, and sales channel management-related functions. If insurance companies (or their outsourcers) introduce single global instances, the need for business continuity becomes even more important since there will always be some processes in use at any time by customers or employees or partners in some parts of the world who require such an instance to accomplish their tasks.

The business of insurance companies is characterized by large volumes of data. For instance, different products require history and contract information to be maintained for a long time, often creating large amounts of transactional and analytical data. This implies that large volumes of complex data need to be handled and secured for both internal and especially external regulatory reporting requirements. In these situations, it is vital to efficiently manage an ever-growing size of content. Using a centralized solution can help reduce management costs and control data retention management.

Insurance companies run solutions that require business continuity. This in turn must be based on infrastructure components, which are based on:

- high availability, by exploiting server and subsystem redundancies and enabling tight integration with server failover for 24x7x365 online systems
- continuous operation, which organizes all planned outages for system maintenance in a nondisruptive manner or even possibly when the production system is still on, as well as capacity customization including nondisruptive backups and federated recovery
- disaster recovery, consisting of tools and procedures to protect against unplanned outages such as disasters, network or site outages
- consistent restart or recovery of a logically corrupted database to any point in time

Two parameters are important in business continuity:

- Recovery Point Objective (RPO) refers to the amount of data at risk. It is measured by the amount of data that would have been processed by the system between two data protection events. It is an indication of the amount of data that potentially could be lost during a disaster recovery.
- Recovery Time Objective (RTO) refers to the amount of time it takes to recover from a data loss event and how long it takes to return to service. RTO refers to the maximum amount of time the system's data is unavailable or inaccessible, thereby preventing normal service.

Security

As a last but most important point, insurance companies need to take special care to protect customer and company-sensitive data. This is vital to the business, and it is a legal requirement. Access to information must be restricted to authorized persons. Access tracing and controls are to be enforced, and all successful and unsuccessful authentication attempts are to be traced for auditing purposes. The data and system administrators able to access sensitive data must be clearly identified, also for legal reasons.

An additional method of preventing information disclosure is data encryption. A secure and reliable digital insurance platform is of fundamental importance for a business process platform for insurance. The chapter on Governance provides more details on this important aspect.

Conclusions

The past few decades have seen a spectacular development of automation in the management of structured information. Simplifying, each decade has been characterized by innovations:

- in the 1960s introduction of computers in the organizations
- in the 1970s development of mainframe computers
- in the 1980s launch of the personal computer
- in the 1990s move to client server systems
- in the 2000s development of the network
- in the 2010s explosion of the mobile

Not all insurance companies have used these innovations to improve the value added to their customers. The basic processes in insurance companies can greatly benefit from them.

The model presented in this chapter focused on how to provide solutions to support the basic processes of insurance to help insurance companies manage them. The next chapter presents new and exciting opportunities. They are certainly extremely interesting, but before moving to advanced solutions, all insurance companies should do their basics and implement the applications described in this chapter.

With regard to practical and theoretical implications, our approach aims at linking processes and digitization tools for supporting insurance companies' management. Due to the different levels of views, this book claims that the artifacts of the proposed model can be adapted to several real-world scenarios. Integrating processes and their digitization can help practitioners make better use of their content and information assets, and accumulate organizational knowledge for improving business processes.

The architecture presented in this chapter provides a starting point for assessing and organizing processes according to their components, and then sharing content within and between organizations. From an academic point of view, the suggested model can be applied and refined by researchers and practitioners to improve its generalizability and broaden its scope. Moreover, the integration of process improvement disciplines such as Lean Six Sigma and digitization, and the continuous process and applications improvement can play a vital role in moving to digital insurance.

The characteristics of the potential customers continue to evolve. To take into account these facts is more and more strategic for the survival and growth of the insurance companies. It is essential that insurance companies keep pace, ensuring that customers are delighted with them. Digital insurance is about matching patterns in people's lives and servicing customers effectively, efficiently, economically, ethically, securely, and through multiple channels. In today's global economy, in which customers and workers are often on the road, solutions must evolve to ensure that the productivity of those individuals remains high despite time spent out of their offices.

Industry leaders continue to raise the bar for what customers, be they businesses or individuals, expect from their insurance companies through digitization. Additionally, it is essential that customers continue to urge their insurance partners to move forward with planned initiatives. Aite Group, therefore, makes the following recommendations to the customers and partners of a financial service:[20]

- Work with the financial institutions to provide them a better understanding of the customer requirements and pain points.
- Ask questions about security to ensure a greater comfort level with the digital insurance solutions.
- Push the insurance partners to continue improving the usability and simplicity of the offerings to match the user interfaces of intermediaries and other providers that are leading the innovation with digital solutions.
- Push digital insurance to provide economic incentives to the customer. A Gallup poll's research showed that more than half of customers would be willing to use massively digital channels if it meant receiving incentives, such as a reduction in the costs of the policies or bigger interest rates on life deposits by more or less 0.25 percent. In contrast,

the use of disincentives to force somehow the migration of customers to digital insurance is, according to Gallup, a practice that can have serious consequences, such as the loss of customers.[21]
- Be clear from the start on the mix strategy, online and offline, for the channels. Immediately work to place the new customers in the channel that the insurance prefers to promote.

The following chapters analyze the challenges, opportunities, and status of new solutions to support digital insurance.

4
Advanced Solutions

Introduction

Information and communication technology (ICT) based solutions have been important for insurance companies. Nevertheless, many insurance companies have devoted fewer resources to insurance information systems as compared to other financial services such as banking. The situation is changing, however, as digital insurance is becoming more and more important for insurance companies. There are several reasons why this is happening that are connected with:

- customers
- technology
- design

This chapter will examine the contribution of technology solutions to support insurance management. The following chapters consider the other two aspects: customers and design. It is important anyway to take into account that an integrated approach to innovation, considering all the aspects, is essential.

Insurance companies need to strive to add value to their customers and to their organizations, and drive competitive advantage. This can be achieved acting on what we call the four P's:

- product and services
- processes
- people
- platforms

An effective approach should be based on the Lean and Digitize method.[1] In order to improve a process, reduce process times, and cut waste, it is necessary essentially to "know" the processes and especially be able to measure them.

In theory, the improvement of the management of insurance companies is relatively easy, since these organizations:

- have been in the past traditionally inefficient
- do not have physical products but essentially manage information

It is time for insurance companies to take the lead in leaning and digitizing. It is possible to carry this out profitably in almost all the insurance sectors:

- New product innovation should take place. Since insurance companies essentially manage information, it should be relatively easy and inexpensive to lean and digitize. Increased digital marketing can improve the opportunity to connect with existing customers, allowing companies to better upsell, cross-sell, and retain valuable customers. The ability to mine the digital data consumers leave behind on the Web, social media, driving apps, and even health-monitoring wearables, can help companies better target customers, price and underwrite policies more accurately, and manage claims more effectively.
- Inquiries should be directed to the customers. In this case, speed is the name of the game. If a customer needs a policy, they would like to have it as soon as possible. Risks should be managed, but with the right balance between customer delight and risk reduction.
- There should be continuous operations. Simplicity and speed are at a premium. The move to lean agencies should be pursued, or to online insurance, or altogether mobile insurance. Security is at a premium, but it should not unduly delay the speed of the operations. Digitization can help quite a bit. In this case, a middle office can take the burden out of the front office. The simple digitization of existing insurance processes (allowing quotes to go straight through processing, for example, and rapid product configuration) could yield strong improvements in the operating margins.
- The back office should be reduced as much as possible. It should be outsourced or offshored and in any case should be strongly automated.

According to a survey conducted by the *Harvard Business Review*, a thoughtful digitization program can deliver up to 65 percent in cost reduction and a 90 percent decrease in turnaround time on key insurance processes, and improve conversion rates by more than 20 percent.[2]

While all insurance companies understand that digital is having an impact on their business, few appreciate how fast and how fundamentally the business is changing. In a McKinsey survey of the digital practices of more than 30 leading US and European Property and Casualty (P&C) and life insurance companies, 39 percent had not articulated a digital strategy across the customer-decision journey at all.[3] While most insurance companies focus their digital efforts on marketing (83 percent) and sales (78 percent), companies have concentrated on the early stages of the customer-decision journey (supporting search and quotations). They have lagged in their pre- and after-sale ability to serve existing customers digitally.

Only 50 percent of companies have budgeted for long-term digital goals. Just 30 percent have a multiyear investment plan to support digital.[4]

From product offering, there are two challenges facing a new insurance company:

- catching up with established players and offering the best products for the richest segments of the market
- innovating and bringing new products and services possibly with new processes, organizations, and business models, not yet in the market

The complication here is that the customer physical touchpoints with digital insurance tend to be fewer and, in most cases, virtual and not physical. This is a different situation with respect to the traditional insurance sales done with agencies or with a direct sales force. Therefore, the focus in digital insurance should be on dynamic organizations and time to market. One possible model to introduce advanced solutions is to use outsourcing. This model has minimal initial costs and the model is scalable. With the right partnership and terms, an insurance company can incentivize the outsourced partner to bring additional business, which could help also in the core insurance business.

This chapter does not consider all possible and foreseeable developments. It concentrates on some of the most interesting ones for each of the following categories:

- mobility
- cloud computing

- big data analytics
- content management systems

This chapter starts with the solutions more visible to the customers (who are one of the main driving forces) and then considers the other ones.

Mobile is expanding at unbelievable rates even if the economic crisis is still affecting many economies in the world. The use of smartphones and tablets is expanding. The total number of mobile phones is overcoming the number of the world population. Mobile can impact heavily on the sales of insurance products. In some cases, it is the ideal solution as, for example, in travel insurance.

In the background, there are two solutions that are influencing the use of digital insurance in insurance companies.

One interesting solution is cloud computing, which is the use of ICT resources on-demand, through the Internet, paying by the use, and with a self-service mode. Cloud computing frees organizations from fixed location data centers. As a consequence, cloud computing combines well with mobile and Web solutions. Also the relationships with partners and the reinsurance and coinsurance businesses could become much easier to operate thanks to the cloud.

Big data analytics are solutions that are extremely important for insurance companies. Two of their uses stand out among the many: marketing support and risk management.

Cloud computing and Big data analytics promise to move ICT from being a system of records to a system of engagement.[5] In other words, ICT can move from being a big archive to the operational support of decisions in insurance companies, such as the decision whether to accept a facultative reinsurance, decide on the premium on new risks, and so on.

This chapter closes with a discussion about an important aspect: content management systems. The management of unstructured information is becoming more and more urgent. It is a subject that should not be tackled "unstructured." For this reason, this final part of this chapter will present a model for managing content in a unified way.

Changing scenarios in insurance information and communication systems

The future is particularly challenging for insurance companies. For a certain number of reasons, insurance companies have not pushed much in the past in terms of automation. This is a traditional attitude that differentiates insurance companies from other financial services such as banks. The latter (especially innovative ones) have traditionally pushed heavily on automated management.

Population growth in Western countries is slowing. In the United States, for example, the population increased by just 0.71 percent for the 12 months ending 1 July 2014, according to the US Census Bureau.[6] In some other countries, such as those in Western Europe, the local population is actually decreasing. This and other factors, including the continuing global socioeconomic crisis; long-term wage stagnation, baby boomer retirements, the housing slump, the rise of the sharing economy among Millennials, and the commoditization of some insurance products, like car insurance, are limiting the insurance industry's growth potential. The industry's pressing objectives are accessing more new potential customers, attracting new ones, and keeping the current ones happy, while finding ways to cross- and upsell and at the same time doing cost-cutting exercises. This is pushing insurance companies to boost also their digital insurance investments, re-examine how they go to the market, and rethink the types and frequency of their customer experiences, which increasingly are digital. Insurance companies will accelerate innovation during the next few years as they race to try to update themselves and especially look for new customers also through new channels.

In the case of financial institutions, retail banks traditionally have been more forward and innovative in the field of digital insurance based solutions. Very likely, the same will happen in the case of insurance companies. In other words, insurance companies providing services to corporations will push less on automation as compared to what will happen to retail insurance. For example, one could expect that areas such as re-assurance will automate more slowly, even if by their nature they could greatly benefit from the support of digital insurance.

This increased use of digital insurance in the world of insurance will very likely affect the following areas:

- There will be major efforts in terms of consolidation of ICT applications. In recent years, there have been many mergers and acquisitions (M&A) among insurance companies. This trend will continue. Consider, for example, the Italian market, in which there are more than 200 active insurance companies, many of them small and medium sized. The expectation is that there will be a continuous consolidation movement, especially with the increasing influence of the European Union and the opening of new markets. Until now, consolidation among insurance companies has been mainly at the corporate level. Now companies need to consolidate in their merged entities their ICT applications, which very often overlap.

- The second requirement for insurance companies is the modernization of their applications. In many cases, the applications for insurance companies, whether in life or property and casualty (P&C) or claims management, date back to last century. A Celent survey covered this subject. They found different results in different parts of the world.[7] Despite its relative digital maturity, insurance companies in the Americas see their existing systems as a major obstacle to digital growth, with 96 percent citing "legacy technology constraints" as the top inhibitor, compared with 80 percent globally. This is also true in Latin America, where significant M&A activity in recent years is creating even greater complexity to the legacy challenge. In this context, 81 percent of insurance companies surveyed in this region say they have the greatest need for new technology resources to deliver their stated digital strategy (compared to 72 percent globally), and big-data analytics has been the most in-demand skill globally. Celent found in another survey that global spending on policy management and other core processing systems is accelerating.[8] It comprised the single largest chunk of software spending by P&C insurance companies in 2013. Investments in core systems accounted for 48 percent of all P&C software purchases, compared to 27 percent the prior year. There are several reasons why this is happening:
    - Legacy platforms struggle to handle the heavier, highly dynamic workloads of Web and mobile apps. The age and complexity of the legacy applications often cannot manage the intense, highly agile, and flexible demands of Web and mobile systems without a virtualized and automated environment in place. This requires the right software in place to process the increasing traffic on the Web and mobile platforms.
    - Legacy systems frequently manage customer interactions in isolation. They have not been architected to bring interactions and information together, in order to actually create an integrated view of the customer relationships.
    - Downtime for upgrades or maintenance is becoming much less acceptable by the customers in today's "culture of immediacy." Customers want to be able to access the systems at any time, including nights and weekends. The consequence is an increasing demand for a continuous instant access to services. This makes the need for seamless application updates all the more important.

    - Legacy systems tend to be completely inadequate to address today's challenges. There is the need to adapt or replace many applications. The effort is significant and presents several difficulties. The funding of this modernization is large. The other difficulty is that the time needed for modernization is substantial. Meanwhile, it is not possible to stop the modifications and upgrades of the existing systems. Modernizing systems has become a race toward a moving target.
- The other major challenge in the near future for insurance companies is the need to introduce new integrated channels. In certain sectors, such as compulsory insurance for liability in the case of motor insurance, there is a fairly standard product and few options of coverage. In this situation, the movement toward direct purchase online by the end customer is very strong. The development in this direction is not only in the use of online channels over the Internet but also in purchasing insurance using mobile phones. Mobile insurance is increasingly an important objective for retail insurance companies. These new channels open a major challenge due to the need to manage a multichannel environment. In this respect, few insurance companies have concrete experiences. Insurance companies traditionally have relied on indirect channels, such as agents, brokers, and other financial institutions. They will need to change and make sure that the different channels are effective and consistent with each other.

The insurance technology researcher Novarica surveyed 88 financial services institutions' CIOs. Almost half of them said they are piloting mobile capabilities for customers.[9] Fewer than 10 percent of these CIOs claimed to have extensive mobile deployments in production. This means that, notwithstanding the rapid proliferation of mobile devices, the trend toward mobile insurance solutions is starting slowly only now.

Increasing automation will provide an increasing amount of data. The problem/opportunity is what to do with all this data, which represent an important asset for insurance companies. Big data analytics solutions can help greatly in managing the use of this data.

Applications of this type may help in managing risks, and therefore provide considerable support for custom and flexible pricing, based on knowledge of the specific situation involved, effective risk mitigation, and improved fraud prevention and detection.

The data may also be used for establishing more effective marketing and sales policies in order to be most effective on the market.

In short, big data analytics will develop in three directions:

- There will be historical analysis to understand the pattern and characteristics of past sales.
- There will be predictive analysis to understand trends and use them to define the best strategies.
- Operational analysis (or Analytics 3.0) will support operational decisions, such as the pricing for a specific customer. It can be used for customer care to choose the most appropriate agent, to help the agents to offer the most appropriate solutions for the customer, and to support the agents in how best to cross-sell and upsell that customer. In this way, it would be possible to increase customer delight, retention, and conversion.

In a survey among industry executives, big data analytics was scored as the disruptor with the maximum impact on insurance industries (78 percent), even greater than increased regulatory oversight (at 40 percent).[10]

There is an increasing need to access these data everywhere: at the customer premises, or on the road, or in some meeting rooms. The consequence is that cloud computing appears to be a very interesting digital solution.

Finally, some of the (big) data are unstructured; hence, there is a need to manage all types of contents.

This chapter will examine all these aspects.

Voice of the customer

The previous chapter covered a large number of digital insurance applications used today in most insurance companies. Cisco conducted a global survey, in early 2013, among financial institutions that included responses from 1,514 customers and 405 insurance professionals across ten countries.[11] The report studied customers' views of how and when they were engaging with their financial services across multiple channels for activities ranging from account monitoring to obtaining financial advice. The majority (69 percent) of American customers would welcome more personal financial services to help simplify the management of their finances over multiple channels, including online, mobile phones, telephones, video conferencing, and insurance agencies.

Customers desire a more seamless and personalized customer experience from the insurance companies with which they work. Customers globally identified the most important attributes when interacting with their insurance or financial advisers as:

- availability (63 percent)
- competence (65 percent)
- efficiency (68 percent)

Customers were willing to exchange more details about their financial habits. They expect financial institutions to be more active in helping them in finding the best insurance products and coverage. In order to do this, customers desire:

- greater protection from identity theft (83 percent)
- personalized service (78 percent)
- more simplicity (56 percent) in managing their finances

Fifty-four percent of global customers expressed a desire for automated systems to provide financial advice or recommendations. The majority (71 percent) indicated that they were comfortable with the increasing use of virtual communications, in addition to in-person financial conversations. Customers from emerging economies expressed a slight preference for on-demand access to expertise (48 percent globally over speaking with a particular individual. The latter choice was favored more in emerging economies [52 percent]).

Customers want personalized services from their financial institutions:

- Seventy-seven percent desired more identity theft security.
- Seventy-three percent wanted advice on increasing their savings through financial services.
- Sixty-seven percent requested more financial education.
- Forty-seven percent wanted an assessment of their financial status and risks as compared to other customers.

The Cisco survey also examined financial services' ability to deliver personal financial services:

- Forty-six percent of American customers feel that their financial services institution has some information that enables them to offer them personal services.
- Fifty-eight percent of American financial institutions feel that they have some information on their customers to offer more personalized services.

With reference to customers' willingness to share private information with financial institutions, the results were the following:

- Fifty-three percent of American customers would be willing to provide their financial institutions with their fingerprints or other biometrics to verify transactions so as to protect them against dangers such as identity theft.
- Globally, 61 percent of customers would share biometric data, with Japanese customers least likely, at only 33 percent, and Chinese customers most likely, at 94 percent.
- Sixty percent of American customers would provide additional personal information in order to receive greater simplicity in managing their finances.

Relative to the insurance companies sharing their personal information, the indications were the following:

- Fifty-seven percent of American customers do not want their financial institutions to share their personal information outside the financial institution, even if it would improve the quality of service in other areas.
- Seventy-two percent of customers in Russia and Germany were unwilling to have their financial services provider share personal information.

The majority of global customers could be virtually connected to their financial service. There was a willingness to have virtual meetings with the personnel of financial services:

- Sixty-three percent of American customers are comfortable communicating with their financial provider using digital solutions (such as texting, e-mail, or video) instead of visiting them.
- Globally, seven in ten customers and 92 percent of financial services institutions are comfortable communicating using virtual solutions.

In terms of the media used to communicate, computers were preferred to smartphones for video connections:

- Twenty-one percent of American customers would favor a smartphone for video conversations with financial services.

- Most customers (79 percent) preferred to use laptop or desktop computers.
- Physical meetings are still important, especially to capture new customers: 46 percent of American customers were open to dealing with a financial service virtually if it offered the best and most secure services. French customers were least likely to meet virtually, at only 44 percent, and Chinese customers most likely, at 91 percent.

Mobile[12]

The number of mobile phones is larger than the global population as of the end of 2013. A report by the US Federal Reserve Board (March 2012) found that 21 percent of mobile phone owners had used mobile banking in the previous 12 months in the United States.[13] The Federal Reserve reports that 48 percent of smartphone owners have used mobile banking in 2012 (up from 42 percent the previous year) and that 21 percent of mobile bankers have deposited a check using their mobile device (double the number from the previous year). While the growth of smartphones might slow down, the adoption of mobile (and hence also of digital insurance) is taking off quickly.

A third of mobile phone users say that they may consider performing some kind of financial transaction through their mobile phone. Some users are interested in performing basic transactions such as querying for a quotation for their insurance policy or reporting a claim. Insurance companies like AXA and Allianz have created digital incubators to identify emerging mobile solutions and the start-ups that can get their innovations to market faster.[14] The pressure is coming from:

- more demanding customers
- shrinking opportunities available to the company to provide value to the customer.

The American companies demonstrate a greater level of digital interaction with customers, including the use of mobile devices, as evidenced by these findings of a Celent survey:[15]

- Seventy-six percent of the respondents to the survey allow customers to conduct transactions and purchases online, compared with sixty-six percent globally.
- Fifty percent of the respondents to the survey enable customers to submit and process claims online versus thirty-nine percent internationally.

- Fifty-seven percent of the respondents to the survey use online customer engagement in product development and market research versus thirty-four percent internationally.
- Forty-four percent of the respondents to the survey enable customers to digitally record claims submissions, compared with twenty-nine percent globally.

This higher level of online and mobile engagement also extends to greater use of social media. For example, Facebook is used by 87 percent of insurance companies in the Americas, compared with 71 percent globally.

In some countries with limited infrastructure, and where it is difficult for people to reach financial institution agencies (like Kenya, Australia, Nordic countries, and so on), the growth in the use of digital insurance could be very extensive. For instance, in Kenya, there are currently 17 million people using the M-Pesa service for person-to-person mobile money transfer.[16]

Digital insurance is attractive, mainly to the younger, more "tech-savvy" customer segment (even if also older generations are more and more using this solution).[17] Actually, the name of this entire generation is the m-generation, in which "m" stands for mobile. The enthusiasts of smartphones are also called smartphonatics.[18]

There are several reasons for using mobile devices for insurance transactions. The main one is convenience, since mobile phones are practically always on and with the customer. Another reason is cost. It is normally very cheap to use the phone for communication. With some telecom contracts, all the traffic is included in the operator fare.

From the point of view of insurance companies, the main benefit of using mobile digital insurance is cost reduction, since it helps these institutions become lean and digitized.

The concerns for customers in using digital insurance are mainly security and handset operability (there are several variations iOS, Android, BlackBerry, Windows, and so on). There are several ways to remediate these issues. A good consultant can be of great help. Cloud computing is an excellent way to overcome some of these disadvantages and, especially, ensure the availability and the reliability essential to guaranteeing the customer delight with this innovation.

Mobile digital insurance is an interesting way to go for insurance companies and for customers. Insurance companies need to take into account that launching mobile digital insurance requires some time. First, it is necessary to do an initial study. Then, the application must be developed and piloted in the market. A thorough testing is important, in order to prevent the end customer's not accepting the application. Finally, the new service should be launched with an excellent marketing campaign. For an insurance company, this would mean launching the application more or less one year after the decision to go ahead with the project. Other insurance companies might launch in advance similar applications and reap the benefits of arriving first on the market. As the case of ING, with online banking, demonstrates, if an organization is the first in the online market, it can get a larger share of the market even outside its traditional territory due to the global nature of the Web. As a consequence, the time to work for the launch or improve digital insurance is now.

The launch and the improvement of digital insurance represent an important moment in the life of an insurance company since this channel will become increasingly important. Insurance companies should use a sound method.

Mobile insurance companies are making insurance available on any personal device. Digital insurance should mass customize the customer experience in accessing the mobile insurance application. This is not a difficult task, thanks mainly to new solutions that are increasingly available, such as big data analytics. This chapter also analyzes this aspect.

The amount of structured and unstructured, internal and external, data available in every organization is increasing exponentially. Data today comes via varied and disparate sources, including customer interactions in channels such as call centers, telematics devices, social media, agent conversations, smartphones, e-mail, faxes, day-to-day business activities, and others. Gartner predicts an 800 percent growth in the availability of data from 2011 through 2016.[19]

Mobile phone use, in particular, is a rich source of data, especially in the emerging world, where the use of mobile phones more and more extends beyond phone calls to trade and insurance. In those countries, mobile data can provide information on which types of insurance company products are best for the customer or on agency availability for consultancy nearby.[20]

Architecture design

The mobile digital insurance applications must offer many of the capabilities that customers consider "must-haves" for a mobile application. This section analyzes this solution in detail against several key performance indicators:

- branding
- mobile modes
- devices
- authentication and fraud prevention
- richness of functions
- usability
- alerts
- support to the sales force
- dynamic rendering
- personalization
- application distribution
- native phone functions

Branding

Branding is an important aspect. The digital insurance application will be the "image" of the insurance company to the customers. It must be appealing and effective.

Strictly connected with branding, there is the need to adopt the right style of communication with the customers and use the connection with him/her through the mobile device to offer more and better services. The insurance company must have a multichannel policy that assures consistency, cross-fertilization, image reinforcement, integration, and so on across all channels, be they physical (agencies, brokers, and so on), or virtual (phone, Web, mobile, and so on).

Mobile modes

Users can access mobile digital insurance in different ways:

- Short Message Service (SMS) is one of the first modes offered to customers to perform simple digital insurance transactions. A customer with a traditional cell phone can conduct some basic insurance transactions, such as receiving alerts or checking the status of the policy. Some companies even provide quotations to prospects including only some basic information.
- Web-based solutions provide mobile Internet, delivered via a wireless application protocol (WAP) or mobile optimized websites (for instance, a micro-site) using the browser of the smartphone. It essentially mimics the experience a user would have using online insurance on his/her computer. The user experience tends to vary greatly depending on the mobile device. The mobile Web is typically the

easiest solution for insurance companies to implement mobile digital insurance. It offers broad functions. It is very consistent with online digital insurance for customers. But, it is not a secure way to use online insurance on a mobile. Sometimes it might be cumbersome to perform entries and view the results of the transactions on the small screen of some smartphones. It is much easier to perform this type of operation with a tablet.

- Customer-based downloaded applications, or simply apps, streamline the mobile experience. The main limitation is that they might be specific to a mobile device type, its operating system, and the network characteristics. Apps can be downloaded on the device from the online stores of many vendors, such as Apple iPhone, Google's Android, BlackBerry, and Windows mobile stores. The insurance application is downloaded through a secure and authenticated process to the mobile device. Once downloaded, the app provides an optimal user experience. Smartphone users tend to prefer these rich customer applications.

There are advantages and disadvantages in each of these modes.[21] A Javelin Strategy Research report on security evaluates the specific security issues that mobile financial services companies face when using these three different channels: mobile web browser, application, and SMS texting.[22] The survey shows the following:

- Forty-four percent of financial institution customers use a mobile browser. It is perceived by the customer to be the most secure. Mobile insurance companies with smartphones view the browser as an extension of their online solutions.
- The second most widely used channel is downloaded apps, used by 25 percent of customers surveyed. The architecture is more secure for mobile insurance companies. App insurance has the potential to replace online insurance altogether and serve as the customer's primary access to insurance companies.
- Nineteen percent of mobile insurance companies use SMS transactions to interface the financial services companies; however, it is declining in popularity. It is the least secure channel and is suited only to simple transactions.

The trend is to move toward rich customer applications. They can assure:

- the best user experience
- the highest security
- the highest transaction speed

Today, most digital insurance offerings include the so-called "triple play." This approach combines all three access modes so that customers can pick and choose the services that best fit their needs.

Devices

One of the reasons for the limited adoption of mobile by some customers, especially in business, is the form factor of mobile phones. The small screen of a smartphone is not the optimal setting for reading and writing the large amounts of information that a person in a business looks at on a daily basis. The rise of tablets could be a solution to this. In addition to capabilities such as the ability to process payments and deliver cash reporting, a mobile app for a company's business customers should be able to deliver solutions that simplify their relationships with the insurance company.

In the case of corporate digital insurance, tablets could give executives the ability to perform big data analytics to support their actions in corporate insurance. For instance, a digital insurance app should provide key indicators on the status of the policies, account balances in different currencies and languages, and many of the functions the insurance company already provides to their business customers in an online environment.

The expectation is that corporate people will be able to use the digital insurance features on tablets for complex transactions requiring larger displays. Corporate people and individuals will use their smartphones for quick approvals, receiving alerts, or similar simple transactions.

Authentication and fraud prevention

Ensuring the highest levels of security is essential for the success of any digital insurance offering. The need for security is increasingly important to customers. They need to be able to authenticate themselves securely when it comes to accessing their accounts. One possibility is to use a token for authentication. Tokens have become the industry standard for large corporate security. The downside is that they require users to carry them. An alternative is to request the customer to call back from their authorized phone number. Biometrics technology, voice pattern, and even facial authentication offer greater convenience than tokens and other security methods by allowing users to prove their identity without having to carry a device or remember a password. Biometrics technology is also a natural fit for mobile solutions.

The chapter on Governance discusses this issue in more detail.

Richness of functions

Integration, security, and usability are by far the most important challenges in launching digital insurance. There are other challenges as well. It is important to provide as many functions as possible. The digital insurance user might need many functions. Designers might want to keep customers away from agencies or contact centers as much as possible. More functions should not prevent simplicity. This is the challenge.

Insurance companies want digital insurance to be able to sell more services and gain more customers or revenues rather than just cannibalizing existing customers. The richer and more convenient the set of functions on the mobile, the more insurance companies will be able to meet this challenge.

Forrester did a survey of mobile applications for insurance in the United States.[23] Some of the results were the following:

- Geico brought home the mobile gold award. With a score of 76 out of 100, Geico earned the designation of the financial institution you can keep in your pocket or purse. The silver award went to Liberty Mutual, with 73, thanks to an especially strong performance when consumers need the most help: the claim.
- Mobile insurance sales performance is led by direct insurance companies.
- Policy information and management is a strength for all.
- Claims are a weakness for most. The moment of truth for insurance customers is the claim experience. And the immediacy and prevalence of mobile position these handy devices as the ideal means for filing and managing claims. A Forrester assessment found that many apps just are not that easy to use or lack some important functions.

Usability

A challenge of digital insurance is the usability of the applications. Digital insurance should not be the source of too many calls to the help desk of the insurance company. Complexity in using digital insurance should not cause the customers to abandon this channel for insurance transactions.

A rich customer application has the ability to deliver the highest-quality user experience. Its absence can deliver customers a poor branding and navigation experience, or even reduce its perceived security. Designing for a mobile application is not just about designing for a smaller screen. It is different from designing websites or online applications. These differences are multiplying rapidly as mobile devices with additional functions and unique hardware characteristics enter the market.

In order to increase the value of the digital insurance experience for the customer, designers must meet the following usability principles:[24]

- A digital insurance solution must have an intuitive and user-friendly interface. Users must be able to quickly access desired information or do the correct transactions without navigating through multiple screens or being forced to push too many keys.
- There should be cross-fertilization between the teams working for the retail side and the commercial side of digital insurance. Many lessons learned from consumer users can also be transferred to commercial solutions for digital insurance.
- Developers should focus on providing the most critical user information on the login page. As a result, at the login stage, users should be able to see a snapshot summarizing all of their relationships with the insurance company, including possible investment and health accounts. Users should also be able to easily group account balances in order to see their total status, in policies, claims, and so on. In this way, they can quickly view the most relevant data in a way that is customized to their specific needs.
- Since the users will be very different, designers should make sure that there will be some kind of error correction feature to protect the customer and the insurance company. To please the maximum number and variety of users, designers should give users the possibility of customizing their application, adding flexibility.

Following the philosophy of Steve Jobs, simplicity in using digital insurance is extremely important. His requirement that to do everything you need with just one button to push, translates in this case to "I want to transact with one click."[25] Customers might accept two clicks, for instance, to be sure that they did not make an error in keying the data in the transaction. No more than two clicks should be required, however. Similarly, labels, messages, or instructions should be extremely clear and crisp and possibly multilanguage.

Alerts

Alerts, especially for pending transactions, are critical for all insurance transactions. Customers are accustomed to this in the PC online channel.

They expect alerts to carry through to mobile. This is even more important because the mobile is always on and with the customer.

Customers of insurance companies should be able to receive notifications with regard to transactions on their policies. They should be able to keep track of their policies at any time with information sent straight to their phones. This basic policy function should provide customers with alerting capability available to all types of digital insurance. This service should generate push and pull alerts depending on customer preferences/settings.

Alerts types can be one or more of the following:

- Scheduled alerts are notifications configured by the user or the insurance company to run periodically at predetermined times in order to communicate valuable insurance information, such as scheduled alerts for the expiration of policies or need for additional documentation for claims, and so on.
- Threshold alerts are triggered when an account or a transaction goes above or below a predetermined amount. This might include claims, aggregated transactions, and/or exceptional individual transactions.
- Security and event-based alerts are triggered at the occurrence of an event, such as a password or credential change.
- Actionable alerts enable users to take action or instruct the insurance company to take action on their behalf. Actionable alerts should leverage all mobile access modes. For example, there could be an SMS prompt where the user responds with an SMS containing one or more keywords, such as "yes," or a push notification automatically prompts the user to log into his/her digital insurance application.
- Service-based alerts might be promotional alerts to inform customers of excellent new product offerings or threats.

Support to the sales force

The mobile can be used for customers' access but also to improve the effectiveness of the employees and intermediaries. Insurance companies are looking to revamp their agent and customer portals to provide an enhanced experience. With the need for increased coverage through face-to-face selling, mobile applications as a policy-selling channel seem to be the most convenient way to connect with prospective customers and reduce turnaround time for closing a transaction. Insurance companies can not only enhance and equip agents with the advanced solutions on a mobile device but also address the challenges agents face when on the road:

- A lack of real-time information and delays due to going back and forth with back office/agencies can result in loss of customers.
- Time-consuming processes to retrieve the lead information, arrange meetings, provide alternate quotes, and collect payments and documents due to dependency on agencies or an Internet connection result in considerable loss of efforts and time.
- The unavailability of agencies or Internet cafes nearby also adds to the long turnaround time.

To address the above-stated pain areas, mobile offers a powerful solution based on providing agents with a next-gen tablet solution. The primary objectives to achieve are:

- providing real-time information to the agents on leads, lead management, financial need analysis, and marketable products
- supporting to the quotation and benefit illustration, product selection, e-Signature, dashboards and case tracking, service corner, and complete offline functions for the above in such a way as to provide one-stop shopping for end-to-end sales processes
- making the complete process paperless including payments and form filling to reduce turnaround time, thus ensuring closure of the deal

A tablet-based application for point-of-sale enablement should have the following characteristics:

- hybrid applications supported on Android, iOS, and Windows
- integration with core insurance applications
- an ability to work online as well as offline to eliminate dependency on network connectivity
- an intuitive interface that uses features of the device, making it superior to an agency portal solution

The new application rolled out for agents in the field should assure increased agent productivity. It should support better customer experience and delight with prompt service.

Dynamic rendering

The mobile digital insurance application needs to understand dynamically the capabilities of the mobile device that is used. It should automatically choose the presentation screens and end-user functions that can be rendered effectively on that specific device with horizontal or vertical displays. It also needs to generate specific screens, scrolling functionality, alerts, and buttons in order to create an optimal user experience.

Personalization

Mobile applications should support personalization such as:

- preferred language and/or currency
- date/time format
- amount format
- default transactions
- standard beneficiary list
- alerts

Application distribution

Due to the nature of the connection between insurance companies and their customers, it would be impractical to expect customers to regularly visit insurance companies' sites or connect to a website for regular upgrade of their digital insurance application. The expectation is that the mobile application itself checks the upgrades and downloads and applies necessary patches (so-called over-the-air updates). However, there could be many issues as far as implementing this approach, such as upgrade/synchronization of other dependent components. In any case, the final decision to update the application should be left to the customer.

Native phone functions

Many interaction points directly influence mobile-design considerations. These include:

- gesture detection (pinching, flicking, dragging, and so on)
- touch detection (allowing for direct interaction with content)
- on-screen, software, or physical keyboard
- location-awareness information and feedback
- (video)camera utilization

Generali and Obis

Generali has reached an agreement with Obi in order to use the mobile channel to reach up to 20 growing markets.

The content of the agreement is to develop on the innovative phone developed by Obi (Worldphone) the native apps labeled tailor-made for Generali.

> The apps are developed taking into account the specificity of each market on which the phones are sold.
> This is an example of how important mobility is becoming in the insurance world and the opportunity to approach it with an ecosystem model.

Big data analytics

Big data analytics are the solutions, processes, and procedures allowing an organization to create, manipulate, store, retrieve, and manage a relatively large amount of data to get information for an organization. The ultimate objective is to aid the decision making process.

This book uses the term "big data analytics," since a large amount of data (big data) in itself cannot really be useful. It is the combination of a relatively large amount of data (big data) and the capability to analyze them (analytics) that can bring large benefits.

A more complete definition of big data analytics is:

- extracting, transforming, loading, and storing a relatively large amount of data
- retrieving and examining (or mining) them
- getting appropriate information
- identifying hidden patterns, unknown correlations, and similar in support of decision-making

in order to get competitive advantages, better strategic and operational business decisions, effective marketing, increased customer delight, and improved risk taking.

Fifteen to twenty percent of data available to insurance companies is in structured form, while the remaining information is available in an unstructured format, such as document, PDF, email, and so on.[26] While managing the overwhelming data flow can be challenging, insurance companies that can capture, store, search, aggregate, and analyze all types of data can obtain real benefits such as increased productivity, improved competitive advantage, and enhanced customer experience. This value, however, does not necessarily come from simply managing big data analytics. It comes from harvesting the actionable insights from them. Insurance companies that can obtain objective-driven business value by applying science to effectively mine data and use them for customer insights, for support, and to offer new products/services will have clear competitive advantages and stay ahead of the curve in this information age.

Big data analytics is connected with analytical solutions that have existed for years but that can now be applied faster, cheaper (for instance using technologies like Hadoop), on a greater scale, and are more accessible. Analytics is the discovery and communication of meaningful patterns in data. It is especially valuable in areas rich with recorded information. Analytics relies on the simultaneous application of statistics, computer programming, and operations research to quantify performance. Data visualization is particularly important in obtaining value from harvesting the data.

These challenges are the current inspiration for much of the innovation in modern analytics information systems, supporting relatively new automatic analysis concepts such as complex event processing, full text search and analysis, semantics, and even new ideas for presenting the information to support successful decisions.

Big data analytics operations can be processed locally. As organizations migrate to the cloud, so will their corporate data. Moreover, cloud-based architectures will become more important as individual entities (that is, both devices and resources) generate continuous data streams that can be collected, stored, processed, analyzed, and reported.

The volume, speed, and power of this type of solutions have transformed the economic environment into a sophisticated data economy. It allows for the execution of complex global transactions at the push of a button. From high-frequency trading to e-commerce, to mobile telephony, computers all over the world are generating huge amounts of data. Like individuals, institutions might be facing an information overload that is limiting the promise and opportunity of technology.

It is estimated that every day, over 2.5 quintillion bytes of data are generated globally. What is more, 90 percent of the existing processable data in the world today has been created in the last two years alone. The term "processeable" can be defined as "able to be processed; suitable for processing" (by other computer applications).[27]

All of these data provide a large amount of information from more sources than ever before – from social media to e-commerce transaction records to cellphone and global positioning system (GPS) signals.

However, because the majority of that data is unstructured and requires unique expertise to understand, organize, and analyze it, most of the information sits idle. The good news is that there is a growing set of big data analytics solutions that are available to help organizations use and monetize this valuable commodity by finding important insights into their activity. It can help in analyzing their customers' transaction flows, which can in turn help them to be more effective, efficient, economical, and ethical with their offerings.

Research has found that big data analytics holds the capability to generate profits by improving the margins coming from the transaction flows.[28] When organized and analyzed, it can highlight flows and offer unique insights into trends, destinations, values, volumes, and fees, which can ultimately drive opportunities for organizations.[29]

Big data analytics is not an entirely new concept. Google, for example, was built on the business of helping persons search through millions of websites and zetabytes of data to provide near instantaneous results with pinpoint accuracy.[30] This capability, which can be almost defined as magic, is accomplished through the use of various big data analytics methods and solutions. In the past decade, a variety of industries in the finance, manufacturing, retail, and technology sectors have started to use big data analytics to improve their processes or to better understand and deliver services to their customers.

In today's ever-changing economic environment, all sectors are faced with rethinking traditional value propositions. Big data analytics is emerging as a cutting-edge option. It is an innovative way to access and visualize key information to be more effective, efficient, economical, and indeed ethical (that is compliant). By unlocking the data available in an organization, persons are able to better understand opportunities for growth and achieve cost savings, be more compliant, and, therefore, are better prepared for success on all fronts.

The superior value of big data analytics is twofold in that it not only provides key information on the business and the market but also offers a look at internal processes and how they can be improved to reflect the changing economic landscape. In some ways, big data analytics acts like a GPS in that it provides support on what the next best step should be in order to reach the targets of the company. This visibility will give organizations the option to fill gaps, improve efficiencies, and ultimately make better decisions. It will also help create customer-centric strategies and improve the overall customer experience.

As digital solutions continue to push for faster, more interconnected organizations, big data analytics will become an increasingly valuable tool. Through this untapped information, organizations will be able to understand their businesses and customers in new and insightful ways that will allow them to develop new products/services, processes, organizations, and business models that will effectively generate margins and additional business opportunities while enhancing their customer experiences and value proposition.

For most of the organizations, using big data analytics to help in decision making is a new approach. Only now are some insurance companies beginning to understand the importance of data as an asset, what information can offer, and are gaining new insights. Diving into big data analytics may seem like diving into uncharted waters for some. Big data analytics is also the future for insurance companies. There is only the need to take advantage of it in order to remain relevant and use the increasing amount of data available for the benefit of the company.

The benefits of big data analytics

Big data analytics is one of the next Big Things in organizations. Big data analytics came into the scene at the beginning of the 21st century. The first organizations to embrace it were online and start-up firms. Firms like Google, eBay, LinkedIn, and Facebook were built around big data analytics from the beginning.

Like many new digital solutions, big data analytics can bring drastic cost reductions, substantial improvements in the time required to perform a computing task, and new product and service offerings.

Big data analytics is similar to "small data," but bigger in size. Having more data requires different approaches:

- methods, tools, and architectures
- solutions for new problems or old problems in a better way

Big data analytics generates value from the storing and processing of very large quantities of digital information that cannot be analyzed with traditional computing techniques.

The use of big data analytics makes sense for the enormous amount of processable data that is more and more available:

- Wal-Mart handles more than one million customer transactions every hour.
- Facebook handles 40 billion photos from its user base.
- Decoding the human genome originally took ten years to process, and now it can be achieved in less than one week.

The reasons for the interest for big data analytics is connected with:

- the growth in the quantity of processable data
- the increase in storage capacities
- the availability of larger processing power
- the availability of data (in different data types)

The characteristics of big data analytics are that it is:

- automatically generated by a machine (for instance, a sensor embedded in a vehicle)
- typically using an entirely new source of data (for instance, use of the Web)
- using data not designed to be computer-friendly (for instance, text streams)

Big data analytics are the results of processes such as:

- transactions
- getting data from the sensors
- interactions in social networks

The data that should be used are:

- produced by the same company
- produced by users, customers, intermediaries, and vendors
- from social media on prospects and customers

Big data characteristics

Big data analytics provides opportunities in existing environments. It also creates new opportunities for the stakeholders of insurance companies. These opportunities were not possible by dealing with structured content in traditional ways. Big data analytics has three characteristics: the so-called three V's.

- Volume. The quantity of data should be relatively large. The word "relative" refers to the organization: a small organization might consider a big data analytics with a relatively lower volume of data with respect to large organizations. Big data analytics refers to the large – and exponentially growing – amount of data flooding into and out of every insurance company and that is internally or externally generated. Of course, the word "big" should be interpreted in relation to a specific organization. Examples of these can be found in a variety of sources including:

- the structured granular call detail records (CDR) in a call center
- detailed sensor data from telematics devices, such as PCs, mobiles, points of sale (POS), radio-frequency identification (RFID) devices and so on
- external information, including open data, marketing research, and other behavioral data
- unstructured data from social media, reports of different types, and so on

- Velocity. Insurance companies must be able to process, access, analyze, and report huge volumes of information as quickly as possible in order to make timely decisions, especially in the operational environment. Insurance companies also need to[31]
    - reduce latency to optimize transparency, cross-selling, and upselling in the different channels
    - provide quick enterprise intranet and extranet documents search to study the impact of different events and decisions
    - decrease business delivery time for reports in a data warehousing environment as there is a need for solutions for the rapid processing of data, in such a way they cannot "age" too much
    - use clickstreams and ad impressions capturing user behavior at millions of events per second
    - exploit machine to machine processes exchanging data between billions of devices
    - take advantage of infrastructure and sensors generating massive log data in real-time
- Variety. Data can come from disparate sources beyond the usual structured environment of data processing. These would include mobile, online, agent-generated, social media, text, audio, video, log files, and more. Big data analytics are not just numbers, data, and strings. Big data analytics are also documents, geospatial data, 3D data, audio, photos and videos, and unstructured text, including log files and social media. Unstructured data outweigh structured data. The processing of such a variety of information is not easy. Traditional database systems were designed to address smaller

volumes of structured data, with fewer updates and with a predictable, consistent data structure. In general, it is possible to classify big data analytics as:

- Structured. Most traditional data sources are structured
- Semi-structured, mixing structured and unstructured data. Many sources of big data analytics are semi-structured
- Unstructured set of data: such as video data, and audio data.

The analysis of unstructured data types is a challenge. Unstructured data differs from structured data in that their format varies widely. They cannot be stored in traditional relational databases without significant effort at data transformation. Sources of unstructured data, such as e-mail, word documents, PDFs, geospatial data, and so on are becoming a relevant source of big data analytics for insurance companies.

There are three other V's that are important in big data analytics:

- There should be a concern about the Veracity of data. This refers to the messiness or trustworthiness of the data. With many forms of big data, quality and accuracy are less controllable. The quality, dependability, reliability, and consistency of data is a critical issue for insurance companies looking to extract from data meaningful information to support their decision-making processes. The consequences are different. The impact of Veracity in big data analytics is much wider than in small data. In some cases, such as in voice-to-text conversions or social network conversations, data quality can result in meaningful information. This is true especially if insurance companies are trying to analyze tacit phenomena, such as in sentiment analysis.
- There must be concern with the Vulnerability. Due to the variety of big data analytics, it might be a challenge to assure data privacy for non/structured data. A later chapter will discuss this aspect in detail.
- Last but not least, big data analytics use should add Value for the customers. Insurance companies that adopt customer-centric approaches can get valuable insights from data analysis. Value refers to the ability to turn the data into information which helps in decision making. It is important that insurance companies make a case for any attempt to collect and leverage data. It is easy to fall into the latest fashion and launch big data analytics initiatives without

a clear understanding of the business value which could come from this approach. In order for insurance companies to derive true value from big data analytics, they must enable innovations in products, processes, organizations, and business models. Value for the customer is the most important of these characteristics. If the customer finds value in the relationship with the insurance company, the organization would also collect value.

It is important to follow the correct process in storing big data analytics:

- selecting data sources for analysis
- defining data models: key value, graphics, and documents
- analyzing the characteristics of the data
- eliminating redundant or duplicated or useful data
- overviewing big data analytics loading, storage, and retrieval.

There are a certain actions that are important in storing big data analytics:

- choosing the correct data stores based on the characteristics of the data
- moving code to data
- implementing multi-language data store solutions
- aligning business goals to the appropriate data store
- integrating disparate data stores
- mapping data to the programming framework
- connecting and extracting data from storage
- transforming data for processing
- monitoring the progress of job flows

It is important to answer some questions when dealing with big data analytics:

- Why should the company use big data analytics?
- What types of solutions are better to use?
- Where is data stored? Is it centralized, distributed, or in cloud storage?
- Where is processing done: mainframe, distributed servers, or in the cloud?

- How is data stored and indexed? Is it in high-performance schema-free databases or in the traditional ways of storing?
- What operations are performed on data? Sequential, analytic, or semantic processing?
- What are the challenges connected with using big data analytics?
- Who are the right talents available that are capable to solve the right problems by using the data available?

Analytics 3.0 and digital insurance

In an article in the *Harvard Business Review*, Tom Davenport presented a model of the development of analytics over time:[32]

- Analytics 1.0 is the business intelligence before the big data analytics. It was mainly devoted to analyzing small internal problems, since the amount of data available was small.
- Analytics 2.0 was a step forward, thanks to the rise of big data analytics. It can also be used for predictive analytics besides historical analysis.
- A new wave is Analytics 3.0. It is a new resolve to apply powerful data-gathering and analysis methods to a company's operations and to its offerings—to embed data smartness into the products and services customers buy.

A statement by Davenport is interesting:[33] "The most important trait of the Analytics 3.0 era is that not only online firms, but virtually any type of firm in any industry, can participate in the given economy."

Table 4.1 shows a synthesis according to Davenport of the characteristics of each generation of analytics.

The development of Analytics 3.0 gives birth to a new architectures. The use of digital solutions existing in many large organizations is not abandoned. It is advisable the use of specialized solutions of big data analytics in the cloud and using open-source and cheap technologies (such as Hadoop).

An example of the use of Analytics 3.0 in insurance is mass private insurance: a low-cost, customer-centric version of insurance:

- It is low cost since it can use the lower costs of processing a large amount of data made possible with big data analytics solutions.
- It is personalized to each customer, thanks to powerful big data analytics.

Table 4.1 The characteristics of the three generations of analytics (adapted from T. Davenport).[34]

Era	1.0 Traditional analytics	2.0 Big data	3. Data economy
Timeframe	Mid-1970s to 2000	Early 2001 to 2020	2021 and in the future
Culture	Competition not on analytics	New focus on data based products and services	Agile method where all decisions are driven (or at least influenced) by data.
Type of analytics	95 percent reporting, descriptive 5 percent predictive, prescriptive	85 percent reporting, descriptive 15 percent predictive, prescriptive (visual)	90 percent+ predictive, prescriptive, automated reporting
Cycle time	Months	An insight a week	Millions of insights per second
Data	Internal, structured	Very large, unstructured, multisource. Explosion of sensor data.	Seamless combination of internal and external data. Analytics embedded in operational and decision processes. Tools available at the point of decision
Technology	Rudimentary BI, reporting tools. Dashboards. Data stored in enterprise data warehouses or marts.	New technologies: Hadoop, commodity servers, in-memory, open source. Master data management. Standards appear for data quality.	New data architectures, beyond the data warehouse. New application architectures. Specific apps, mobile. Data dictionaries. Full data governance.
Organization	Analytical people segregated from business and ICT. Back room statisticians	Some chief data officers appear in some advanced companies. Data scientists are on the rise. Talent shortage. Educational programs starting.	Centralized teams, specialized functions among team members, dedicated funding. Chief analytics officers. Training and education programs.

This would require:

- recording the behavior of the customer through his/her accesses, transactions, and, if available, social networks, with his/her consent
- processing all these data versus a model that might provide useful information for marketing, investment, or risk-averse actions
- suggesting or taking actions with the customers, which could add value to them

Such use of the data would work particularly well in the case of digital insurance. Mobile would also add information on the location of the customer. If he/she is in a mall, it would be possible to provide her/him with some proximity information on the nearest agency or merchant.

From a privacy point of view, it would be necessary to obtain the customer's permission to trail his/her activity. In some cases, for instance, if the customer has some funds available, he/she might appreciate suggestions on how to invest the funds available in unit-linked insurance product. The acceptance of the suggestion sent by the insurance company to the customer via mobile might even not require pushing a key on the smartphone, but simply a "double shake" of the mobile device.

A similar type of function would be particularly useful in the case of mobile corporate/institutional insurance. The insurance company should send (on request) alerts to the corporate treasury telling about the need to renew a policy or switch to a different value of coverage. That would help the treasury in properly covering corporate risks. Such services would be particularly appreciated in the case of small and medium size insurance enterprises (SME), where the managers would not have time to follow liquidity or would not have the necessary skills to optimize insurance coverage.

Value creation from big data analytics

According to McKinsey, big data analytics can create value for customers and organizations in five ways by[35]

- increasing transparency, making data more easily accessible to relevant stakeholders
- creating and storing more transactional data in digital form, in such a way that organizations can collect accurate, detailed performance data in real time or near-real time, thus enabling proofs of concept to identify needs and improve performance, but especially to offer new products and services to add value to the customer

- providing insurance companies the means to improve customer segmentation and then better develop and tailor products, services, processes, and promotions to each specific segment (in the limit, to each specific customer, the so-called one-to-one relationship or mass personalized insurance)
- including advanced analytics to provide actionable customer insights that minimize risks and improve decision-making
- being useful for organizations looking to create new business models and improve products/services, processes, and organizations

Leading-edge insurance companies should start to exploit big data analytics in at least 12 different ways.[36] Each of them would add value to the customers and the insurance company in one or more of the ways described:

- Customer channels should be combined from an informational point of view. By combining and making transparent direct customer connections (e-mail, call center, agent, portal, SMSs, reports, and so on) with indirect customer connections such as social media, blogs, log files, and so on, a more holistic, 360-degree view of each customer can be obtained. This helps create a personalized and consistent communication response, enabling marketing to achieve better brand value and gain competitive advantages, while directly influencing the bottom line by becoming leaner, thanks to the reduction in processing and communication costs.
- The call center and middle offices workload should be optimized. Analyzing network data from the call center switches (call detail records) and combining them with transactions helps in understanding who performed, what activity was performed, and how efficiently. It can be used to provide training guidelines for employees and intermediaries or simply to tune the computer telephony integration system (CTI). Temporal call patterns analysis on voluminous and raw telecom and processing data can help assist in staffing optimization as well.
- Insurance companies can use data to find prescriptive and predictive information. They can investigate how big data analytics can improve the user experience by sensing data and responding in near-real time. Prescriptive analytics can provide alerts on risky behavior in terms of transactions.
- Cross-sell and upsell to potential customers should be leveraged. By analyzing text and speech in a near-real time environment, insurance

companies are presented with new opportunities to convert the call center from a cost center to a service-to-sales (S2S) center by providing cross-sell, upsell capabilities, or simply selling to uninsureds.

- Natural language processing (NLP) and text analytics for social media should be used, as well as speech analytics for call center conversations. Digital insurance can improve their sentiment analysis to better meet customer service improvement objectives, even if not explicitly disclosed to the company.
- Using social media to introduce new products and services, marketing can exploit social media to introduce new products and services. They can target customers in specific regions in a cost-efficient and effective way as compared to capital-intensive paper, television, and Web promotions. In this way, they can innovatively change the business model. Insurance companies can experiment with different segments, and then upgrade their strategies to a higher (regional, national, or international) level.
- By closing the loop between pricing risk, transactions, and financial effects, risk officials can evaluate the loss and fraud propensity of existing customers in order to better price risk for new prospects, especially in the property and casualty (P&C) insurance. This helps in minimizing the risks and to a large extent, pricing the risk appropriately. It can help also in improving real-time risk decisions.
- External data should be leveraged for more accurate pricing. Using real-time location and business characteristics, data can lead to more appropriate pricing on customer risk based on how, when, and where customers use the insured goods.
- Search capabilities should be enhanced. Unfortunately, not many insurance companies are using big data analytics to discover innovative ways to search their intranet or extranet contents in order to provide fast search capabilities in unstructured documents. These can be used by their financial departments, as well as in call-center scenarios to provide real-time recommendations.
- Comprehensive customer delight surveys and feedback should be created. Most financial services organizations perform customer surveys using a relatively small customer sample size. Big data analytics enables insurance companies to survey their entire customer base (and possibly prospects through social media), processing the survey results in a fast and cost-effective way. Thus, they can obtain a more correct picture of what would be available from their customer service responses.

Woolworths Australia

Woolworths in Australia has used retail shopping patterns to predict financial risk.[37] It found that customers who drink lots of milk and eat lots of red meat are significantly better from an auto insurance risks point of view than customers who drink alcohol, eat lots of pasta and rice, and fill their gas tanks at night.

Harnessing and harvesting big data analytics for digital insurance

Big data analytics platforms do not replace existing traditional data management and analytics platforms. They simply complement, extend, and improve upon existing environments and capabilities. Big data analytics consists of two processes: harnessing, which involves collection, extraction, transformation, loading, administration, and management of data, and harvesting, which is the skills and solutions required to apply science to the data, in order to derive actionable and meaningful insights from the data to drive actions and help in decision making.

The harvesting and harnessing processes are complementary to one another. They are two sides of a big data analytics initiative.

Harnessing big data analytics

At the most basic level, the harnessing process consists of:

- the collection of data
- the extraction, transformation, and loading of data
- the management of data
- the setting up of an ecosystem that can not only create big data analytics but sustain it as well

In the past, the data-harnessing process was much easier than it is today. The benefits of using this data were more limited. Today, the complexity arises from:

- a combination of additional sources of data, like social media or open data
- the complex solutions that exist to provide insurance companies access to those data as well as the ability to analyze them
- the diversity of data. Gartner estimates that between 80 percent and 90 percent of all data produced is unstructured.[38] Insurance companies can tap into a treasure trove of unstructured data of all varieties: text, audio, video, adjustor notes, click streams, and log files, for instance, and combine them with other structured types such as

currency exchanges, investments performances, demographics and geographic data, competition information, and so on

Harvesting big data analytics

Big data analytics harvesting can be classified in two ways. Big data analysis uses descriptive and predictive models to gain valuable knowledge from data. It uses this insight to recommend actions or to guide decision-making and communication. The latter is called operational big data analytics.

Data cannot be consumed in their raw form. They must be processed into a consumable form before they can be both interpreted and acted upon.

The harvesting process utilizes solutions and algorithms that enable insurance companies to:

- analyze
- deliver actionable insights
- support process intelligence
- get real value from big data analytics

One more emerging challenge is dynamic regulatory needs. For example, in the insurance industry, Solvency II and capital adequacy needs are likely to force even smaller insurance companies to adopt internal risk models. In such cases, cloud computing and open-source solutions can help smaller insurance companies adopt risk analytics and support agency-level monitoring by applying predictive analytics. Once big data analytics is introduced for compliance reasons, it can also be used for marketing and risk reduction.

Organizations may commonly apply analytics to insurance companies' data, to describe, predict, and improve business performance. Specifically, areas within analytics include:

- enterprise decision management
- marketing optimization and marketing mix analytics
- web analytics
- sales force sizing and optimization
- price and promotion modeling
- predictive science
- risk analysis
- fraud analytics

Skill sets such as statistics, data mining, econometrics, business analytics, visualization techniques, and more are in high demand as they provide a solid foundation for deriving useful insights from harvesting the data. Academic institutions have started trying to fill the supply-demand gap by offering various teaching programs to prepare for the next generation of skills needed to mine actionable insights, such as the ones necessary to train data scientists.

Celent surveyed many insurance companies.[39] European insurance companies mentioned company structure or culture constraints (90 percent), lack of skills (70 percent), and channel conflicts (67 percent) as their top three challenges in executing their digital insurance strategy. Although company structure/culture is also the top global challenge (albeit at a lower 68 percent), lack of skills (50 percent) and channel conflict (46 percent) are viewed as less of a challenge globally. European non-life insurance companies feel particularly challenged by the scarcity of skills/expertise and channel conflicts: 79 percent and 74 percent cite these challenges, compared to only 66 percent for life insurance companies. Big data analytics and solutions capabilities are most needed by European insurance companies, suggesting that the recruitment activity will be intense in search of people armed with these skills.

While the ability to successfully harness and harvest data is critical to a big data analytics strategy, the harvesting process is where insurance companies can extract real true value from their data, with the help of analytics and process management. Defining use cases and hypotheses becomes crucial when following a focused "top-down" approach to creating actionable insights.

Although this is a focused approach, many times insurance companies need to do some initial work in order to perform data exploratory analysis in order to come up with the use cases that can exploit big data analytics. This initial bottom-up approach is a prerequisite for determining and prioritizing use cases to support proof of concepts (PoCs) for big data analytics.

Real value is derived when actionable insights can make a positive difference in achieving the strategic objectives and especially finding ways to add value to the customers and eliminating waste in internal processes.

Analytics can be used to harvest the data in different fields. The following sections examine in more detail the fields of:

- marketing
- risks and fraud
- portfolio analysis
- operations

Progressive

Progressive USA has sold more than one million snapshot policies in which driving behaviors are monitored, and the data collected helps it tailor its pricing.[40] Harvesting digital data has enormous potential in the current environment in which people leave vast amounts of information behind from the websites they visit, the words they search, and the social media posts they make. Several companies are already mining data on social media to provide their (physical or virtual) agents with real-time information about their policyholders' life events (moves, job changes, car and real-estate investments, new babies, and so on) for sales, and similarly are using digital data to curb fraudulent claims.

Marketing optimization. Big data analytics supports both strategic marketing decisions (such as how much to spend overall on marketing, how to allocate budgets across a portfolio of brands, and the marketing mix). It can also support more tactical campaigns in terms of getting customer insights or clustering, or promoting a specific product in a specific market. This would help in targeting the best potential customers with the optimal message, in the most cost-effective medium and messages, at the ideal time, and, thanks to the mobile, in the right place.

Marketing has evolved from a creative process into a highly data-driven process. Marketing organizations can use big data analytics to:

- define where, when, to whom, and how to conduct campaigns
- determine the outcomes of campaigns or efforts
- guide decisions for investments and customer targeting
- use demographic studies, customer segmentation, conjoint analysis, and other techniques on large amounts of customer purchases, surveys, and panel data to understand and communicate marketing strategy

Web analytics allows marketers to collect session-level information about interactions on a website. Those interactions provide the big data analytics with the information to track the referrer and search keywords, IP addresses, and activities of the customers or prospects. With this information, a marketing person can improve the marketing campaign, the site creative content, the target market, and the information architecture.

Analysis solutions connected with big data analytics that are frequently used in marketing include:

- online campaigns
- marketing mix modeling or, as it is commonly referred to, attribution modeling, in the digital or mixed-media context
- pricing and promotion analyses

- customer analytics, for instance, segmentation
- web analytics and optimization of websites
- sales force optimization

All these solutions now frequently work in conjunction with the more traditional marketing analysis techniques.

Risk and fraud analytics. The use of risk scores is aimed at predicting the individual's delinquency behavior (so called customer intelligence). Scores are used to evaluate the insurance worthiness of each applicant and rate it for the processing of policy applications. Insurance companies use predictive models to reduce uncertainty across the risk scores for individual customers. Big data analysis can also help in preventing and detecting frauds.

Portfolio analysis. Business analytics can support portfolio analysis. In this case, an insurance company has a collection of accounts of varying value and risk. The accounts may differ according to the social status (wealthy, middle class, poor, and so on) of the insureds, the geographical locations, their net value, and many other factors. The insurance companies must balance the return on the insurance transactions with the risk of losses for each insurance transaction.

It is important to evaluate the portfolio as a whole. The lowest-risk insurance customers tend to be the rich people. There are a very limited number of wealthy people. They do not necessarily need insurance from insurance companies. However, there are many low-earning people who can request policies, but at a greater risk. A balance must be struck that maximizes return and minimizes risk. Big data analytics solutions may combine time series analysis with many other methods in order to make decisions on when to insure these different market segments, or decisions on the premiums to charge to members of a portfolio segment to cover the losses among members in that segment.

Generali

Generali, the Italian insurance group, uses big data analytics in the actuarial department to monitor portfolio performance and to improve its motor-product rating engine.[41] The billing and collections departments of the company use analytics to measure and improve call-center performance. Generali analyzes the large volume of data and uses big data analytics to simplify business operations, to make accurate decisions, and to increase the return on investment. This approach supports Generali's business strategy and competitive position and improves its management infrastructure.

Operational analytics. Operational analytics includes, but is not limited to (and some of these actions overlap):

- many things that happen at the time of customer interactions
- ad serving, web page personalization, and so on
- on-the-fly fraud or risk assessment
- automated price resetting
- automated risk analysis
- much of what might in general be called the "next best action"

In its simplest terms, operational analytics is done on the fly as part of the operational business processes. By way of contrast, investigative analytics is done at the speed of research, not the speed of operational business processes.[42] There are borderline cases in this version of the dichotomy too, such as when the analytics are highly urgent, yet otherwise investigative in nature.

UnipolSai

The online management of claims in UnipolSai has a history spanning several years. It passed through several stages[43]

- The first phase was bringing online the front end of the claims department through a platform capable of linking all actors working in this field.
- The second phase can be defined as the "evolution of online." It introduced more sophisticated support features, the real-time monitoring of performance indicators of the claims management (Business Intelligence (BI) on speed, loads of treatment, average cost, and so on). In support of organizational processes established by the management, projects were developed for the dematerialization, automatic expired date management, claims virtual desktops, electronic files, workflows, advanced data management, interaction with wireless devices, and so on. At the same time, it has been possible to turn to increasingly stringent operational synergies with all the intermediaries network who interact with the settlement network – professional trustees, car body repairs, spare parts retailers, health circuits – and move on to platforms that make possible automatic antifraud activities.
- The third phase can be labeled high online integration. It was developed in UnipolSai with a project referred to as Bibos – Business Intelligence Bilancistica Operativa Sinistri (BI operational financial reporting for claims). BI no longer plays only a statistical role. It becomes a key element for analyzing the processes in the different contexts of the claims processing. In particular, the transition to the third phase is determined by the fact that the online application, in addition to directly managing the data of the operational environment in its relational data structure, intercepts the

events that affect the management accounting and the financial reporting. In this way, it can support the timely monitoring of the accounts. It is therefore an integrated reporting in which indicators that refer to different contexts are connected according to the level of details required by the individual types of users involved. This reporting is made available through a specific interface that makes available the output generated in an intuitive and effective visualization.

- The fourth phase allows the integration of the claims data with the requirements of Solvency II. It supports the consolidation and the integration with the systems that are not directly connected to claims.

In this way, the BI can meet with one tool and a single source of data all the needs of an insurance company in the field of claims. At the same time, the solution respects the requirements of data quality to comply with the internal policies and the technical architecture. The flexibility of the platform allows people to take actions on the rules of aggregation and monitoring of data, using the wealth of historical data available. The claim solution becomes an important tool also with respect to the Solvency II regulations.

At Group level Fondiaria Sai, the reference database for BI contains over 70 million occurrences per year in an archive of several terabytes. These occurrences are only the movements affecting the accounts and the budget. In order to get the total number of elements stored, it is necessary to add the classic indicators that are at least of a similar dimension.

The main areas of intervention supported by Bibos are the management of claims, their administration, their control, and the evaluation of the actuarial losses. It can help also in other areas such as risk management.

Big data analytics and digital insurance

Case literature and economic theory suggest a potential connection between data driven decision (DDD) making and productivity. By analyzing a large sample of firms, a study found that DDD is associated with higher productivity and market value, and that there is some evidence that DDD is associated with certain measures of profitability (Return on Equity – ROE, that is asset utilization).[44]

A survey on the relationship between big data analytics and digital insurance revealed some very interesting results.[45] Customer churn and engagement are one of the top issues for most insurance companies. Several studies and models have proven that churn remains one of the biggest destroyers of enterprise value. Some insurance companies are aware of the importance of the support in this field that can be provided by a big data analytics solution. When it comes to understanding customers, many companies are still unsure of how to effectively assess and use their data to improve customer loyalty and lower attrition. The survey revealed that:

- approximately 44 percent of financial services claims do not have the right resources in place to take advantage of big data analytics
- sixty-eight percent say that one-to-one targeting and personalized product offers are or will be an important business driver for their big data analytics initiative
- seventy-six percent of financial services stated that the business driver for embracing big data analytics is to enhance customer engagement, retention, and loyalty
- seventy-one percent acknowledge that, in order to increase their top line, they need to better understand customers, which big data analytics will help them do: that is the so-called customer intelligence
- fifty-five percent of financial institutions feel that having a real-time view of data provides a significant competitive advantage, since the availability of batch processed data is ineffective

Insurance companies can and should deliver an excellent user experience to their customers. Companies should move beyond taking care only of the insurance products and consider the heart of the transaction. In this way, they can add value and provide meanings to customers and intermediaries at the same time. Customers should be able to use the insurance company's applications from any device for any service: be it real or virtual, with the same security and ease of use to which they are already accustomed. Digital insurance should become a "brand wrapper" for insurance companies instead of a disintermediation.

Insurance companies are at a vulnerable point when it comes to losing customers to competitors. Insurance companies own very useful data. Data can help these institutions to better understand what their customers need and what they are interested in. The insurance companies should quickly find a way to access and use these data to their benefit, as well as working with the customer on how they can better control financial services. Through opt-in programs, for example, insurance companies can greatly improve customer retention rates. They can also improve profitability from each customer. In this way, they can win in the insurance competition for more and satisfied customers.

Bought By Many

Bought By Many, a free, members-only service based in the United Kingdom, helps people find insurance for the out of the ordinary way people have bought insurance in the past. Its motto is: "Insurance made social."[46] The company uses social media and search engine optimization to assemble groups of people who need niche personal insurance – travel insurance for people with a special sickness, for example. They do this search using public available data. The company is working for creating a "social thumbprint" of each of these groups to help identify an individual's insurance needs. The company intends to use the social data they get to improve an individual's insurance experience.

The company also wants to analyze claims experience and what people are claiming for. They can use this data to analyze which groups of people have better or worse claims experiences and are more or less likely to claim. Insurance companies can use that information to drive pricing. If they can do all of that using publicly available information, that is hugely compelling.

Quality of big data analytics

Implementation

Big data analytics solutions encompass a new generation of software and architectures designed to extract value in velocity, from a relatively large volume of data, and from a variety of structured and unstructured information, on how to provide better value to the customer and the enterprise. This is achieved by enabling rapid data capture, discovery, and/or analysis. According to Novarica, the organizations that will be able to profit from the potential value of big data analytics will be those that have created a culture in which business leaders trust analytics and act on the insights provided.[47] All insurance companies should take steps to create that culture today if it does not already exist in their organizations.

The key for success in this initiative is to start small with a proof of concept (PoC). In a PoC, for example, the business could use a big data analytics solution to speed up long-running processes of extraction, transformation, and loading (ETL) in a traditional data warehouse environment using structured data. This would allow situations to be overcome in which the company is missing meeting the service level agreements (SLAs) requested by its customers.

It is important for insurance companies to develop good business use cases for meeting the strategic objectives of the lines of business. A robust sponsorship from a C-level executive is required. This is essential not only for funding but also for evangelizing and communicating the objectives, needs, and solutions to the entire organization, including intermediaries and vendors.

Although the initial scope and investment in terms of people, solutions, technologies, and infrastructure might be small, the architecture should keep the long-term view in mind. For the right data harnessing and harvesting, good collaboration between ICT and business is essential to iteratively experiment and drive actionable insights. Insurance companies can then use incremental successes to obtain increased funding for the next phases and/or use cases.

As insurance companies identify and understand the scenarios for applying big data analytics within their businesses, they will need to improve their existing processes with a Lean and Digitize approach. This is necessary to be able to:

- take into account the data "variety"
- have good "veracity"
- increase "volume"
- grow the need for real-time "velocity"
- protect the "vulnerability" of the data
- derive objective-driven actionable "value" for the customers and the organization

Insurance companies that are able to develop a fact-based culture can learn how to harness the power of big data analytics, and harvest the valuable information and insights that big data analytics can provide. This would allow them to create competitive advantages and positively impact their brand and their top and bottom lines (see Table 4.2 for some successful use of big data analytics).

Table 4.2 Examples of successful uses of big data analytics

Insurance company	**Project**
Allstate Financial	Using annuity legacy data to minimize risk.
AXA UK	Using internal and external data to pinpoint risks, manage accumulations, and, if necessary, respond to a catastrophe
CNA	Using big data analytics to fight fraud
Celina Mutual Insurance Company	Mastering machine learning for predictive analytics
Farm Bureau	Incorporating predictive analytics in workers' compensation underwriting
Markerstudy	Using big data analytics as a competitive solution in the UK market

Source: The examples are drawn from the finalists and winners of the Celent Modern Insurers in recent years.

Big data analytics impacts on ICT

Big data analytics is a force presenting opportunities and challenges to ICT organizations.

To work on big data analytics insurance companies must make efforts to:

- identify sources
- collect data and create a structure for supporting the initiative
- organize, process, and provide a value
- use and expand the results

In terms of professionals, there is the need for:

- enterprise architects
- business analysts
- data scientists

Big data analytics can potentially create more than 4.4 million ICT jobs in big data analytics, with 1.9 million in just the United States in the next few years. India alone will require a minimum of 100,000 data scientists in the next couple of years in addition to data analysts and data managers to support the big data analytics space.[48]

Challenges of big data analytics

There are challenges to the growth of big data analytics:

- the evaluation of the benefits for the organizations
- the data quality (see the chapter on Governance)
- the impact on the organization

Benefits of big data analytics

Surveys have found that organizations are using big data analytics to target customer-centric outcomes, tap into internal data, and build a better information ecosystem. Big Data is already an important part of the $64 billion database and data analytics market. It offers commercial opportunities of a comparable scale to enterprise software in the late 1980s, the Internet boom of the 1990s, and the current social media explosion.

The potential value of big data analytics is huge. It is estimated that better use of data has:

- $300 billion potential annual value to US health care
- $600 billion potential annual consumer surplus from using personal location data

- 60 percent potential in increasing retailers' operating margins.

The future of big data analytics is bright. The estimates are:

- $15 billion on software firms only specializing in data management and analytics.
- This industry on its own is worth more than $100 billion and growing at almost 10 percent a year which is roughly twice as fast as the software business as a whole;
- In February 2012, the open source analyst firm Wikibon released the first market forecast for big data analytics, listing $5.1B revenue in 2012 with growth to $53.4B in 2017;
- The McKinsey Global Institute estimates that data volume is growing 40 percent per year, and will grow 44 times between 2009 and 2020.

Impact on the organization

Big data analytics can bring permanent changes to managers' and employees' roles and responsibilities.[49] If pricing is automated, for instance, it is hard to hold the managers working in the pricing departments solely responsible for the profit and loss of the business going forward. Whoever designed and implemented big data analytics is now responsible. As managerial responsibilities evolve or are eliminated altogether, organizations will have to adapt by redefining roles to best leverage and support the continuous development of these digital solutions in the use of big data analytics to predict the severity of claims. Automated systems instantly compare a filing with millions of claims records, cutting down on the need for human intervention. In this scenario, insurance company claims employees no longer process all claims. They focus on the exceptions: those with the highest level of complexity or those representing the most severe damage. Focus is required, since job redesign is time consuming, and it can be taken on only if automated solutions and new roles have been developed and tested to meet whatever surprises the volatile market environment brings to them.

XL Group

XL Group (XL) is a global insurance company based in Ireland. The company decided to develop advanced analytical solutions for its underwriters who make risk decisions and price policies before they know the costs.[50] XL formed a team led by an actuary, to develop and implement predictive, multivariant analytics, using internal and external data. After four years, XL has seen its claims per dollar of premium written fall significantly in those businesses that were early adopters of predictive models. That is a significant source of recurring profits derived from having a new proprietary way of identifying risks.

Cloud computing

Cloud computing promises access to massively scalable hardware and software distributed on the Internet through services accessible from any device, fixed or mobile.[51] The result is that cloud computing can be considered a disruptive innovation and a leap forward in the digital solutions (see Figure 4.1).[52] An example is that a customer relationship management (CRM) application can be selected from a catalogue and immediately used after the specific configuration is done and the interfaces built.

This section describe the fundamentals of the cloud computing model by clarifying:

- the principles that underlie it
- the offerings available
- the benefits
- the challenges, especially in terms of security
- the vendors in the cloud computing arena
- the importance of cloud computing for SMEs and start-ups

Information and communication technologies, in particular those underlying the model of cloud computing, provide innovative solutions to manage multiple tasks with efficiency and savings. They could present challenges and risks to privacy that are important to take into

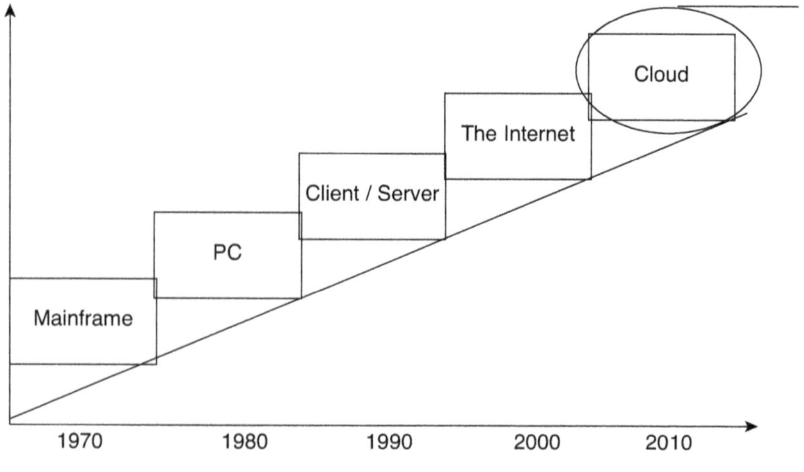

Figure 4.1 The ICT solution evolution

account. Prior to a company's moving to the cloud, the processing and storing of data and documents or adopting of new organizational models, it is necessary to obtain responses to some questions, carefully choosing the surest solution available for the institution's activities or for its business.

The Internet is traditionally represented with a cloud. That is why this new paradigm of computing is named cloud computing.

Cloud computing enables access on demand to shared resources that reside in massively scalable data centers. You can access them from any telecommunication network and any Internet-connected device.

The main feature of the new model is that it transforms ICT from an internal cost center to a set of external services that are agile, responsive, and paid according to consumption, to be used not only as business solutions but as a means by which to manage the organization and especially to more easily innovate it. The service vendor of cloud computing takes care of the ICT infrastructure and the services it provides to client organizations. The latter need normally pay only for what they consume. The client organization can benefit, because the resource sharing allows substantial reductions in operating costs and, above all, it does not require investments.

Definition of cloud computing

The term "cloud computing," or simply the cloud, refers to a model of use of computing resources, based on the management, normally

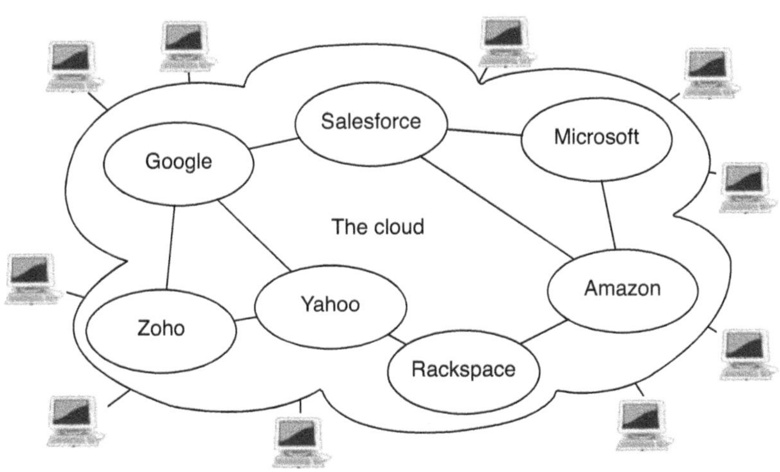

Figure 4.2 Some cloud computing examples

outside of the organization, of the computer infrastructure, and/or platform and/or applications. Their access is through a telecommunications network, usually the Internet.

According to the USA National Institute of Standards and Technology, cloud computing[53] "is a model for enabling ubiquitous, convenient, on-demand network access to a shared pool of configurable computing resources (for instance, networks, servers, storage, applications, and services) that can be provisioned and released with minimal rapid management effort or service vendor interaction." Individuals often use cloud computing without even knowing it. Some of the most popular e-mail services (such as Outlook or Gmail) or data storage (for instance, Dropbox) are "in the cloud." Even many of the functions offered by smartphones are based on the cloud: for example, those that use geolocation for advising on the locations of nearby agencies or shops and for allowing a person to listen to music or access to online games, as well as many other functions and apps (mobile applications).

There are various types of cloud computing, which are classified in several ways. In particular, the model of cloud computing consists of (see Figure 4.3):

- five essential features
- three models of service
- four implementation models

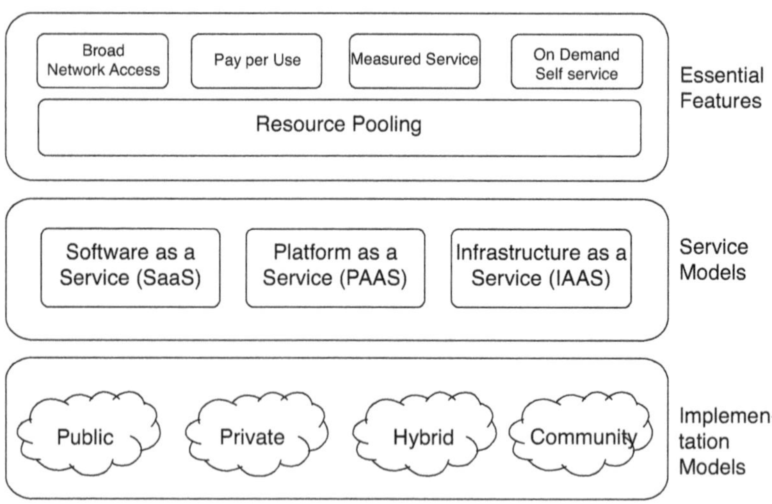

Figure 4.3 Nist model's view of the cloud definition

Essential features

A solution, provided as a cloud-based solution, must meet a number of very specific features:

- access through a network (preferably the Internet)
- capability on demand
- self-service
- pay-per-use
- multi-tenancy
- virtualization

These points can be detailed:

- Access through a network (preferably the Internet). Thanks to the development of broadband connections, today practically all the organizations already have access to the Internet.
- Capability on-demand. The request on-demand of higher or lower capability based on the needs of business, also referred to as "elasticity," is one of the more important features of cloud computing. This means that customers who subscribe to services organizations that use a certain number of resources can subsequently increase or reduce the use of these resources freely without modification to the contractual elements. Theoretically, cloud computing is a model with infinite resources that are immediately available.
- Pay-per-use. The request for services by an organization often is not constant over time. There are peaks of utilization that are sometimes predictable (for instance, at the end of the month) or unpredictable, according to the specific needs of the business and the demand for its products and services. In such contexts, the elasticity of cloud computing is very beneficial. It allows the use of the necessary resources at the right times. In such cases, a form of payment based on consumption is very appropriate. The measurability of the resources used makes ICT a utility similar to electricity, water, or gas.
- Multitenancy. Multitenancy is an architectural principle in which a single instance of a computer resource is used by more organizations, denominated clients or tenants. This principle is fundamental to cloud computing because it allows the sharing of resources across multiple client organizations, providing cheaper services.
- Self-service. Cloud solutions are typically "off the shelf." They are immediately available and usable by users. They are, to some extent,

self-managed and self-serviced by changing configuration parameters. Access to the configuration parameters of the services is usually done through a web browser, or by client applications for mobile and fixed devices provided directly by the service vendor cloud.
- Virtualization. Virtualization consists of the "dematerialization" of a physical resource, such as a server, in an abstract resource equivalent realized by software. Physical resources (processors, memory, storage, and similar devices) are shared among many virtual hosts.

Models of service

Cloud computing transforms the ICT infrastructure components in services. This lead to three basic delivery models, named with the following abbreviations: IaaS, PaaS, and SaaS (see Figure 4.2). These models, which also define the strategic and organizational solutions through which a vendor acquires competitive benefits, can also be referred to as the business models for the provision of cloud computing (see Figure 4.4 and Table 4.2):

- Infrastructure as a Service – IaaS (cloud infrastructure made available as a service). The cloud service vendor offers, according to a model "pay by use," hardware solutions and basic software (memory spaces, operating systems, virtualization programs, and similar resources). Examples of the infrastructure could be remote virtual servers that the company can use to replace or increase the systems resources already present within the premises of the organization. These vendors are typically specialized market players, which operate a technological infrastructure, complex and often distributed in different geographic areas. Examples of IaaS are S3 (Simple Storage Service) and EC2 (Elastic Compute Cloud) provided by Amazon Web Services, offering respectively, storage space and processing systems (servers).
- Platform as a Service – PaaS (platform software provided via the Internet as a service). The vendors offer advanced solutions for software development that meet customer requirements. Typically, this kind of service is addressed to organizations that use them to develop and host their own application solutions (for example applications for financial management, accounting, or logistics), in order to fulfill internal needs, or to provide their services to third parties. In the case of PaaS, the services provided by the vendors limit the need for the user to introduce internal solutions or additional specific hard-

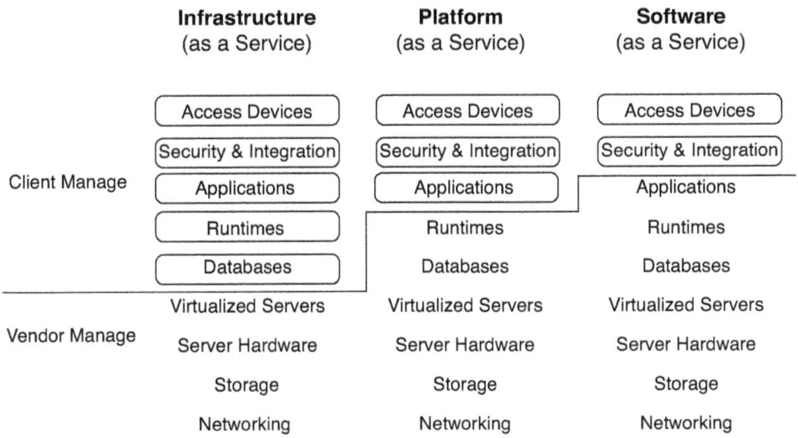

Figure 4.4 A comparison of management responsibilities between traditional ICT infrastructure and cloud computing

Table 4.3 Examples of models of service

IaaS	**PaaS**	**SaaS**
Infrastructure as a Service	**Platform as a Service**	**Software as a Service**
Utility computing data center providing on-demand hardware resources	Hosted application environment for building and deploying cloud applications	Applications typically available via browser
Examples: HP Adaptive	Examples: Salesforce.com	Examples: Google Apps
Rackspace	Amazon E2C	Salesforce.com
Amazon E2C&S3	Microsoft Azure	Office 365
	Telecom Italia Nuvola Italiana	

ware or software. Examples of PaaS are the software development environments Google App Engine, Microsoft Azure, and Force.com.

- Software as a Service – SaaS (application software delivered as a service in the cloud computing model). The vendor delivers a number of application services by making them available to the end users through Internet. This is the case, for example, with applications commonly used in offices, such as email services. They are provided in web mode, such as processing spreadsheets or word processors, the management of protocols and the rules for accessing computer documents, contact lists, and shared calendars, but also advanced electronic mail services or ERPs. Examples of SaaS are Google Docs, Google Mail (Gmail), Sales Cloud 2 (Salesforce.com), or Zoho CRM. SaaS, although it existed before cloud computing as Internet software providers (ISP), reaches its highest level of service quality and availability when it respects the principles of the cloud.

Models of deployment

There are four different models of the deployment of cloud computing (see Figure 4.6):

- The private cloud is a computer infrastructure (a computer network connected to provide services), mostly dedicated to the needs of a single organization or a group of companies of the same holding, located on its premises or in management-entrusted third-party vendors (in the traditional form of server hosting), over which the owner of the data can exercise full control.

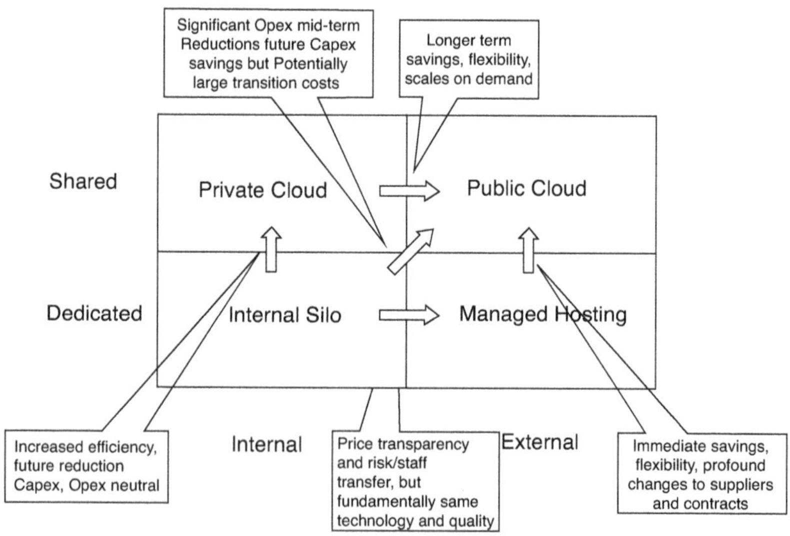

Figure 4.5 The benefits of migration to the cloud

Source: Adapted by the author from R. Hall (2012), "Radical IT as a Service," *Richmond Events: The IT Directors' Forum*, 17 May.

- The public cloud includes resources owned by a vendor that specializes in the provision of services that makes available to users, companies, or administrations in a multitenant environment its systems through the sharing and the provision of Internet computing, processing capacity, and storage data.
- The hybrid cloud is characterized by solutions involving the use of services provided by on-premises infrastructure beside services acquired from public clouds.
- The community cloud has resources shared by several organizations for the benefit of a specific community of users, for instance, the SMEs in a cluster.

The client organization that uses the services provided as cloud computing needs the connection to the Internet and the local ICT infrastructure to access remote services. Depending on the services used, the level of quality of service (QoS) for the connectivity needs to be defined. This results in a drastic reduction of investment costs (or capital expenses, also called CapEx), because the costs of the ICT infrastructure (purchase of new equipment, software licenses, upgrades of hardware and software, and so on) are no longer required: the applications, the platforms, and the ICT infrastructure in the cloud are completely managed by the service provider in the cloud. With the cloud model, the savings compared to the management on-premises can fluctuate on average between 35 percent and 65 percent.[54] The savings can be passed to the business or used for the innovation of the organization.

Benefits of cloud computing

The main benefits of cloud computing are:

- the efficiency of centralization (and the resulting economies of scale)
- a drastic reduction of the time and costs for accessing new services/resources
- a significant reduction in the risks associated with the implementation of new applications such as budget overruns (which occurs in more than 50 percent of cases[55]), the risk of technological obsolescence, the dimensioning of the systems, or the failure to use the application (a possibility less unusual than people think)
- a substantial reduction in the time for the activation of new solutions or new computing resources

- the ability to develop new solutions in few weeks on platforms that provide the services required (PaaS)
- the virtually continuous usability of processing services (IaaS) allows any organization to access the resources necessary in times that are a fraction of those normally required in traditional settings
- a total flexibility and scalability (up and down) of services used. Cloud computing may scale up and down services with ease and does not require binding contract structures. This creates a flexibility that is very important today
- better integration with the needs of the lines of business

With cloud computing, the role of ICT is strengthened, since the override of an uncontrolled situation becomes less likely. There is normally also an improvement in the collaboration between business units.

Nationwide

In the last 80 years, Nationwide has grown from a small mutual auto insurance company owned by policyholders to one of the largest insurance and financial services companies in the United States, with more than 38,000 employees. Headquartered in Columbus, Ohio, this Fortune 500-listed company is the number one provider of public-sector retirement plans and the seventh-largest auto insurance company in the United States. Nationwide's 3,000 distributed servers were inefficient and costly. To increase business agility and prevent the increase in costs, Nationwide started a virtualization journey that ultimately led to the cloud.[56] They consolidated their distributed server landscape with Linux virtual servers running on mainframes, creating a multiplatform private cloud optimized for all its different workloads. This cloud deployment reduced power, cooling, and floor space requirements by 80 percent and reversed expenditure on a distributed server landscape, saving an estimated US$15 million over the first three years.

Risk assessment

It is important to choose the right type of cloud and the service model that is best suited to the organization's needs. If the company decides to go for a public cloud, it is necessary to clarify that almost all the processes are outsourced and the data are located "far away" from the direct control of the customer. The concept of the cloud can appear "virtual." In fact, the cloud computing model can handle many practical services, such as the distribution of the products of a company, the services of the registry of a local, regional, or nation-wide organization, travel reservations, medical analysis, online insurance, and much more.

Before opting for a certain type of cloud, it is important that the company and the security department verify the type of data that they intend to locate in the cloud (for instance, personal data, particularly sensitive or critical data for the business, such as confidential work or patents or trade secrets), and assess the possible risks and possible consequences of that choice. The client organization might not have the ability or the power to negotiate a reformulation of the contract proposed by the vendors; however, a customer organization can choose between different vendors.

Security management

Some issues to clarify with the potential vendors of cloud computing, and especially to include in the contract, are the following:

- Security measures. The cloud service vendor must have systems in place to protect against viruses, hacker attacks, or other hazards for the information that are more effective than those that the individual organization could afford. Before choosing a cloud partner, the customer organization must always consider that, in relying on a remote vendor, it may lose control over its data directly and exclusively. On the other hand, a reliable vendor is able to ensure far greater security than that many organizations can afford on their own premises with their limited and not always up-to-date resources.
- Vendor of cloud computing services. The chosen service may be the result of a "chain of transformation" of services provided by other service vendors, other than the one with which the customer enters into the contract of service.
- Availability of service and emergency plan. The virtual service, in the absence of adequate safeguards regarding the quality of the network connectivity, may occasionally deteriorate in the presence of cyberattacks or peaks of high traffic, or even become unavailable when abnormal events or failures that prevent accessibility to ICT resources and data occur. A business continuity (BC) plan is essential.
- Retrieving data. Natural disasters or cyberattacks could affect the operations of some data centers in the cloud. It is particularly important to identify procedures for data and disaster recovery, and quantify the economic impact on the organization of the loss or deletion of data stored only in the cloud.
- Confidentiality. Vendors might store the data of individuals and organizations that might have different interests and needs or even conflicting and competing objectives with other tenants of the same

cloud computing vendor. It is therefore appropriate to assess the guarantees that are offered by the vendor aimed to protect the confidentiality of information transferred to the cloud.

- Location of the server. The identification of the place in which the data is stored or processed has immediate consequences on both the law that is applicable in the event of a dispute between the customer and the vendor, and in relation to national regulations or laws governing the processing, storage, and security of data. Privacy regulations, in order to protect the persons concerned, provide that the data can be accessed in countries outside the EU only in specific cases and when both countries offer adequate protection with respect to what is requested by EU regulations. Some regulations require also that at any moment the organizations using the cloud should be informed of where their data are stored. This information may be used to establish the jurisdiction and the law applicable in the case of disputes between the insurance company and the service vendors, but especially to determine the level of protection of the data.
- Migration. The adoption by the service vendor's own solutions can, in some cases, make it difficult for the organization to migrate data and documents from one system to another in the cloud or the exchange of information with other organizations or individuals who use different vendors of cloud services, endangering the portability and interoperability of data. It is particularly important not to be locked-in by a vendor at the termination or change of the contract.
- Insurance on damage. The current regulatory uncertainties can make it difficult and costly to be able to obtain adequate compensation for damages suffered as a result of violations, loss of data, or even temporary interruption of the service cloud.

Important aspects in cloud computing

The privacy guarantors for the protection of personal data in some countries have prepared guides to provide some indications that apply to all users, in particular corporations and government. The aim is to take into account, especially in the contractual terms with the cloud computing vendors, some important legal, economic, and technological aspects.

The main recommendations, in addition to those previously mentioned, are as follows:[57]

- It is necessary to check on the reliability of the vendor. Users should verify the experience, expertise, and reliability of the vendor before transferring to the cloud their valuable systems and data, taking into account their institutional or business needs, the amount and type of information they want to allocate, the risks, and the security measures.

- It is important to assure data portability. It is advisable to use cloud computing services based on open formats and standards, which facilitate the transition from one system to another in the cloud, even if they are managed by different vendors.
- The availability of data in case of need should be ensured. It is appropriate to ask that the contract with the vendor specify well adequate guarantees about the availability and performance of the cloud services.
- The organization should select the data to move to the cloud. Some information, such as that related to trade secrets and all sensitive data (such as that related to health, ethnicity, political opinions, or trade union memberships), require, by their sensitivity, special security measures.
- The data should not be lost sight of. It is always advisable that the insurance company should weigh carefully the type of service offered. It is necessary to check whether the data will remain available to the operator with which it entered into the contract, or if the vendor works as an intermediary, or offer a service based on digital solutions made available by other third-party operators.
- It is important to assess the suitability of the contractual conditions for the provision of the cloud services with particular reference to the obligations and responsibilities in the event of loss and unlawful dissemination of data stored in the "cloud," and any conditions for the withdrawal from service and switching to another vendor or to in house operations.
- It is important to check the times and methods of data retention. In the acquisition phase of the cloud service and, in the contract clauses with the vendor, it is important to clarify whether and when data retention will take place in the cloud. It is necessary to ensure, where not already provided by law, the cancellation of the data of the owner at the end of the contract for the cloud services.
- The staff, both of the customer and of the vendor, in charge of processing data using cloud computing services, should be well trained, in order to limit the risks of illegal access, data loss or, more generally, treatment that is not allowed.

Assessment of costs/benefits of a cloud computing solution

The organization that is planning to move to the cloud must prepare a detailed business case for the adoption of the cloud.[58]

The costs when an organization has the data center on-premises are:

- purchase of hardware and its installation
- purchase of licenses and related maintenance
- customization and configuration
- hosting
- back-up facility for the disaster recovery
- replication between data centers
- proper and timely installation of updates and patches
- support to the end user
- support for the maintenance
- resources engaged in the physical and logical security

Costs related to a cloud computing solution are:

- fees based on consumption
- integration with applications that remain in-house
- customization and configuration
- support to the end user
- connection to the cloud (usually the Internet)

The cost reduction of a cloud solution in respect to an in house implementation tends to be around 35 percent to 65 percent, taking into account the reduced costs of capital expenses.

Table 4.3 shows some examples of financial services using cloud solutions. The box shows some vendors offering cloud computing solutions.

Vendors in the cloud computing market

Amazon

Amazon has emerged as the champion in the world of cloud computing. This company is among the largest vendors of cloud infrastructure with its Elastic Compute Cloud (EC2) offering. It is also providing cloud platforms for the development and deployment of applications (PaaS). An Accenture research analyst, Liu Huan, estimated that Amazon Elastic Compute Cloud (EC2) runs on 450,000 servers.[59] Amazon offers a competitive pricing for storage services (S3 Simple Storage Service). Amazon, like most of the big cloud vendors, does not reveal much about the location of its data centers or its turnover, estimated at a billion dollars on a global basis.

Google
Google is a major player in Internet technology with its platform Google App Engine and its e-mail service. It has good products related to productivity in the office and sharing/collaboration on data and documents. The main strength of the company is its scalable service that allows customers to pay for what they use, with no start-up costs or recurring fees. Google has several customers in the financial sector, for example BBVA and some small savings banks.

Microsoft
Microsoft is active in the cloud with its platform Windows Azure and Office 365. Office 365 brings together Microsoft Office, Microsoft SharePoint Online, Microsoft Exchange Online, and Microsoft Lync Online into a single cloud service to date, available through a monthly predetermined subscription. The cloud service Windows Azure provides developers with the ability to host, develop, and manage Web applications. Azure provides a complete set of services, including computing environments, scalable storage, database functions, and a network of content distribution. Microsoft Office 365 is very active on the markets: the Microsoft and 21Vianet cloud computing partnership provides for example the possibility for its customers to use China-based cloud computing resources that operate a version of Microsoft's cloud computing technology.

Salesforce
Salesforce is a vendor of software as a service, mainly in support of the sales force and the optimization of their work. Salesforce specializes in the distribution of business applications through the cloud. Force.com is a platform-as-a-service that allows developers to use the infrastructure of Salesforce to develop additional applications that integrate with Salesforce. This company is well known for offering new product features and new capabilities on an ongoing basis.

IBM
SmartCloud is a family of services and solutions of cloud computing organizations for developing secure hybrid cloud, integrating private and public components. IBM has depth, expertise, open standards, and consolidated infrastructure which allow client organizations to reach high levels of innovation and efficiency.

Telecom Italia
Nuvola Italiana is the offering in several countries of Telecom Italia, the largest telecom operator in Italy. Nuvola Italiana is targeted to SMEs. In order to reach such a dispersed and diverse target, Telecom Italia offers Nuvola Italiana through a franchising network and make available a host of tools supporting migration to the cloud.

Table 4.4 Examples of financial services using cloud solutions

Financial services institutions	Cloud benefits
Auva	Auva is Austria's largest social security and emergency hospital insurance vendor. It maximizes service availability through virtualization.
Aviva	Aviva provides support to improve enterprise productivity and collaboration.
Axa	Among the largest insurance companies in Europe, Axa, thanks to the cloud, provides its sales force and service organization with better tools.
DnB NOR	Norway's largest financial services group uses the new platform for a risk evaluation process.
Lloyd's	Lloyd's, the world's only specialist insurance market, virtualizes the environment to cut operating costs, increase resource utilization, and take advantage of its new data centers.
Urban Lending Solutions	This financial services vendor uses Hyper-V for increased speed with $1 million savings.

Perspectives on cloud computing

The promise of cloud computing is very attractive: it is flexible and adapts well to the needs of the organizations. Organizations pay for what they consume. The cloud allows fixed costs to be transformed into variable costs. It eliminates large investments, replacing them with operating costs over time. Finally, it can make the ICT infrastructure redundant and fault tolerant. The model is particularly suitable in the contexts in which computing needs are discontinuous in time. In these cases, cloud computing resources are exploited to the maximum while internal ICT resources might not always be fully utilized. Cloud computing is very interesting for start-ups that can focus on the business elements and neglect most of the structural and economic aspects related to the technological ICT infrastructure.

Other important elements to consider include the portability of the applications developed in the cloud, the level of service provided (service level agreement – SLA), the backup, and the restoring of the applications, as well as the legal regulations in cases of disputes.

Cloud computing for insurance companies and start-ups

The cloud is being widely adopted for applications that are important to business success, according to a study by Forrester Research conducted on behalf of Infosys, a provider of consulting and outsourcing services[60].

A majority of the 300 organizations in the United States, the United Kingdom, Germany, France, and Australia, surveyed by Forrester in July and August 2014 (81 percent), said they are either using or planning to use critical applications in the cloud in the next two years.

The survey found that cost savings is no longer the primary driver for leveraging cloud services, with 77 percent of organizations considering agility to be the key driver.

Other highlights of the study are that 77 percent of respondents are either using or planning to use infrastructure as a service (IaaS), platform as a service (PaaS), or software as a service (SaaS) for a range of business applications within two years from the date of the survey. 66 percent agree that they should prioritize the development of a comprehensive cloud strategy for their digital resources.

In addition, 70 percent of businesses want to work with a cloud implementation vendor that offers a single point of accountability, and 66 percent are either concerned or very concerned about the complexity involved in managing and governing a hybrid cloud environment.

Unified content management

People often talk about unified communications in referring to the use of a single tool (be it a computer or an electronic appliance) for all possible modes of communication: voice, data, e-mail, video, and so on. It is a concept that is interesting for the possibility of not only reducing the number of devices that are used (phone, tablet, PDA, computer, and so on) but also centralizing in a single device (and in one software) all communications. In this situation, there would not be the need to move from one device to another in order to communicate.

From the point of view of the organization, this also means focusing more and more on a unified management of all possible content. This term refers to the entire set of unstructured information that is used to support the processes of an organization. This can be done either with reference to structured data or unstructured data, such as documents, voice, video, e-mail, or other forms of information. The media are not the contents but their support.

Today there are no solutions for managing in a unified way all possible contents. People talk of enterprise content management (ECM); however, this term often refers to the containers and not to the overall management of the content. Traditional computer science has developed very sophisticated methods and models for managing structured data. Much less has been done so far with regard to the data or information when they are not structured or, more generally, to any type of content.

An estimation for unstructured information in an organization is that it normally represents between 70 percent to 90 percent of all the information in the organization.[61] There are several reasons for this situation. In the past, there was no structured data, as there was no need to structure it because there were no automatic solutions for the management of unstructured information. People tend to be very good at manually managing unstructured data. For example, the manual production of unstructured information is easier than the production of structured information. The latter requires a lot more effort in terms of compliance with standards or formats or conventions.

Some numbers can help in assessing the situation:[62]

- The so-called knowledge workers spend up to ten hours a week searching for information.
- Up to 10 percent of the time, and therefore of the cost of labor in the organizations, is wasted in ineffective searching of content.
- Sixty percent of the top managers say their organizations should do a better job of taking advantage of available information.
- Managers argue that up to 50 percent of the results of a search for information is not useful.
- Forty percent of the time of an office worker is spent to managing unstructured data.
- Between 16 and 20 percent of operating revenues are spent correcting problems associated with incorrect data.
- Seventy-eighty percent of organizations have more than a repository of contents and 43 percent more than six.[63]

The aim of this section is to describe a generalized model for the management of the content in support of digital insurance. This is particularly important in connection with the Lean and Digitize business process improvement initiatives. The model provides a set of methods that can be used to improve processes and at the same time help in their digitization.

A study conducted by Paivarinta and Munkvold (2005) is useful in this regard[64]. In their study, the authors identify a framework for an enterprise content management system (ECMS) implementation. The framework of Paivarinta and Munkvold, shown in Figure 4.6, provides a

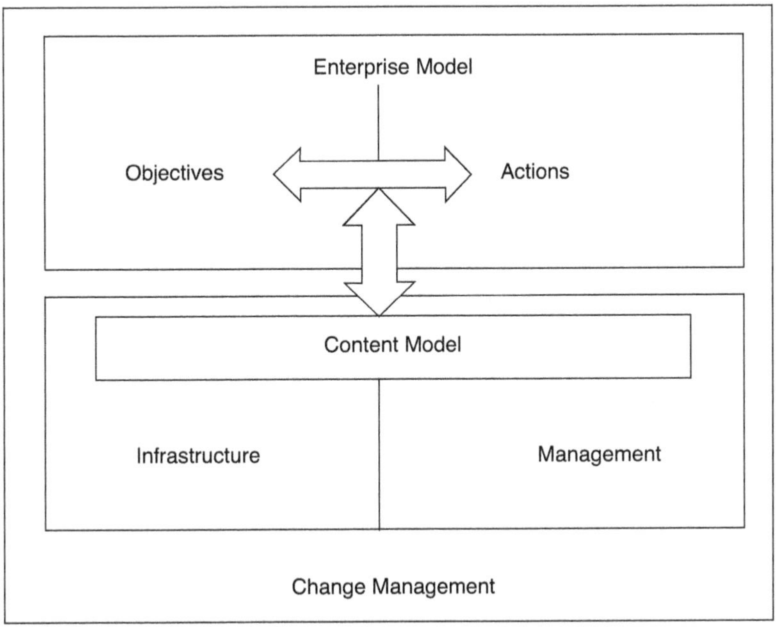

Figure 4.6 Framework for ECMS implementation

Source: Adapted by the author from T. Paivarinta, B.E. Munkvold (2005), Enterprise Content Management: An Integrated Perspective on Information Management, *2005. HICSS'05. Proceedings of the 38th Annual Hawaii.*

basis for business and ICT managers to understand and facilitate ECMS implementation in an organization. These authors state that ECMS should support organizational objectives and the desired enterprise model. Actions based on objectives result in more or less anticipated and desired impacts, interplaying with future objectives. ECMS is realized through the design and implementation of the content model, including all information content relevant from the viewpoint of the enterprise model. The implementation of ECMS is supported by the digital solution infrastructure, the administrative resources, and the practices in place. Change management is needed to cultivate an optimized fit between the enterprise and its content model, infrastructure, and management over time.

Paivarinta and Munkvold mention that an ECMS implementation should be aligned with the enterprise architecture to ensure that "it can build meaningful information and communication systems to support the operations." The concept of an enterprise architecture, as underlined in Chapter 2, is important because it refers to what needs to be done in an enterprise, including the idea of the business, the required support operations, who does what, and how an insurance company can reach its customers, intermediaries, and vendors.

The enterprise architecture is supportive both as regards the structured and nonstructured data. It also applies to content that are not data, but rather voice, pictures, video, and similar. The architecture allows evaluation of the solutions for managing the contents used in an organization. Moreover, the architecture highlights the processes connected with the management of contents and then allows organizations to focus on their improvement if the management of content is not optimal.

Content management in insurance companies

Content management is extremely important in insurance companies. For instance, applications should seamlessly integrate with the intermediaries, the customers, and the insurance management systems, with just one click necessary to file and retrieve documents. This allows the company to reduce policy- and claims-processing times and costs while enhancing the customers' experience.

In property and casualty insurance, there is the need to seamlessly integrate with partner information and finance applications. It is necessary seamlessly to retrieve stored documents and automatically file, name, and link documents to transactions within the company's insureds and finance applications.

In life and health insurances, companies manage hundreds of pages of support documentation associated with life, disability, accidental, and medical insurance policies, and claims. It is necessary to manage applications, policies, reinsurance, enrollments, claims, and client correspondence. The solutions must provide a secure place to centrally store the client information so that authorized personnel can view the same files at the same time without having to make copies.

For policy underwriting and claims processing, insurance companies face the challenge of managing the information, people, and procedures specific to policy underwriting and claims processing. There is the need for workflow automation, so that it is possible to notify, track, and report on the company processes. With the integration of workflows with business intelligence, organizations can maximize resources by identifying bottlenecks and level loaded resources.

Model of the Ten plus One S

The model presented in this section is referred to as the Ten plus One (10 + 1) S (also referred in this chapter as unified content management

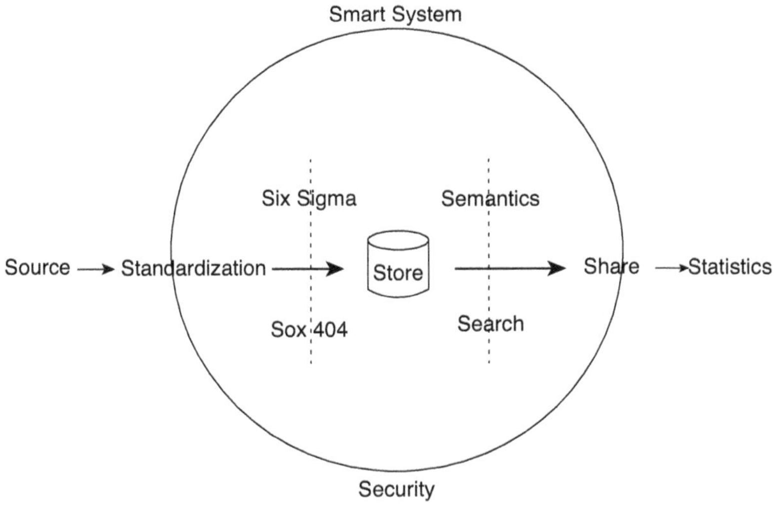

Figure 4.7 The model of the 10+1 S

[UCM]), because the main processes related to the management of the content can be classified into ten words starting with "S," plus an additional S summarizing the previous ten.[65]

Figure 4.7 summarizes the UCM model. The following paragraphs examine each of the processes that comprises the model. For each process, the potential digitization support is summarized. The right approach to follow in improving these processes can be synthetized as Lean and Digitize: the processes should be at the same time freed of any waste ("Lean") and automatized ("Digitize").[66]

Source

The source generates the content. The source of the content could be very diverse. It can be internal or external to the organization. It can be more or less reliable. Its origin can be identified or not identified, and therefore can be secure or not.

The enterprise content management system (ECMS) represents a type of solution useful in organizing and facilitating the collaborative creation of documents and other content. Technically, the ECMS is a server side application, divided into two parts:

- the back end, or the administration section, which deals with organizing and supervising the production of the content

- the front end, that is, the section of the application that the user access to accomplish changes, updates, and insertions/deletions

Standardization

The first process to which to submit the raw content is its standardization at the maximum level possible, so as to facilitate the subsequent classification or search. This operation can also be named in some cases as normalization.

To manage the contents, an interesting tool consists of the extensible markup language (XML). This is a standardized markup language for information within documents. Being a data format for exchanging structured documents, XML contains a set of rules that expand the amount and types of information that can be provided on the data contained in the documents.

Six Sigma

The Six Sigma approach, or rather, Lean Six Sigma, is another step, which concerns the management and improvement of content quality.[67] Lean Six Sigma is the right mix between the work on the quality required by Six Sigma and the speed of the processes of the lean approach. This combination can reduce the complexity and the defect improvement processes, improving both the quality and speed. These aspects are particularly important especially in basic services.

Prior to automating and digitizing, it is essential to streamline the processes. Lean identifies waste (*muda* in Japanese) in the processes, by eliminating and reducing process time and minimizing costs. To do this, the lean approach poses some questions: "Is this content essential?", "Is it in all its parts?", "How can the quality of the content be assured?", "Is it essential to develop and store the essential documents?" "Which are the really mandatory processing?" Once these questions are answered, and acted upon accordingly, the organization can move to automate the processes.

Data quality assessment determines the quality of the critical data fields that are of key importance to the insurance company.

Storage

With the model of the Ten plus One S, all the content can be managed in a unified manner, thanks to the storing of the content in a repository, which makes the content quickly accessible to all interested parties.

The UCM solutions are object-oriented systems for the management, storing, and production of documents. In them, the documents are represented by the collection of logical components, or "objects." They can be combined and physically mapped within a layout page by page. The objects are organized, stored, accessed, and processed through a system of database management. At a minimum, this repository contains objects of constituents based on the information, texts, images, voices, or graphics. Objects can also contain other data specifying the physical characteristics, relationships with other objects, and access restrictions.

Security

Another "S" refers to security concerns: it is critical to manage the security of content access, processing, and storing. Digital data can be compressed into very minute spaces and in large quantities. This increases its vulnerability and the risk that it can be copied and used fraudulently.

It is important to design carefully:

- the access control, to secure the contents and identify who is authorized to read, create, modify, or delete contents
- the access permissions to allow the permissions for revisions by authors, publishers, and employees and allow users the right to create, edit, or view the content
- the audit of the content, which requires analyzing sample materials and looking for information that is similar/identical as well as to eliminate the unnecessary duplication of contents

A comprehensive secure UCM solution must provide the appropriate level of protection, at the right time, while simultaneously being practical in today's dynamic business environment.[68] Protecting all types of content is not the same as protecting the right content. Today, many point solutions exist for protecting content, but these are often not integrated into a holistic and comprehensive secure UCM strategy. Digital solutions like document encryption, information rights management (IRM), and data loss protection (DLP) address different use cases and security requirements.

Semantics

Semantics is important in the use of content. It is critical to recognize and access similar information, stored with different wordings but taking into account the links among them. Three critical enablers of semantic technology are classification, metadata, and ontologies. The combined application of these three core components may aid in overcoming the challenges of a unified content management as traditional content management evolves into semantic content management.[69]

Sharing

It is important to define the processes for sharing information. These processes should foster collaboration, not only within the organization but also outside, with vendors, customers, intermediaries (be they agencies brokers, or promoters), and other partners.

Web content management systems support managing the contents (text, graphics, links, and so on) for their distribution on a web server. Normally, this application provides solutions with which users with limited knowledge of programming languages or markup languages (such as XML) can create and manage content with relative ease.

Search

Another "S" is the possibility of searching or researching data. Google and other companies, such as the vendors of packages of enterprise resource planning (ERP) are introducing interesting solutions. They work primarily as an appliance adaptable to many types of content, both structured and unstructured. The search solutions are still not very effective on voice or video. Some interesting software can search also images and videos.

The transactional content management system (TCMS) assists in managing the contents of transactions and in particular those relating to e-commerce.

Sox 404

Another "S" is connected to the Sox 404 and other regulations, involving mainly the financial aspects and processing by ICT companies. It includes a number of roles and activities that ensure compliance on electronic and manual transactions as well as in the storage of content.

The Sarbanes-Oxley Act is a federal law of the United States, enacted in 2002, in response to a number of scandals that occurred in that country, such as those related to Enron, Tyco International, Adelphia, Peregrine Systems, and WorldCom.[70] The law is named after two US Senators, Paul Sarbanes and Michael Oxley, who sponsored the legislation. It is considered one of the major reforms of business practices since the time of Franklin D. Roosevelt.

The Sox 404 establishes standards mandatory for all American companies listed on the USA stock exchange and for their accounting firms.[71] There are sections in the law with significant impacts on digital solutions and in particular on the verification of the existence of adequate control and responsibility of the management, mainly in assuring security but also the protection of third parties, such as customers. In other nations, there are laws and similar regulations that must be respected.

Often organizations face this compliance issue without an organic and responsive approach. The context in which insurance companies need to work today requires the ability to structure an integrated approach to governance, risk management, and compliance.

Over the last few years, there has been a new awareness toward these issues. The impulse comes mainly from the introduction of regulations such as Sarbanes-Oxley or Solvency II regulations that impose new models for managing information and data, often related mainly to the field of accounting.

The need to comply with the regulations has important organizational effects. In most cases, the activities necessary for compliance have been entrusted to the finance directors. They have been invested with new responsibilities for monitoring and assure quality processes. This has resulted in an evolution of the job descriptions of these figures requiring to take an active role in the definition of the business strategy of their organizations.

Governance, risk management, and compliance systems (GRCS) are software solutions that can act as a central nervous system to capture, track, and report on regulatory and corporate compliance policies. These platforms provide the solutions needed to embed compliance and governance into day-to-day business activities. Solutions of this type help position the insurance companies in meeting ongoing regulatory requirements and identifying risks, while at the same time gathering information that helps to proactively run the business.

Statistics

The production of dashboards and statistics on all the content, be it structured or unstructured, is an interesting and very useful field. Not surprisingly, the leading companies in the field of statistics software have made acquisitions in the UCM areas, not only to produce statistics on the number or type of documents but above all for processing their content.

The publication content management system (PCMS) assists in managing publications (manuals, books, aid, guides, and references) during the life processing of the contents.

Smart system

The Ten plus One S model synthesizes and integrates the main processes connected with the management of the content for adding value to the organizations. Solutions that can support the Ten plus One S can be indicated as smart systems. They should also include a unified strategy of content management, which corresponds to the One S in addition to the Ten S's. This would be a repetitive method of identifying all the requirements of the content. Initially, it requires creating content suitable to be reused, then managing it in a well-defined repository, and finally assembling the content on demand to meet the needs of its users. A strategy of this type can help in reducing the cost of creating, managing, storing, and distributing content and ensuring that content effectively supports the needs of the organization and of individual users.

Aegon

Aegon, a multinational life insurance, pensions, and asset management company, won a Celent Model Insurer award in 2015 for operational excellence in noncore systems/ICT management.[72] Aegon, jointly with a technology company, designed and created an enterprise-wide customer correspondence management framework as part of an effort to transform Aegon's legacy systems into a modern application portfolio. This framework delivers consistent customer communication across multiple channels (Web, mobile, e-mail, and print). This project exemplifies a vision of the digital insurance in which organizations move away from implementing disparate and piecemeal digital touch point projects, and toward a continuous system of optimization.

Dynamic content

In a manner similar to UCM, often people talk of master data management (MDM). The basic concept of MDM is to leave the data in their computer application and to retrieve it when access is needed to produce reports, statistics, or similar reports, or to combine them with data from other sources. This concept is based very much on the technological method of the service-oriented architecture (SOA) or on the presence of the so-called information servers.

In MDM, there are two significant trends that combine:[73]

- the need to actively (not passively) govern content and structured data in a uniform manner
- the need to apply MDM principles to nonmaterial data, such as reference data

It turns out that these are not dissimilar trends – they are just operating, today, in different environments. They will come together. The issue is that content management solutions and technologies are notoriously bad at assuring a "single view" of content!

A similar concept can also be applied to the content. In this case, it is called dynamic content. This is the content that is assembled in real time to meet specific uses, providing exactly what is required, when it is required, and in the format in which it is required.

At the base of the MDM, and therefore of the dynamic content, is the S that has been defined in this section as Standardization. It refers in this case to the normalization of the content. It serves to eliminate redundancies due to the collection of content from dissimilar sources. The process includes:

- identification of the source
- the collection of content
- the processing
- normalization rules

One possible use of dynamic content is related to third parties (both customers and vendors or other partners) that must assemble all the content. An example is an interaction with a customer, which may be based on both structured data and unstructured data, or via voice (call center or phone call), or anything else.

Using this tool, there would be the need to store all the content in a single repository, making it possible to have all the updated content in one place.

The future of content management

The future is not easy to predict, but in the case of content, it is certain that its management, and in particular a unified management, is a challenge that will find many solutions. Already, many ICT and consulting vendors are addressing this topic to provide solutions.

Illinois Mutual Life Insurance Company (IMLIC)

Implementing a content management system (CMS) in several departments helped the Illinois Mutual Life Insurance Company speed turnaround time, elevate productivity, and reduce the time it takes to answer a policy information request by 75 percent.[74] The CMS was integrated with multiple proprietary applications without programming, giving users in policy services, underwriting, sales, and other departments instant access to supporting documents from the systems in which they work daily. Instead of sending paperwork between departments, users route documents to colleagues electronically in the workflow of the CMS, resulting in faster policy processing and reducing redundant effort. When customers call with questions, IMLIC employees instantly retrieve specific policy documents using CMS, thus eliminating callbacks and boosting customer delight.

Conclusions

Innovation is key to the success of insurance companies in today's world. There are plenty of opportunities in new solutions more and more available to insurance companies to innovate in terms of products, processes, organizations, and business models.

ICT solutions continue to progress. This chapter has considered four innovative aspects:

- mobile
- cloud computing
- big data analytics
- content management

Mobile has been expanding at very high rates even during the economic crisis. It is having an impact on many economies throughout the world. The use of smartphones and tablets is expanding. The total number of mobile phones is almost equal to the world population. The sales of smartphones and tablets are expanding faster than those of traditional dumb phones and PCs. Mobile is impacting heavily on the sale of insurance products. In some cases, it is the ideal solution: think of travel insurance, for instance.

In the background, there are other digital solutions that are influencing the use of ICT in insurance companies. One is cloud computing, which is the use of ICT resources on-demand, through networks (mainly Internet), paying by use and providing a self-service mode. Cloud computing frees companies from fixed location data centers. As a consequence, they combine very well with mobile. Also reinsurance, coinsurance, and partnerships become much easier to manage, thanks to the cloud.

Big data analytics are solutions that are extremely important for insurance companies. Two uses stand out among the many: marketing support and risk management.

These solutions promise to move ICT from being a system of records to a system of engagement. In other words, ICT can move from being a big archive to become the support of operational decisions in insurance companies, such as whether to accept reinsurances, decide on the premium on new risks, and so on. Big data analytics is essential to providing a personalized experience in digital insurance. Financial services institutions are moving in this direction. However, it is necessary to speed up the process. The combination of digital insurance with cloud computing can further simplify the process and make it possible to enjoy the benefits of big data analytics in a quicker and less expensive way.

Management of all the contents necessary for operating digital insurance will become more and more important. UCMs can help in this endeavor.

The launch and the improvement of digital insurance represent an important moment in the life of an insurance company, since this channel will become increasingly important. Financial institutions should use a sound method. The approach proposed here is the Lean and Digitize method. The next chapter on Governance presents the method.

5
Governance

Introduction

Governance is important in general, but particularly in the case of digital insurance. It is a subset discipline of corporate governance, focused on digital support for an insurance company and its performance and risk management. The interest in digital insurance governance is due to the ongoing need within organizations to focus value creation efforts on strategic objectives and to manage better the performance of the solutions responsible for creating value for all stakeholders.[1]

Digital solutions are causing profound changes in the relationships between companies, the customers, and other partners. Therefore, they have become the source of new challenges for the management and of potential risks.

To underline the importance of governance for insurance companies, it should be noted that the Bank of England stressed its significance in order for the insurance companies to prepare for Solvency II implementation. To assure that supervisory authorities and firms are prepared for the implementation of Solvency II on 1 January 2016, the system of governance and the own risk self-assessment (ORSA) were included in European Insurance and Occupational Pensions Authority's (EIOPA) preparatory guidelines. The Bank of England reminded firms of the following key points:[2]

- Companies are encouraged to review their system of governance procedures and take the opportunity to use the preparatory phase to make any changes required to assure they meet the Solvency II Directive.
- The Prudential Regulatory Authority (PRA) expects companies, when asked, to be able to explain what governance changes they need to

make to satisfy the guidelines, how they plan to make those changes, what progress there has been to date and any particular difficulties they face.
- The PRA does not prescribe the format or content of the ORSA supervisory report, recognizing that it needs to reflect the specific risk profile and governance mechanism of each firm and group.

This chapter is dedicated to analyzing the most important aspects of the governance of digital insurance. It covers aspects related to project management, data governance and quality, and security.

Project management and data governance are important in assuring the effectiveness, the efficiency, the economics, and the ethics of digital insurance.

Security is particularly important, since it is the main concern of many customers. Systems, smartphones, and tablets are used to process an increasing amount of sensitive information. Access must be managed and controlled to protect the account information, the privacy of the users, the intellectual property, and the reputation of the insurance company.

Smartphones and PCs are preferred targets of attacks. These attacks exploit weaknesses related to devices that can come from means of communication, such as short message service (SMS), multimedia messaging service (MMS), Wi-Fi networks, the Global System for Mobile Communications (GSM), application software vulnerabilities, and weak behavior on the part of the average user.

Various security countermeasures are being developed and applied to digital solutions, from more stringent security in different layers of software to actions to increase the awareness of the user. This chapter describes some good practices to be observed at all levels, from design to use.

Lean and Digitize project management

Currently, every organization (and particularly insurance companies) must struggle to meet the needs of customers in terms of products and services as they relate to quality and price. They need at the same time to reduce the costs of the operations and the time to deliver the services. To achieve these objectives, it is crucial to focus on process improvement. The most effective methods for driving process improvement are Lean Thinking and Agile Management. These methods consider primarily the analysis and the subsequent optimization of the physical and organizational flows. They leave aside the study of the management automation and the interactions between information systems and telecommunications networks, and physical and organizational activities. The risk is that, once the physical and organizational improvements are defined, the automation might clash with the management of the processes due to the constraints imposed by those systems.

However, only after this rationalization and redesign of the new processes takes place does it make sense to introduce or improve automation effectively, efficiently, ethically, and economically.

To obtain the most competitive advantages, the integration of automation and improvements through Lean Thinking and Agile Methodology is of fundamental importance. This is especially true in many insurance companies, in which productivity has not increased in recent decades; hence, the need for a holistic approach is important to streamline and improve processes from all points of view. This approach should be:

- complete and operational
- structured (through the use of the Six Sigma method, which can be considered part of the Lean Thinking)
- driven by the need to add value to the customer (in accordance with the approach of Lean Thinking)
- adding agility to the business, in order to reach flexibility
- not limited to a specific sector, but taking into consideration end-to-end processes
- based on automation to enhance the benefits of Lean Six Sigma improvements with a rational use of information systems and telecommunications

We have defined this approach as Lean and Digitize.[3] The next section describes this method.[4]

By using a Lean and Digitize approach, the insurance companies can enhance activities that add value with automation. A rule of thumb says that 50 percent of the improvement of processes is independent of the automation, while the remaining 50 percent of improvements require automation.[5] These percentages are changing. Automation is becoming more and more important.

It is essential to apply this method and its tools with a team approach with all the involved areas of the organization, quality management, and support organizations (such as marketing, finance, or operations). In this way, the new initiatives are not used to solve specific problems or challenges, but rather become rooted in the culture of the organization. A Lean and Digitize approach can save up to 30 percent.[6]

A digital insurance transformation using Lean and Digitize

The Lean and Digitize method is important in transformation management since a digital insurance project needs to cover what are called the four P's:

- products or services
- people
- processes
- platform

Several stages compose the Lean and Digitize (short for Lean Six Sigma and Digitize) innovation process in digital insurance. To be successful, Lean and Digitize innovation must adopt a process that this chapter describes as the 7 D's: define, discover, design, develop, digitize, deploy, and diffusion. It is essential to apply this methodology and its tools in strong partnership between the sectors of the organization involved, quality and support departments (such as information and communications technology [ICT], finance, or operations).[7] Stakeholders from all parties need to align in setting up and staffing the improvement project team. Perhaps more importantly, organizations must treat the initial application of the Lean and Digitize innovation process to digital insurance as the beginning of an iterative cycle. This cycle should generate continuous improvement and leads to a change in the culture of the organizations toward lean thinking.[8]

It is important to blend process improvement and digital solutions. Based on research and experience, one can profitably use the Lean and Digitize innovation process. In reference to lean innovation, Lean and Digitize innovation can be summarized as follows. It can be divided into seven stages and 29 steps, as described below and shown in Figure 1.6. At the end of each stage there are tollgates, where the project needs to be checked by a digital insurance steering committee, before moving to the next stage.

The seven stages are the following:

Stage 1: Define

In this stage, the environment is defined to set the ground for the move to digital insurance.

1. context: identify the needs or the requests of the customers, shareholders, and employees; the challenge of competitors; and the respect for compliance (for example, legislation, and regulations)

2. culture: detect the culture of the organization, of the community, and of the nation in which the insurance organization is located
3. vision: tackle the problems of effectiveness, efficiency, economy, ethics, and quality of the innovation
4. strategy: define the possible content of the innovation
5. kick-off: launch the project during a special meeting and notify all the stakeholders
6. governance: define how to manage the project and set up the team
7. voice of the customer: listen to the voice of the customers (VoC) associated with the potential innovation and verify it

Stage 2: Discover

In this stage, new ideas are discovered for potential development within the digital insurance project.

8. invention: the creation of something new through an organization's own creative process
9. selection: finding and evaluating an innovation to potentially develop or adopt
10. metrics: translate the innovation and the VoC into critical-to-quality (CtQ) factors
11. as-is: map the existing situation in terms of products, processes, organization, or business models

Stage 3: Design

In this stage, the framework and the sequence of activities are defined.

12. lean: define with the support of the team in workshops and meetings how to innovate
13. *kaizen* plan: define the improvement intervention plan
14. architecture design: define the rules, policies, and process structure of the potential innovation

Stage 4: Develop

In this stage, an idea is developed into a usable innovation.

15. build: develop the chosen solutions
16. packaging: surround the core solution with complementary products and services that together form a solution that can be effectively used for a given purpose by the target adopter

17. configure: decide which solution features will be used, whether they will be used as is or with adaptations, how the solution will integrate with other solutions the organization already has in place, how related organizational components (for example, structures, processes) will be changed, and how the organization will absorb and make use of the solution
18. change management: manage the transformation

Stage 5: Digitize

In this stage, the automation is applied at the deepest possible level.

19. implementation: implement the digitized solution
20. test: conduct unit tests, system tests, integration tests, user acceptance tests, and operations acceptance tests

Stage 6: Deploy

In this stage, the solution is implemented and the ancillary activities are performed.

21. deploy: implement the chosen solution
22. document: issue the documentation related to the innovation
23. verify: control the improvements
24. internal and external benefits: assess the benefits, both external (in other words, take notice of customers, shareholders, and employees' satisfaction) and internal (in other words, assess the profitability, market share, and internal improvements related to the new process)
25. lessons learned: learn from the initiative
26. celebration: acknowledge the team's work

Stage 7: Diffusion

In this stage, it is necessary to assemble and arrange the resources necessary to a) persuade and enable a population of organizations or individuals to adopt and use the innovation and b) to diffuse or spread it across a population of potential users.

27. assimilation: when individuals and other units absorb the innovation into their daily routines and the work life of the firm
28. appropriation: involves such tasks as managing intellectual property and the ecosystem of complementary products and services so that profits are protected from suppliers, customers, and imitators

29. transformation: the technology and organization to take advantage of the new opportunities brought about by the innovation; transformations can also happen at the market and societal levels

Stages 3, 4, and 5 should be done with an Agile approach, doing several cycles, or "sprints" in the Agile terminology. An Agile approach is a development method based on iterative and incremental development, where requirements and solutions evolve through collaboration between self-organizing, cross-functional teams.[9] It promotes adaptive planning, evolutionary development and delivery, and a time-boxed iterative approach. It encourages rapid and flexible responses to change. It is a conceptual framework promoting tight interactions throughout the development cycle.

The Agile Manifesto is based on 12 principles.[10] They can be customized in connection with the Lean and Digitize digital insurance project:

1. Customer and organization delight should be pursued by the rapid and flexible delivery of useful innovations.
2. Requirement changes should be welcomed, even late in the innovation process.
3. Incremental working innovations should be delivered frequently (for example, every few weeks rather than months or even years).
4. Incremental working innovations are the principal measures of progress.
5. Development should be sustainable; the team must be able to maintain a constant pace.
6. There should be close, daily cooperation between business people and the innovation team.
7. In-person conversation is the best form of communication (co-location but also virtual teams properly managed).
8. Projects should be built around motivated individuals, who should be trusted and trust.
9. Continuous attention should be paid to technical excellence and good design.
10. Simplicity – the art of maximizing the amount of work not done – is essential.
11. Teams should be self-organizing.
12. Adaptation to the changing environment is encouraged.

Many tools can be used in conjunction with the process described. They can derive from the tools used in Lean thinking, Six Sigma, Agile

Management, and digitization. This chapter does not consider the latter ones, because they are extensive and well covered in many publications. The following discussion does not consider all the possible tools that can be used but only the most appropriate ones.

One of the best tools for process design is quality function deployment (QFD), commonly known as the House of Quality. It identifies the potential customer value of the innovation based on the customers' (be they internal or external) needs and an innovation's (normally a product) quality characteristics. The analysis through QFD is used to determine when a new innovation is useful, so excess resources are not consumed for innovation that may not add much value.

Another useful tool is TRIZ (a Russian acronym for theory of inventive problem solving). The requirements for innovation can be defined by introducing the TRIZ problem-solving approach in finding innovative solutions to technical problems, especially in product development processes. TRIZ is implemented to define the solutions necessary to improve these processes. The use of TRIZ is beneficial with the lean practice because it efficiently utilizes resources in the processes to eliminate waste.

Yamashima, Ishida, and Mizuyama describe a method, named the innovative product development process (IPDP).[11] It systematically integrates QFD with TRIZ and enables the effective and systematic creation of technical innovation for new products. In IPDP, the target products' functions and mechanisms are deployed in parallel into hierarchical structures. The mechanism that most requires technical innovation is specified from an analysis of customers' needs by calculating a mechanism weight. Then, the technical problems to be solved are defined by considering the relationship between the specified mechanism and the corresponding functions or quality characteristics. The application of TRIZ helps in developing the "technical" innovation.

Another important tool is prototyping, which is both a culture and a language.[12] Just about anything can be prototyped – a new product or service, a process, even an organization or a business model. What counts is moving the ball forward, achieving progress in a continuous way even on pieces of a goal.

In the case of innovations, digital mock-up (DMU) is a concept that allows the description of a product, usually in 3D, for its entire life cycle.[13] The product design, manufacturing, and support engineers work together to create and manage the DMU. One of the objectives is to have important knowledge of the innovation to replace any hard prototypes with virtual ones. As an extension, it is frequently referred to as digital prototyping or virtual prototyping. The benefits of DMU are:

1. reduced time-to-market by identifying potential issues earlier in the design process
2. reduced product development costs by minimizing the number of prototypes that need to be done in the market
3. increased product quality assurance by allowing a larger number of design alternatives to be investigated before a final one is chosen

There are several practices connected with the Agile approach, such as extreme programming from software engineering, which enables the team to work together to determine goals and shared objectives; the rational unified process from both systems and software engineering with its iterative development methodology, the focus on eliminating waste from lean manufacturing, and the daily scrum update meetings from product development. These processes enable the innovation team to adapt to changing requirements, reduce the project risk, increase the visibility of team progresses, involve stakeholders and practitioners from the beginning of projects, and speed up the creation of value that the team brings to the business.

Innovation in organizations is important. A key to effective and efficient innovation is the ability to commercialize new products quickly and economically, while leveraging the benefits of global outsourcing. The growing role of global outsourcing in innovation represents a paradigm shift that has had a large impact on innovation and commercialization.[14] It is important to explore the use of external innovation and commercialization resources, from contract employees to short-run operators. The digital insurance team can synthesize their research into many areas in which innovation operators can most effectively leverage outsourcing throughout the innovation continuum. Opportunities include developing strong strategic partnerships with outside vendors, buying innovative start-ups, using rapid prototyping resources to support agile development, using short-run manufacturers to test products and markets before building to volume, and using expert contractors to reduce fixed personnel costs.

These tools and approaches are helpful in creating an environment open to promote effective, efficient, and economical digital insurance innovation.

Nationwide Mutual Insurance Company

Nationwide Mutual Insurance Company & Affiliated Companies (Nationwide) is a group of large US insurance and financial services companies based in Columbus, Ohio. At Nationwide, the lean development system governs how the work is executed, improved, and monitored in the overall system.[15] The development system:

- creates an efficient process sequence with the lowest possible waste;
- standardizes routine work items to allow Nationwide knowledge workers the freedom to concentrate on value-added activities; and
- empowers team members to continuously improve upon the standards covering the entire application development and maintenance cycle (ADC) with their ideas.

Standardized work is the basis for continuous improvement, with:

- waste elimination;
- increased productivity;
- improved morale; and
- foundation for improvement activities.

Nationwide purses the enabling of *kaizen*, that is, continuous improvement, and the A3's relentless pursuit of perfection, based on using as an analysis tool a A3 sheet of paper.[16] Continuous incremental improvement (*kaizen*) is an approach of continuous improvement that pervades all areas and aspects of the organization. It is embedded in Nationwide's culture and becomes a part of everybody's way of working.

Nationwide ADC continuous improvement:

- applies to both formal *kaizen* events and *kaizen* eyes – everyday continuous improvement to eliminate or at least reduce waste;
- is driven by the practitioners;
- provides a governance mechanism for pushing changes into the Nationwide processes;
- utilizes the A3 tool to assure PDCA thinking as well as other lean tools such as the Five Whys, Fishbone, and similar.

Without the lean management system, the gains of implementing a lean development system cannot be supported and maintained.

Data management

Data quality and governance: an increasing challenge for organizations

In the past, the attention of management and academicians was very much concentrated on the quality of products and their development and management. Since then, more and more attention has been devoted to the processes. The idea is that if the processes are sound, the quality of the product would also be good.

At the basis of the processes there is data. Thanks to the spreading of information and telecommunication technology, of sensors, and of mobile, more and more data are available. A very interesting development is big data analytics: This term refers to data that are processeable and that have three characteristics: large volume, the need to access them in velocity, and with a great variety (structured and unstructured, internal and external, and so on).

Data analysis is also labeled business intelligence. This is the use of data to extract information in support of the decision making process. If this is the sequence, it is very important that the quality of the data be excellent. If that is not the case, at the end of the chain (data=>information=>decision), the decisions might be incorrect.

Until now, attention to the quality of the data has been relatively limited. In the world of big data analytics, this is no longer possible, however. It is now time to move from the certification of products to the certification of data.

This can be achieved by applying Lean and Digitize to data management. This means acting on the four P's: products, people, processes, and platforms:

- In the case of insurance companies, the design, marketing, and delivery of the Products must take into account the need to assure the quality of the data connected with them. More and more regulations and attention are moving in this direction.
- To act on People means essentially to take care of the data governance. Data governance is an integral part of corporate and ICT governance. It combines leadership, organizational structures, and processes to assure that data provide value to the insurance company. For effective, efficient, and economical data governance, it is essential to define a proper organization.
- Organization is essential to define Processes. In the case of data, the important processes to consider are relative to the creation, transformation, and loading of data into the archives. The auditing and vetting of data already present in the databases are also important. To be more precise, the subprocesses to consider are:
  - data creation/capture/extraction and recording at the start of the process
  - data manipulation/transformation (label preparation, moving data to a ledger, data enrichment, and so on)

  - classification and tagging of data (class, observation, and so on) and its recording
  - documentation of the data (capturing and recording the metadata)
  - digitization/transfer of the data
  - data storage and archiving
  - data presentation and dissemination (on paper and electronic publications, web-enabled databases, and so on)
  - data use (analysis, transformation, and integration)
- Once the proper organization and improved processes have been identified, it is necessary to evaluate the tools that can help in the certification of data (the platforms). The tools are essential in the case of big data analytics due to the sheer volume of the data, its diversity, and the speed at which it is necessary to perform the processes.

Generali acquisition of MyDrive Solutions

The Generali Group, an Italian headquartered multinational insurance company, acquired MyDrive Solutions, an English start-up founded in 2010. MyDrive is among the leading companies in the use of data analytics tools to profile driving styles. The objective is the identification of innovative and tailor-made products for the customers and favorable tariffs for low risk drivers.[17]

This is a way for Generali to enhance its operating platform and to develop innovative, smarter products, tailored to the customers' specific needs, benefiting from connectivity and exploiting all the potential of big data analytics.

MyDrive uses customer data gathered from a series of technological instruments, such as black boxes, installed on the vehicle, or smartphones, to build predictive algorithms and to define behavioral scores of the users, enabling those who choose new products to receive customized commercial offers.

MyDrive is now specialized in motor insurance. It will expand big data analysis activities to a vast series of sectors, from fraud prevention to sophisticated customer segmentation.

Definitions of data management

There are some basic definitions of data management:[18]

- Master data management (MDM) is the practice of developing and maintaining consistent definitions of business entities (such as customers, products, operational financial aspects and content, and partners). MDM's entity definitions and reference data facilitate the sharing of data across the digital insurance organization and possibly outward to business partners, such as the intermediaries, be they agencies, brokers, comparators, or similar. In this way, MDM can improve data-driven initiatives, such as business intelligence, integrating business units via common data, 360-degree views, operational efficiency, the compliant use of data, and customer interactions that span multiple touch points.

- Data quality (DQ) is a family of data-management tools and business-quality practices, applied repeatedly over time as the state of quality evolves. The objective is to assure that data is accurate, up-to-date, fit for their intended purpose, and capable of adding value to all stakeholders.
- Data governance (DG) is the creation and enforcement of policies and procedures for business use and the operational management of data. Common goals of data governance are defining ownership, improving data quality, remediating its inconsistencies, sharing data widely, leveraging its aggregate for competitive advantages, managing change supported by the use of data, and complying with internal and external regulations and standards for data quality (for example, Iso 14041).[19]
- Data stewardship (DS) is usually performed by a business manager who knows how data affects the performance of his or her business unit or the enterprise. In addition to daily management responsibilities, a data steward collaborates with data management specialists and data owners to direct data management work to support the achievement of the insurance company goals and priorities.

Data as a critical success factor for digital insurance

For the success of any initiative, it is important to understand the critical success factors for generating an excellent customer experience. Due to the high risk and low switching cost, building customers' initial trust and keeping it are critical for digital insurance.

An empirical study showed that structural assurance and information quality are the main factors affecting initial trust. Initial trust affects perceived usefulness, and both factors help in predicting usage intention.[20] Marketing is devoting more and more importance to the user experience connected with the products, and even more in providing services. Thus digital insurance needs to take all possible actions to improve the initial trust in order to facilitate customers' adoption and usage of insurance products and services.

For the customers the perceived security in the use of digital insurance is important. As big data analytics become more used in understanding customers, assuring data quality is a big challenge. A white paper produced by Experian QAS surveyed 300 ICT and business leaders across several industry verticals. Some results are the following:[21]

- On average, twenty five percent of the data collected by the organizations surveyed was inaccurate.
- Eighty-two percent of the respondents said their organizations have an analytics department for improving customer intelligence.
- Forty-three percent of them acknowledged that they are not able to maintain accurate information for daily operations.

Organizations will never be able to fully realize the potential of big data analytics if they cannot make up for the possible inaccurancy of data. To start improving the quality of their data, Experian's research suggests that organizations need to link customer records across all of their departments (for instance using MDM), improve their data collection processes across all channels, vet the data before loading it in the system, and make sure they are getting accurate information from third-party sources.

Due to the lack of direct experience, users need to rely on their own perceptions, such as information and system quality, to form their trust in digital insurance. Both information quality and system quality are factors affecting information system success. The aspects important in data certification are:[22]

- accuracy, which refers to the closeness of measured values, observations, or estimates of the real or true value (or of a value that is accepted as being true)
- precision (or resolution), which can be divided into two main types:
  - Statistical precision is the closeness with which repeated observations conform to themselves. There is not a direct relationship to the true value, and there might be high precision, but low accuracy.
  - Numerical precision is the number of significant digits in which observations are recorded, and it has become far much more common with the advent of computers.

Information quality must also satisfy other requirements, such as timeliness and understandability. Users expect to access digital insurance to acquire their correct insurance information at any time from anywhere. If the information provided is irrelevant, inaccurate, or out of date, users may question whether digital insurance providers have enough ability and willingness to provide quality services. Information quality affects initial trust. For example, if mobile digital insurance is asynchronous with the call center information, users may get wrong information about policies. This may decrease or destroy altogether the users' trust in digital insurance.

Information quality may also affect the perceived utility of digital insurance. Users rely on quality information to manage their insurance, which can improve their living and working performance and effectiveness. In contrast, low-quality information decreases users' perceived utility of digital insurance. Prior studies have noted the effect of information quality on initial trust for example in health infomediaries. Information quality also affects the perceived usefulness of data warehousing software.[23]

Insurance companies should devote more and more time to data and information quality. It is interesting to note that the central Bank of Italy, in a recent directive for the Italian financial services (issued on 2 July 2013), devoted a full chapter to the subject of data governance, which includes the subject of data quality.[24] The Bank of Italy is now in charge of supervising the insurance companies.

New India Assurance Co. Ltd.

The first major implementation challenge in New India Assurance Co. Ltd. (NIACL) was the migration of policy and customer data to a centralized solution.[25] Given the starting point of 1,100 separate branches, the transition required also to put emphasis on data quality in order to remove duplicate data and resolve data conflicts. The data migration resulted in the consolidation of all master data, a cleansed dataset across the entire company, and centralized validation schemes for ongoing data quality. Various tools were used for performance tuning and load balancing to assure excellent delivery to support a large customer base across the country.

From a centralized database, the NIACL solution is now able to provide multichannel access to information on products, policies, customers, and claims.

This approach was of great help in aiding NIACL competitive positioning in the insurance market. NIACL can price policies based on large-scale actuarial data. Using advanced analytics, NIACL can take advantage of its large customer base and nationwide scope to launch and sell competitive insurance products. The resulting underwriting rules and policies can be deployed instantly across the entire sales network.

Master data management

ICT must guarantee that the system supports the following functions:

- data dictionary
- the ability to collect definitions of business terms from disparate business functions
- the ability to update the definitions by authorized users
- the ability to publish the business terms
- the ability to show functional lineage of a business term
- a data quality framework, including deduplication of the data and its vetting
- a framework/model to capture the quality of the key metrics
- a reporting function to publish the quality metrics for periodic measurability and auditability

Master data management of disparate data systems requires data transformations as the data extracted from the disparate source data system is transformed and loaded into the master data management hub.[26]

Processes commonly included in master data management (MDM) are data governance, source identification, data collection, data transformation, normalization, deduplication, rule administration, error detection and correction, data consolidation, data storage, data classification, taxonomy services, item master creation, schema mapping, product codification, data enrichment, and data utilization.

An MDM system requires data networks, a data warehouse, data marts or the so-called cubes, an operational data store, data mining, data analysis, data visualization, data federation, and data virtualization.

There are essentially three ways in which master data may be collated and distributed to other applications:

- data consolidation, which is the process of capturing relevant data from multiple sources and integrating them into a single hub (Operational Data Store or ODS) for replication to other destination applications
- data federation, which is the process of providing one virtual view of relevant data from multiple sources to multiple destination applications
- data propagation, the process of copying relevant data from one application to another, typically through point-to-point interfaces or web services in legacy applications

The implementation of MDM is important for insurance companies, especially since such implementation could realize other positive benefits for a business through big data analytics at little incremental cost.

The field of data management is in development.[27] A new technology, virtual master data management, utilizes data virtualization and a persistent metadata server to implement a multilevel automated MDM hierarchy.

Security

Challenges of security

Digital insurance transactions might be executed from some remote locations and through the transmission of insurance information over the air or on public networks. The security of such transactions is one of the most complex challenges that need to be addressed jointly by application developers, network service providers, insurance companies' ICT departments, and the customers themselves.

The following aspects need to be managed for offering a secure infrastructure for digital insurance transactions:

- the physical part of the device, be it a PC or a mobile or similar, should be fully protected with antivirus software, local firewall, and similar
- user ID/password authentication of the digital insurance users should be very effective. It would be ideal to use a physical or virtual token to authenticate the access. One-time passwords (OTPs) do not rely on traditional character-based passwords. OTPs must be used by the customer each time he/she wants to perform sensitive transactions using online or digital insurance devices. When the request is received, the password is sent to the customer's phone via SMS or read on the OTP. The password expires once it has been used or once its scheduled timing has expired
- data being transmitted over the air should be encrypted
- data stored in the device by the users should also be encrypted
- extreme caution should be taken in allowing users and ICT persons to store the data in external devices, such as fob keys or CDs

Potential threats

Customers are concerned that fraudsters use sophisticated and malicious techniques to:

- thwart existing authentication controls
- gain control of customer accounts
- transfer funds to money mules that facilitate the movement of those funds beyond the reach of insurance companies and law enforcement

Many of these schemes target small to medium-sized business customers since their policies are generally higher than consumer policies and their transaction activity is generally more intense making it easier to hide fraudulent transfers. Frequently they cannot afford strong defenses with respect to large business customers.

A user is exposed to various threats when he/she accesses a system. For instance, in the last two quarters of 2012, the number of unique mobile threats grew by 261 percent, according to ABI Research.[28]

Insurance companies should be aware of the types of potential threats that can affect their digital insurance services.[29] These threats can disrupt the operations of their systems, and transmit or modify the user data. For these reasons, the applications deployed must guarantee privacy, protection, and the integrity of the information they handle. In addition, since some apps can themselves be malware, their functions and activities should be limited (for example, accessing location information via the Global Positioning System [GPS] or address book, transmitting data on the network, sending SMS, and so on).

There are two prime targets for attackers in the case of digital insurance:[30]

- Data: Transactions used in digital insurance may contain sensitive data like personal data, card numbers, authentication information, private and sensitive information, and so on.
- Identity: Devices are more and more customizable, so the device or its contents are associated with a specific person. For example, every mobile device can transmit information related to the owner of the mobile phone contract. An attacker may want to steal the identity of the owner of a personal computer, smartphone, or tablet to commit other offenses.

The possible attacks are:

- Based on the networks, for instance, the Global System for Mobile (GSM) networks. The attacker may try to break the encryption of the network. Once the encryption algorithm of the network is broken, the attacker can intercept all unencrypted communications made by the victim's device.

- Access point twins in which an attacker can try to eavesdrop on Wi-Fi communications to derive information (for instance, user name or password). These types of attack are highly vulnerable, especially in the case of mobile devices since often Wi-Fi is the only means of communication that attackers have to access the Internet.
- Based on vulnerabilities in software applications.
- Based on flaws in the operating system or the firmware.

There is also spam. In theory, there is a regulation to prevent spam. The Privacy and Electronic Communications (EC Directive) Regulations 2003 in the United Kingdom are the overriding antispam legislation in that country.[31] In other countries, it is necessary to take into account of the local legislation. The global nature of the Web is not helping in this direction.

Consequences

When an attacker is able to infect a device or an application, he/she can attempt several things:

- manipulating the device as a zombie machine, that is to say, a machine with which the attacker can communicate and send commands that will be used to transmit sensitive transactions
- recording conversations between the user and others, and sending them to a third party, which can cause user privacy and economic security problems
- stealing a user's identity, usurping the user's identity, and thus impersonating the owner. This raises security concerns where devices can be used to place orders, view financial institution accounts, or are used as an identification device

A tool used effectively by fraudsters is a key logging malware. A key logger is a software program that records the keystrokes entered on the device on which it is installed and transmits a record of those keystrokes to the person controlling the malware over the Internet. Fraudsters use key loggers to steal the login ID and password, and challenge the financial institution customers.

Other types of more sophisticated malware allow fraudsters to perpetrate man-in-the middle (MIM) or man-in-the browser (MIB) attacks on their victims. In a MIM/MIB attack, the fraudster inserts him-/herself between the customer and the financial institution. He/she hijacks the online session. In one scenario, the fraudster is able to intercept the authentication credentials submitted by the customer and log into the user's account. In another scenario, the fraudster does not intercept the credentials, but modifies the transaction content or inserts additional transactions, not authorized by the user, that transfer funds to accounts controlled by the fraudster.

MIM/MIB attacks may be used to circumvent some strong authentication methods and other controls, including OTP tokens. Since the OTP is generally only good for 30–60 seconds after a password is generated, the fraudster must intercept and use it in real time in order to compromise the customer's account.

Controls

Customers should be aware of the security techniques that can be used to help detect and prevent the types of attacks described above. Some of these techniques have been in use for some time, while others are relatively new.

Countermeasures

The security mechanisms in place to counter threats can be divided into different categories, since not all function at the same level. They range from the management of security by the operating system to behavioral education of the user. The threats prevented by the various measures are not the same, and depend on the case. Considering the cases mentioned above, in the first, one would protect the system from corruption by an application, and in the second, one would prevent the installation of suspicious software.

Application control

Antivirus and firewall. Antivirus software can be deployed on a device to verify that it is not infected by a known threat, usually by signature detection software that detects malicious executable files. A firewall, meanwhile, can watch over the existing traffic on the network and assure that a malicious application does not seek to communicate through it. It may equally verify that an installed application does not seek to establish suspicious communication, which may prevent an intrusion attempt.

Transaction confirmation. In the same vein, it is important to confirm certain actions on the application by a user decision. The Turing test helps in distinguishing between a human and a virtual user. It often comes as a captcha (Completely Automated Public Turing Test to tell Computers and Humans Apart). This is a request to the user to type a certain sequence of characters that have been partially hidden or obstructed. It is difficult for a computer program to solve such a test, and therefore suspicious activities must be subject to approval or denial by the user.

An easier way is to confirm certain relevant transactions (such as money payments) is by using a physical or virtual token.

Security software

Above the operating system security, there could be a layer of security software. This layer is composed of individual components to strengthen various vulnerabilities to prevent malware, intrusions, identification of a user as a human, and user authentication.

The security layer contains software components considered to be effective for the security from experiences. On smartphones or tablets, this software must deal with greater constraints.

The following sections help clarify some of the security software available.

Authentication. Insurance companies should take a layered approach to security and authentication. For example, in the first layer, insurance companies may require customers to register their device to an existing online account. In the second layer, they may require customers to enter a password each time they access their account via their devices. However, none of the controls discussed ensures the absolute prevention or detection of a successful attack, because the types of attacks are innovated continuously.

Customers should be aware that a number of institutions are requiring "out-of-band" authentication or verification of high-value and/or anomalous transactions. Out-of-band authentication means that a transaction that is initiated via one delivery channel (for instance, a mobile device) must be reauthenticated or verified via an independent delivery channel (for instance, a telephone) in order for the transaction to be completed. Out-of-band authentication is becoming more popular given that customers' mobiles are increasingly vulnerable to malware attacks.

However, out-of-band authentication directed to or input through the same device that initiates the transaction may not be effective since that device may have been compromised. For business customers, someone other than the person who first initiated the transaction can provide the out-of-band authentication or verification. It can also be combined with other administrative controls.

The Federal Insurance Companies Examination Council provides some guidelines to improve security.[32]

Institutions should no longer rely on one form of customer authentication. A one-dimensional customer authentication program is simply not robust enough to provide the level of security that customers expect and that protects institutions from financial and reputation risk.

Layered security controls do not have to be complex.[33]

Financial services institutions have continued to innovate in response to the increasing cyber threat environment.

Other control methods for customer authentication include keystroke dynamics and biometrics based responses. Additionally, institutions can look to traditional and innovative business process controls to improve security over users' online activities. Some examples include:

- establishing, requiring, and periodically reviewing volume and value limitations or parameters for the activities a user can functionally accomplish while accessing the online system
- monitoring and alerting on some events which are not usual by that user
- establishing individual transaction and aggregate account exposure limits based on expected account activity
- registering and tracing those users who are being provided a particular privilege, service, mobility, or access and/or blacklisting them
- requiring business customers to deploy double control routines over higher risk functions performed online

ERGO Direkt

TÜV Süd tested ERGO Direkt's mobile website for quality, security, and transparency for the first time in 2014, and awarded it the "s@fer-shopping" seal of approval. ERGO Direkt was therefore the first company in the German insurance industry to receive this certification for a website designed for mobile devices.[34] The audit included the quick navigation and easy usage of the website, from the initial contact by the customer to cancel an insurance policy. Another important point was assuring that personal data is securely kept.

Access control. The key aspect that differentiates the mobile channel from other self-service channels, such as the Web or mobile, is the concept of "known device." Device identification is a key part of security because it is the second factor of a two-factor identification security model. In the context of rich-customer applications security, the application has the capability for local storage and data processing. This allows for the support of security features in addition to those supplied in a native mode by a phone and by telecommunication operators. For example, each instance of a downloaded application should have its own unique ID and PIN, allowing validation of server requests and detection of potential spoofing activities.

Because a dedicated ID is delivered with each application download, the rich-customer application inherently delivers multifactor authentication. The mobile or web solution should be integrated into the insurance company's existing multifactor authentication infrastructure.

Examples of other strong authentication measures include hardware and software tokens or biometrics.

Device fingerprinting. A device fingerprinting process further increases security capabilities by dynamically capturing device-specific elements such as network operator, device type, and IP address. These elements are then used to determine which transactions may be allowed, providing a higher level of certainty for insurance companies and users alike, especially when dealing with high-value transactions.

Biometrics identification. An effective way to identify customers is biometrics. Biometrics is a technique of identifying a person by means of his or her morphology (through recognition of the fingerprint, or the iris of the eye or the face, for example) or behavior (the signature or style of writing, for example). One advantage of using biometrics security is that users do not need to remember a password or other secret combination to authenticate and prevent malicious users from accessing their device. In a system with strong biometrics security, only the recognized user can access the smartphone or the tablet. Commercial devices with such identification are becoming more and more available in the market.

Decades of improvements in voice and facial recognition are also helping reduce false negatives and friction – facial recognition takes two seconds. And a growing exasperation with forgotten, lost, or stolen passwords may drive people toward face- or voice-based logins.

Anti-malware software. Anti-malware software may provide a defense against key loggers[35] and MIM/MIB attacks. Anti-malware is a term used to describe various software products referred as antivirus or antispyware. Anti-malware software helps in preventing, detecting, blocking, and removing adware, spyware, and other forms of malware such as key loggers. Anti-malware is generally signature based. Some advanced versions of malware continuously alter their signature.

Transaction monitoring/anomaly detection software has been in use for a number of years. Similar to the manner in which the card industry detects and blocks fraudulent transactions, systems are now available to monitor digital insurance activity for suspicious transactions.

Manual or automated transaction monitoring/anomaly detection can assist in preventing many fraudulent actions whenever they are perceived as clearly out of the ordinary when compared with the customer's established patterns of behavior. Automated systems may also look at the velocity of a transaction and other similar factors to determine whether the transaction is suspicious.

Encryption

It is possible to encrypt in several ways:

- Encryption of stored data. PC, smartphones, and especially tablets have a significant memory size, and their storage capacity is increasing. They can carry several gigabytes of data. The user must be careful about what stored data it carries and whether it should be protected. No private data should be stored locally inside the application. All sensitive information held in memory, such as passwords, pins, and encryption keys, should be possibly erased or overwritten by the application itself. Furthermore, when a user decides to change the device, he or she must remove all personal data on the device.
- Transmission encryption. Because it is always possible that data that is exchanged can be intercepted, communications, or even information storage, should rely on encryption to prevent a malicious entity from using any data obtained during the communications. This poses the problem of key exchange for encryption algorithms, which requires a secure channel.
- The primary option for encryption is transport layer security (TLS). Many devices support TLS. It provides a proven, industry standard security protocol for the transport of data from the phone to the financial institution's internal servers.

Resource monitoring. When an application passes the various security barriers, it can take some actions for which it was designed. When such actions are triggered, the activity of a malicious application can sometimes be detected if one monitors the various resources used on the device. Depending on the goals of the malware, the consequences of infection are not always the same. Malicious applications are not intended to harm the devices on which they are deployed.

Memory, network, or any other resource usage is inherent in any application. However, if one finds that a substantial proportion of the resources is used by an application, it may be flagged as suspicious. The application should send an alert or stop the transactions altogether.

This observation is essentially an alert, because some legitimate applications can be very resource intensive in terms of resource utilization, the best examples being streaming video or downloading images.

Network control. On a device, many applications are bound to connect via the network, as part of their normal operation. Unusual activity can be monitored, and if necessary, stopped, by examining abnormal network activity.

Penetration testing. An application penetration testing (or just pen test) is the simulation of an attack on a web or a mobile site with the aim of evaluating the effectiveness of an application's security controls. The objective is to find the risks posed by possible exploitable vulnerabilities. The penetration test model is built around a manual testing process by friendly hackers. This process can go much further than the generic responses, false positive findings, and lack of depth provided by automated application assessment tools.

Device and app penetration testing can help organizations pinpoint and correct flaws in their applications and devices, as well as understand the risks posed by new platforms or applications.

Insurance companies should regularly conduct penetration testing as new features are added to applications and new threats appear in the environment.

Experience dictates that pen tests are very useful in learning a lot about the holes in the security. They greatly help developers in improving their work.

Security recommendations for digital insurance. Understanding security risks and implementing the highest levels of security into digital insurance offerings through a broad range of measures is critical to the success and adoption of digital insurance. In fact, 43 percent of the finance departments that responded to Aite Group's October 2010 survey stated that they would not adopt financial services via a mobile device due to concerns about security.[36]

In order to improve security, there are many actions that should be taken. Their effectiveness is not 100 percent. However, they certainly can reduce in a substantial way the risks connected with the use of digital insurance.

User awareness

User awareness is the most important measure to adopt to improve security. It is important not only to prevent security breaches but also to improve the detection and remediation of security issues.

Much malicious behavior can cause harm due to the carelessness of the user. The user has a large responsibility in the cycle of security. He/she may:

- leave the device without a password
- fail to give precise control of permissions granted to applications added to the device
- share the password with other persons

Insurance companies should not aim to scare their customers away from using digital insurance. They should launch campaigns to increase awareness of the danger of being careless with a device or application.

These precautions are important also if the user is an employee of an organization that uses corporate digital insurance. Detailed below are some precautions that a user can take to improve security.[37]

Users should be careful to protect their devices through simple actions and precautions, such as:

- locking the device when not using it
- not leaving their device unattended
- not trusting messages received or strange behavior of applications
- not storing sensitive data in the device
- encrypting sensitive data that cannot be separated from the device

Users should not believe everything that may be presented by an application. Some information may be phishing or attempting to distribute a malicious application.

When installing applications, it is good to warn the users against sets of permissions that, grouped together, seem potentially dangerous, or at least suspicious. Along with the app stores, a new feature for mobile apps has appeared: remote revocation.[38] First developed on Android devices, this procedure can remotely and globally uninstall an application on any device that has it.

New versions of various software components of a device, including operating systems and their releases or patches, are published regularly. They can correct many flaws over time.

The mass distribution of applications is accompanied by the establishment of different permissions mechanisms for each operating system. It is necessary to clarify these permissions mechanisms to users, as they differ from one system to another.

Forensic

Digital forensics is the examination of hardware or software in the pursuit of evidence to disprove or prove an allegation.

Devices are rooted in their own operating systems, file systems, file formats, and methods of communication. Dealing with this creates unique problems for examiners. Performing a forensic exam on a device requires use of special software and special knowledge of the way these devices work, as well as where possible evidence could be stored.

A sound forensic foundation requires:[39]

- evidence collection
- evidence preservation
- analysis
- reporting

These foundations are the core of dealing with all types of traditional digital devices. However, when it comes to nontraditional devices like handhelds, these foundations change based on how a forensic examiner might apply them.

Montana Department of Public Health and Human Services

In June 2014, a computer server at the Montana Department of Public Health and Human Services was hacked, affecting 1,062,509 individuals – a number that nearly matches the state's population. An investigation found the server likely was initially attacked in July 2013. Breached information included patient names, addresses, birth dates, and Social Security numbers, employee names, and bank account numbers. All individuals were offered a year of credit and identity protection services.

Utah Department of Public Health

The Utah Department of Public Health in April 2012 announced the hacking of a server holding information on 780,000 Medicaid and Children's Health

Insurance Program (CHIP) recipients. About 280,000 individuals had their Social Security numbers stolen and were offered a year of credit monitoring services. Other breached information included names, birthdates, and addresses. The server, which held Medicaid eligibility determination transactions, was in the State's Department of Technology Services, and the head of the department subsequently lost his job.

Triple-S Management

Triple-S Management, a Blue Cross and Blue Shield plan serving more than one million members in Puerto Rico, in 2010 learned that it was hacked by employees of a competitor who downloaded data on more than 475,000 insured individuals into its own information systems. The employees had gone rogue, and the competitor itself reported the breach to Triple-S. The hacking employees used active user IDs and passwords specific to Triple-S' database to access the information. The likely target was financial information related to the government insurance plan rather than individuals' information.

USAA

The use of facial recognition for authentication is rare in insurance companies' applications. United Services Automobile Association (USAA), the San Antonio, Texas, financial services company, chose facial recognition so that it could deliver biometrics to the largest base of Android and iOS users possible – all smartphones have cameras that make face capture quick and easy.[40]

The advantage of face over voice recognition is that it takes two seconds or less to take a picture of the user's face. Voice requires a certain amount of dialogue, usually around 20 or so seconds, in order to validate the signature of the voice.

Voice recognition is also heavily reliant on environmental factors like background noise.

The key point is that the company must use device identification in the background, so each time a member logs in, an encrypted token is sent from his or her phone to USAA, which is matched against the ID of the device registered at enrollment. So for a fraudster to successfully impersonate a member with a photo or video (or trying to mimic his/her voice), he or she would also have to steal the member's mobile device. The other security mechanism is that USAA requires the member to blink, which rules out the use of a static photo.

Security experts give USAA's approach high marks, especially for the facial recognition technology that watches the eye region of an image and looks for the user to blink. The combination of requiring the right device, a face match, and a blink at the right time should prove to be far more accurate and secure than a password, thumbprint, or a fingerprint.

USAA is also allowing voice recognition, in part for circumstances like driving a car, when taking a photo would be inconvenient. The program asks members to read a short phrase out loud.

Conclusions

Governance is sometimes neglected in the implementation of innovations. However, its importance cannot be minimized. Governance has many important aspects: project management, data quality, security, and so on. Security is certainly also the biggest threat for digital insurance. Security management has to be able to cope with the possible magnitude of the attacks. Due to the computing and storage power of the digital applications, the extent and the size of the damage could be substantial.

However, there are solutions to help prevent and to manage security threats. The real effective defense against threats depends on the actions that insurance companies that are pushing digital insurance can take. In this respect, actions to increase the awareness of the users are very important.

As the next chapters detail, the future will be more interesting but also more challenging in terms of security.

6
Regulatory Framework

Introduction

Digital insurance can be a success due to many reasons, such as:

- convenience for the customer and the insurance company
- easy and relatively inexpensive access to telecommunication networks
- low market barriers
- the increasingly global nature of the business and the interactions between people

Digital insurance, similar to e-commerce, requires transparent and clear regulations as the contracting parties are not in physical contact.

The introduction of a digital media has made many potential customers suspicious of such innovation. On the part of the customer, there are concerns about the privacy and security of personal data (especially, for instance, PIN numbers or credit card information) and the potential misuse of private data while carrying out electronic transactions. On the part of insurance companies, there are concerns about fraud and money laundering issues. Regulators are concerned on both aspects (fraud and money laundering) plus the respect of taxation and accounting principles.

The contracting parties, therefore, should be fully compliant with the law and regulations to protect them for digital transactions they execute when, for instance, using mobile devices. The customer should be able to rely on the privacy of his or her personal data. A clearly defined regulatory framework is essential to boosting customer confidence and increasing acceptance among the potential customers of digital insurance, as well as to ensuring its smooth functioning.

Legal regulations aim to safeguard and balance the interests of both the customers, the financial institutions, and the community at large by setting rules and regulating the market, as well as controlling the usage of existing and emerging solutions. They tend to impose a high level of restrictions that govern legally carried-out transactions.

There are multiple regulators. A CIO of a leading insurance company in Europe summed up the situation with these words: "Regulators aim to protect consumers, which is laudable, but there are now multiple regulators with sometimes conflicting agendas. This creates much difficulty for us."[1]

The good news is that most of the digital insurance transactions are processed just like any other financial input or output transactions. As such, when dealing with digital insurance, one can focus on those functions that are different with respect to other channels, such as remote device connection (RDC) or financial institution web and mobile apps.

This chapter describes some of the most relevant aspects in terms of compliance with regulations in the case of insurance companies.[2]

Regulations for insurance organizations: from Solvency II to customer protection

One of the challenges for all companies, and particularly for financial services organizations, is compliance. Take, for example, the case of an insurance company. It needs to comply by 2016 and early 2017 with:

- regulations known as Solvency II, international regulations with very strict requirements in terms of liquidity, among other matters. Very likely there will be further regulations along similar but more stringent lines
- generally accepted accounting standards (GAAP)
- the second Insurance Mediation Directive (IMD2), which provides local regulators with the option of banning commission payments and includes specific requirements on product oversight and governance
- the Packaged Retail Investment Products (PRIPS) initiative
- the second Market in Financial Instruments Directive (MiFID2)
- the EU data privacy regulations
- anti-money laundering regulations
- anti-terrorist regulations
- equality legislation

The objectives of all these regulatory initiatives are to assure greater transparency in terms of the information provided to customers, revisions to the relationships with intermediaries, and greater governance and oversight over new and existing products.

All these regulations are likely to create significant changes to product and sales procedures and internal controls going forward. These initiatives will have a great influence on the governance of insurance organizations, control and risk frameworks, sales processes, customer operations, and information and communications technology (ICT). These changes will have strategic impact on intermediary relationships and product pricing. Insurance companies should develop and implement as soon as possible plans for ensuring that the regulation deadlines can be achieved and appropriate market strategies can be executed to maintain or gain market share.

Regulations are felt, particularly in some parts of the world, as an inhibitor to digital transformation. For instance, Celent surveyed these aspects in the Asia-Pacific region. Some of its findings follow.[3] The Asia-Pacific insurance companies recognize challenges in the legacy technology issues (63 percent) but also on regulation (44 percent), a lack of a compelling business case (41 percent), and perceived customer/data security issues (40 percent). The "slow pace of delivery by insurance companies," which is considered the second-strongest global inhibitor, ranks fifth in the Asia-Pacific region, with the regulatory environment is far more of a concern. The focus on regulatory concerns may be explained by the number and diversity of regulatory jurisdictions in the Asia-Pacific region. Regulatory environments vary from traditionally prescriptive to more permissive regimes. Asian regulators have historically been more protective of a less sophisticated customer class, taking a more prescriptive approach. The region has undergone a rapid, wide-ranging evolution in the regulatory environment in recent years. New customer protection regulations may impose tighter compliance requirements on insurance companies, for example, related to the education and training of sales and customer service staff. Evolving regulations will certainly affect the ways that insurance companies can respond to the digital insurance challenge.

Solvency II

The Solvency II Directive (2009/138/EC) is a European Union (EU) directive that codifies and harmonizes EU insurance regulations.[4] Primarily, this directive concerns the amount of capital that EU insurance companies must hold to reduce the risk of insolvency.

Following an EU Parliament vote on the Omnibus II Directive on 11 March 2014, Solvency II comes into effect on 1 January 2016. This date has been previously pushed back many times.

EU insurance legislation aims to create a single EU insurance market and enhance customer protection. The third-generation Insurance Directives established an "EU passport" (single license) for insurance companies to operate in all member states if they fulfill the EU conditions. Many member states concluded that the EU regulations were not enough, and took up their own reforms, which still led to differing regulations, hampering the goal of a single market.

Since the initial Solvency I Directive 73/239/EEC was introduced in 1973, more elaborate risk management systems have developed. Solvency II reflects new risk management practices to define required capital and manage risk. The Solvency I Directive was aimed at revising and updating the current EU solvency regime. Solvency II has a much wider scope. A solvency capital requirement has the following objectives:

- to reduce the risk that an insurance company would be unable to meet claims
- to reduce the losses suffered by policy holders in the event that an insurance company is unable to meet fully all claims
- to provide early warning to supervisors so that they can intervene promptly if capital falls below the required level
- to promote confidence in the financial stability of the insurance sector

Solvency II is somewhat similar to the banking regulations of Basel II. It has three main areas (pillars):

- Pillar 1 consists of the quantitative requirements (for example, the amount of capital an insurance company should hold).
- Pillar 2 sets out the requirements for the governance and risk management of insurance companies, as well as for the effective supervision of insurance companies.
- Pillar 3 focuses on disclosure and transparency requirements.

The contents of the Solvency II directive are:

- Title I General rules on the taking-up and pursuit of direct insurance and reinsurance activities

  - Chapter I Subject matter, scope and definitions
  - Chapter II Taking-up of business
  - Chapter III Supervisory authorities and general rules
  - Chapter IV Conditions governing business
  - Chapter V Pursuit of life and non-life insurance activity
  - Chapter VI Rules relating to the valuation of assets and liabilities, technical provisions, own funds, solvency capital requirement, minimum capital requirement, and investment rules
  - Chapter VII Insurance and reinsurance undertakings in difficulty or in an irregular situation
  - Chapter VIII Right of establishment and freedom to provide services
  - Chapter IX Branches established within the community and belonging to insurance or reinsurance undertakings with head offices situated outside the community
  - Chapter X Subsidiaries of insurance and reinsurance undertakings governed by the laws of a third country and acquisitions of holdings by such undertakings
- Title II Specific provisions for insurance and reinsurance
- Title III Supervision of insurance and reinsurance undertakings in a group
- Title IV Reorganization and winding-up of insurance undertakings

Solvency II requirements

Effective data management is at the root of most Solvency II requirements. Insurance companies have usually generated risk reporting internally, even if they depend to some extent on externally provided data. Without modifications, this internal-only strategy is not sustainable in the face of the Solvency II requirements. The UK Financial Services Authority's (FSA's) internal model approval process (IMAP) thematic review findings explicitly identify data management as an area in which insurance companies need to do substantial work to achieve compliance.[5]

Reporting and analysis requirements outlined in Solvency II are more demanding than any existing reporting framework for insurance companies. Some of the biggest challenges are:

- establishing and monitoring the source of key data
- assigning ownership
- implementing quality metrics

Pillar 1

The pillar 1 framework sets out qualitative and quantitative requirements for the calculation of technical provisions and solvency capital requirement (SCR) using either a standard formula given by regulators or an internal model developed by the (re)insurance company. Technical provisions comprise two components: the best estimate of the liabilities (that is, the central actuarial estimate) and a risk margin. Technical provisions are intended to represent the current amount the (re)insurance company would have to pay for an immediate transfer of its obligations to a third party.

The SCR is the capital required to ensure that a (re)insurance company would be able to meet its obligations over the next 12 months with a probability of at least 99.5 percent. In addition to the SCR capital, a minimum capital requirement (MCR) must be calculated. This represents the threshold below which the national supervisor (regulator) would intervene. The MCR is intended to correspond to an 85 percent probability of adequacy over a one-year period, and is bounded between 25 percent and 45 percent of the SCR.

For supervisory purposes, the SCR and MCR can be regarded as "soft" and "hard" floors respectively. A regulatory ladder of intervention applies once the capital holding of the (re)insurance undertaking falls below the SCR, with the intervention becoming progressively more intense as the capital holding approaches the MCR. The Solvency II Directive provides regional supervisors with a number of actions they can take to address breaches of the MCR, including the withdrawal of authorization from selling new business and the winding up of the company.

Pillar 2

The 2011 Report on the Fifth Quantitative Impact Study (QIS5) for Solvency II by the European Insurance and Occupational Pensions Authority (EIOPA) underlined that 20 percent of the firms reported that their data (relating to core Pillar II data such as valuations, asset reference, and pricing and policyholder static) were not absent or substantially incomplete. Eighty percent reported gaps where required data was unavailable or where the quality and completeness were under question.[6] Some data were normally managed manually using spreadsheets, requiring a full audit and application of governance policy.

Overall, firms responding to the EIOPA survey reported six different initiatives necessary to deliver Pillar II requirements:[7]

- data quality (validation)
- gap analysis (identification and mitigation)
- processes (data governance)
- control (focusing on external source controls)
- look-through (requirements on pooled fund valued position and security reference data)
- infrastructure (data warehouse and workflow)

Fifty-seven percent of EIOPA survey respondents said they had high or medium exposure to third-party providers such as risk modelers, third-party fund managers, custodians, and ex-EEA parent companies.[8] It is necessary that data audits extend across all these external providers.

Good quality data is the starting point for a successful Solvency II process, and many insurance companies have responded by establishing dedicated teams whose tasks are to focus on data governance and quality. Many companies have launched projects to improve the availability of the data required by Solvency II from their systems.

Pillar 3

The requirements under Pillar 3 of Solvency II are sufficiently clear. Their interpretations, however, are different country by country. For instance, in Belgium and the United Kingdom, there are requirements to involve auditors. In the Netherlands, this is not the case. Organizations are seeking to ensure that transitional reporting is reliable and that disclosures are clear and of high quality, recognizing that the recipients of these documents look carefully at them for the first time.

Capital optimization is also receiving a new focus as firms look to change the composition of their balance sheets. While not all firms are going for internal model approval, they are all subject to the governance requirements set out under the directive. They have to complete and submit to their regulator(s) a Forward Looking Assessment of Own Risks (FLAOR) or Own Risk and Solvency Assessment (ORSA) as preparation for Solvency II.

All these regulations require not only platforms but also products, processes, platforms, and people (called the Four P's in this book). The forward looking assessment needs to be integrated into decision-making, ensuring activities such as business planning and stress and scenario testings are aligned to what is required under Solvency II. There will be gaps, which need to be overcome or at least remediated. Organizations need to identify the gaps and consider how to ensure their governance structures are robust and their ORSA processes are effective.

Markets in financial instruments directive (MiFID)

MiFID II/MiFIR introduces changes that will have a large impact on the EU's financial markets. There are transparency requirements for a broader range of asset classes, the obligation to trade derivatives on-exchange, requirements on algorithmic and high-frequency trading, and new supervisory tools for commodity derivatives. It also strengthens the protection for retail investors through limits on the use of commissions, conditions for the provision of independent investment advice, stricter organizational requirements for product design and distribution, product intervention powers, and the disclosure of costs and charges.

MiFID II/MiFIR empowers the European Securities and Markets Authority (ESMA) to propose regulatory technical standards (RTS) and implementing technical standards (ITS).

Generally accepted accounting principle (GAAP)

GAAPs are generally known as accounting standards or standard accounting practices. They are the standard framework of guidelines for financial accounting used in any given jurisdiction. These include the standards, conventions, and rules that accountants should follow in recording and summarizing and in the preparation of financial statements.

Many county and city governments in the United States choose to "opt out" of GAAP practices as they operate on a cash basis, as opposed to an accrual basis.

Regulations on customer and data protection

The regulations applicable to digital insurance are guided generally by five principles:[9]

1. legal enforceability of contracts
2. customer protection
3. privacy of data (no unnecessary, unauthorized data access and collection)
4. confidentiality of data (protecting data from misuse)
5. right of self-determination (to carry out or reject a communication)

Digital insurance, being a relatively recent phenomenon, has not yet attracted much attention from lawmakers as an independent business field. Its web and mobile transactions in many countries are governed by the electronic commerce and telecommunication regulations. More and more regional and national regulations are issuing specific regulations for the financial services industry. Some European nations have issued regulations that are expected to provide a reliable and modern legal framework in order to better exploit the benefits of these new solutions while ensuring a high degree of customer protection.

Many of these regulations have their origins in multilateral treaties, such as those of the EU or the United Nations (UN). Other international organizations, such as the Organization for Economic Cooperation and Development (OECD), the World Trade Organization (WTO), and the World Intellectual Property Organization (WIPO), have been actively supporting member countries in formulating regulatory frameworks. These international regulations are important due to the international characteristics of the Internet, even if the degree of regulations might differ across states.

The EU has issued 12 directives to ensure legal certainty and customer confidence. They define the regulatory framework for (among others)[10]

- legally binding electronic commercial contracts
- determination of jurisdiction and applicability
- customer and data protection
- protection of intellectual property rights (IPR)
- dispute resolution
- cyber crimes
- taxation regimes

These EU directives define the regulatory framework for member states while ensuring compliance with international treaties, most importantly, the Model Law on Electronic Commerce passed by the United Nations Commission on International Trade Law (UNCITRAL).[11]

Regulations on digital insurance products, services, and practices continue to evolve alongside the solutions that supports these next-generation solutions. It is imperative for insurance companies that are entering the new world of digital insurance to keep up to date on the rules and requirements. Not respecting the law subjects the financial institution not only to the risks of regulatory scrutiny and possible fines but also undermines customers' confidence in the financial institution's ability to provide adequately and fairly the latest solutions to protect their customers.

In terms of vendor partners and solution providers working with the financial institution (for instance, in the United States) in the execution of the customer's strategy for digital insurance, it is important to verify some points:[12]

- Does the information security program of the vendor comply with the Gramm-Leach-Bliley Act, if in the US?
- Are the proper disclosures and notifications accessible to customers?
- Are updates easily communicated and accepted by the customers?

In addition to getting the answers to these questions, it is important for insurance companies to have a compliance team (or an individual assigned to compliance) in place to keep track of changing regulations that may affect digital insurance applications. This team should report at a very high level in the organization. This is a requirement by the central regulators in many countries.

Regulations can be tricky. While they may not seem to have an impact on a specific application, there can be an indirect impact that could put the insurance company in a bad situation if it is not in compliance by the stated deadline.

When insurance companies launch digital insurance, they need to consider also how to authenticate their customers in the digital insurance environment. This is especially important since security is very important for the customers and the regulators. The American Federal Financial Institutions Examination Council (FFIEC) Guidance on Authentication in an Internet Banking Environment is a good source to consult. The guidance was originally issued in October 2005, with a supplement issued in June 2011. While neither specifically mentions digital insurance, the *FDIC Winter 2011 Supervisory Insights* refers readers to the guidance.[13] It requires financial institutions to perform a full risk assessment for every new technological innovation to be renewed every year.

The protection of the private sphere of the customer and the prevention of unauthorized use of personal data have been of primary concern for lawmakers in order to safeguard the public interest, on the one hand, and to increase customer confidence in the digital form of commerce, on the other hand. The EU defines and protects personal data as "any information relating to any identified or identifiable natural person."[14]

For this purpose, several stringent regulations have been put in place. For instance:[15]

1. Personal data may only be collected, processed, or used with the explicit and written consent of the user.
2. If the user is offered the choice to give his/her consent electronically, the provider/vendor must guarantee that such consent can only be given by an unambiguous and deliberate act by the user.
3. The text of such consent should be accessible at any time by the user.

4. The consent may be withdrawn by the user at any time.
5. Personal data cannot be processed for any other purpose than the one for which it has been explicitly collected.
6. There should be separate processing of user data for the use of different services.
7. Data that is no longer required must be deleted without delay.
8. Customer profiles, even if anonymous, can only be created with the consent of the customer.
9. The user may demand from the financial institution information on the data on the user that is stored at the institution.
10. There are also territorial regulations: personal data on European citizens cannot be accessed outside the EU.
11. Violations of these regulations by the financial institution or the failure to inform the user of his or her rights constitute an administrative offense, punishable with a monetary fine.

Before an insurance company begins to move to become a digital insurance company and continuously afterward, it is important to review existing disclosures to see if they also cover all new and existing channels. If not, the institution needs to send out updated disclosures. The updates should include any limit and restriction for digital insurance. It should also remind customers when data storage and device usage charges will apply and on which transactions.

These regulations are basic, general norms. The law provides for exceptions in extraordinary situations. Government authorities have the power to authorize such exceptions.

Digital transaction investigation and monitoring

Once a customer uses digital insurance services, there is a host of new and old compliance to consider. In the United States, the financial institution is responsible for Regulation E errors. Primarily, all of the traditional rules for error resolution still apply, such as the definition of "error," limitations on customer liability, investigations timing, and provisional credit.

How the financial institution investigates reported errors becomes more complex because people tend to share devices in a way that they do not share their wallets.

In many countries, there are regulations for tracing the use of the devices and of the applications. They are useful for compliance but also for the security of the insurance company.

Digital insurance and mobile commerce

It might be interesting to analyze the German law-regime for the mobile commerce closely connected to digital insurance,[16] since it is typical of regulations in many countries in Europe.

Digital commerce is organized in Germany under the Information and Telecommunication Services Act (*Informations- und Kommunikationsdienste Gesetz*, known as *IuKDG*). This act consists of a large subset of related clauses. The cornerstones of this law-regime are:[17]

1. the Act on Legal Framework Conditions for Electronic Commerce (*Gesetz über rechtliche Rahmenbedingungen für den elektronischen Geschäftsverkehr*, also known as the *Elektronischer Geschäftsverkehr-Gesetz*, or EGG)
2. the Teleservices Act (*Teledienstgesetz*, known as TDG)
3. the Teleservices Data Protection Act (*Teledienstedatenschutzgesetz*, known as TDDSG)
4. the Conditional Access Services Protection Act (*Zugangskontroll-diensteschutzgesetz*, known as ZKDSG)
5. the Interstate Agreement on Media Services (*Mediendienstestaats-vertrag*, known as MDStV)

Another relevant law that is not a part of the IuKDG is the Act of Distant Sales (*Fernabsatzgesetz*). These regulations follow an EU directive on Electronic Commerce (2000/31/EC). The regulations are integrated in Book 1 (General Part) and Book 2 (Law of Obligations) of the German Civil Law.[18]

Online sales to customers

When a company launches digital insurance, it is essential that they protect the customer not only in terms of the solidity of the insurance company (see, for instance, Solvency II) and the protection of personal data (Data Privacy) but also from the point of view of the transparency, simplicity, and fairness in the market for customer financial products or services. An increasing percentage of customers already use digital and remote channels. In addition, more and more customers are interested to use these channels when and where they are available. It is expected that, due to market developments in this area, potential customer damages may become an increasing issue for financial supervisory authorities.

EIOPA was established in consequence of the reforms to the structure of supervision of the financial sector in the EU. The reform was initiated by the European Commission, following the recommendations of a Committee of Wise Men, chaired by Jacques de Larosière, and supported by the European Council and Parliament.[19]

Before and during the financial crisis in 2007 and 2008, the European Parliament called for a move toward more integrated European supervision in order to ensure a true level playing field for all actors within the EU and to reflect the increasing integration of financial markets in the Union. As a result, the supervisory framework was strengthened to reduce risk and the severity of future financial crises. EIOPA is part of a European System of Financial Supervisors that comprises three European Supervisory Authorities, one for the banking sector, one for the securities sector, and one for the insurance and occupational pensions sector, as well as the European Systemic Risk Board.

EIOPA expresses opinions on different issues related to its areas of competence.[20] Opinions are provided upon a request from the European Parliament, the Council, or the Commission, as well as on EIOPA's own initiative. Opinions aim, inter alia, at building a common EU supervisory culture and consistent supervisory practices, as well as ensuring uniform procedures and consistent approaches throughout the EU.

EIOPA has provided an "Opinion" concerning customer protection issues related to product sales via the Internet.[21] This Opinion may apply to sales and distribution channels that include Internet sales, even where such sales are not explicitly referred to. This opinion is particularly relevant for digital insurance initiatives.

This Opinion is addressed to the National Competent Authorities (NCAs). EIOPA has invited the NCAs to increase their level of awareness of and monitoring of the market with regard to the use of the Internet as a distribution channel.

Customers can find lot of information online. Digital research can help empower customers in making an informed choice. This may help mitigate general information asymmetries that exist between customers on the one hand, and insurance distributors and insurance undertakings on the other. The surfeit of information online, and the different ways this can be filtered or presented, can also present challenges for customers. Behavioral economics has found that, in general, most people do not conduct sufficient searches for information, even in a context where plenty of information is available. They instead tend to rely on rules of thumb that can be subject to biases and distortions. Most customers do not read standard disclosure documents outlining the details of products ("fine prints") when buying online. They focus only on the price of the product or service.

On the other side, distributors, such as comparators or even insurance companies themselves, sometimes do not provide sufficient advice when distributing their products, or the information displayed is not enough. This may lead customers to buy products and services that insufficiently meet their needs and requirements or on the contrary include services not really necessary.

Customers wishing to research policies via the Internet may not be fully aware that they may inadvertently enter into unsolicited contracts. This can be particularly the case given the various options and fields to check off, also taking into account that sometimes such fields are checked off as default options by the distributor. Such inadvertent and unsolicited contracts may be caused by a lack of comprehension of the online purchasing process.

Additionally, the potentially transient nature of online information increases the challenge. It is difficult to monitor emerging digital distribution channels or distribution by e-mail. Supervisors may also face challenges due to the existence of different supervisory tools for online sales supervision, like a monitoring tool only for advertising and websites of supervised entities.

If not remedied, these issues could lead to a number of undesirable outcomes. Customers might buy insurance that is unsuitable, risk concluding an invalid or unsolicited contract, or fail to conclude a contract. That is, their needs and demands would not be met. Customers may choose an insurance policy based solely on the price offered, where material differences in quality and coverages should also be considered. They may not seek or receive other information important for the decision-making process, such as disclosure documents, information on the distributor's customer services, and the level of any guarantee provided.

Directive 2002/65/EC concerning the distance marketing of customer financial services set down fundamental rights for consumers.[22] For example, the Directive establishes an obligation to provide customers with comprehensive information on the provider, the financial service, the distant contract and means of redress, before a contract is concluded; the consumer's right to withdraw from the contract during a cooling-off period; a ban on abusive marketing practices seeking to oblige customers to buy a service they have not solicited ("inertia selling"); and rules to restrict other practices such as unsolicited phone calls and e-mails ("cold-calling" and "spamming"). Nevertheless, a cooling-off period would not necessarily address all issues with unsolicited contracts identified in the EIOPA Opinion.

EIOPA's Customer Trends Report in 2013 found several issues related to the disclosure of information, new channels for sales, and the marketing of products and services, especially via the Web, including social networks.[23] In 2014, EIOPA issued a Report on Good Practices on Comparison Websites.[24] The Report found that customers tend to rely very much on the price of products shown in the initial list of the comparators, rather than the underlying terms and conditions. Misleading information may be provided to customers due to conflicts of interest stemming from close commercial links among insurance companies and commercial comparison websites. Comparison websites may not necessarily be suitable for certain types of insurance products, for instance some life insurance products, such as the unit-linked policies.

Future requirements applicable in the EU for the provision of services to customers will include *inter alia* better information to consumers. In this respect, Regulation 1286/2014 of the European Parliament and the Council on key information documents for packaged retail and insurance-based investment products (PRIIPs) introduces a common standard for key information documents. It can improve the transparency of PRIIPs offered to retail investors, irrespective of the distribution channel used.

In its Opinion, EIOPA reminds NCAs that the fact that distributors out online distribution should not affect their ability to comply with existing and future requirements applicable in the EU for the provision of such services to consumers.

EIOPA issued some recommendations for the NCAs to take the necessary and proportionate supervisory actions to ensure that:

- online distributors comply with a duty of advice, if such a duty exists in national law or when sales are so promoted
- customers are provided with appropriate information on the selling process of the online distributor with a view to avoiding unsolicited, or mistakenly concluded, contracts

EIOPA recommends that NCAs, where relevant, prevent customer detriment by taking a more proactive approach to how they:

- collect information on online distribution activities used by distributors
- identify challenges and address issues with newly established online distribution channels at national or international level

In some countries, there are specific regulations to follow. For instance in Italy there is the Regolamento Ivass n. 5/2006. In the near future, insurance companies and intermediaries should expect the issuance of more and more regulations and guidelines, similarly, for instance, to what happened in the past for the sales of travel and leisure programs via distributors and the Web.

The support to compliance

The biggest challenges for complying with the multitude of regulations are:

- data quality
- consistent classification and identification of data
- data-reconciliation issues

Systems need to produce consistent and accurate information based on multiple models and real-time calculations, which correlate across divisions and asset classes. Digital solutions must be robust enough to deal with data integrity, usability, and be compliant. They also need to be flexible enough to build quick interfaces and reporting systems for other external financial systems and standard feeds as applicable.

Insurance organizations need to refresh their systems in order to produce financial information precisely and timely and tailor reports to International Financial Reporting Standard(s) (IFRS), local Generally Accepted Accounting Principles (GAAP), or Solvency II requirements. Many organizations have automated the processes in order to run them in a similar way to those around the production of the report and accounts.

Although a significant challenge, European insurance companies need to get the most out of limited resources and look to see how the volume of developments can be spread across the year(s).

There are many regulations. However, there are solutions that can work to satisfy them. Many financial institutions, mostly small and medium, are currently maintaining the data in Excel spreadsheets. They would like to host the information in a solution that fits the functional and technical infrastructure within the insurance company. In order to meet these project requirements, and the deadlines of the Solvency II, one very interesting solution is master data management (MDM). The previous chapter presents this solution from a functional point of view.

MDM has the objective of providing processes for collecting, aggregating, matching, consolidating, quality-assuring, persisting, and distributing such data throughout an organization to ensure consistency and control in the ongoing maintenance and application use of this information.

Conclusions

This chapter, although absolutely not exhaustive, necessarily correct, and especially updated in this dynamic environment, provides an overview of some legal regulations to be kept in mind when designing and introducing digital insurance.

Regulatory compliance is a critical aspect also for insurance companies. Although compliance with regulations is required, it certainly does have a material impact on the operations of digital insurance. This is not necessarily anything new, but the complexity of the task has changed with more regulations coming into play. Regulatory costs are already having a significant impact on the investments and operations in insurance companies.

Compliance and innovation are not necessarily mutually exclusive.[25] Systems investments for the purposes of regulatory compliance and those that are driven by innovation criteria can be intrinsically linked. The regulatory requirements both make the insurance environment more secure and are complementary to the approach of building a simpler business for the customers and the insurance companies, which focuses on doing less complex operations but doing them better. Customers and regulators are both looking for greater operational stability, improved reporting/transparency, and for developments to keep pace with solutions advancements. The benefits of investment in these areas are mutually shared. For example, enhanced transaction monitoring and the overall integration of risk management tools help ensure the security of financial systems. This, in turn, improves customers' protection against exposure in global transaction flows.

7
Digital Insurance Throughout the World

Introduction

The launch of successful digital insurance is not simple. There are many sources of uncertainty, and many aspects are innovative. The opportunities and the costs are many and varied. For this reason, it is important to learn from past errors, especially if committed by other companies.

Digital insurance is spreading in many parts of the old and the new world. Digital insurance could also be popular in countries where most of the population is uninsured or underinsured. In the majority of these places, insurance companies' agencies can only be found in large cities. Customers are forced to travel many miles to the nearest financial institution agency to obtain consultancy or buy insurance services.

This chapter describes the status, the plans, and the opportunities of digital insurance all over the world. It is not at all exhaustive nor can be updated at the time of reading, since the world of digital insurance is very dynamic and growing fast. Nor is there an intent to present best practices in this chapter. The main objective is to present the status of a certain number of implementations of digital insurance in different parts of the world.

Digital insurance across the world

The move from the physical to the virtual world, from person-to-person interaction to person-to-machine or even machine-to-machine, is changing the insurance industry. The potential integration and coordination among diverse and separate delivery channels are critical to creating new customer experiences and delighting customers.

Celent analyzes periodically the differences between insurance companies in the Asia-Pacific, Europe, the Middle East and Africa, Latin America, and North America in terms of their digital transformation initiatives, investments, and programs.[1] Celent's excellent analysis is at the basis of many considerations, and especially statistics, in this chapter together with similar documents of other institutions and the author's personal experiences. This information is presented in a synthetic format. We urge readers interested to go to the original document or future ones which will be produced.

In presenting some of the findings of Celent, it is important to consider their definition of digital transformation. For Celent, digital transformation is the strategy of transferring as many manual tasks as possible to digital activities.[2] This strategy can be achieved in different ways, including:

- leaning and automating processes
- selling products with new channels
- leveraging digital devices and mobile solutions in general
- dematerializing documents and communication
- data gathering, management, and analytics

Celent states that digital transformation is a major investment driver for insurance companies globally. Digital insurance will trigger further spending over the next several years. The next wave of digitization will be related to exploiting new solutions which will introduce disruptive innovation in insurance.

Europe

Forrester Research produced a report on the status and perspectives of insurance companies in Europe.[3] The years ahead will be challenging ones for the European insurance industry. The expectation is for moderate growth in certain insurance services and low interest rates, which will affect the business environment. Successful insurance companies look to seize opportunities to maximize their digital insurance solutions and make better use of the data they capture in order to personalize products and services. Insurance companies have traditionally lagged behind the retail and the banking sectors in innovation. Within general insurance in Europe, the increased use of comparators by customers, especially for motor insurance, combined with low retention rates, determines a continuous pressure on margins. Insurance companies need to look at servicing customers in more effective, efficient, economic, and ethical ways. They must find new approaches for encouraging loyalty and brand stickiness, and providing excellent customer experiences and new services for traditional and continuously evolving customer needs, anticipating them as much as possible.

A growing number of insurance companies are scaling up their analytical capabilities. Their aim is to be in a better position to use data in a more integrated way, drawing meaningful insights at virtually every stage of the insurance life cycle, from customer targeting to product design and pricing, underwriting, claims, and reporting.[4] Regulatory initiatives require better liquidity, greater transparency on the information provided to the customers, revisions to relationships with intermediaries, and greater governance and oversight on new and existing products and services, and their risks.

The disintermediation of life and pensions has also put more pressure on insurance companies to maximize direct channels. One possible solution lies in improving the client interfaces. The key themes are technology, big data analytics, mobile, content management, and, in general, innovation. In order to make more out of customer interactions, insurance companies must modernize their legacy systems, which are in most cases obsolete and unable to support new requirements. They must provide customers with a wider range of digital solutions and communication channels, while making better use of customer and market data to tailor products and services to the individual customer: the so-called mass personalized insurance.

Within personal lines, where products are increasingly commoditized (partly as a result of price-driven distribution via the comparators' channel), there is an environment in which differentiation becomes more challenging. Solutions are moving towards personalization, but it will take time. Initially, new products tend to be targeted to young customers, even if it they are not normally a rich part of the market. European insurance companies have started to invest in using data, which is increasingly available in a processable format, in innovative ways in order to appeal to these dynamic markets. European insurance companies face a juggling act to use these opportunities to personalize products, to find other ways of adding value, to build greater loyalty, and to increase customer retention and profitability. The challenge is that they must comply with various legal, regulatory, accounting, and tax challenges, which are a drag on resources. Having a robust reactive, but especially proactive, strategy can enable insurance companies to remain competitive in the future. By keeping their products simple and transparent and investing in areas such as big data analytics and innovation, insurance companies can be potentially in a better position to create and increase their relationships with their customers and differentiate their offerings from the old and the new competition.

One of the priorities is that insurance companies must refresh their finance functions. Solvency II and other accounting and fiscal regulations (such as the International Financial Reporting Standards [IFRS] 4 Phase II) are more and more demanding on finance and risk departments. European CFOs, CROs, and CIOs must maintain a strong focus on meeting the various and increasing regulatory requirements.

Celent surveys show that Europe is lagging behind other regions in current capability and immediate investment plans. Insurance companies rate themselves at the lowest digital maturity level. In many industry sectors in Europe, and particularly in nonfinancial services, the customer services environment and loyalty management are well developed, but that is not the case with many insurance companies.

The analysis of European insurance companies' surveys highlights some clear regional differences:

- Insurance companies perceive different challenges.
- There is still a slow pace of delivery of new solutions, which is acknowledged by insurance companies.
- Many insurance companies believe they have a long way to go.
- Companies are spending less on digital in the near term, but have (dream?) significant long-term investment plans.
- Insurance companies remain positive about their digital future.

Many European insurance companies also have multiple legacy systems due to the merger and acquisition trends of the last few years. These old and varied systems in the combined enterprises do not easily lend themselves to customer-centric digital activity. The Celent survey points out that the resulting costs and complexity issues have pushed digital down the insurance companies' agenda and, especially, their budgets. A difficulty is the presence of legacy systems. Interestingly, virtually no one in the surveys believes that a lack of customer demand for digital is an inhibitor. However, costs and complexity have prevented the European insurance industry from responding better over recent years to the new challenges. This situation should rapidly change.

Another important aspect is the high proportion of independent agents or intermediaries and the significant shift in their power over the customer relationship in recent years. Nearly 50 percent of the Celent survey respondents cite this as an inhibitor to digital growth. Getting a direct relationship with customers is the highest driver of digital strategy in Europe by some margin (39%, ahead of the second-place driver, enriching the customer experience at 23%).

The vast majority of the companies surveyed by Celent cite the slow pace of delivery by insurance companies as the most significant inhibitor.

Moreover, the increasing number of comparators is making direct relationships with the customers rather elusive. Physical intermediaries have been replaced by virtual brokers: the comparators!

The gap between how European insurance companies rate their current levels of digital maturity and the global average is wide. Additional disparities between European insurance companies and others include the following:[5]

- Sixty-seven percent rate themselves as a one out of five for managing and building brand loyalty through digital channels, compared with 53 percent globally.
- Seventy-six percent rate themselves as basic in using digital solutions to reduce cost to serve customers, compared with 55 percent globally.
- Twenty-eight percent admit they currently have no business case for their digital strategy, compared to 10 percent globally.

Despite this relatively low current self-assessment, European insurance companies have, like their global peers, ambitious future objectives. In some areas, such as reducing cost to serve and getting the right operating model in place, they have rated higher than their average digital ambitions.

Overall, European insurance companies intend to spend less on near-term digital investment than other regions. This situation very likely reflects the current state of some European markets, in which a large number of new businesses for coverage, such as personal motor insurance, are already online. This is a rate of digital penetration in the sales process that is unmatched by any other market. However, the region customers' long-term plans are for many more investments. More than one-third of European insurance companies expect to increase digital spending by more than 50 percent over the next five years, compared with 18 percent globally. Of course, in the meantime some insurance companies have a long way to grow to become more efficient and reducing costs, while adding more value to their customers.

Despite their challenges, European insurance companies are more positive than those in other regions about their success to date. An interesting case is provided by Belgium.[6] The operational ratio held steady at 14.3 percent, keeping Belgian non-life insurance companies in the bottom one-third percentile globally in terms of operational performance. Belgian non-life insurance companies continue to focus on improving efficiency and controlling costs through the use of solutions such as telematics, legacy-system replacement, and big data analytics aimed at powering advanced predictive tools. They are getting very interesting results.

The Americas

The scope of the Americas region in the Celent survey comprises a very diverse range of countries. For example, direct insurance and direct-to-customer marketing are only just emerging in Latin America. They are much more developed in North America. Nonetheless, the region has much in common across many indicators of digital advancement, from budgetary spending to customer engagement:

- There is a high level of support for digital solutions.
- Legacy technology constraints are the top inhibitor of digital growth.
- There is a greater sense of urgency.
- Insurance companies show more digital interactions and mobile engagements.
- Insurance companies have a positive assessment of digital leadership and success so far.

The Americas spend more on digital than the rest of the globe. One-third of American respondents to the Celent survey say they spend between 10 percent and 30 percent of their information and communications technology (ICT) development budget on digital, compared with 19 percent globally. Company business models support digital more effectively and efficiently.

The slow pace of delivery by insurance companies is the second-highest inhibitor of digital growth in this region. The internal organization is seen as a challenge by both life and non-life insurance companies. For life companies, creating a culture of innovation is the greatest challenge. Among non-life companies, 87 percent cite internal company structure or culture constraints as a major challenge, compared with 64 percent globally.

Both the greater awareness of digital challenges and the greater progress to date may reflect a more acute sense of urgency for innovation in the Americas. These are parts of the world with a high percentage of young persons and a digital-oriented society. Insurance companies are over a third more likely than the global average to think customers will switch companies if they do not go all the way to digital. This is the leading consequence mentioned by insurance companies in the region, while it is in third place globally, behind concerns over losing competitive advantage and ability to innovate in the market.

In mentioning digital drivers, Americas insurance companies mention reducing cost to serve customers and intermediaries as far more important than other aspects in these parts of the world with respect to other ones. In 2013, the operational ratio in the United States deteriorated an additional 12 percentage points to 22.1 percent, making it the highest of all the countries examined.[7] Continued heavy investment in complex initiatives, such as customer-centric business models and integrated solutions explain the industry high costs for servicing customers.

Non-life insurance companies are investing in advanced and improved security solutions as they strive to keep up with the stringent regulations aimed at improving customer protection and preventing fraud. US non-life insurance companies were more accomplished when it came to acquiring customers. The ratio of acquisition of new customers continued a steady decline from 2010 on. Almost 63 percent of customers already use online channels to compare rates and get quotations.

As direct channels continue to gain momentum, US non-life insurance companies will likely continue to reduce acquisition costs, while also working to improve customer experience.

To succeed in the United States, companies active in life insurance and annuities must expand their digital capabilities with new Web, social media, and mobile solutions that empower customers and intermediaries with self-service features, while also making insurance products easier to understand, compare and buy, and reduce costs.[8]

A major opportunity to widen margins that exists for insurance companies in the United States is to leverage big data analytics and cloud computing to transform back office systems and processes. These decisions must be carefully followed, by taking into account the danger of security risks and regulatory issues they might bring.

The soft pricing conditions in the United States are eroding profit margins, compelling insurance companies in the property and casualty sector (P&C) to focus on expense management and operational efficiency, reducing costs through technology upgrades, process optimization, selective offshoring, and enhanced risk management. The use of data analytics and modeling techniques to improve underwriting and back office processes is an important opportunity for US P&C insurance companies to improve their revenues.

On the distribution front, insurance companies plan to optimize the channel mix, adding distribution outlets, expanding the use of comparators, and selling direct-to-customer models, while providing customers with enhanced product price transparency and real-time support and service.

Many customers turn to online banking and investment services to manage their finances. They seek similar opportunities from providers of insurance, with very good chances for insurance companies that develop the right products combined with online alerts and transactional models.

For instance, building an enterprise information excellent infrastructure via more robust big data analytics helped insurance companies in Canada pinpoint new growth opportunities, optimize claims outcomes, reduce the incidence of claims fraud, and mitigate bottom-line risks.[9]

Insurance companies in the region are more likely to consider being customer-centric in order to stay one step ahead of their competitors and use digital insurance to increase market share. Particularly within the high-growth markets of Latin America, digital insurance is seen as strategically important for reaching out to the new middle class, which is buying insurance for the first time.

A key challenge for many insurance companies in Latin America is to modernize their operations and distribution models to adapt to rising business and customer expectations of digital, mobile, Web, and social interactions, particularly for commercial lines of insurance in which intermediaries are still retaining control.[10]

The Asia-Pacific

Asia-Pacific insurance companies have far less clarity around the barriers to digital progress and future investments than their global peers. One reason may be that the region's emerging nations are at an earlier stage in their digital roadmap. The Celent findings are more representative of Asia than Australia, due to the large number of Asian countries. As a matter of fact, Australia aligns more with the digitally developed European and US markets. There are many reasons why the Asian markets are very different with respect to US and European markets. The reasons are connected with the culture, the industrial development, the openness of the markets, and so on.

The Celent survey found that the situation in the Asia-Pacific is characterized by the following:

- Digital strategy clarity is lacking.
- Integrating digital with other distribution channels is a top challenge.
- Customer experience and internal efficiency are driving digital strategy.
- Regulatory restrictions are a higher concern.
- Social media and mobile tools have a lower perceived value.

A significant number of Asia-Pacific respondents to the Celent survey did not know (or weren't willing to discuss) their current levels of digital development expenditure. Such lack of clarity is mirrored also looking forward. This may reflect the greater geographic complexity of the region or the deferral of strategic planning to the group level at this time.

Another reason for the lack of clarity may be a weaker sense of urgency and top-of-mind awareness. In 2013, GDP growth for Asia was forecast at 5.75 percent, compared to a 3.5 percent global average, with almost negative values in Europe. Such prosperity, combined with lower insurance penetration and density rates in this region, means digital innovation is not yet deemed necessary to secure customer growth. Insurance companies have focused on targeting market share, often by expanding their sales forces. This may explain why regional respondents rate the consequences of not embracing digital insurance significantly below global levels.

However, there could be a false sense of security: 16 Asian countries are in the top 30 countries in terms of Internet use in the world. Together, they account for 42 percent of the world Internet population. A 2012 McKinsey survey of Indian Internet users found that, for example, about 66 percent of users bought health insurance online.[11] In India, ICT investments have had the most noticeable impact on the insurance industry. In this country, insurance industry is undergoing a drastic transformation in response to growing demand and regional competition. According to Kaylan Banga of Netscribes, an India-based research company, ICT spending in the insurance industry will have a compound annual growth rate (CAGR) of 14 percent until 2015. This growth is attributed to the large appetite for ICT in various sectors of indian rapidly evolving market, including fierce competition among companies.[12]

Digital insurance presents a significant opportunity to Asian insurance companies to reach customers in remote areas. Failure to recognize this would cost insurance companies dearly.

Insurance companies are challenged to invest in big data analytics and modeling capabilities, as well as Web and mobile digital sales, distribution, and customer service solutions, given an increasingly technologically sophisticated population.[13]

Underlying the importance of agency distribution in the Asia-Pacific, many insurance companies (especially in life insurance) consider that integrating digital and media with other distribution channels is the top challenge they face in delivering their digital strategy. The prevalence of an inefficient agency channel and high support costs is reflected in regional respondents' to the Celent survey which rank higher the intermediaries' current use of digital to improve the efficiency and quality of customer interactions with respect to the rest of the world. The fact that Asian insurance companies are far more likely than their global peers to have mobile strategies for their intermediaries is another sign of the dominance of the agent network.

To confirm this situation, Asia-Pacific insurance companies view the benefits of digital insurance through a slightly different perspective. Like their global peers, enriching the customer experience is the key driver of digital strategy. However, increasing internal efficiencies ranks second. Only a few insurance companies in the region see regaining more direct control of the customer relationship as a driver, compared to their global counterparts.

Conclusions

The surveys cited in this chapter and the author's personal experience show that the approach to digital insurance is diverse in different parts of the world. However, it is the way to go. The disruptive forces of globalization and digital solutions will push toward a more common environment. The laggards need to play catch-up.

The future developments in digital insurance will push even more in this direction, as the next chapter on the Future shows.

8
The Future

Introduction

Digital insurance is a clear investment priority as insurance companies attempt to add value to their services and capitalize on the features unique to digital solutions. New, interesting developments are on the horizon.

Digital insurance shares some key functional trends with other sectors of financial services, like mobile banking.[1] With the advent of technology and the increasing use of mobile devices, the use of digital insurance functions will enable the customers to connect across the entire customer life cycle in a much more integrated and complete way than before. With this scenario, the digital insurance objectives of achieving new revenue streams, building relationships with customers, and reducing costs will transform to enable new objectives. Insurance companies will target higher-level goals such as building the brand of the insurance company. Emerging technology and functions will enable the creation of new ways of lead generation, of prospecting, of managing insurance, and of developing deep customer delight and hence relationships. Digital insurance will be the basis for a superior customer experience with bidirectional communications.

Following are some of the key functional trends in the world of digital insurance:[2]

- communication enrichment, such as video interaction with agents and consultants
- pervasive transactions capabilities: comprehensive websites, including plenty of functions that are not only related to insurance activities

- customer education: "test drives" for demos of insurance services and investment options and great support for coaching and helping the customer
- connections with new customer segments: connections with digital natives through games and social networks customized to support insurance companies' offerings (for instance, through the so-called gamification, that is the application of typical elements of game playing [such as point scoring, competition with others, rules of play] with insurance services, typically as an online marketing technique to encourage engagement with the service offered by the insurance company)
- content monetization: micro-level revenue themes such as travel tickets, e-books, or news download
- vertical positioning: offerings over digital insurance-specific industries or alternative investments
- horizontal positioning: offerings over digital insurance across all industries
- personalization of experiences for multiple roles and hierarchies in business insurance in contrast to the simple enhancements in the current context
- building of a better insurance brand while enhancing the "customer experience"

This chapter does not consider all possible and foreseeable developments. It concentrates on some of the most interesting ones for each of the following categories:

- the application innovations
- the technological innovations
- the network innovations

The following sections examine some of the solutions that insurance companies will be able to use to reach the previously listed objectives.

Application innovation

There are many new application innovations which are interesting in connection with digital insurance. This chapter examines only the ones more promising in the short term.

Integration of risk and finance management

There is an ongoing trend in the integration of actuarial and finance functions with consideration of the risk mitigations and regulatory compliance. In a survey conducted by Ernst & Young, nearly 40 percent of respondents had complete or nearly complete integration of risk and finance management, while a further 42 percent had partial integration with plans for full integration by 2020.[3]

An integration between these two functions would enable finance to become a better business partner in the cycle of planning, budgeting, forecasting, and monitoring of the business. A real success factor will be how such information is used throughout that cycle. It can be useful in highlighting possible action plans and opportunities. On the other side, simply keeping risk and finance performance in sync and on track will be a key success factor.

The pressure on insurance companies' finance functions will grow over time, with Solvency II, IFRS 4, and their successors putting additional demands on finance and risk management functions. Change is the only constant. Financial and risk management and staff need to demonstrate they can be effective and efficient in the change and enhancement of the digital competencies, which are more and more an integral part of their jobs.

Finance needs to adapt not only to new reporting requirements but to new innovating financing ways. In particular, companies should carry out dry runs ahead of Solvency II. With so many pressures and the need to get priority projects over the line, CFOs and CROs all around the world are maintaining a strong focus on meeting the increasing and diverse regulatory requirements.

There will certainly be new compliance regulations after Solvency II (maybe Solvency III+), which will advance this aspect. However, this development can also bring better management of the insurance business.

Artificial intelligence

With life products, for instance, actuaries and life insurance functions are continually faced with a common business problem in using lots of data, that accumulate almost randomly, into useful information. Generally, actuaries employ standardized symbols in representing insurance quantities. Aided by the number-crunching ability of today's computers, new and powerful applications have been developed. Some of these applications employ artificial intelligence (AI) intertwined with knowledge engineering.

AI denotes a set of software or machines that shows some kind of "intelligence". It is based on a discipline that has the goal of creating more advanced solutions to tackle with problems. Major AI researchers and textbooks define this field as "the study and design of intelligent agents." In this case, an intelligent agent is a system that monitors its environment and takes actions that maximize their probability of success.

The central objectives of AI research include reasoning, knowledge, communication, perception, and the ability to move and manipulate objects. General intelligence is still among the field's long-term goals. As of now, most of the approaches include statistical methods, computational intelligence, and traditional symbolic AI. AI can use a large number of tools, including semantic search and mathematical optimization, logic, methods based on probability and economics, and many others. The AI field is interdisciplinary. It is based on the convergence of a number of sciences and professions, including computer science, mathematics, psychology, linguistics, philosophy, and neuroscience, as well as other specialized fields such as artificial psychology.

Nobody doubts that in time AI will be very effective. For the time being, however, AI has been the subject of optimism but has also suffered stunning setbacks. Today, it has become an essential part of the technology industry, providing support in solving a certain number of the most challenging problems in computer science.

AI is defined as a set of machine competencies that use acquired knowledge and to solve new tasks "efficiently," while performing under new conditions. This is made possible by expert rules and algorithmic representations, adapted and adaptable to specific problems.

In the case of risk management for insurance, the system developed becomes knowledge based when actuarial formulas are written into AI algorithms and both, combined, result in computational intelligence. Knowledge-based systems are essentially computational systems that recognize, and therefore swiftly manipulate, all forms of actuarial definitions. In so doing they can create a viable link between actuarial symbols and algorithmic syntax. Until now the major applications of AI have been in the field of life insurance.

Robotics process automation

A variation of AI is the use of robotics process automation (RPA) in insurance. RPA is the application of technology that allows insurance companies to configure computer software and/or a robot to capture and redo existing human applications for processing a transaction, manipulating data, triggering responses, and communicating with other digital systems.[4]

RPA is revolutionizing the way people think about and administer business processes, ICT support processes, workflow processes, remote infrastructure, and back-office work. RPA provides substantial improvements in accuracy and cycle time and increased productivity in transaction processing. At the same time, it elevates the nature of work by removing people from simple, repetitive tasks.

The technology of RPA can provide a solution to a wide range of activities:

- process automation
- ICT support and management
- automated assistance

The robots in process automation can be composed of two different parts, similar to what happens with humans:

- the brain
- the arm

RPA can automate both, and, when it does, it can get excellent results especially in activities such as:

- judgment-based analysis: the "brain" part manages the workflow and validation across many activities and their sequence
- complex data entry-rule-based decisions: the "brain" part drives validation and the execution of the "arm" driven automation
- simple data entry, use of macros, optical character recognition (OCR) or intelligent character recognition (ICR), and so on.

This solution is particularly interesting for an insurance company whose general processes are manual-intensive. On the other hand, the combination of AI with the manual capabilities of a robot-like solution can bring big benefits.

In the case of insurance companies, RPA can be used in several fields, some of which could be:

- automated quotes and letter generation
- automated data extraction and presentation for the customer relationship center
- automatic claims processing

Anticipatory computing

Anticipatory computing is one of the most interesting solutions, useful for digital insurance. It refers to information technology designed to anticipate the user's requirements and take action in advance of the user requesting it.

Examples of anticipatory computing include Google Now and MindMeld. Google Now is an intelligent personal assistant developed by Google that is available for the Android and iOS operating systems. Google Now employs a natural language user interface to answer questions, make recommendations, and perform actions by delegating requests to a set of web services. Along with answering user-initiated queries, Google Now passively delivers information to the users that it predicts they might want, based on their search habits or actions.

Anticipatory computing, when combined with big data analytics and mobile solutions, could be useful for processing massive amounts of historical and recent data. In such a situation, big data analytics can help users in decision making. Big data analytics processing usually happens through a batch-processing model. But if a company is able to process data in real time, it results in real-time analytics. If these real-time analytics are fed into some kind of a predictive model and the results are used to help users in decision making user's, then we have what is defined as anticipatory computing. If the output of the predictive model is directly fed into an automated decision-making process, it ensures a desired outcome. This is prescriptive analytics. This roadmap essentially is shaping the future.

If we join three solutions: anticipatory computing, real-time big data analytics, and mobile, we have a very powerful system indeed. The mobile allows sensing of the environment, record data, commands, voices, chat conversations, and so on in real time. The opportunity becomes to use all these data in real time using anticipatory computing. If the user starts talking about a pregnant woman, the digital insurance app might come up suggesting a customized insurance. If the user is talking about a trip, digital insurance could suggest travel insurance.

In the IPG Media Lab's 2013 outlook report, titled "2013: The Year of Anticipation and Refinement"[5] it is states that "Anticipatory Computing will be the trend to watch in the years to come." This report quotes the Expect Labs (which launched MindMeld) CEO's view on anticipatory computing: anticipatory means listening and delivering information before a person asks for it. The next generation of computing platforms, whether they are smartphones, tablets, or something built into our glasses, or on our wall, will all have the technical ability to access rich streams of information, and will be listening in the background as a person does other things. The way we search for information right now could and should be dramatically improved.

It is possible that systems accessing different streams of data to anticipate what a person might need next may make some people feel uncomfortable and intruded upon. These systems must have a mechanism to switch off the anticipatory features.

It looks like more and more systems will become anticipatory in the future, and as the saying goes, "It is not the data or technologies in themselves that are the problem, it is how they are used." On the other side, real-time data analytics is not a dream. It is now possible with the so-called in memory processing.

Social networks

Social networks are becoming more and more important as a way of connecting people. In some cases (for instance, private communications), the number of messages transmitted through social networks has become larger than through traditional e-mails. Insurance marketing and sales can greatly benefit from the channel of social networks.

The social network has proven to be a fertile ground for experimentation and innovation. While most companies think of social media first in terms of customer acquisition or customer service, there are several other ways in which insurance companies have or can put social media to use.

These include:

- using on-board social media to create a platform for independent agents to come and share ideas, experience, and expertise
- capturing feedback and input from customers for use in product design, which is an excellent way to gain insight into what customers want in terms of (virtual or physical) agency design, new products, and other features
- using off-board social media such as Facebook and LinkedIn to develop a customer recruiting presence, especially among younger individuals more likely to use and/or frequent these sites
- employing social media to complement call centers, helping reducing the number of incoming calls and, in effect, helping customers answering other customers' questions thanks to the creation of communities
- putting a "human face" on the company by publicizing charitable activities, sustainability initiatives, and other initiatives not directly related to insurance products

McKinsey sees a very bright future for social technologies or solutions. The company defines social solutions as digital technologies used by people to interact among themselves and together to create, enhance, and exchange content.[6] Social solutions characteristics:

- are enabled by information technology.
- provide distributed rights to create, add, and/or modify content and communications.
- enable distributed access to consumer content and communications.

Celent surveyed the state of insurance in many countries.[7] It found that Twitter is used by 68 percent of the Americas' companies versus 42 percent globally and that LinkedIn is used by 57 percent in the Americas region, compared with 35 percent globally. Reflecting this higher level of use, 91 percent of companies monitor the customers sentiments about their brands online and in social networks, against a global ratio of 75 percent. In Latin America, countries such as Colombia have leapfrogged many developed countries and now have more active social network users than London and Paris.

The same Celent survey found that Asian insurance companies are less likely than their global counterparts to use social media and mobile tools to interact with customers and agents: 30 percent use mobile apps, lower than half the global ratio of 61 percent. Facebook use is much higher at 60 percent, but still short of the global percentage of 71 percent. The infrequent use of apps and social media in Asia may suggest that insurance companies do not intend to rely on such tools for business purposes. This is also reflected in a lower use of online and social media monitoring (56 percent, compared with 75 percent globally).

Lack of interest in social media may reflect a more general reluctance to use digital to engage in customer dialogue, at least for some types of communication. Asian insurance companies are more likely than their global counterparts for interacting digitally with customers at financial stages (for instance, quotes, transactions, and payments). For example, 83 percent of Asian regional insurance companies provide online quotes, and 70 percent offer online purchase/transaction capabilities (72 percent and 66 percent globally). In contrast, 82 percent provide company and product information, and 49 percent educate customers about their brand values, compared to 92 percent and 63 percent globally.

American Family Insurance

The US life insurer American Family Insurance has launched an initiative called "Be a Fan, Be a Winner." It allows Facebook users to earn free merchandise from their favorite sports team, simply by becoming Facebook fans of both their team and American Family. The application links fans of two different Facebook pages.

The insurance company is partnering in a FanFare pilot with teams and organizations across the United States. As an added benefit, American Family Insurance is donating one dollar to the American Red Cross for each of its first 5,000 Facebook fans. The program was launched in August 2009, and has been successful in increasing American Family's exposure to new customers while helping with customer acquisition and retention. At the same time, American Family is doing a charitable activity.

Generali France

Generali France has launched various initiatives in the field of social media. Among others, Generali France has been tightly engaged in www.generation-responsable.com, an Internet website based on the social network model to federate initiatives.[8] In addition, Generali has created and maintaining its own Twitter account.

Generali France launched a new type of insurance, Kontsurnous (a play on the words "Count on us" in French). It allows customers to group in "tribes" and, through a loyalty program, to share the benefits collected from insurance subscriptions. The tribe collects points for each car insurance contract signed by its members. All members of a community have a right to a share of points collected by all other members of the tribe. "K-points" collected by the tribe even benefit members who become victims of an accident, providing up to 100 percent insurance excess reimbursement.

Prices are customized according to the behavior of the community. This onboard program differs from traditional loyalty programs that provide nontransferable individual benefits.

Generali France has also nurtured a culture of innovation within their company via a LinkedIn closed group dedicated to Generali employees.

MetLife

The US insurance company MetLife taps Facebook Custom Audiences for look-a-like modeling.[9] Beginning with a rich set of call center/customer relationships management systems (CRM), demographic, and behavioral data, it uses Facebook to identify new prospects for several insurance products based on key segments such as "young and driven" and "mature planners."

As soon as MetLife got on the Facebook platform, its segments went out the door. MetLife was able to find out what content resonates with which individual. In turn, Facebook delivered MetLife a 49 percent decrease in cost per lead with a 2.4x increase in lead-to-sale ratio.

This prospecting is not limited to Facebook. While MetLife might be able to reach certain targets vertically within Facebook, it shatters the attribution and targeting necessary to reach potential customers horizontally, across various online properties.

Friendsurance

The German insurance broker Friendsurance developed a way to encourage potential customers to apply for insurance as a group to save money.[10] The savings come because customers in the group underwrite all the small claims themselves, which allows them to qualify for lower premiums and rebates on the coverage that the insurer provides for bigger claims. This approach is also called peer-to-peer insurance. This creates value for the insurance company by lowering the administrative costs of managing small claims as well as the likelihood of fraudulent claims, since that would reduce the annual rebate across the group. The system also works because groups are likely to be careful about letting in members who might be high risk. Finally, the model reduces the costs of customer acquisitions. According to Friendsurance, customers save 50 percent on average, and some groups have saved as much as 70 percent.

Technological innovations

Internet of (every)thing

The future will bring many new solutions. Internet of Things (IoT) is one of the most impressive. Cisco calls it also the "Internet of Everything" (IoE). IoT provides the possibility of using Internet to connect not only humans but also objects. Actually, the real disruptive solution will be the possibility of connecting processes.

Businesses and people act on processes. These are essentially a series of activities that help to reach a target. In the case of businesses, the target could be a sale. In the case of people, it could be reaching a personal target, such as having a good dinner at a restaurant or buying a property.

Most of these processes today are absolutely unconnected between themselves. People will need to move from one activity to the following one, at best supported by an automatic workflow. Most of the time, people are moving without any help at all.

The IoT will change this situation drastically. Thanks to various types of sensors, embedded more and more in objects, IoE will be able to sense where a person is, what he/she is doing, and which object or human he/she is in contact with. IoT together with anticipatory computing, will be able to forecast what we could be doing next and then help accomplish it.

Somebody might be afraid of this "big brother." This is certainly true for some activities, but for other ones it will be a great support. Think of the black boxes mounted on vehicles. The IoT will provide a huge amount of data. The IoT is the interconnection of uniquely identifiable embedded computing devices within the existing Internet infrastructure. Typically, IoT is expected to offer advanced connectivity of devices, systems, processes, and services. It covers a variety of protocols, domains, and applications. The interconnection of these embedded devices (including smart objects) is expected to usher in automation in nearly all fields. In insurance, IoT can refer to a wide variety of devices such as heart monitoring implants, biochip transponders on farm animals, automobiles with built-in sensors, home appliances for monitoring fires, or field operation devices that assist in remote monitoring plenty of apparatus and situations and even people's health.

According to Gartner, Inc., there will be nearly 26 billion devices on the IoT by 2020.[11] ABI Research estimates that more than 30 billion devices will be connected via wireless to the IoT by 2020.[12] According to a survey done by the Pew Research Internet Project, a large majority of the technology experts and engaged Internet users who responded – 83 percent – agreed with the notion that the Internet/Cloud of Things, embedded and wearable computing will have widespread use and beneficial effects by 2025.[13] IoT consists of a very large number of devices that are connected to the Internet. It allows (near)real-time remote monitoring of a specific situation and makes possible a much more flexible pricing of insurance products. For instance, it will be possible to collect more information on the customer behavior. Some insurance companies are already doing just this, by using telematics data from cars and commercial vehicles to price their auto and transport policies.

The real challenge is how to use the IoT. Once again, it will go back to the capabilities of each organization. Certainly, it will change the job of ICT from information and communication technologies to ICT as Innovation, Collaboration, and Transformation. This is really a challenge for ICT managers. They will be called to move from being chief information officers to chief innovation officers. Whether they will be able to cope with the challenge will depend very much on the person.

Zurich Italy[14]

Zurich Connect introduced a new mobile application for smartphones called Save As You Drive. Zurich Connect created this application in partnership with Vodafone Italia, to monitor in real time the driving style of its customers. The new app is able to record the driver's behavior at the wheel, taking advantage of some characteristics of the device to analyze the mobile speed, braking, acceleration, and frequency with which potentially dangerous maneuvers are carried out.

Based on these parameters, 30 days after the first use and driving for at least 200 Km, Save As You Drive provides a score on the skills of the driver. The most virtuous receive as a reward an extra discount on auto insurance.

Promoting greater awareness on behavior behind the wheel in terms of safety and cost savings, the app promotes environmental sustainability with the measurement of energy efficiency-related guidance, showing how it is possible, driving in a virtuous way, to reduce the emissions of a car and save on fuel consumption, in addition to reducing the cost of car insurance. Save As You Drive promises, therefore, great help for the more effective management of corporate fleets. The app also provides the services and contents available in the Zurich-Connect.it Mobile Version, from budgeting for all products (cars, motorcycles, vans, home), the management of the policy and its renewal in self-service. It is available for smartphones running Android and iOS, and is downloadable for free from the Play Store and the Apple Store.

Wearable technology

Wearable technology, tech togs, or fashion electronics are clothing and accessories that incorporate computers and advanced electronic technologies.[15] Their designs often incorporate practical functions and features. They may also have a purely aesthetic purpose.

Wearable technology is related to both the fields of ubiquitous computing and the history and development of wearable computers. With ubiquitous computing, wearable technology shares a vision of computers as a pervasive technology into all products and services with frictionless interaction. Through the history and development of wearable computing, this vision has been both contrasted and received with enthusiasm.

The calculator watch, introduced in the 1980s, was one original piece of worn electronics that became widespread. Google Glass is a more recent example.

According to ABI Research, due to the relative ease of compatibility with smartphones and other electronic devices, the wearable technologies market will spike to 485 million annual device shipments by 2018 in Italy alone.[16] In the United States, the device business was at over US$ 14 billion in 2014.[17] Truly disruptive new solutions, in the form of e-textiles, will also begin to establish major sales in a few years' time with heavy fashion, industrial, and commercial consequences.

All these new devices will make the use of digital insurance simpler and faster. Nearly two-thirds of insurance companies expect wearable technologies to have a significant impact on their industry, according to a survey of more than 200 insurance executives as part of Accenture's annual Technology Vision report.[18]

Insurance companies are using solutions to track customers and encourage safe behaviors. For instance, if fitness trackers can achieve low-level United States food and drug administration (FDA) approval, they could be linked to company-wide health insurance premiums. Auto insurer Progressive Corporation runs a monitoring program known as Snapshot that rewards customers who drive fewer miles, avoid hard braking, and minimize travel from midnight to 4 a.m. Health insurance companies have also gotten into the game, with 80 percent of all large companies tying their plans to wellness programs to control costs, according to the consultant Towers Watson.[19]

John Hancock Life Insurance

Manulife Financial Corporation's John Hancock Life Insurance discounts premiums by as much as 15 percent for policyholders who track and perform well on metrics such as daily exercise, annual health screenings, and flu shots. New customers receive a Fitbit Inc. fitness tracker to monitor their every step.[20]

The objective is to make life insurance more immediate and relevant in the daily lives of Manulife policyholders and help them connect their financial well-being to their long-term health.

The program is run by Discovery Ltd.'s Vitality Group division, which operates wellness programs for companies.

CarePredict combines wearables with beacons to monitor elderly patients and thus help them in living on their own.[21] A senior's activities are tracked throughout his/her home, establishing a typical daily "Tempo" score. When the senior deviates from the norm, the system alerts a caregiver to check in.

Network innovation

5G networks

The new technology protocol for transmission that is currently being deployed is 4G. The shift toward smartphones and tablets forced operators to seek more efficient ways to use the spectrum. 4G is about ten times faster than 3G. New standard releases beyond 4G are in progress by standardization bodies. They are not considered as new mobile generations, but rather they are under the 4G transmission umbrella. 5G is already looming. It is a technology to support the major phase of mobile telecommunication standards beyond the 4G/IMT-Advanced standards. As of 2014, no official document had been made public by telecommunication organizations or standardization bodies such as 3GPP, WiMAX Forum, or ITU-R.

5G and beyond make possible and cheap live video transmissions. This helps a lot in the case of health insurance of elderly patients. 5G will be able to provide connectivity to billions of devices that in the future will require access to the Internet, ranging from driverless cars to smart cities. IoT requires a network that is not only faster but also broader.[22]

Web 2.0

Web 2.0 is a term used to indicate a generic state of evolution of the Internet and particularly the World Wide Web.

Some have attempted to define the Web 2.0 as a set of websites with interface, ease, and speed of use that make them similar to traditional applications that users are accustomed to installing on their personal computers. Others have tried to define Web 2.0 in terms of the tools of mass collaboration throughout the network, sometimes also referred to as social networks. For these sites, special programming technologies are used, such as Ajax (Gmail widely uses this technique to be simple and fast), which, among other things, allow users to customize the interface.

Proponents of the term Web 2.0 say that this differs from the initial concept of the Web, retroactively labeled Web 1.0, because it departs from the classic static websites, from e-mail, from the use of search engines, the linear navigation and proposes a World Wide Web more collaborative, dynamic and interactive for its users.

An example would be social commerce, the evolution of e-commerce in an interactive way, allowing greater participation of customers, through blogs, forums, feedback systems, and so on, and even the definition of new products. In Italy, for example, Ducati has used these tools to define a new motorcycle.

Web 2.0 is strongly connected to social. It would allow a process of collaboration in the creation and updating of content. This process can ensure consistency in the elements of the contents and allow the reuse of it when it is required.

In organizations, the Web 2.0 can improve the management of explicit knowledge (documents, e-mail, Web, social networks, and so on). It also lets organizations analyze how relationships develop between the various actors of the community (social network analysis). This can help a company, especially in innovative projects, move toward organizational structures able to collaborate better.

Other topics of interest in the Web 2.0 relate to a way of working based on voluntary cooperation, or customer management tools through CRM 2.0 that is open to the involvement of customers in the after sale, through participation in a social or business community.

Web 3.0

Recently, people have started to talk about Web 3.0. It is in its early stages of definition. There is no precise definition of what it will be. It is expected that in the Web 3.0, which presumably will be introduced gradually, there will be a wider integration with video content, in a much more advanced way with respect to what today some sites (like YouTube) allow. Under these assumptions, the Web 3.0 would generalize the unified content management, presented as part of the chapter on New Solutions, at the level of the Web, and therefore globally.

Conclusions

In the case of the insurance industry, there is a change in the paradigm. The current economic and financial global crisis, born in 2008 but still continuing, is a powerful accelerator in this respect. In this sense, the crisis is welcome since it is finally waking up to new solutions the insurance companies, with most of them for a long time been static and conservative.

These upcoming changes are not exclusive to insurance companies. Especially all organizations that interact directly with customers need to change. The reason is simple: the customers are changing, the level of preparation and education is greater, and the world is more global.

People are more and more connected. Therefore, the model of the services needs to change in a drastic way. This is a threat but it is also a great opportunity. Consequently, the shares of the markets of the players in the insurance services sector will change.

In particular, it is essential to change the structure of the costs in the insurance companies. To reach this result, it is essential:

- to earn more with the services
- to reduce the costs in a drastic way

In a nutshell, it is necessary to do (much) more with (much) less.

Digital insurance is a great opportunity on these aspects. As an example, today, many insurance company customers pay their bills either manually or through the agencies or the banks. Insurance companies should push more and more on direct payments. This can be also achieved by providing to the customers small benefits, alerts, suggestions, opportunities, and so on.

In terms of a reduction in costs, it is necessary to take into account that the younger generations love new technological solution. This is a great opportunity for insurance companies. Today, roughly 80 percent of transactions are done in the agencies. In the future, they will not be more than 30 percent. This implies a drastic reduction in the number of agencies and their different positioning. If customers use agencies for obtaining financial advice and consultancy, there is no reason to be on the streets. It will be possible to move to upper floors or even to a remote location and connect via videophones or traditional phones.

Insurance companies will need to customize the relationship with each customer in such a way as to assure an excellent customer experience for them. Insurance companies, which will move in this direction, will gain big competitive advantages. This creates the need to move from mass insurance to mass personalized insurance. It is essential to understand the need of each customer and how to satisfy (and indeed delight) him or her. Of course, insurance companies cannot afford the costs that today they incur in their insurance activities. There is a need of reducing the costs of mass personalized insurance. Technology once again can help. The big data analytics solutions help in this respect. Big data analytics is an advanced way of dealing with data, whether varied (structured or unstructured) or in very large volume. It especially offers the possibility of increasing the velocity in accessing, retrieving, and processing data. Variance, Volume, Velocity, Veracity, Vulnerability, and Value are the main benefits of big data analytics solutions.

Next to the classic design science and research approach, there is a need to use qualitative research methods within this context of future innovation avenues. Information-intensive organizations, such as insurance companies, are an excellent test bed for testing new design science and especially observational and experimental evaluation methods.

A framework for business process improvement should address all the four aspects: products, process, platforms, and people.

Stay tuned, digital insurance will bring many more exciting solutions.

Conclusions

Insurance companies need to further innovate in these four ways:

- products (services)
- processes
- organizations
- business models

This book examines each one of these ways and tries to describe what can be expected.

Innovation in products

The insurance companies must be more personal and tailor-made. Insurance companies today find themselves stuck with legacy systems. These systems are so cumbersome and poorly documented that is very difficult for companies to migrate to modern systems. Insurance companies cannot assume that their customers will accept for ever to suffer from such inertia.

New solutions and regulations will make it easy for customers to abandon the insurance company they are using and move on to another company. There will be a strong push to insurance companies for customization based on customer insight such as behavioral-based pricing of financial services, which will be based on big data analytics. Customers whose behavior makes them more profitable and/or reliable to insurance companies will receive preferential pricing to keep them delighted and loyal. Personal financial management platforms will provide the perfect data set to put this new service model in place.

The insurance company of the future will be a hub for identity and security. If there is one service that a customer would be willing to pay for (and it does not really exist today), it is using the insurance company as an insurance and health data locker for all their assets and life.

Value-add digital features offer potential revenue growth. Insurance companies can realize the full potential of digital insurance by offering personalized customer experiences and advanced capabilities, according to a study by Cognizant and Monitise.[1] The study surveyed more than 700 customers from a diverse group of US financial institutions, age ranges, annual incomes, genders, diverse ethnics groups, education levels, and employment backgrounds to understand their digital insurance expectations, emerging trends, and current and future needs.

Customers are increasingly expecting insurance companies to help improve their lifestyles by providing any time, anywhere, any device capabilities, customized user experiences, shopping and social features, and value-added services. The Cognizant and Monitise study states new advanced solutions represent a new opportunity for insurance companies to drive customer loyalty, attract new business, and generate more revenue.

Key findings in this study include the following:[2]

- any time, anywhere, any device capabilities: Customers are looking for better functions as they seek more options. This strongly relates to the segmentation of customer interest and behavior. Remote access and real-time alerts are important features across segments that could induce customers to switch insurance companies.
- customized user experiences: Tablets have emerged as a unique and valued user interface, with 41 percent of survey respondents wanting to use tablets compared with smartphones, and 60 percent of tablet owners preferring a tablet for benefiting from digital insurance. Customers are now using both devices for different purposes and want features optimized to suit each device's form factor. Feature personalization, like rearranging tabs and functions, is also important to more than 75 percent of the customers surveyed. Offering this flexibility can give insurance companies a competitive edge and help them retain customers.
- better customer experiences: Customers want their insurance companies to offer better shopping and social experiences. They also prefer offers from insurance companies rather than from other intermediaries and merchants. On the other side, by providing discounts and offers from merchants (such as travel companies or auto rentals) on customers' devices, insurance companies can increase insurance purchases. Customers are also open to using social networking features on digital insurance apps/websites for accessing information on new products, sharing opinions, and providing suggestions;

- value-added services: Customers are seeking services that drive security, ease mobile payment use, and provide insights on insurance and claims patterns. They are willing to invest in these products. More than one-third of customers surveyed are willing to pay for advanced security features such as biometrics. Nearly 30 percent of respondents are willing to pay for mobile services capabilities.

Innovation in processes

Technological development in the mobile sector, like 5G and improved displays of devices, will likely change the current scenario and further expand and improve wireless service consumption. It is interesting to understanding how all these innovations would impact on processes.

Data input may still be a bottleneck in the consumption of some financial services. This is a field in which one can expect major developments. Near field communication (NFC), barcode readers, or picture-taking phones can be used to reduce the burden and perceived uncertainty of the customer and to increase convenience in mobile policy paying by copying the account numbers, index numbers, and the sums payments and due dates from the printed bill or a driver license into the mobile phone. The customer only needs to accept or reject the policy.

Imaging technology would be able to reduce by up to 80 percent the amount of data that new customers have to enter. Biometrics, using facial and voice recognition technology, will be more and more common. Voice commands will become more available and reliable. For thousands of years, persons have interacted via words. Such interactions will reduce also the size of the devices used for communicating and processing. Wearable devices will become more and more common.

These innovative processes require additional regulatory analysis and implementation. Primarily, it is necessary to determine which liability rules apply as determined by the manner in which the data, images, and voice are ultimately cleared.

Innovation in organizations

With more and more remote users, the traditional organization of insurance companies in the front office and the back office will become insufficient. An increasing number of insurance companies have three logical levels. They correspond to the three areas that constitute the benchmark architectural reference of the financial services sector (see Figure C.1).

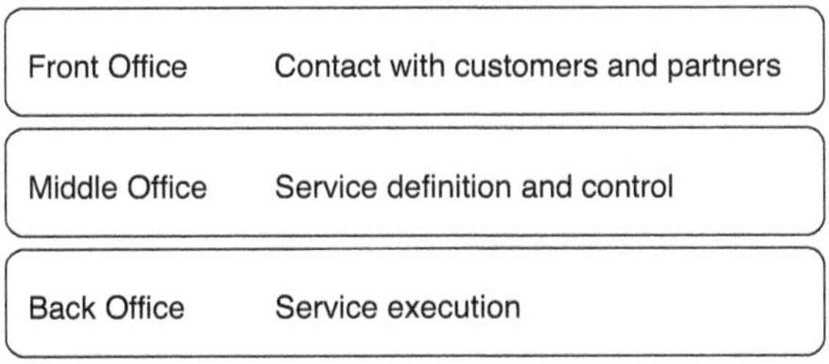

Figure C.1 The three-tier structure to serve the customer

The front office is the trade side. It is composed of all customer-centric services that can be activated directly by the intermediary operators in contact with the customer or, more and more, by the customer themselves. It is directly linked to the channels and will become more and more automated and direct.

The middle office ensures the control and processing of transactions. It represents the point of conjunction between the customer side (front office) and the operational side (back office). The middle office includes all those activities that have the goal of maximizing the match between supply and demand. Its relevance has increased with the widespread use of online and digital insurance.

The back office is the operational side. It is composed of all the product-oriented administration services that do not require direct contact with the customer or the intermediary.

The middle office is a great way to speed up the front office operations. At the same time, it makes available a much cleaner input to the back office.

From a strategic business perspective, this organizational innovation in insurance companies will be the driver that will lead to:

- a focus on customers rather than products
- customer interaction through multichannels, with the concept of everywhere, every time, and in every possible way
- leaner front, middle, and back offices
- process management strongly integrated with digitization
- business and information and communications technology (ICT) alignment
- innovation in business models

To survive and prosper, insurance companies will therefore have to adapt not only their traditional offering but also get into markets that today are totally unrelated to them. As a successful example, CIC, a French financial institution, began selling mobile phones and related plans a few years ago.[3] It now has a significant portion of the insurance market, and also has one of the French market's highest ratios of customers who use digital insurance services.

In other words, it is necessary to create a digital insurance ecosystem (see Figure C.2). Insurance companies can, for example, decide to use their customer data to make relevant coupon offers and provide other marketing activities to their customers.

As a matter of fact, it is becoming a popular notion in the financial services industry that the key to customer adoption of digital insurance is providing targeted and timely offers to customers that will entice

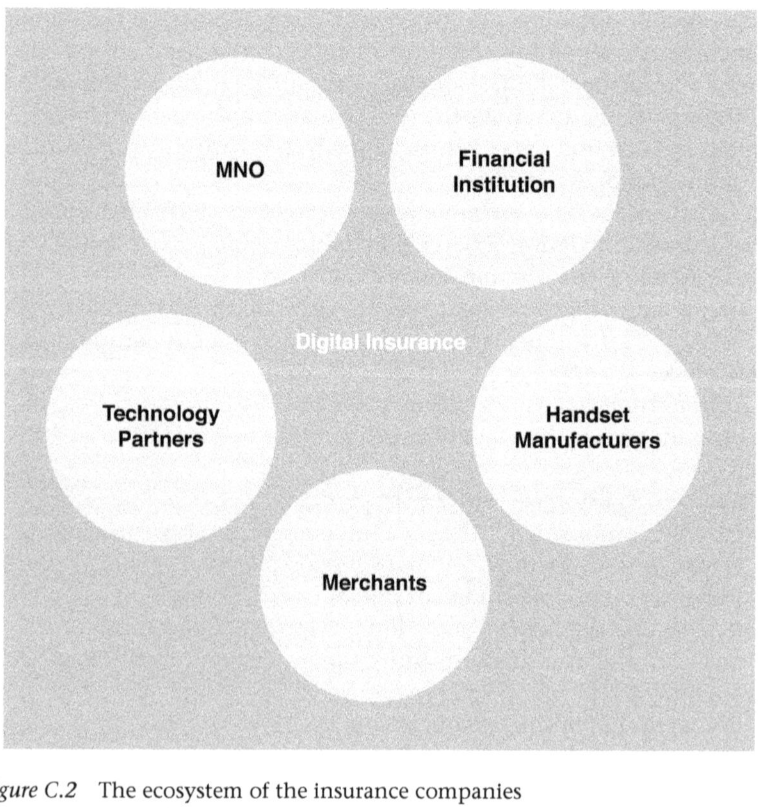

Figure C.2 The ecosystem of the insurance companies

them to communicate and pay with their phones. Many also believe that this puts insurance companies in a strong position in the mobile ecosystem because of the data that insurance companies have and/or they will have even more in the future, thanks to the Internet of Things (IoT), and can process to develop relevant offers.

A survey undertaken by Ngdata and Clear2Pay led to the hypothesis that 80 percent of financial institutions customers thought that insurance companies can make digital insurance more enticing for customers by offering targeted marketing activities. Three-quarters of the respondents said that their financial institutions would be interested in facilitating commerce between merchants and their customers through such activities.[4] The data behind those marketing activities will determine how enticing the offers are and how successful the digital insurance initiatives will be. Some insurance companies have realized this and are looking at new ways to leverage more customer data (by using big data analytics) to push adoption through better and easier marketing and e-commerce activities.

Arming customers with real-time information regarding their current insurance position is useful. However, combining financial data with GPS technology will enable insurance companies to provide value-added services not traditionally associated with insurance companies, as well as counter the threats of nontraditional competitors. An example is location-specific services such as customized or special offers. A message on the smartphone or tablet can inform the customer that he or she can get a discount on the travel insurance on the flight that he or she is boarding. The smartphone can also act as a payment device. Embracing the smartphone as a device to replace debit or credit cards also provides insurance companies the possibility of offering new financial services.

Innovation in business models

A more difficult but more rewarding innovation is based on new business models. More and more today it is necessary to think in terms of platforms[5] and ecosystems.[6,7]

A survey by Accenture's Technology Labs in collaboration with Accenture Research, a business leader, found that 75 percent of insurance companies believe that, in the future, industry boundaries will dramatically blur as platforms reshape industries into ecosystems. Most insurers are still tied to a business model based on pooling risk, calculating average pricing, and generating gross premium income. This model will come under increased threats in the future as the IoT, big data analytics, digital channels, and artificial intelligence (AI) enable insurance companies to assess and price risk directly and individually. The result pointed out by Accenture is the move from a "Me Economy" to a "We Economy."[8]

The ICT services provider Tech Mahindra is taking a different approach to the challenge of using data to push relevant offers to customers. All of the customer data that can be used today to make relevant offers is often divided up among many organizations. Telco providers, insurance companies, and banks all have different data on the same customers, and combining all of that data across the organizations could lead to more relevant offers than any one of those organizations could provide on its own.

With that in mind, Tech Mahindra designed a platform called the Global Inter-Carrier Gateway for Context Aware m-Commerce that can combine data from different organizations to produce offers for mobile customers.[9] The platform connects with insurance companies, financial services, mobile network operators, payments processors, merchants, and card networks. It is unclear if this initiative will succeed. Certainly it is a possible and interesting development of the financial services ecosystem.

If customer adoption of digital insurance depends heavily on customer data, then insurance companies are going to have to figure out also how they want to use their data to participate in the financial services space, and with whom – if anyone – they are willing to share that data, of course in full respect of data privacy issues.

Finally, imagine an entrepreneur with an idea, and an insurance company delivering everything from the incorporation of the organization to the insurance policy for the assets and the employees of the new company. It would be very interesting. Understanding potential customers before they become real ones is one of the most innovative, and rewarding thing an insurance company can do.

According to the *Harvard Business Review* (2014),[10] a thoughtful digitization program can result in a 65 percent cost reduction, a 90 percent reduction in turnaround time on key insurance processes, and improve conversion rates by more than 20 percent.

The future is limited only by our imagination.

Notes

Introduction

1. Financial Institution Group (2012), "The Triple Transformation: Achieving a Sustainable Business Model," *2nd McKinsey Annual Review on the Banking Industry*, October.
2. Carney, E. (2015), "Is Google Buying CoverHound? The Curious Case of the California Insurance License," *WSJ Blog*, January.
3. Nicoletti, B. (2014), *Mobile Banking: Evolution or Revolution*, Palgrave-MacMillan, London.
4. Nicoletti, B. (2014), op. cit.
5. Nicoletti, B. (2012), *The Methodology of Lean and Digitize*, Gower Press, London.
6. Nicoletti, B. (2013), *Cloud Computing for Financial Services*, Palgrave-MacMillan, London.
7. Bower, J.L., Christensen, C.M. (1995), "Disruptive Technologies: Catching the Wave," *Harvard Business Review*, 73(1) (January–February 1995), pp. 43–53.
8. Davies, A. et al. (2012), *Systemic Innovation*, A Social Innovation Europe Report.
9. Nicoletti B. (2012), op. cit.
10. The world is very dynamic. As a consequence, we urge interested readers to follow my blog for updates: www.leandigitize.com.

1 Innovation in Financial Services

1. R. Dobbs, J. Manyika, J. Woetzel (2015), No Ordinary Disruption: The Four Global Forces Breaking All the Trends," *Public Affairs*, May 12.
2. J. Schumpeter (1927), The Explanation of the Business Cycle, *Economica*, 7, 286–311.
3. P. Drucker (1985), *Innovation and Entrepreneurship*, HarperCollins, New York, NY.
4. A. Brem, E. Viardot (Eds) (2013), *Evolution of Innovation Management*, Palgrave-MacMillan, London, UK.
5. J.E. Stallworth (1988), *Improving the Quality of Life for the Black Elderly: Challenges and Opportunities*, U.S. Government Printing Office, Washington, DC.
6. Council on Competitiveness (2004), Innovate America, *National Innovation Initiative Summit and Report*, Washington, DC, Dec. 15.
7. F. Gens (2014), IDC Predictions 2015: Accelerating Innovation – and Growth – on the 3rd Platform, http://itsyn.com/sites/default/files/IDC percent20Forecast percent20for percent202015.pdf, Accessed 10 April 2015.
8. A.D. Chandler (1990), *Strategy and Structure: Chapters in the History of the Industrial Enterprise* (Vol. 120), MIT Press, Cambridge, MA.

9. H.J. Leavitt, H. Bahrami (1988), *Managerial Psychology: Managing Behavior in Organization* (5th ed.), University of Chicago Press, Chicago, IL.
10. R. Verganti (2013), *Design Driven Innovation: Changing the Rules of Competition by Radically Innovating What Things Mean*. Harvard Business Press, Cambridge, MA.
11. B. Nicoletti (2014), Lean and Digitized Innovation, in *Engineering, Technology and Innovation (ICE), 2014 International ICE Conference on IEEE* (pp. 1–7), June, Bergamo, Italy, 23 June.
12. B. Nicoletti (2015), Optimizing Innovation with the Lean and Digitize Innovation Process, *TIM Review*, March.
13. CapGemini-Efma (2015), *World Insurance Report 2015*, file:///C:/Users/Nicoletti/Downloads/WorldInsuranceReport_2015_Web.pdf, Accessed 10 April 2015.
14. CapGemini-Efma (2015), op. cit.
15. H. Broeders, S. Khanna (2015), Strategic Choices for Banks in the Digital Age, *McKinsey Quarterly*, January.
16. http://www.assicurazione.it/DirectLine.html, Accessed 9 April 2015.
17. B. Nicoletti (2012), *The Method of Lean and Digitize*, Gower Publishing, Aldershot, UK.
18. H. Broeders, S. Khanna, (2015), op. cit.
19. Manyikam J. et al. (2011), Big Data: The Next Frontier for Innovation, Competition, and Productivity, *McKinsey Global Institute*, May.
20. J.F. Gasc, E. Sandquist, E. (2014), Seizing the Opportunities of Digital Transformation, *Accenture White Paper.*
21. L. Galvagni (2015), Generali aumentera' i dividendi, *Il Sole 24 Ore*, 1 May, p. 28.
22. D. Garth (2011), The Insurance Tipping Point: Innovation and Transformation, *Journal of Insurance Operations*, March.
23. A.M. Perrault (2007), An Exploratory Study of Biology Teachers' Online Information-Seeking, *School Library Media Research*, 10.
24. D. Garth (2011), op. cit.
25. J.F. Gasc, R. Caillet, T.D. Meyer (2014), The Digital Insurer Double the Profits: How High-Performance Insurers Can Create Business Value from Digital Transformation, *Accenture Research Paper.*
26. —— (2013), Genialloyd, al via piattaforma multidevice, *Insurancetrade.it.*
27. J. Cusano (2014). From Digital Wallflower to Digital Disrupter, *Accenture Research Paper.*
28. R. Narsalay and R. Viswanathan (2015), India's path to digitalization, *Accenture Research Paper.*
29. J.F. Gasc, E. Sandquist, E. (2014), Seizing the Opportunities of Digital Transformation, *Accenture Research Paper.*
30. D. Lovell (2013), Are Aggregators the Right Option for Your Car Insurance? *ASDA Money*, 19 November.
31. P. Evans, P. Forth (2015), Navigating a World of Digital Disruption, *BCG Report.*
32. —— (2013), Reaching Maturity in Digital Insurance Will Call for a Focus across Several Dimensions, *Ernst & Young White* Paper, EYG no. EK 0135.
33. —— (2015), Investments in Digital by Insurance Industry Requires Greater Focus on Customers, *Infosys Survey*, 14 April.

34. M. Fitzerald (2014), Innovation at Tokio Marine and Nichido Fire Insurance Company: Evolution of a Digital Customer Engagement Platform, *Celent Case Studies*, 28 November.
35. J. Hockling (2014), Insurance and Technology Evolution and Revolution in a Digital World, *Morgan Stanley Research Blue Paper*, 8 September.
36. D. Garth (2011), op. cit.
37. http://www.parkrun.co.za/news/, Accessed 8 March 2015.
38. M. Porter (1998), *Competitive Strategy: Techniques for Analyzing Industries and Competitors*, Free Press, New York, NY.

2 The Management of Digital Insurance

1. B. Nicoletti (1976), "Appunti su un modello di sviluppo per l'informatica aziendale," *Sviluppo e Organizzazione*, 7(35), Lug.-Ago., 53–56.
2. Similar categories are elaborated from F. Georgi, J. Pinkl (2005), "Mobile Banking in Deutschland – Der zweite Anlauf," *Die Bank*, Issue 3/2005, 57–61.
3. R. Tiwari, S. Buse (2007), *The Mobile Commerce Prospects: A Strategic Analysis of Opportunities in the Banking Sector*, Hamburg University Press, Hamburg.
4. B. Meara (2015), Celent Model Bank 2015 Part 2: Case Studies of Omnichannel Banking, *Celent Paper*, March.
5. I. Bright (2013), "European Consumers Empowered by Digital Insurance", ING, 1 July, http://www.ing.com/Our-Company/Press-room/Press-release-archive/PressRelease/European-consumers-empowered-by-mobile-insurance-1.htm, accessed 11 April 2015.
6. B. Niehaves, S. Köffer, and K. Ortbach (2012), "IT Consumerization – A Theory and Practice Review", *AMCIS 2012 Proceedings*. Paper 18, July 29.
7. http://it.infor.com/product-summary/erp/ln/, accessed 6 May 2015.
8. N. Jones (2014), Top 10 Mobile Technologies and Capabilities for 2015 and 2016, *Gartner Research*, 12 Feb.
9. B. Nicoletti (2012), *Lean and Digitize*. Gower Publishing, Farnham, UK.
10. A. Mamiit (2015), "Google Plans to Sell Auto Insurance: Be Ready US Insurance companies," *Tech Times*, 9 January.
11. Consumers and Mobile Financial Services (2012), *Federal Reserve Board Publication*, March, http://www.federalreserve.gov/econresdata/mobile-device-report-201203.pdf, accessed 15 April 2015.
12. F.D. Davis (1989), "Perceived Usefulness, Perceived Ease of Use, and User Acceptance of Information Technology," *MIS Quarterly*, 13(3), 319–340.
13. C. Kim, M. Mirusmonov, I. Lee (2010), "An Empirical Examination of Factors Influencing the Intention to Use Mobile Payment," *Computers in Human Behavior*, 26(3), May, 310–322.
14. P.G. Schierz et al. (2010), "Understanding Customer Acceptance of Mobile Payment Services: An Empirical Analysis," *Electronic Commerce Research and Applications*, 9(3), May–June, 209–216.
15. S. McKechnie, H. Winklhofer, C. Ennew (2006). "Applying the Technology Acceptance Model to the Online Retailing of Financial Services." *International Journal of Retail & Distribution Management*, 34(4/5), 388–410.
16. M.L. Fleming, M.D. Hatfield, M.K. Wattana, K.H. Todd (2014). "Exploratory Study of Emergency Physicians' Use of a Prescription Monitoring Program

Using a Framework of Technology Acceptance." *Journal of Pain and Palliative Care Pharmacotherapy*, 28(1), 19–27.
17. Adapted by the author from M.L. Fleming, M.D. Hatfield, M.K. Wattana, K.H. Todd (2014). "Exploratory Study of Emergency Physicians' Use of a Prescription Monitoring Program Using a Framework of Technology Acceptance." *Journal of Pain and Palliative Care Pharmacotherapy*, 28(1), 19–27.
18. B. Nicoletti (2014), *Mobile Banking: Evolution or Revolution?*, Palgrave-Macmillan, London.
19. J.F. Gasc, R. Caillet, T.D. Meyer (2014), The Digital Insurance Company Doubles the Profits: How High-Performance Insurance Companies Can Create Business Value from Digital Transformation, *Accenture Research Paper.*
20. Tower Group (2010), Top 10 Business Drivers, Strategic Responses, IT Initiatives In US Digital Insurance And Payments, Tower Group Research Paper.
21. S.H. Hsieh, C.T. Liu, L.Y. Tzeng (2014). "Insurance Marketing Channel as a Screening Mechanism: Empirical Evidences from Taiwan Automobile Insurance Market." *The Geneva Papers on Risk and Insurance: Issues and Practice*, 39(1), 90–103.
22. D. Ryan (2014), *Understanding Digital Marketing: Marketing Strategies for Engaging the Digital Generation*. Kogan Page Publishers, London, UK.
23. Policy and Charging: The Path to Service Personalization (2013), Ericsson White Paper, May.
24. Jerome E. McCarthy (1960). *Basic Marketing. A Managerial Approach*, Richard D. Irwin, Homewood, IL.
25. C. Lovelock, P.G. Patterson, J. Wirtz (2014), *Services Marketing*. Pearson Australia, Melbourne, VIC.
26. S. Hollensen (2015). *Marketing Management: A Relationship Approach*. Pearson Education, New York, NY.
27. E. Hsu (2014). "Mobile Marketing." *Haettu, 18,* 1–9.
28. T. Catlin, P. Patiath, I. Segev (2014), Insurance Companies' Untapped Digital Opportunity, *McKinsey on Marketing and Sales*, March.
29. Value Partners (2012), *Mobile Financial Services: A Competitive (and Fragmented) Landscape*, Value Partner report published in collaboration with Fiserv.
30. Osservatorio Digital Insurance (2013), *Mobile Banking: Banca e cliente cavalcano l'onda*, Politecnico di Milano e AbiLab, Giugno.
31. P. Crossman (2011), "What's the ROI of Digital Insurance?" *Bank Technology News*, May.
32. P. Crossman (2011), op. cit.
33. C. Yee, C. Rashad Yazdanifard (2014). "How Customer Perception Shape Buying Online Decision." *Global Journal of Management and Business Research*, 14(2), 13–20.
34. Consumers and Mobile Financial Services 2014 (2014), *Board of Governors of the Federal Reserve System*, March.
35. B. Nicoletti (2014), op. cit.
36. Javelin Strategy Research (2013), Javelin Identifies $1.5 B in Mobile Banking Cost Savings by Leveraging Omnichannel Approach, *Javelin Research Report*, July, https://www.javelinstrategy.com/news/1424/92/Javelin-Identifies-1-5-B-in-Mobile-Banking-Cost-Savings-by-Leveraging-Omnichannel-Approach/d,pressRoomDetail, accessed 17 August 2013.

37. Javelin Strategy Research (2013), op. cit.
38. J.F. Gasc (2015a), "Are Insurance Companies Getting Enough Bang from Their Digital Investments Buck?," *Accenture Insurance Blog*, 17 February, http://insuranceblog.accenture.com/are-insurers-getting-enough-bang-from-their-digital-investments-buck/, accessed 22 Jul. 2015.
39. J.F. Gasc (2015b), Double the Profits: How High-Performance Insurance Companies Can Create Business Value from Digital Transformation, *Accenture Report*.
40. J.F. Gasc (2015a), op. cit.
41. T. Catlin, P. Patiath, I. Segev (2014), op. cit.
42. The Digital Insurance Company (2013), Accenture 2013 Consumer-Driven Innovation Survey: Playing to Win, *Accenture Report.*
43. T. Catlin, P. Patiath, I. Segev (2014), op. cit.
44. T. Catlin, P. Patiath, I. Segev (2014), op. cit.
45. A. Humphrey (2005), SWOT Analysis for Management Consulting, *SRI Alumni Newsletter (SRI International)*, December.
46. Javelin Strategy Research (2013), Mobile Deposit Changing the Role for Agency Interactions, *Javelin Research Report*, San Francisco, 9 July.
47. Javelin Strategy Research, (2013), op. cit.
48. Iso, ISO/IECJTC1/SC35-UserInterfaces, http://www.iso.org/iso/iso_catalogue/catalogue_tc/catalogue_tc_browse.htm?commid=45382&published=on, accessed 8 May 2015.
49. B. Nicoletti (2013), *Cloud Computing in Financial Services*, Palgrave-Macmillan, London.
50. M. Josefowicz (2013), Bring Your Own Device (BYOD) at US Insurance Companies, *Novarica Research Report*, Feb.
51. J. Busch (2013), What's Next, *ISM Risk Conference*, Chicago.
52. B. Nicoletti (2014), op. cit.
53. IBM (2013), *IBM BusinessConnect 2013: Realize the Art of the Possible*, 6–9 July, Bucharest.
54. S. Zhen (2013), "Every Banking App," *American Banker*, 5 August.
55. H.T. Krause et al. (1999), *Insurance Information Systems*, 3rd Edition, Insurance Institute of America, Malvern, PA. See also I. Lloyd (2014). *Information Technology Law*. Oxford University Press, Oxford, OX.
56. H.T. Krause et al. (1999), op. cit.
57. H.T. Krause et al. (1999), op. cit.

3 The Digital Insurance Basic Systems

1. "M&A in Insurance: Start of a New Wave?" (2015), *Sigma*, No. 3.
2. In compiling this chapter, we have taken into account a book that we recommend, although it is a little bit dated: H.T. Krause et al. (1999), *Insurance Information Systems*, 3rd edition, Insurance Institute of America, Malvern, PA.
3. S.N. Lee, D. Ko, S. Park, S. Kim (2014), "An Approach To Building Domain Architectures Using Domain Component Model and Architectural Tactics," *International Journal of Engineering Systems Modelling and Simulation*, 6(1), 54–61.

4. IBM Industry Models for Insurance (2012), *IBM White Papers*.
5. IBM Insurance Framework (2010), *IBM Presentation*.
6. B. Kohleret al. (2014), Reference Architecture for SAP – SAP for Insurance, *SAP White Paper*, 17 December.
7. See endnote 2.
8. R.M. Hanley (2014), "Is Digital and Social Media Marketing Right for Your Business?," *Irmi*, February.
9. B. Nicoletti (2014), *Mobile Banking*, Palgrave-Macmillan, London.
10. M. Fitzgerald. (2013), "Stand-Alone Insurance Portal Solutions: An Overview of Vendor Offerings," *Celent Vendor Reviews*, 28 June.
11. J.M. Raol, K.S. Koong, L.C. Liu, C.S. Yu (2003), "An Identification and Classification of Enterprise Portal Functions and Features," *Industrial Management & Data Systems*, 103(9), 693–702.
12. C.M. Jonker, R.A. Lam, J. Treur. (1999, July). A multi-agent architecture for an intelligent website in insurance. In*CIA* (Vol. 99, 86–100).
13. J. Kolko (2014), *Well-Designed: How to Use Empathy to Create Products People Love*. Harvard Business Press, Cambridge, MA.
14. C. Stephanidis (ed.) (2011), Universal Access in Human-Computer Interaction. *Users Diversity*. Proceedings of the 6th International Conference, UAHCI 2011, held as Part of HCI International 2011, Orlando, FL, 9–14 July 2011 (Vol. 6766). Springer Science & Business Media, New York.
15. K. Monks (2015), Mobile and Web Self-Service Roadmaps: Where Are Life Insurers Headed?, *Celent Industry Trends Report*, 16 April.
16. SAP, SAP Business Wrehouse,, https://help.sap.com/saphelp_nw74/helpdata/en/b2/e50138fede083de10000009b38f8cf/frameset.htm, accessed 6 May 2015.
17. Ergo investe sulla gestione delle relazioni con i clienti (2012), *Insurancetrade.it*.
18. M. Corso et al. (2008), Le Intranet nelle Banche Italiane, *Rapporto Abi Lab Politecnico di Milano*, November.
19. J.F. Gasc, R. Caillet, T.D. Meyer (2014), The Digital Insurer Double the Profits: How High-Performance Insurers Can Create Business Value from Digital Transformation, *Accenture Research Paper*.
20. C. Barry, D. Albertazzi (2011), Corporate Mobile Banking: A Look at JP Morgan ACCESS Mobile, *Aite Paper*, October.
21. B. Youra (2015), "The State of Banking in 2015: Our Experts Weigh in," *Gallup Opinion*, 29 January.

4 Advanced Solutions

1. B. Nicoletti (2012), *Lean and Digitize*, Gower Publishing, Abingdon, UK.
2. T. Catlin, P. Paliath, I. Segey (2014), "Insurance Companies' Untapped Digital Opportunity," *Harvard Business Review*. 24 March.
3. M. Chui et al. (2012), *The Social Economy: Unlocking Value and Productivity through Social Technologies*, McKinsey Global Institute Report, July.
4. T. Catlin, P. Paliath, I. Segey (2014), op. cit.
5. J. Bersin (2012), "The Move from Systems of Record to Systems of Engagement," *Forbes*, 16 August. http://www.forbes.com/sites/joshbersin/2012/08/16/

the-move-from-systems-of-record-to-systems-of-engagement/, accessed 27 July 2015.

6. G. Toppo, P. Overberg (2014), "U.S. Population Growth Slows to Just 0.71 Percent," *USA Today*. 7 October.
7. K. Monks, N. Michellod (2014), *Digital Transformation in Insurance: Differences across Continents*, Celent Industry Trends Report, 12 September.
8. C. McMahon (2015), "Top 5 Tech Trends," *Digital Insurance Networking News*, January.
9. M. Hillebrand (2014), "6 Key IT Segments That Insurance Companies Will Enhance in 2015," *Property Casualty 360*, 30 September.
10. 2015 World Insurance Report (2015), *Cap Gemini-Efma Report.*
11. Cisco (2013), Cisco Customer Experience Research Retail Insurance Results Global Data, ://newsroom.cisco.com/documents/10157/1142732/CiscoCustomerExperienceReport_for_Retail_Insurance_Global.pdf, accessed 15 August 2013.
12. B. Nicoletti (2014), *Mobile Banking: Evolution or Revolution*, Palgrave-Macmillan, London.
13. *Consumers and Mobile Financial Services* (2012) Federal Reserve Board Publication, March http://www.federalreserve.gov/econresdata/mobile-device-report-201203.pdf, accessed 15 August 2013.
14. E. Carney (2012), "The Future of Insurance Is More Mobile Than Ever," *Forrester Research*, 3 February.
15. K. Moks, N. Michellod (2014), op. cit.
16. W. Jack, T. Suri (2010), The Economics of M-PESA, *MIT Sloan White Paper*.
17. G. Agarwal (2007), "Financial Inclusion through Mobile Phone Insurance: Issues and Challenges," *Cab Calling*.
18. R. Shevlin (2012), *The Global Rise of Smartphonatics: Driving Mobile Payment and Insurance Adoption in the United States, EMEA, and Asia-Pacific*, Aite Group Report, 14 May.
19. McKinsey Co. (2011), *Big Data: The Next Frontier for Innovation, Competition and Productivity*, McKinsey Global Institute Report, May, http://www.mckinsey.com/insights/business_technology/big_data_the_next_frontier_for_innovation, accessed 13 August 2013.
20. R. Kirkpatrick. (2013), "Big Data for Development," *Big Data*. March, 1(1), pp. 3–4. doi:10.1089/big.2012.1502.
21. Mobile Marketing Association (MMA) (2009), "Digital Insurance Overview (NA)", *Mobile Marketing Association Paper*, January, http://www.mmaglobal.com/minsuranceoverview.pd, accessed August 19, 2013.
22. (2011), "Javelin Reveals the Most Secure Digital Insurance Channels," *Business Wire*, 20 December, http://www.businesswire.com/news/home/20111220005887/en/Javelin-Reveals-Secure-Mobile-Insurance-Channels, accessed 9 August 2013.
23. E. Carney. (2014), "Forrester Research Takes Six US Mobile Auto Insurance Apps Out for a Test Drive," *Forrester Research*, 14 November.
24. C. Barry, D. Albertazzi (2011), Corporate Digital Insurance: A Look at JP Morgan ACCESS Mobile, *Aite Paper*, October.
25. L. Eadicicco (2014), "Steve Jobs Thought Two-Buttons for a Mouse Was a Failure in Design," *Business Insider*, 11 March.

26. R. Feldman, J. Sanger (2007), *The Text Mining Handbook: Advanced Approaches in Analyzing Unstructured Data*, Cambridge University Press, Cambridge, UK.
27. T. Hey, S. Tansley, K. Tolle (eds) (2009), The Fourth Paradigm, *Microsoft Research*, Redmond, WA.
28. "Banking on Big Data" (2014), *Banking Technology*, 3 December.
29. S.C.W.C. Albright, W. Winston, C. Zappe (2010), *Data Analysis and Decision Making*. Cengage Learning, Boston, MA.
30. J. Cutroni (2010), *Google Analytics*. Amazon Media EU S.a r.l., Luxembourg.
31. A. Bhargava (2014), A Dozen Ways Insurers Can Leverage Big Data for Business Value, *Tata Consultancy Services White Paper*.
32. T.H. Davenport (2013), "Analytics 3.0," *Harvard Business Review*, December.
33. T.H. Davenport (2013), op. cit.
34. T.H. Davenport. (2013), op. cit.
35. McKinsey Co. (2011), op. cit.
36. R. Thomas (2011), IBM Big Data Success Story, *IBM Paper*.
37. P. Evans, P. Forth, (2015), Navigating a World of Digital Disruption, *BCG Report*.
38. N. Lohit (2013), "Big Data, Bigger Facts," blogs.sap.com, 5 July. http://blogs.sap.com/innovation/big-data/big-data-bigger-facts-098520, accessed 4 October 2013.
39. K. Monks, N. Michellod (2014), *Digital Transformation in Insurance: Differences across Continents*, Celent Industry Trends Report, 12 September.
40. T. Catlin, P. Patiath, I. Segev (2014), Insurance Companies' Untapped Digital Opportunity, *McKinsey on Marketing and Sales*, March
41. Carolyn J. Dawson (2011), "EMC Documentum xCP Helps Generali Transform Business Processes", *Insurance Technology*, 4 November.
42. —— (2011), Terminology: Operational analytics, *DBMS2*, Nov.
43. P. Italiano (2015),"Gestione sinistri: l'online ad alta integrazione", *Insurancetrade.it*, 4 April.
44. E. Brynjolfsson, M. Lorin, H.K. Heekyung (2011), "Strength in Numbers: How Does Data-Driven Decisionmaking Affect Firm Performance?," ssrn.com, April 22, http://ssrn.com/abstract=1819486 or http://dx.doi.org/10.2139/ssrn.1819486, accessed 5 May 2015.
45. —— (2013), The emerging big returns on big data, *A TCS Global Trend Study*
46. S. Mendel, (2015), "Digital Insurance for the Long Tail", *Bcg Perspectives*, 1 May.
47. —— (2013), Novarica Customer Webinar, Novarica, 13 August.
48. J. Bughin, J. Manyika (2012), *Internet Matters: Essays in Digital Transformation*, McKinsey Report, March.
49. D. Court (2015), "Getting Big Impact from Big Data," *McKinsey Quarterly*, No. 1.
50. S. Ransbotham, S. Kiron, P. Kirk Prentice (2015), "The Talent Dividend," *MIT Sloan Management Review*, 25 April.
51. B. Nicoletti (2012) *Cloud Computing in Financial Services*, Palgrave-Macmillan, London.
52. P. Evans, P. Forth (2015), *Navigating a World of Digital Disruption*, BCG Report.

53. P. Mel, T. Grance (2011), "The NIST Definition of Cloud Computing," *NIST Special Publication* 800–145. September.
54. B. Nicoletti, C. Andreoli (2014), Total Cost Management and Cloud Computing, *Icec 2014*, Milan, Italy, 20–23 October.
55. R.D. Archibald and D. Prado (2014), The Importance of Knowing Your Project, Program, and Portfolio Management Maturity: PPPMM, *PM World Journal*;Feb., Vol. 3 Issue 2, p. 1.
56. http://www.enisystems.com/eninew/latest/blue/news/IBMSystem_z_Software_Virtualization_Virtualization_Server_Smarter_Computing.pdf, accessed 25 April 2015.
57. The suggestions from the Italian Garante della Privacy are contained in a Vademecum: http://www.garanteprivacy.it/web/guest/home/docweb/-/docweb-display/docweb/1895296, accessed 25 April 2015.
58. B. Nicoletti, C. Andreoli (2014), op. cit.
59. B. Darrow (2012), Amazon Is No. 1. "Who's Next in Cloud Computing?" 14 March, gigaom.com, https://gigaom.com/2012/03/14/amazon-is-no-1-whos-next-in-cloud-computing/, accessed 9 April 2015.
60. B. Violino (2014), "81 Percent of Companies Shifting Mission Critical Apps to Cloud," *Forrester Research Study*, November 25. B. Nicoletti, C. Andreoli (2014), op. cit.
61. —— (2005), Intelligent Document Integration Automates Insurance Policy Forms for Big Cost Savings, *InformationWeek*, 28 March.
62. McCormick, J., (2005), "Charging Ahead", *Baseline*, 24 June.
63. —— (2005), "Intelligent Enterprise," *Forrester Research Paper*, June.
64. T. Paivarinta, B.E. Munkvold (2005), op. cit.
65. B. Nicoletti (2009), Gestione Integrata della Documentazione Tecnica, *L'Impiantistica Italiana*, Anno 22, no. 4, Lug.-Ago., pp. 1–12.
66. The paper assigns to each process one specific application. Some of the applications can actually do more than just supporting that specific process.
67. B. Nicoletti (2012), *Lean and Digitize*. Gower Publishing, Farnham, UK.
68. Ensuring Security and Compliance of Your EMC Documentum Enterprise Content Management System: A Collaborative Effort of EMC Documentum and RSA (2009), *EMC White Paper for Applied Technology*
69. M. Fisher, A. Sheth (2004), "Semantic Enterprise Content Management," in M.P. Singh (ed.), *The Practical Handbook of Internet Computing*. CRC Press, Bora Raton. FL.
70. —— (2002), The Sarbanes Oxley Ac, Sarbanes-Oxley Compliance Toolkit http://www.soxlaw.com/, accessed 28 April 2015.
71. 107th US Congress (2002), *Public Law* 107–204, 30 July.
72. —— (2015), HCL Congratulates Aegon on Celent Model Insurer Award, *BusinessWire*, 26 March.
73. A. White (2010), "IBM's Big Data and Analytics Analyst Summit, NY, Day 1," blogs.gartner.com, http://blogs.gartner.com/andrew_white/category/enterprise-content-management-ecm/, accessed 5 May 2015.
74. —— (2013), Case Insurance Illinois Mutual Life Insurance Company, *Perceptive Software*, http://www.perceptivesoftware.co.uk/content/dam/psw/www-perceptivesoftware-com/pdfs/en_gb/psl_cs_illinoismutual-1108_uk.pdf, accessed 9 April 2015.

5 Governance

1. W. Van Grembergen (ed.) (2004), *Strategies for Information Technology Governance*. Igi Global, Hershey, PA.
2. http://www.bankofengland.co.uk/pra/Pages/solvency2/default.aspx, accessed 25 April 2015.
3. B. Nicoletti (2012), *The Methodology of Lean and Digitize*, Gower Publishing, Aldershot, UK.
4. B. Nicoletti (2012), op. cit.
5. B. Nicoletti (2006), "Nuovo Pignone, l'arte di fondere Lean Management e Six Sigma," *Computerworld Italia*, 6 December, 1–2.
6. B. Nicoletti (2015), "Optimizing Innovation with the Lean and Digitize Innovation Process," *TIM Review*, March.
7. B. Nicoletti (2012), op. cit.
8. J.P. Womack and D.T. Jones (2003). *Banish Waste and Create Wealth in Your Corporation*. Free Press, New York.
9. D. Socha, T.C. Folsom, J. Justice (2013), Applying Agile Software Principles and Practices for Fast Automotive Development. In *Proceedings of the FISITA 2012 World Automotive Congress* (pp. 1033–1045). Berlin, Germany: Springer.
10. K. Beck et al. (2001), "Principles behind the Agile Manifesto," http://agile-manifesto.org/principles.html, accessed 25 January 2015.
11. T. Yamaguchi, H. Sakaniwa, H. Hayami (2005), "An Innovative Product Dev elopment Process for Resolving Fundamental Conflicts," *Journal of the Japan Society for Precision Engineering, 71*(2), 184–188.
12. T. Kelley (2001). "Prototyping Is the Shorthand of Innovation," *Design Management Journal* (Former Series), *12*(3), 35–42.
13. P. Subramaniyam, K. Srinivasan, M. Prabaharan (2011), "An Innovative Lean Six Sigma Approach for Engineering Design," *International Journal of Innovation, Management and Technology, 2*(2), 166–170.
14. T.J. Marion, J.H. Friar (2012). "Managing Global Outsourcing to Enhance Lean Innovation," *Research Technology Management, 55*(5), 44–50.
15. T. Paider, D. Potts, (2011), *Nationwide Application Development Center*, http://www.thepathtoagility.com/wp-content/uploads/2012/03/Lean percent-20Framework percent20Nationwide.pdf, accessed 9 April 2015.
16. B. Nicoletti (2012), op. cit.
17. Generali (2015), Generali acquires MyDrive Solutions, a leading company in motor insurance technologies, Generali Company Press release, 23 July.
18. P. Roussom (2014), Seven Tips for Unified Master Data Management, *TDWI Research Report.*
19. J.B. Guinée (2002). "Handbook on Life Cycle Assessment Operational Guide to the ISO Standards," *The International Journal of Life Cycle Assessment, 7*(5), 311–313.
20. T. Zhou (2011), An Empirical Examination of Initial Trust in Mobile Payments, *Internet Research, 21*(5), 527–540
21. J. Camhi (2013), 3 "Keys to Improve Data Quality," *Bank Systems Technologies*, 21 June, http://www.banktech.com/business-intelligence/3-keys-to-improving-data-quality/240157060?cid=nl_bt_daily&elq=b7ed8ddc2625499dbf6869cf41f9fd22, accessed 11 April 2015.

22. A.D. Chapman. (2005), Principles of Data Quality, version 1.0, *Report for the Global Biodiversity Information Facility*, Copenhagen.
23. T. Zhou (2011) "An Empirical Examination of Initial Trust in Mobile Banking," *Internet Research, 21*(5), 527–540.
24. Banca d'Italia (2013), *Nuove disposizioni di vigilanza prudenziale per le Banche, Circolare del 17 dicembre 2006 – 15° Aggiornamento del 2 luglio 2013.*
25. P. Das (2015), *New India Assurance*, tcs.com, http://www.tcs.com/resources/case_studies/Pages/New-India-Assurance.aspx?utm_source=feedburner&utm_medium=feed&utm_campaign=Feed percent3A+tcscasestudies+percent28TCS percent3A+Case+Studies percent29&utm_content=FeedBurner+user+view, accessed 28 April 2015.
26. —— (2015), Enterprise Archtecture, Sainsbury ebooks, UK http://samples.sainsburysebooks.co.uk/9781743336670_sample_143931.pdf, accessed 8 May 2015.
27. K. Roebuck (2012). *Enterprise Information Management (EIM): High-Impact Strategies– What You Need to Know: Definitions, Adoptions, Impact, Benefits, Maturity, Vendors*. Emereo Publishing. London, UK.
28. AI Research (2013), *BYOD and Increased Malware Threats Help Driving Billion Dollar Security Services Market in 2013*, http://www.abiresearch.com/press/byod-and-increased-malware-threats-help-driving-bi, accessed 11 April 2015.
29. Digital Insurance Overview (NA) (2009), *American Management Association*, January.
30. M. Bishop (2004), *Introduction to Computer Security*, Addison Wesley Professional, Boston, MA.
31. —— (2003), The Privacy and Electronic Communications (EC Directive) Regulations 2003, http://www.legislation.gov.uk/uksi/2003/2426/contents/made, accessed 1 May 2015.
32. The Board of Governors of the Federal Reserve System, Federal Deposit Insurance Corporation, National Credit Union Administration, Office of the Comptroller of the Currency, Office of Thrift Supervision, State Liaison Committee (2011), Supplement to Authentication in an Internet Banking Environment, *Paper of the Federal Insurance companies Examination Council*, SR 11–9.
33. —— (2002), Authentication in an Internet Banking Environment, *FFIEC IT Examination Handbook* (2003), Information Security Booklet.
34. "ERGO Direkt Mobile Website Rated Exceedingly Trustworthy: TÜV Süd Awards 'S@Fer-Shopping' Seal of Approval" (2015), ergo.com, www.ergo.com, accessed 7 April 2015.
35. A computer program that records every keystroke made by a computer user, especially in order to gain fraudulent access to passwords and other confidential information.
36. Aite Group (2011), Corporate Digital Insurance: A Look at J.P. Morgan ACCESS Mobile, *Aite Report*, http://www.jpmorgan.com/treasury/jpm_access/doc/Corporate_Mobile_Banking_A_Look_at_JP_Morgan_ACCESS_Mobile.pdf, accessed 11 April 2015.
37. (Huawei Ascend W1 – User Guide (2013), *Huawei Paper*.
38. Securing your Mobile Device, Eastern Illinois University, Charleston, IL, http://www.eiu.edu/its/security/mobile2.php, accessed 8 May 2015.

39. A. Schroader (2008), *Handheld Forensics*, http://www.elsevierdirect.com/downloads/SyngressFreeE-booklets/ITManagement/1597491381.pdf, Syngress, Waltham, MA, accessed 11 April 2015.
40. P. Crossman (2015), "Biometric Tipping Point: USAA Deploys Face, Voice Recognition," *INN Breaking News*, 3 February.

6 Regulatory Framework

1. 2015 World Insurance Report (2015), *CapGemini-Efma Report.*
2. This chapter describes some basic regulations that are relevant for Digital insurance transactions. This information aims to provide a general overview of the legal framework governing digital insurance. It neither intends nor claims to provide all-exhaustive, updated, and correct information on the subject.
3. K. Monks, N. Michellod (2014), Digital Transformation in Insurance: Differences across Continents, *Celent Industry Trends Report*, 12 September.
4. —— (2009), Directive 2009/138/Ec of the European Parliament and of the Council, http://eur-lex.europa.eu/LexUriServ/LexUriServ.do?uri=OJ:L:2009:335:0001:0155:en:PDF, accessed 8 May 2015.
5. —— (2013), Financial Services Authority Annual Report 2012/13, https://www.fca.org.uk/static/documents/annual-report/fsa-annual-report-12–13.pdf, accessed 9 May 2015.
6. European Commission (2014), Economic Review of the Financial Regulation Agenda, http://ec.europa.eu/internal_market/finances/docs/general/20140515-erfra-working-document_En.pdf, accessed 9 May 2015.
7. Solvency II: the Data Challenge (2015), *Rimes White Paper.*
8. Solvency II: the Data Challenge (2015), *Rimes White Paper.*
9. R. Tiwari, S., Buse, C. Herstatt (2006), "From Electronic to Mobile Commerce: Opportunities through Technology Convergence for Business Services," *Tech Monitor*, September.
10. R. Tiwari, S. Buse (2007), *The Mobile Commerce Prospects: A Strategic Analysis of Opportunities in the Banking Sector*, Hamburg University Press, Hamburg, Germany.
11. United Nations (2001). UNCITRAL Model Law on Electronic Signatures with Guide to Enactment 2001, http://www.uncitral.org/pdf/english/texts/electcom/ml-elecsig-e.pdf, accessed 9 May 2015.
12. K. Christensen (2013), "Non-compliance Creates Significant Risk with Digital Insurance Products," 8 August, ATM Marketplace, http://www.atmmarketplace.com/blog/10913/Non-compliance-creates-significant-risk-with-mobile-banking-products, accessed 9 August 2013.
13. J.M. Kopchik (2011), "Digital Insurance: Rewards and Risks," *FDIC Winter 2011 Supervisory Insights*, FDIC, 8(2), Winter.
14. EU Regulation 45/2001, Article 2
15. R. Tiwari, S., Buse, C. Herstatt (2008), "From Electronic to Mobile Commerce," *CACCI Journal*, 1, Reprinted from the *Asia-Pacific Tech Monitor*, September–October, 2006, 38–45.
16. R. Tiwari, S. Buse (2007), op cit.
17. R. Tiwari, S. Buse (2007), op cit.

18. R. Becker (2002), *Bürgerliches Gesetzbuch, BMJ*, 1.
19. —— (2015), About EIOPA, https://eiopa.europa.eu/about-eiopa, accessed 9 May 2015.
20. —— (2015), EIOPA Opinions, https://eiopa.europa.eu/publications/eiopa-opinions, accessed 1 May 2015.
21. EIOPA-BoS-14/198 (28 January 2015) https://eiopa.europa.eu/Publications/Opinions/Opinion_on_sale_ percent20via_the_internet percent28published percent29.pdf, accessed 1 May 2015.
22. EurLex (2002), Directive 2002/65/EC of the European Parliament and of the Council of 23 September 2002 concerning the distance marketing of consumer financial services and amending Council Directive 90/619/EEC and Directives 97/7/EC and 98/27/EC, http://eur-lex.europa.eu/legal-content/EN/TXT/?uri=celex:32002L0065, accessed 28 April 2015.
23. EIOPA (2014), Third Consumer Trends Report, https://eiopa.europa.eu/Publications/Reports/EIOPA-BoS-14–207-Third_Consumer_Trends_Report.pdf, accessed 9 May 2015.
24. EIOPA (2014), Report on Good Practices on Comparison Websites ,https://eiopa.europa.eu/Publications/Reports/Report_on_Good_Practices_on_Comparison_Websites.pdf, accessed 9 May 2015.
25. P.L. Kimmelman (2010), The School Leadership Triangle: From Compliance to Innovation, Corwin, Thousand Oaks, CA.

7 Digital Insurance Throughout the World

1. K. Monks, N. Michellod (2014), Digital Transformation in Insurance: Differences Across Continents, *Celent Industry Trends Report*, 12 September.
2. K. Monks, N. Michellod (2014), op. cit.
3. A. Freiling (2015), 2015 European Insurance Outlook, *Ernst & Young Research Paper*.
4. CapGemini-Efma (2015), World Insurance Report 2015, https://www.capgemini.com/thought-leadership/world-insurance-report-2015, accessed 10 April 2015.
5. K. Monks, N. Michellod (2014), op. cit.
6. CapGemini-Efma (2015), op. cit.
7. CapGemini-Efma (2015), op. cit.
8. CapGemini-Efma (2015), op. cit.
9. S. Crawford (2015), 2015 Global Insurance Outlook, *Ernst & Young Report*.
10. CapGemini-Efma (2015), op. cit.
11. K. Lam, J. Sengupta (2013). Retail Banking in Asia, *McKinsey Report*, March.
12. PR Newswire (12 April 2012). ICT in Insurance Industry in India 2012. *Digital Journal*.
13. S. Crawford (2015), op. cit.

8 The Future

1. S. Gupta, M. Kaur, A. Kang, A. (2013), "Role of Mobile Banking in Today's Era," *International Journal for Science and Emerging Technologies with Latest Trends*, 11(1), 5–9.

2. S.R. Vaidya (2011), "Emerging Trends on Functional Utilization of Mobile Banking in Developed Markets in Next 3–4 Years," *International Review of Business Research Papers*, 7(1), 301–312.
3. A. Freiling (2015), 2015 European Insurance Outlook, *Ernst & Young Research Paper*.
4. H.P. Fung (2014), Criteria, Use Cases and Effects of Information Technology Process Automation (ITPA). *Institute for Robotic Process Automation*, 7.
5. 2013: The Year of Anticipation and Refinement (2013), *IPG Media Lab Outlook*.
6. M. Chuiet al. (2012), The Social Economy: Unlocking Value and Productivity through Social Technologies, *McKinsey Global Institute Report*, July.
7. K. Monks, N. Michellod (2014), "Digital Transformation in Insurance: Differences across Continents," *Celent Industry Trends Report*, 12 September.
8. http://www.insurancenetworking.com/blogs/insurance_social_networks_french_insurers-28194–1.html, accessed 15 March 2015.
9. K. Liyakasa (2015), "MetLife Navigates the Path through Publishers' Walled Gardens," *AdExchanger*, 26 January.
10. "Social Insurance Company Relies on Communities to Reduce Premiums" (2011), *Springwise*.com, 18 May.
11. J. Rivera, R. van der Meulen (2013), Forecast: The Internet of Things, Worldwide, 2013, *Gartner Report*, 12 December.
12. Internet of Everything Research Service (2013), *ABI Research Report*, 9 May.
13. J. Anderson, L. Rainie (2014), The Internet of Things Will Thrive By 2025: Main Report: An In-depth Look at Expert Responses, *Pew Research Center*, 14 May.
14. "Mobile Marketing and Service: La Partita Si Fa Seria!" (2015), *Osservatorio Mobile Marketing & Service*, 29 January.
15. H. Zervos (2015), Textile Integration of Electronic Functionality: Market Forecasts for the Next Decade, *Research Innovation and Science for Engineered Fabrics Conference (RISE)*, 9–12 February, Miami, FL.
16. ABI Research (2013), "Wearable Computing Devices, Like Apple's iWatch, will exceed 485 Million Annual Shipments by 2018, http://www.abiresearch.com/press/wearable-computing-devices-like-apples-iwatch-will, accessed 13 August 2013.
17. H. Zervos (2015), op. cit.
18. Accenture Technology Vision for Insurance 2015 – Digital Insurance Era: Stretch Your Boundaries (2015), *Accenture Research Report*.
19. D. Bloomfield (2015), Time to Jog: Hancock Offers Insurance Discount for Good Behavior, *Bloomberg New*, 8 April.
20. D. Bloomfield (2015), op. cit.
21. J.P. Gownder (2014), Smart, Connected Devices Reshape Customer Experiences in Healthcare and Insurance, *Forrester Research*, 12 December.
22. D. Thomas (2015), "Mobile Groups Race to Develop 5G Technology," *Financial Times*, 4 May.

Conclusions

1. —— (2013), Segmented Consumer Experience and Digital Wallet Capabilities Hold Keys to the Future of Mobile Banking, Finds Cognizant and Monitise

Study, 30 July, http://www.monitise.com/news/press_releases?id=786, accessed 1 August 2015.

2. —— (2013), Segmented Consumer Experience and Digital Wallet Capabilities Hold Keys to the Future Of Mobile Banking, Finds Cognizant and Monitise Study, 30 June. http://www.monitise.com/americas/news-and-events/press-releases/2013/0730.php, accessed 18 October 2014.
3. M. Bauer-Leeb, E. Lundqvist (2011), "Social Entrepreneurs and Business Angels," http://unltd.org.uk/wp-content/uploads/2012/11/BVC_Baseline_paper_FINAL.pdf, accessed 22 October 2014.
4. J. Camhi (2013), "How Big Data Can Drive Mobile Payments Adoption," *Bank Systems Technology*, http://www.banktech.com/payments-cards/how-big-data-can-drive-mobile-payments-a/240156872, accessed 11 August 2014.
5. B. Edelman (2015), "How to Launch Your Digital Platform," *Harvard Business Review*, April.
6. P. Drews, I. Schirmer, S., Mumm, M. Morisse (2014). An Empirically Grounded Ontology for Analyzing IT-based Interventions in Business Ecosystems, Twentieth Americas Conference on Information Systems, Savannah, 1–11.
7. Timothy Alborn and Sharon Ann Murphy, eds. (2012), *Anglo⊠American Life Insurance, 1800*–1914, 3 vols. (London: Pickering & Chatto, 2012. Vol. 1, pp. xxiii+ 394; Vol. 2, pp. xx+ 432; Vol. 3, pp. xxvi+ 436).
8. Accenture Technology Vision 2015 (2015), techtrends.accenture.com, http://techtrends.accenture.com/us-en/it-technology-trends-2015.html, accessed 12 May 2015.
9. J. Camhi (2013), op. cit.
10. T. Catlin, P. Paliath, I. Segey (2014), "Insurance Companies' Untapped Digital Opportunity," *Harvard Business Review*. 24 March.

References

Afuah, A. (2003), *Innovation Management: Strategies, Implementation, Profits*, Oxford University Press, Oxford, UK.

Agarwal R., Prasad J. (2000), A Field Study of the Adoption of Software Process Innovations by Information Systems Professionals. *IEEE Transaction on Engineering Management*, *47*(3), 295–308.

Agarwal, R., Venkatesh, V. (2002), Assessing a Firm's Web Presence: A Heuristic Evaluation Procedure for the Measurement of Usability, *Information Systems Research*, *13*(2), 168–186.

AIIM (2013), What Is Enterprise Content Management (ECM)?, *Association for Information, Image Management*, http://www.aiim.org., accessed 20 February 2015.

Alavi M., Leidner D.E. (2001), Review: Knowledge Management, Knowledge Management Systems: Conceptual Foundations, Research Issues. *MIS Quarterly*, *25*(1), 107–146.

Allen, D. (2008), *Enterprise Content Management Best Practices: ECM Strategy 100 Most Asked Questions*. Qld: Emereo Publishing, Newstead, NY.

American Productivity & Quality Center (2007), Executive Summary of Knowledge Management, *Best-Practice Report*, http://www.apqc.org/portal/apqc/ksn?paf_gear_id=contentgearhome&paf_dm=full&pageselect=detail&docid=10820, accessed 5 May 2015.

Amidon, D.M., Mahdjoubi D. (2003), An Atlas for Knowledge Innovation: Migration from Business Planning to Innovation Strategy. In *Handbook on Knowledge Management, Volume 2: Knowledge Directions*, (Holsapple C.W., Ed.), 331–353, Springer-Verlag, Berlin/Heidelberg, Germany.

Anand, B. (2003), *Health Insurance*, MFL Net Services, Hyderabad, India.

Ansah-Adu, K.,Oh, C., Abor, J. (2012), Evaluating the Cost Efficiency of Insurance Companies in Ghana, *The Journal of Risk Finance*, *13*(1), 61–76.

Arshad, N.I., Milton, S.K., Bosua, R. (2014), "Enterprise Content Management Systems-Use Supports Standardized Business Processes," *International Journal of Engineering & Technology*, *14*(2), 10–15.

Ashby, S. (2011), "Risk Management, the Global Banking Crisis: Lessons for Insurance Solvency Regulation," *Geneva Papers on Risk, Insurance – Issues, Practice*, *36*(3), 330–347.

Ba, S., Pavlou, P.A. (2002), Evidence of the Effect of Trust in Electronic Markets: Price Premiums, Buyer Behavior. *MIS Quarterly*, *26*(3), 243–266.

Balasubramanian, S., Konana, P., Menon, N.M. (2003), "Customer Satisfaction in Virtual Environments: A Study of Online Investing," *Management Science*, *49*(7), 871–889.

Barros, C.P., Nektarios, M., Assaf, A. (2010), "Efficiency in the Greek Insurance Industry," *European Journal of Operational Research*, *205*(2), 431–436.

Benton, D. et al. (2010), How Cloud Computing Will Transform Insurance, Accenture Paper, http://insuranceblog.accenture.com/wp-content/uploads/2013/07/Cloud_for_Insurance_POV_Final.pdf, accessed 17 August 2014.

Bishop, M. (2004), *Introduction to Computer Security*, Addison Wesley Professional, Boston.

Black, N.J., Lockett, A., Ennew, C., Winklhofer, H., McKechnie, S. (2002), "Modelling Customer Choice of Distribution Channels: An Illustration from Financial Services," *International Journal of Financial institution Marketing, 20*(4), 161–173.

Black, S.P., Rossi, J.P. (2015), *Entrepreneurship and Innovation in Automobile Insurance: Samuel P. Black, Jr. and the Rise of Erie Insurance*, Routledge, New York.

Blair, B.T. (2004), "An Enterprise Content Management Primer," *Information Management Journal, 38*, 64–66.

Boiko, B. (2002), *Content Management Bible*. John Wiley & Sons, New York.

Bonner D. (2000), *In Action: Leading Knowledge Management*, Learning. ASTD, Alexandria, VA.

Boston Consulting Group (BCG) (2010), The Solvency II Challenge: Anticipating the Far-Ranging Impact on Business Strategy, www.bcg.com, accessed 9 May 2015.

Brem, A., Viardot, E. (Eds.) (2013), *Evolution of Innovation Management*, Palgrave-Macmillan, New York.

Bruce, L., Bondy, K., Street, R., Wilson, H. (2009), "How New Multichannel Thinking Can Deliver Competitive Advantage," *Journal of Direct, Data, Digital Marketing Practice, 10*(4), 329–335.

Buchner, A. (2006), *Marketing Life Insurance Online*. Jupiter Research, New York.

Butt, M. (2007), "Insurance, Finance, Solvency II, Financial Market Interaction," *Geneva Papers on Risk, Insurance – Issues*, Practice, *32*(1), 42–45.

Campbell, C.B. et al. (2002), "Embedded Value of Life Insurance Product Lines," *Boston Annual Meeting 2002 Record*, 28(3).

Carter, F.J., Jambulingam, T., Gupta, V.K., Melone, N. (2001), "Technological Innovations: A Framework For Communicating Diffusion Effects," *Information & Management, 38*(5), 277–287.

Casualty Actuarial Society (CAS) (2012), CAS Research Working Party on Risk-Based Capital Dependencies, Calibration, Report 1 Overview of Dependencies, Calibration in the RBC Formula. 1, www.casact.org, accessed 8 May 2015.

Chen, Y.S., Chang, H.Y. (2009), "Taiwan's Insurance Industry Left Stranded," *Common Wealth Magazine, 417*, 1–7.

Chien, S.C. (2005), *The Principle, Practice of Insurance Accounting*, San-Ming Publisher, Taipei.

Choi, B.P. (2010), "The U.S. Property, Liability Insurance Industry: Firm Growth, Size, Age," *Risk Management, Insurance Review, 13*(2), 207–224.

Chow-Chua, C., Lim, G. (2000), "A Demand Audit of the Insurance Market in Singapore," *Managerial Auditing Journal, 15*(7), 372–382.

Claessens, S., Kose, M.M.A., Kose, M.A., Laeven, M.L., Valencia, F. (2014), *Financial Crises: Causes, Consequences, and Policy Responses*. International Monetary Fund, Washington, DC.

Coelho, F., Easingwood, C. (2003), "Multiple Channel Structures in Financial Services: A Framework," *Journal of Financial Services Marketing, 8*(1), 22–34.

Comité Européen des Assurances (CEA) (2007), Consequences of Solvency II Costs for Insurers Administrative Costs, *Technical Report*.

Committee of European Insurance, Occupational Pension Supervisors (CEIOPS) (2009a), CEIOPS Advice for Level 2 Implementing Measures on Solvency II: Assessment of Group Solvency, www.eiopa.europa.eu., accessed 18 May 2015.

Committee of European Insurance, Occupational Pension Supervisors (CEIOPS) (2009b), Lessons Learned from the Crisis, www.eiopa.europa.eu., accessed 18 May 2015.

Committee of European Insurance, Occupational Pension Supervisors (CEIOPS) (2010), Solvency II – Calibration Paper, www.eiopa.europa.eu., accessed 18 May 2015.

Committee of European Insurance, Occupational Pensions Supervisors (CEIOPS) (2009), Lessons Learned from the Crisis: Solvency II, Beyond, accessed 18 May 2015.

Cox, J., Dale, B.G. (2001), "Service Quality, E-Commerce: An Exploratory Analysis," *Managing Service Quality, 11*(2), 121–131.

Crispo B. et al. (2012), Security Protocols XIX: 19th International Workshop, Cambridge, UK, March 28–30, 2011, *Lecture Notes in Computer Science/Security, Cryptology*.

Crouhy, M., Galai, D. (2014), *The Essentials of Risk Management*, 2nd Edition, McGraw-Hill, New York.

Cummins, J., Phillips, R. (2009), Capital Adequacy, Insurance Risk-Based Capital Systems, *Working Paper*, rmi.gsu.edu, www.rmi.gsu.edu, accessed 19 May 2015.

Cummins, J.D., Rubio-Misas, M. (2006), "Deregulation, Consolidation, Efficiency: Evidence from the Spanish Insurance Industry," *Journal of Money, Credit, Banking, 38*(2), 323–355.

Cummins, J.D., Weiss, M.A. (2000), "Analyzing Firm Performance in the Insurance Industry Using Frontier Efficiency, Productivity Methods," in G. Dionne (ed.), *Handbook of Insurance*, Kluwer Academic Publishers, Boston, MA., 767–829.

Cummins, J.D., Xie, X. (2013), "Efficiency, Productivity, Scale Economies in the U.S. Property-Liability Insurance Industry," *Journal of Productivity Analysis, 39*(2), 141–164.

Customers, Mobile Financial Services (2012), *Federal Reserve Board Publication*, March, http://www.federalreserve.gov/econresdata/mobile-device-report-201203.pdf, accessed 15 August 2013.

Darlap, P., Mayr, B. (2006), "Group Aspects of Regulatory Reform in the Insurance Sector," *Geneva Papers on Risk, Insurance – Issues, Practice 31*(1), 96–123.

Data Monitor Research Store. (2010), UK Private Motor Insurance 2010, available athttp://www.datamonitor.com/store/Product/toc.aspx?productId=DMFS2495, accessed 23 April 2015.

Davenport, T.H., Beck, J.C. (2001), *The Attention Economy: Understanding the New Currency of Business*, Harvard Business School Press, Boston.

Dawes, J., Mundt, K., Sharp, B. (2009) "Consideration Sets for Financial Services Brands," *Journal of Financial Services Marketing, 14*(3), 190–202.

Diacon, S., O'Brien, C. (2002) Persistency in UK Long-Term Insurance: Customer Satisfaction, Service Quality, *CRIS Discussion Papers III*, University of Nottingham, Nottingham, UK.

Diacon, S.R. (2001), The Efficiency of UK General Insurance Companies, Working Paper, Centre for Risk, *Insurance Studies*, University of Nottingham, Nottingham, UK.

Diacon, S.R., Starkey, K., O'Brien, C. (2002), "Size, Efficiency in European Long-Term Insurance Companies: An International Comparison," *Geneva Papers on Risk, Insurance – Issues, Practice, 27*(3), 444–466.

Dilnutt, R. (2006), "Enterprise Content Management: Supporting Knowledge Management Capability," *International Journal of Knowledge, Culture, Change Management, 5*, 73–84.

Dilnutt, R. (2006), "Surviving the Information Explosion," *IEE Engineering Management, 16*, 39–41.

Dinh, T.L., Rickenberg, T.A., Fill, H.G., Breitner, M.H. (2014), "Towards a Knowledge-based Framework for Enterprise Content Management," in *System Sciences (HICSS), 2014 47th Hawaii International Conference on*, January, 3543–3552.

Doff, R. (2008), "A Critical Analysis of the Solvency II Proposals," *Geneva Papers on Risk, Insurance – Issues, Practice, 33*(2), 193–206.

Dunham, K., Abu Nimeh, S., Becher, M. (2008), *Mobile Malware Attack, Defense*, Syngress Media, Waltham, MA.

Eckstein, A., Liebetrau, A. (2014), *Insurance & Innovation 2014: Ideen und Erfolgskonzepte von Experten aus der Praxis*, Verlag Versicherungswirtschaft Gmbh, Karlsruhe, Germany.

Eling, M., Gatzert, N., Schmeiser, H. (2008), "The Swiss Solvency Test, Its Market Implications," *Geneva Papers on Risk, Insurance – Issues, Practice 33*(3), 418–439.

Eling, M., Luhnen, M. (2010a), "Efficiency in the International Insurance Industry: A Cross-Country Comparison," *Journal of Banking Finance, 34*(7), 1497–1509.

Eling, M., Luhnen, M. (2010b), "Frontier Efficiency Methodologies to Measure Performance in the Insurance Industry: Overview, Systematization, Recent Developments," *Geneva Papers on Insurance – Issues, Practice, 35*(2), 217–265.

Eling, M., Schmeiser, H., Schmit, J. (2007), "The Solvency II Process: Overview, Critical Analysis, Risk Management," *Insurance Review, 10*(1), 69–85.

Engau, C., Hoffmann, V.H. (2011), "Corporate Response Strategies to Regulatory Uncertainty: Evidence from Uncertainty about Post-Kyoto Regulation," *Policy Sciences, 44*(1), 53–80.

European Commission (EC) (2002), "Directive 2002/87/EC of the European Parliament, of the Council of 16 December 2002 on the Supplementary Supervision of Credit Institutions, Insurance Undertakings, Investment Firms in a Financial Conglomerate," *Official Journal of the European Union*, www.eur-lex.europa.eu, accessed 9 May 2015.

European Commission (EC) (2009), "Directive 2009/138/EC of the European Parliament, of the Council of 25 November 2009 on the Taking-Up, Pursuit of the Business of Insurance, Reinsurance (Solvency II)," *Official Journal of the European Union*, www.eur-lex.europa.eu, accessed 9 May 2015.

European Commission (EC) (2010), QIS5 Technical Specifications, www.ec.europa.eu, accessed 9 May 2015.

European Commission (EC) (2011), Solvency II: Frequently Asked Questions (FAQs), www.ec.europa.eu, accessed 9 May 2015.

European Commission (EC) (2011), "Directive 2011/89/EU of the European Parliament, of the Council of 16 November 2011 amending directives 98/78/EC, 2002/87/EC, 2006/48/EC, 2009/138/EC as Regards The Supplementary Supervision Of Financial Entities in a Financial Conglomerate," *Official Journal of the European Union*, www.eur-lex.europa.eu, accessed 9 May 2015.

European Insurance, Occupational Pensions Authority (EIOPA) (2011), QIS5 Results: General Findings, Surplus, Preparedness, www.eiopa.europa.eu/

fileadmin/tx_dam/files/consultations/QIS/QIS5/HearingQIS5slides%20 [Compatibility%20Mode].pdf, accessed 9 May 2015.

European Insurance, Occupational Pensions Authority (EIOPA) (2012), Request for the EU-U.S. Dialogue Project for Public Comment on the Technical Committee Reports; Comparing Certain Aspects of the Insurance Supervisory, Regulatory Regimes in the European Union, the United States, https://eiopa.europa.eu, accessed 9 May 2015.

Evans, P., Forth, P. (2015), Navigating a World of Digital Disruption, *BCG Report.*

Federal Assembly of the Swiss Confederation (2004), Insurance Supervision Act, www.finma.ch., accessed 9 May 2015.

Filipović, D., Kupper, M. (2007), "On the Group Level Swiss Solvency Test," *Bulletin of the Swiss Association of Actuaries, 1*(1), 97–115.

Fill, H.G. (2009), Design of Semantic Information Systems using a Model-based Approach, *AAAI Spring Symposium*, Stanford University, Stanford, CA.

Financial Services Authority (2008), "Review into General Insurance Comparison Websites," May, available at http://www.fsa.gov.uk/pages/Doing/Regulated/Promo/thematic/review_gi_comparison.shtml, accessed 16 August 2014.

Fiorina, P. (2009), Key Trends in Mobile Financial Services in the European Union, *Research Paper by Celent Group.*

Flier, B. et al. (2001), "The Changing Landscape of the European Financial Services Sector," *Long Range Planning, 34*(2), 179–207.

Gayathri, H., Vinaya, M.C., Lakshmisha, K. (2006), "A Pilot Study on the Service Quality of Insurance Companies," *Journal of Services Research, 5*(2), 123–138.

Glau, K., Scherer, M. (2015), *Innovations in Quantitative Risk Management*, Springer, Munich.

Gogerty, N. (2014), *The Nature of Value: How to Invest in the Adaptive Economy*, Columbia Business School Publishing, New York.

Grahlmann, K.R., Helms, R.W., Hilhorst, C., Brinkkemper, S., Amerongen, S.V. (2012), "Reviewing Enterprise Content Management: A Functional Framework," *European Journal of Information Systems, 21*, 268–286.

Grahlmann, K.R., Hilhorst, C., Amerongen, S.V., Helms, R., Brinkkemper, S. (2010), Impacts of Implementing Enterprise Content Management Systems, in *18th European Conference on Information Systems South Africa.*

Gupta, H. (2007), "The Role of Insurance in Health Care Management in India," *International Journal of Health Care Quality Assurance, 20*(5), 379–391.

Gupta, V.K., Govindarajan, S., Johnson, T. (2002), "Overview of Content Management Approaches, Strategies," *Electronic Markets, 11*(4), 281–287.

Gurtner, S., Soyez, K. (2014), *Challenges and Opportunities in Health Care Management*, Springer Verlag, Heidelberg, Germany.

Hampton, J. (2014), *Fundamentals of Enterprise Risk Management: How Top Companies Assess Risk, Manage Exposure, and Seize Opportunity*, AMA, New York.

Han, Y. (2004), "Digital Content Management: The Search for a Content Management System," *Library Hi Tech, 22*(4), 355–365.

Harrison, N. (2005), The Darwin Information Typing Architecture (DITA), Applications for Globalization, *Professional Communication Conference*, 115–121.

Hayes-Roth, F. (2005), Model-Based Communication Networks, VIRT: Filtering Information by Value to Improve Collaborative Decision-Making, *10th International Command, Control Research, Technology Symposium.*

Hislop D., Newell S., Scarborough H., Swan, J. (2000), Innovation Processes: The Management of Knowledge. *Knowledge Management: Concepts, Controversies Conference*, University of Warwick, Coventry, UK.

Holsapple C.W., Joshi K.D. (2000), "An Investigation of Factors that Influence the Management of Knowledge in Organization," *Journal of Strategic Information Systems*, *9*(2–3), 235–261.

Holzmüller, I. (2009), "The United States RBC Standards, Solvency II, the Swiss Solvency Test: A Comparative Assessment," *Geneva Papers on Risk, Insurance: Issues, Practice*, *34*(1), 56–77.

Horton, J. (2007), "The Value Relevance of Realistic Reporting: Evidence from U.K. Life Insurers," *Accounting, Business Research*, *37*(3), 175–179.

Hsiao, C.N. (2003), "To Probe Deeply into the Customer Relationship Management Strategy, Operation Flow of Life Insurance – Ex. Nan Shan Life Insurance Co, Ltd.," Master's thesis, Sun Yat-Sen University, Taiwan.

Hsu, W. (2010), "Don't Let New Insurance Accounting to Scare Away Foreign Insurers," *United Daily News*, A17, 27 March.

Huang, W., Eling, M. (2013), "An Efficiency Comparison of the Non-life Insurance Industry in the BRIC Countries," *European Journal of Operational Research*, *226*(3), 577–591.

Hughes, I. (2008), "Customer Loyalty in the UK General Insurance Market," *Journal of Direct, Data, Digital Marketing Practice*, *10*(1), 29–42.

I.VW-HSG/Accenture (2010), "Insurance in 2015 – Determining the Position: New Coordinates in the German-speaking Insurance Market," www.ivw.unisg.ch, accessed 9 May 2015.

I.VW-HSG/PricewaterhouseCoopers (PwC) (2011), "Antworten mit Fragezeichen. IFRS 4 Phase II," www.ivw.unisg.ch, accessed 9 May 2015.

IfB-HSG/KPMG (2011), "Regulatorischer Wandel – Chancen und Risiken für die Versicherungsbranche," www.kpmg.com, accessed 9 May 2015.

Institute of Direct Marketing. (2008), Internet First Point of Call for Financial Information. 17 April, http://www.theidm.com/resources/daily-newsfeed/internet-first-point-of-call-for-financial-info/, accessed 9 September 2014.

Institute of Direct Marketing. (2009) Internet to Beat TV by 2010. 14 April, http://www.theidm.com/resources/daily-newsfeed/internet-to-beat-tv-by-2010, accessed 9 September 2014.

Institute of Direct Marketing. (2009) Marketing Budgets Fall. 13 January, http://www.theidm.com/resources/daily-newsfeed/marketing-budgets-fall/, accessed 8 September 2014.Insurance Times. (2009), "Insurers Do Not Reward Loyalty," 16 January, available at http://www.insurancetimes.co.uk/story.asp?sectioncode=13&storycode=376344, accessed 8 September 2013.

Insurance Times. (2010), "IAGs UK Claims Cut Margin," 2 June, available at http://www.insurancetimes.co.uk/story.asp?sectioncode=13&storycode=384718, accessed 9 June 2013.

International Association of Insurance Supervisors (IAIS) (2008), Guidance Paper on the Role, Responsibilities of a Group-Wide Supervisor, www.iaisweb.org, accessed 9 May 2015.

International Association of Insurance Supervisors (IAIS) (2009), Issues Paper on Group-wide Solvency Assessment, Supervision, www.iaisweb.org, accessed 9 May 2015.

International Association of Insurance Supervisors (IAIS) (2010), Guidance Paper on the Treatment of Non-Regulated Entities in Group-Wide Supervision, www.iaisweb.org, accessed 9 May 2015.

Jasperson, J., Carter, P.E., Zmud, R.W. (2005), "A Comprehensive Conceptualization of Post-Adoptive Behaviors Associated with Information Technology Enabled Work Systems," *MIS Quarterly, 29*, 525–557.

Jauhiainen, E. (2014), *Deployment of XML for Office Documents in Organizations*, University of Jyväskylä, Finland.

Joseph, M., Stone, G. (2003), "An Empirical Evaluation of US Bank Customer Perceptions of the Impact of Technology on Service Delivery in the Banking Sector," *International Journal of Retail & Distribution Management, 31*(4), 190–202.

Joseph, M., Stone, G., Anderson, K. (2003), "Insurance Customers' Assessment of Service Quality: A Critical Evaluation," *Journal of Small Business, Enterprise Development, 10*(1), 81–92.

Kader, H.A., Adams, M., Hardwick, P. (2010), "The Cost Efficiency of Takaful Insurance Companies," *Geneva Papers on Risk Insurance – Issues, Practice, 35*(1), 161–181.

Kalakota, R., Robinson, M. (2002), *M-business: The Race to Mobility*, McGraw-Hill, New York.

Khambadkone, K. (2011), "Are You Ready for Big Data?" InfoGain, http://www.infogain.com/company/perspective-big-data.jsp, accessed 23 August 2013.

Khare, A., Dixit, S., Chaudhary, R., Kochhar, P., & Mishra, S. (2012), Customer behavior toward online insurance services in India. *Journal of Database Marketing & Customer Strategy Management, 19*(2), 120–133.

Klein, R.W. (2012), "Principles for Insurance Regulation: An Evaluation of Current Practices, Potential Reforms," *Geneva Papers on Risk, Insurance – Issues, Practice, 37*(1), 175–199.

Klumpes, J.M. (2005), "Managerial Use of Discounted Cash-Flow or Accounting Performance Measures: Evidence from the U.K. Life Insurance Industry," *Geneva Papers on Risk, Insurance Issues, Practices, 30*(1), 171–186.

Klumpes, J.M., O'Brien, C.D., Reibel, A. (2009), "International Diversity in Measuring the Fair Value of Life Insurance Contracts," *Geneva Papers on Risk – Insurance Issues, Practices, 34*(2), 197–227.

Klumpes, P.J.M. (2007) Consolidation, Efficiency in the Major European Insurance Markets, *Working Paper*, Imperial College, London, UK.

Krause, H.T. et al. (1999), *Insurance Information Systems*, 3rd Edition, Insurance Institute of America, Malvern, PA.

Laffey, D., Gandy, A. (2009), "Comparison Websites in UK Retail Financial Services," *Journal of Financial Services Marketing, 14*(2), 173–186.

Le Dinh, T., Rinfret, L., Raymond, L., & Dong Thi, B. T. (2013), Towards the reconciliation of knowledge management and e-collaboration systems. *Interactive Technology and Smart Education, 10*(2), 95–115.

Leverty, J.T., Grace, M.F. (2010), "The Robustness of Output Measures in Property-Liability Insurance Efficiency Studies," *Journal of Banking & Finance, 34*(7), 1510–1524.

Liedtke, P.K. (2007), "What's Insurance to a Modern Economy?" *Geneva Papers on Risk, Insurance – Issues, Practice, 32*(2), 211–221.

Life Insurance Council. (2010) (online) http://www.lifeinscouncil.org, accessed 14 February 2010.

Liu WT (2004) "A Study of Diffusion of Information Technology in the Organization: To Discuss on TAM, TTF." Master's thesis, *Soochow University*, Taiwan.

Lorson, J., Schmeiser, H., & Wagner, J. (2012), Evaluation of Benefits and Costs of Insurance Regulation – A Conceptual Model for Solvency II. *Journal of Insurance Regulation*, *31*(1), 125.

Luarn, P., Lin, T.M.Y., Lo, P.K.Y. (2003), "An Exploratory Study of Advancing Mobilization in the Life Insurance Industry: The Case of Taiwan's Nan Shan Life Insurance Corporation. Internet Research. Electronic Networking Applications," *Policy*, *13*(4), 297–310.

Luhnen, M. (2009), "Determinants of Efficiency, Productivity in German Property-Liability Insurance: Evidence for 1995–2006," *Geneva Papers on Risk, Insurance – Issues, Practice*, *34*(3), 483–505.

Mahlberg, B., Url, T. (2003), "Effects of the Single Market on the Austrian Insurance Industry," *Empirical Economics*, *28*(4), 813–838.

Marchand, D. (Ed.) (2000), *Competing with Information*, John Wiley & Sons, West Sussex, UK.

Marwa, S.M. (2005), "Exploration of SERVQUALS Efficacy aia the Diagnosis, Improvement of Service Quality in Kenya's Insurance Industry," PhD thesis, Lancaster University, Lancaster, UK.

McNay, H.E. (2002), Enterprise Content Management: An Overview, *Proceedings of the International Professional Communication Conference*, Portland, OR.

Mehta, S.C., Lobo, A. (2002), MSS, MSA, Zone of Tolerance as Measures of Service Quality: A Study of the Life Insurance Industry. *Second International Services Marketing Conference*, University of Queensland, Australia.

Mescan, S. (2004), "Why Content Management Should Be Part of Every Organizations Global Strategy," *Information Management Journal*, *38*, 54–57.

Microsoft, Taiwan (2005), "The Quiet Revolution of Cathay Life Insurance Co.," microsoft.com, http://www.microsoft.com/taiwan/business/km/cathay.htm, accessed 13 May 2015.

Miles, D. (2011), *State of the ECM Industry 2011*, AIIM International, Silver Spring, MD.

Mintel Research. (2009), "Motor Insurance – UK, May 2009," oxygen.mintel.com, http://oxygen.mintel.com/sinatra/oxygen/display/id=395477/display/id=479856, accessed 23 August 2014.

Monetizing Mobile (2011), *KPMG Paper*, July.

Money Week (2008), "Take Care When Using Price Comparison Sites," 27 August, available at http://www.moneyweek.com/personal-finance/take-care-when-using-price-comparison-sights-93874.aspx, accessed 9 May 2015.

Moneywise (2008), "New Warning over Price Comparison Sites," 13 November, available at http://www.moneywise.co.uk/news-views/2008/11/12/new-warning-over-price-comparison-sites, accessed 8 September 2013.

Montoya-Weiss, M.M., Voss, G.B., Grewal, D. (2003), "Determinants of Online Channel Use, Overall Satisfaction with a Relational, Multichannel Service Provider," *Journal of the Academy of Marketing Science*, *31*(4), 448–458.

Moon, J.W., Kim, Y.G. (2001), "Extending the TAM for a World-Wide Web Context," *Information & Management*, *38*(4), 217–230.

Morgan Stanley, Oliver Wyman Group (2010), Solvency 2: Quantitative & Strategic Impact – The Tide is going Out, *Technical Report.*

Munkvold, B.E., Paivarinta, T., Hodne, A.K., Stangeland, E. (2006), "Contemporary Issues of Enterprise Content Management," *Scandinavian Journal of Information Systems, 18*, 69–100.

Nakano, R. (2002), *Web Content Management: A Collaborative Approach*. Addison-Wesley, Boston, MA.

Nandram, S.S. (2014), *Organizational Innovation Integrating Simplification: Learning from Buurtzorg Nederland*, Springer Verlag, Munich.

Naone, E. (2011), "The New Big Data," *MIT Technology Review*, 22 August.

National Association of Insurance Commissioners (NAIC) (2009a), "Issues for Consideration in the Solvency Modernization Initiative," www.naic.org, accessed 9 May 2015.

National Association of Insurance Commissioners (NAIC) (2009b), "NAIC, State Insurance Regulators Involved in the U.S. FSAP," www.naic.org, accessed 9 May 2015.

National Association of Insurance Commissioners (NAIC) (2009c), "Risk-based Capital – General Overview," www.naic.org, accessed 9 May 2015.

National Association of Insurance Commissioners (NAIC) (2010a), Insurance Holding Company System Model Regulation with Reporting Forms, Instructions; Model #450 8/5/10 – as adopted by Financial Condition (E) Committee, www.naic.org, accessed 9 May 2015.

National Association of Insurance Commissioners (NAIC) (2010b), Insurance Holding Company System Regulatory Act, Model #440 08/05/10 – as Adopted by Financial Condition (E) Committee, www.naic.org, accessed 9 May 2015.

National Association of Insurance Commissioners (NAIC) (2010c), Memorandum, 26 February 2010, www.naic.org, accessed 9 May 2015.

National Association of Insurance Commissioners (NAIC) (2011a), Group Capital Assessment Proposal for U.S. Compliance with the International Association of Insurance Supervisors (IAIS) Insurance Core Principles (ICP) on Group Capital, to Observe Financial Sector Assessment Program Recommendations, www.naic.org, accessed 9 May 2015.

National Association of Insurance Commissioners (NAIC) (2011b), Own Risk, Solvency Assessment (ORSA) Guidance Manual, www.naic.org, accessed 9 May 2015.

National Association of Insurance Commissioners (NAIC) (2011c), Solvency modernization initiative – Roadmap, www.casact.org, accessed 9 May 2015.

National Association of Insurance Commissioners (NAIC) (2011d), Solvency modernization initiative – Update as of January 2011, www.naic.org, accessed 9 May 2015.

National Association of Insurance Commissioners (NAIC) (2011e), White Paper on High-Level Corporate Governance Principles for Use in U.S. Insurance Regulation, www.naic.org, accessed 9 May 2015.

Nicoletti, B. (2011), "Applicare il Lean & Digitize nei servizi finanziari," *Bancamatica*, Gen.–Feb., 12–14.

Nicoletti, B. (2011), "Tra smartphone e prepagate: le opportunità per i pagamenti," *Bancamatica*, Nov.–Dic., 16–18.

Nicoletti, B. (2012), *Lean and Digitize*, Gower Publishing, London.

Nicoletti, B. (2013), *Cloud Computing in Financial Services*, Palgrave-Macmillan, London.

Nicoletti, B. (2014), *Mobile Banking*, Palgrave-Macmillan, London.

Nonaka, I., Toyama, V., Hirata, T. (2008), *Managing Flow: A Process Theory of the Knowledge-Based Firm*, Palgrave-Macmillan, New York.

Nordheim, S., Paivarinta, T. (2004), Customization of Enterprise Content Management Systems: An Exploratory Case Study, *37th Annual Hawaii International Conference on System Sciences*, Waikoloa, Hawaii.

Noulas, A.G., Hatzigayios, T., Lazaridis, J., Lyroudi, K. (2001), "Non-parametric Production Frontier Approach to the Study of Efficiency of Non-Life Insurance Companies in Greece," *Journal of Financial Management, Analysis, 14*(1), 19–26.

O'Callaghan, R., Smits, M. (2005), A Strategy Development Process for Enterprise Content Management, *13th European Conference on Information Systems*, Regensburg, Germany.

Oracle. (2007), The Benefits of a Unified Enterprise Content Management Platform, *Oracle White Paper*, February.

Ortega, D. (2011), "Mobility: Fueling a Brainier Business Intelligence," *IT Business Edge*, http://www.analyticsasaservice.org/analytics/, accessed 1 August 2015.

Out-Law News. (2008), "Insurance Comparison Sites Have Cleaned Up Their Act, says FSA." 12 November, http://www.out-law.com/page-9589, accessed 8 September 2014.

Päivärinta, T., Munkvold, B.E. (2005), Enterprise Content Management: An Integrated Perspective on Information Management, *Proceedings of the 38th Annual Hawaii International Conference on System Sciences*, Waikoloa, Hawaii.

Parasuraman, A. (2000), "Technology Readiness Index (TRI), Multiple-Item Scale to Measure Readiness to Embrace New Technologies," *Journal of Service Research, 2*(4), 307–320.

Pennington, L.L. (2007), "Approaches/Practices: Surviving the Design, Implementation of a Content Management System: Do the Benefits Offset the Challenges?" *Journal of Business, Technical Communication, 21*(1), 62–73.

Perry, R., Lancaster, R. (2002), *Enterprise Content Management: Expected Revolution or Vendor Positioning*, The Yankee Group, Boston.

Porteous, D. (2006), "The Enabling Environment for Mobile Banking in Africa," Bankablefrontier, www.bankablefrontier.com/publications.php, accessed 29 August, 2014.

Porter-O'Grady, T., Malloch, K. (2014), *Quantum Leadership*. Jones & Bartlett Publishers, Burlington, MA.

Pottier, S.W. (2010), "Life Insurer Efficiency, State Regulation: Evidence of Optimal Firm Behavior," *Journal of Regulatory Economics, 39*(2), 169–193.

PricewaterhouseCoopers (PwC) (2010), "Getting Set for Solvency II," *Technical Report.*

Pullman, G., Gu, B. (2008), "Guest Editor's Introduction: Rationalizing, Rhetoricizing Content Management," *Technical Communication Quarterly, 17*, 1–9.

Quaddus, M., Intrapairot, A. (2001), "Management Policies, the Diffusion of Data Warehouse: A Case Study Using System Dynamics-Based Decision Support System," *Decision Support Systems, 31*(2), 223–240.

Reimer, J.A. (2002), "Enterprise Content Management," *Datenbanken Spektrum, 2*, 17–35.

Rickenberg, T.A., Neumann, M., Hohler, B., Breitner, M.H. (2012), Enterprise Content Management – A Literature Review, *Proceedings of the 18th AMCIS.*

Rickenberg, T.A., Neumann, M., Hohler, B., Breitner, M.H. (2012), Towards a Process-Oriented Approach to Assessing, Classifying, Visualizing Enterprise Content with Document Maps, *Proceedings of the 20th ECIS.*

Robertson, J. (2004), "Open-Source Content Management Systems," *KM Column,* January.

Rockley, A, Kostur, P., Manning, S. (2003), *Managing Enterprise Content: A Unified Content Strategy,* New Riders Publishing, San Francisco.

Schatt, D. (2014), *Virtual Banking: A Guide to Innovation and Partnering,* Wiley Finance, New York.

Scheer, A.W., Nüttgens, M. (2000), *ARIS Architecture and Reference Models for Business Process Management* (376–389), Springer Verlag, Berlin.

Schmid, B.F., Lindemann, M.A. (1998), "Elements of a Reference Model for Electronic Markets," in *System Sciences, 1998, Proceedings of the IEEE Thirty-First Hawaii International Conference on,* Vol. 4, 193–201.

Schutts, M.I. (2007), "The Implications of Mobile, Financial Services Convergence, the Transformation Potential of M-Banking," *The Policy Paper Series,* no. 6, July.

Scott, R. (2000), "Shaping the Future of the Life Agency Force," *Coverage, 26*(1), 22–26.

Sharp, A., McDermott, P. (2001), *Workflow Modeling: Tools for Process Improvement, Application Development,* Artech House, Boston, MA.

Sinha, T. (2004), "The Indian Insurance Industry: Challenges, Prospects," Zurich: Swiss Re, www.icpr.itam.mx/papers/SinhaSwissRe.pdf, accessed 8 May 2015.

Smith, H.A., McKeen, J.D. (2003), "Developments in Practice VIII: Enterprise Content Management," *The Communications of the Association for Information Systems, 11,* 647–659.

Stair, R.M., Reynolds, G. (2008), *Fundamentals of Information Systems,* 5th Edition, Course Technology, Stamford, CT.

Sun, C.Y. (2009), "The Negative Spread in the Life Insurance Is the Worst in the World," *United Daily News,* AA1, 26 November.

Suresh M.C (2010), Cloud Computing: for Banking, Financial Services Institutions, *TCS White Paper,* Mumbai, India.

Swiss Federal Office of Private Insurance (FOPI) (2004), *White Paper of the Swiss Solvency Test,* www.finma.ch, accessed 8 May 2015.

Swiss Federal Office of Private Insurance (FOPI) (2006), *Technical Document on the Swiss Solvency Test,* www.finma.ch, accessed 8 May 2015.

Swiss Federal Office of Private Insurance (FOPI) (2007), *Directives on Corporate Governance, Risk Management,* the Internal Control System, www.finma.ch, accessed 8 May 2015.

Swiss Financial Market Supervisory Authority (FINMA) (2010a), *Annual Report 2010,* www.finma.ch, accessed 8 May 2015.

Swiss Financial Market Supervisory Authority (FINMA) (2012), *FINMA Policy on Insurance Supervisory Colleges,* www.finma.ch. accessed 8 May 2015.

SwissRe (various years), World Insurance, *Sigma,* Zurich, Switzerland. "A Third of Financial Institutions Have Mobile Detection" (2012), *Mapa Research.*

Tsoukatos, E. (2008), "Applying Importance-Performance Analysis to Assess Service Delivery Performance – Evidence from Greek Insurance," *EuroMed Journal of Business*, *3*(2), 144–162.

Tsoukatos, E., Rand, G.K. (2006), "Path Analysis of Perceived Service Quality, Satisfaction, Loyalty in Greek Insurance," *Managing Service Quality*, *16*(5), 501–519.

Tyrväinen, P., Päivärinta, T., Salminen, A., Iivari, J. (2006), "Characterizing the Evolving Research on Enterprise Content Management," *European Journal of IS*, *15*(6), 627–634

UMTS Glossary (2005), UMTS Forum – Glossary, http://www.umts-forum.org/glossary.asp?id=180, 18.05.2005, accessed 20 October 2013.

Van Bragt, D., Steehouwer, H., Waalwijk, B. (2010), "Market Consistent ALM for Life Insurers – Steps Toward Solvency II," *Geneva Papers on Risk, Insurance – Issues, Practice* *35*(1), 92–109.

Van Rossum, A. (2005), "Regulation, Insurance Economics," *Geneva Papers on Risk, Insurance – Issues, Practice*, *30*(1), 43–46.

Vaughan, T.M. (2009), The Implications of Solvency II for U.S., *Insurance Regulation*, www.naic.org, accessed 9 May 2015.

Veen, J. (2004), "Why Content Management Fails," *Adaptive Path*, 16 October.

Vom Brocke, J., Derungs, R., Herbst, A., Novotny, S., Simons, A. (2011), The Drivers behind Enterprise Content Management: A Process-Oriented Perspective, *19th European Conference on Information Systems*, Helsinki, Finland.

Vom Brocke, J., Simons, A., Cleven, A. (2008), A Business Process Perspective on Enterprise Content Management: Towards a Framework for Organisational Change, *Proceedings of the 16th ECIS*.

Vom Brocke, J., Simons, A., Cleven, A. (2008), A Business Process Perspective on Enterprise Content Management: Towards a Framework for Organisational Change, *16th European Conference on Information Systems*, Galway, Ireland, 1680–1691.

Vom Brocke, J., Simons, A., Cleven, A. (2010), "Towards a Business Process-Oriented Approach to Enterprise Content Management (ECM), The ECM-Blueprinting Framework, Information Systems," *E-Business Management*, *9*, 475–498.

Von Volker P. (2011), 2025 – *Die Versicherung der Zukunft Gebundene Ausgabe*, Verlag Versicherungswirtschaft Gmbh, Karlsruhe, Germany.

Vong, J., Song, I. (2014), *Emerging Technologies for Emerging Markets* (Topics in Intelligent Engineering and Informatics), Springer Science, Singapore.

Walsh, M.L. (2014), *The Manager's Instant Guide to Sustainability*, ICMA, Washington, DC.

Ward, D., Zurbruegg, R. (2000), "Does Insurance Promote Economic Growth? Evidence from OECD Economies," *Journal of Risk and Insurance* *67*(4), 489–506.

Ward, D., Zurbruegg, R. (2002), "Law, Politics, Life Insurance Consumption in Asia," *Geneva Papers on Risk, Insurance – Issues, Practice* *27*(3), 395–412.

Watson, J. (2008), "New Customer Acquisition: Five Ways to Make It Work Again," 15 May, available at http://www.theidm.com/resources/idm-insights/new-customer-acquisition-five-ways-to-make-it-work-again/, accessed 17 May 2010.

Webb, I., Grace, M.F., Skipper, H.D. (2002), The Effect of Banking, Insurance on the Growth of Capital, Output, Working Paper 02, *Center for Risk Management*, Insurance.

Wedgwood, I.D. (2015), *Lean Sigma: Rebuilding Capability in Healthcare*. Pearson Education, New York.
Worthington, A., Hurley, E. (2002), "Cost Efficiency in Australian General Insurers: A Non-Parametric Approach," *The British Accounting Review, 34*(2), 89–108.
Yang, H.L., Wang, C.S. (2008), "Locating Online Loan Applicants for an Insurance Company," *Information Review 32*(2), 221–235.
Yao, S., Han, Z., Feng, G. (2007), "On Technical Efficiency of China's Insurance Industry after WTO Accession," *China Economic Review, 18*(1), 66–86.
Zeithaml, V.A., Parasuraman, A., Malhotra, A. (2000), A Conceptual Framework for Understanding e-Service Quality: Implications for Future Research, Managerial Practice, *Marketing Science Institute*. Report no. 00–115, Cambridge, MA.

Glossary

Accident: An unforeseen and unintended event.

Accident-only policies: Policies that pay only in cases arising from an accident or injury.

Actual cash value (ACV): The value of the customer asset, based on the current cost to replace it minus its depreciation.

Adjusted SCR: The Solvency Capital Requirement level that includes any supplementary capital requirement determined through the Solvency II's Pillar 2 Supervisory Review.

Adjuster: An individual used by an insurance company to evaluate losses and settle policyholder claims. Also see "Public insurance adjuster."

Administrative expense charge: An amount deducted, one time or periodically, from the policy.

Adoption rate: How quickly it takes the public at large to adopt new solutions.

Advertising based pricing model: A pricing model with services to customers for free at low cost. The vendor obtains most of its revenues from advertisers whose ads are delivered to the customer together with the service.

Agency: An office where insurance is sold. It may be directed toward a specific insurance, such as property and casualty, pension, life and health insurance, or a combination of them. Also, it might be an independent organization or an insurance company subsidiary.

Agent: A person who sells insurance policies.

Agility: How quickly the organization responds, as the customer's resource load scales up or down, allocating the needed resources to the activity.

Android: An open platform developed by Google and, later, the Open Handset Alliance. It consists of the operating system (on which the middle-ware and applications run), the middle-ware (allowing applications to talk to a network and to one another), and the applications (the actual programs that the platform will run).

Annuity: A contract in which the buyer deposits money with a life insurance company for investment. The contract provides for specific payments to be made at periodic intervals for a fixed time or for life.

Anti-money laundering (AML): The effort through legislation, regulation, and systems to track, identify, and stop the laundering of illicit funds within the legal financial system.

App: Short for application. It is a program or piece of software, especially as downloaded by a user to a mobile device.

Application: A process requiring some customer information that an insurance company uses to decide whether to issue a policy and its premium. In ICT, it indicates an application module.

Application module: Software program that uses the basic software, hardware, and network environments to achieve a specific function related to the purposes of the organization.

Application programming interfaces (API): A specification for the interfaces used by software components to communicate with each other. An API may include specifications for routines, data structures, object classes, and variables.

Application/App store: The virtual location used for the distribution of digital applications available on many mobile devices.

Appraisal: An evaluation of an insured property claim by appraisers to determine property or damaged property values. Many policies provide this process to negotiate claim disputes. In this process, the customer and the insurance company hire separate damage appraisers. The two appraisers choose a third appraiser to act as an "umpire." The appraisers then review the claim. The umpire rules on any disagreements. The umpire's decision is binding on the customer and the insurance company, but only for the loss amount. If there is a dispute above what is covered, the customer can still pursue a settlement of the coverage issue after the appraisal process takes place. The customer is required to pay for his/her hired appraiser and half of the umpire's costs.

Assignment: The transfer of all or part of a policy owner's legal title and rights to a policy to another person. It is possible to change this type of transfer at a later date on respect to the application process.

Audit and compliance: The ability to collect data useful for audit and compliance work.

Authentication: The authentication procedure of verifying the identity of a user manually or by a system or service.

Authorization: Procedure that checks whether a customer or another person inside or outside the organization has the right to perform a certain action, for instance, to transfer funds or access to the organization data.

Automation: The automated handling of services. It is also the percentage of requests to the ICT applications handled without any human contribution.

Availability: Percentage, calculated on a periodic basis and net of planned service stops, in terms of time of service coverage.

Avatar: An icon or figure representing a virtual person in a website, which can provide help on the use of an application module.

B2B: Business to business. It refers to organizations that interface to other organizations, rather than consumers.

B2C: Business to consumer. It refers to organizations that interface to consumers, rather than to business.

Back office: Administration and support personnel in a company. They carry out functions like settlements, clearances, record maintenance, regulatory compliance, HR, finance, and accounting.

Bancassurance: The marketing and sale of insurance products through bank distribution channels. This process allows banks and insurance companies to get new customers and create additional products through different distribution channels.

Basel 2 and 3: The second and third of the Basel accords were signed in 2004 by the G10 central financial institution governors (Basel 1 was signed in 1998). Basel 2 is a package of measures designed to introduce new rules for prudent credit risk management. Financial institutions are required to put aside equity to reduce the risks of their lending and investment activities. In this way, it is possible to improve the robustness of the financial institution and bring greater transparency to financial institutions' solvency. In 2010, further proposals were introduced for international banking regulation in the Basel 3 accord and more might be introduced in the future.

Basic software: The set of software programs that enables a user to perform basic operations such as building and actually running an application or managing a database. Typical examples of basic software are the operating system, the editors, the utilitites, the compilers, and the management systems of databases.

Benchmarking: The comparison of processes and/or measures to other processes and/or measures implemented by well-organized entities.

Beneficiary: The person, people, or entity designated to receive the benefits from an insurance policy or annuity contract.

Best estimate liability: The expected or mean value (probability weighted average) of the present value of future cash flows to settle contract obligations. It is projected over the contract's runoff period, taking into account all up-to-date financial market and actuarial information.

Binder: A temporary insurance contract that provides proof of coverage until a permanent policy is issued.

Blog: A contraction of the term "web log." It is a type of website, usually maintained by an individual, with regular entries of commentary, descriptions of events, or other material such as graphics, photos, or videos relative to a specific subject.

Bordereau: A report providing policy, premium, or loss data with respect to identified specific risks. This report is periodically furnished to a reinsurance company by the ceding insurance or reinsurance companies.

Broad network access: Facilitates network capabilities and their access. Heterogeneous thin or thick customer platforms promote the use of the platform. Notebooks, tablets, PCs, PDAs, smartphones, and similar devices are the input devices that can access the network.

Broker: An insurance intermediary who/that deals with the insurer on behalf of the insured. Since they are not the legal representatives of insurance companies, brokers, unlike agents, often do not have the right to act on behalf of insurance companies, such as to bind coverage. While some brokers might have agency contracts with some insurance companies, they remain obligated to represent the interests of insureds rather than of insurance companies. For example, some state insurance codes impose a fiduciary responsibility to act on behalf of their customers or provide full disclosure of all their compensation from all sources.

Business intelligence (BI): BI is a broad category of applications and technologies for gathering, storing, analyzing, retrieving, and providing access to data to help users make better organization decisions. BI applications include the activities of decision support systems, querying and reporting, operational analytical processing, statistical analysis, forecasting, and data mining. In some cases, it is also indicated simply as Analytics, even if the latter word can have a wider meaning.

Business process management (BPM): The management of processes in order to improve them substantially.

Business process outsourcing (BPO): The practice of outsourcing some or all of the business's back-office processes or subprocesses to an external organization or service provider. Examples are call centers processing, help desk, and information and communication technology (ICT) support.

Business process re-engineering (BPR): The drastic re-engineering of business processes to either reduce costs or improve the flow in a process to add value to the customer.

Caller line identification (CLID): A system that identifies a customer based on the phone number he/she uses to call a service provider.

Cancellation: Termination of an insurance policy by the company or insured before the renewal date.

Carrier: A company or health maintenance organization (HMO) that provides health-care coverage.

Cash value: The amount of money the life insurance policy owner will receive as a refund if the policy owner cancels the coverage and returns the policy to the company.

Casualty insurance: Insurance that is primarily concerned with the losses caused by injuries to persons and legal liability imposed on the insured for such injury or for damage to property.

Certificates of coverage: Printed material showing members of a group health benefit plan and the benefits provided by the group master policy.

Churn: Customers moving from a service provider within one specific product category to another, based on price, value, or some other factors.

Churning: Can occur when an agent persuades a customer to borrow against an existing life insurance policy to pay the premium on a new one.

Claim: A policyholder's request for reimbursement from an insurance company under an insurance policy for a loss.

Claimant: A person who makes an insurance claim.

Client: In this book, it refers to the customer. It could be either external or internal to the organization. In some cases, the word "client" indicates the access device. In this latter meaning, there will be always in this book a specification (such as a thin client).

Cloning: Refers to copying the identity of one mobile phone to another, thereby allowing the perpetrator to represent himself/herself as the victim. The intent normally is to use the phone for calls and other services billed to the victim's cell account. In the case of mobile insurance, cloning could give the hacker access to the victim's insurance accounts.

Cloud: A metaphor for a global network. It was initially used to refer to the telephone network. It is now commonly used to refer to the Internet or to the cloud computing services.

Cloud computing: A computing capability that provides convenient and on-demand network access to a shared pool of configurable computing resources. These resources can be rapidly provisioned and released with minimal management effort or vendor interaction. Cloud computing has six essential characteristics: pay-per-use, self-service, broad network access, resource pooling, rapid elasticity, and measured service. In general terms, cloud computing enables Infrastructure as a Service (IaaS), Platform as a Service (PaaS), Software as a Service (SaaS), Business Process as a Service (BPaaS), or similar services.

Coinsurance: Coinsurance occurs when two or more title insurance underwriters proportionally insure a given transaction via separate title policies. The amount of risk is shared in equal or different proportions with their policy amount. The same term is used also with a different meaning. Coinsurance is a co-sharing agreement between the insured and the insurance company under an insurance policy that provides that the insured will cover a set percentage of the covered costs after the deductible has been paid. It is similar to co-pay insurance plans, except that co-pays require the insured to pay a set money amount at the time the service is rendered.

Coinsurance provision: An insurance provision that penalizes the insured's loss recovery if the limit of insurance purchased by the insured is not equal to or greater than a specified percentage of the value of the insured property. The coinsurance provision specifies that the insured recovers no more than the following: the amount of the loss multiplied by the ratio of the amount of insurance purchased (the limit of insurance) to the amount of insurance required (the value of the asset on the date of loss multiplied by the coinsurance percentage), less the deductible. The amount of the loss that is not payable to the insured as a result of failure to comply with the coinsurance provision is referred to as a coinsurance penalty. In commercial insurance policies, it is sometimes possible to avoid the possibility of a coinsurance penalty with an agreed value provision.

Company profile: A summary of information about an insurance company, including its license status, financial data, complaint history, and a history of regulatory actions.

Comparator: Online insurance comparators are software that meets all the necessary information to determine the profile of insurers and associated with the type of insurance claims. The results are ranked on the best options from the cost benefit point of view or similar criteria, which might be decided by the user.

Complaint: A written communication primarily expressing a grievance against an insurance company or agent.

Complaint history: Information collected or maintained by the organizations or by the regulatory bodies relating to the complaints received against a particular insurance company, agent, or premium finance company and the results of the complaints.

Compliance: Respect for the internal and external compulsory rules of the organization.

Computer security incident: Every event that involves a violation or imminent threat of violation of the rules and business practices in the field of information security (for instance, computer frauds, attacks through the Internet, malfunctions, and faults).

Computer-telephony integration/interface (CTI): A system that integrates telephone systems with computer networks.

Configuration management: Refers to the ability to federate configuration data or applications for services.

Consumption-based or use-based pricing model: A pricing model in which the vendor charges its customers based on the number of services the customer consumes, rather than on a fixed fee. For example, an insurance company might charge for the use of the asset, such as the miles run by the insured's car.

Contract: In most cases, as in this book, an insurance policy. A policy is considered to be a contract between the insurance company and the policyholder.

Conversion privilege: The right to change (convert) insurance coverage from one type of policy to another. For example, it is the right to change from an individual term insurance policy to an individual whole life insurance policy.

Coverage: Used to specify the type of insurance or protection.

Credential: The secure, encrypted information associated with a specific use which is supposed to access the object.

Credentials information: Refers to information used by a user to authenticate a system or service. They are included in the definition of the tools that provide or store information (for instance, password generators of a non-reusable smart card) or something that reminds the user (for instance, a password) or represents him or her (for instance, biometric characteristics).

Credit life insurance: Special type of coverage usually designed to pay off a loan or charge account balance if the policyholder dies.

Some lenders or sellers may require credit life insurance before they will approve a credit. If credit life is required, the lender or seller cannot require the policyholder to purchase it from them or a particular insurance company. If the policyholder has an existing life policy, the creditor has to accept an assignment of benefits under their existing policy instead of requiring them to purchase a credit life policy. Insurance regulators normally regulate credit life insurance premium rates for loans of 10years or less. Premium rates for loans that are more than 10-years old normally, are unregulated. It is similar to payment protection insurance (PPI) which has a wider risk coverages, for instance loss of the job.

Crisis: A situation formally declared as a service interruption or the deterioration of one or more critical processes or as systemically important as a result of incidents or disasters.

Cross-selling: A method of targeting and selling new products to an existing customer.

Customer: The contracting recipient of a contract.

Customer relationship management (CRM): An information system for managing relationships with the customers. In principle, it helps managing the whole customer life cycle, from the acquisition of new customers to the growing of relationships with the customer, to loyalty building with customers who have multiple relations with the organization. It allows the optimization of relationships with customers by increasing loyalty, cross-selling products and services, and so on.

Customer service representative (CSR): The staff working in a call center to assist customers with inquiries.

Data governance and compliance: Data governance requires applying governance to the organization's own data infrastructure and also the data infrastructure that the organization partially controls. Data governance has two key drivers: understanding compliance and risk and organization performance goals.

Database: A set of computer files organized in such a way as to be quickly accessed, normally using tables.

Deductible: The amount the insured must pay in a loss before the payment from the insurance company.

Default: A payment application or credential that is set to be used unless another payment application or credential is selected.

Detection and forensics: It is the activity to separate legitimate from illegitimate activity, before, during, or after a break in security.

Digital natives: They are the Y-Generation, or the younger users of technology.

Disruptive innovation: It describes innovations that improve products or services in unexpected ways and change both the ways things are done and the market. For example, cloud computing is often referred to as a disruptive technology. It has the potential to completely change the way in which ICT services are procured, deployed, and maintained. Cloud computing can also change in a drastic way the products and processes of the organization. Cloud computing impacts heavily also on the organization of the companies or institutions.

Durability: A measure of how likely it is that the data is lost.

Earned premium: The portion of a policy premium that has been used to actually buy coverage, or that the insurance company has earned. For instance, if a policyholder has a twelve-month policy that was paid for in advance, two months into the policy, there would be two months of earned premium. The remaining ten months of premium is unearned premium.

ECM: Enterprise Content Management is the management of all contents (data, structured and unstructured documents, emails, voice, video, and so on). The relative system is called enterprise content management system or ECMS.

ECN: Electronic Communications Network is an electronic network that facilitates trading between stock or commodities exchanges.

Economic balance sheet (EBS): A balance sheet statement based on one of those accounting approaches using market-consistent values for all current assets and current obligations relating to the business.

Ecosystem participants: Set of organizations or individuals that can work together in order to gain synergies.

Effective date: The date on which an insurance policy becomes effective.

Emergency situation: Caused by accidents or disasters affecting the operator, and is characterized by the need to take appropriate technical and managerial exceptional actions aimed at reassuring business continuity.

Encryption: Coding to protect the customer's information assets.

End user (or customer): The final user of digital insurance mobile payment and connectivity services.

Endorsement: A written agreement attached to a policy expanding or limiting the benefits otherwise payable under the policy. Also called a rider or appendix.

Enterprise resource planning (ERP): The extension of the Manufacturing Resource Planning II to the remaining functions in the organization, such as engineering, finance, and personnel administration and management. It consists of a software package with a single data model that facilitates the horizontal and vertical integration of all inter-organizational processes, improves process efficiency, and monitors processes through special Key Performance or Process Indicators (KPI) according to quality, service levels, costs, and timeliness. Some components of an ERP are: accounting, industrial accounting, payrolls, procurement, warehouse management, production, project control, sales, distribution, and facility maintenance.

Escrow: Money or documents placed in the hands of a third party until specified conditions are met.

Exclusions or limitations: Provisions that exclude or limit coverage of certain named accidents conditions, or services, as well as some sicknesses or accidents that occur under specified circumstances.

Expiration date: The date on which an insurance policy expires.

Face value: The initial amount of benefit provided by the policy as shown on the face page of the contract. The actual benefit may be higher or lower depending on the options selected, outstanding policy loans, or premium owed.

Facebook: A hugely popular online social network founded in 2004 for helping persons (called friends) stay in touch and share content.

Facultative reinsurance: A form of reinsurance whereby an exposure the ceding company wishes to reinsure is offered to the reinsurance company and is contained in a single transaction. The submission, acceptance, and resulting agreement is required on each individual risk that the ceding company seeks to reinsure. In other words, the ceding company negotiates an individual reinsurance agreement for every policy it intends to reinsure. The reinsurance company is not obliged to accept or to submit every new opportunity. Facultative is different from reinsurance treaties that govern a given set of reinsurance policies.

Federation: The act of combining organizations, data or identities across multiple systems or companies.

Fee for service: An insurance plan that allows the customer to go to any physician or provider the customer choose, but requires that the customer pay for the services himself and file claims for reimbursement. (Also known as an indemnity plan.)

Financial institutions (FI): They are the institutions that handle financial transactions and are normally the place where people deposit or transact their money.

Frequently asked questions (FAQ): These functions list the questions and answers asked frequently by the users.

Front office: Marketing, sales, and service departments that come in direct contact with the customers, and liaise directly or through a middle office with the back-office (administrative) departments to maintain a two-way flow of information.

Gap insurance: Insurance that pays the difference between the actual cash value of the damage and the amount to be paid on the customer claim. Some gap policies may also cover the amount of the deductible.

Generally accepted accounting principles (GAAP): They are the standard framework of guidelines for financial accounting used in any given jurisdiction. They are normally known as accounting standards or standard accounting practice.

Generation Y (Gen Y): A term commonly used by marketing professionals to describe the segment of the population born between 1977 and 1994, especially in the USA. This generation is sometimes called digital natives.

Generation Z (Gen Z): It is a term commonly used by marketing professionals to describe the segment of the population born between 1995 and 2000, especially in the USA. This generation is sometimes called m-generation, due to their frequent use of mobile devices.

Geo-location: It is the technique of identifying the geographical location of a person or device by means of digital information.

Gilder's law: George Gilder proposed this law stating that bandwidth grows at least three times faster than computer power.

Global systems for mobile communications (GSM): The primary standard for digital mobile phones, and currently is in use by 80 percent of the global mobile market.

Governance: Governance defines who is responsible for what, and the policies, processes and procedures that persons or groups need to follow. It refers to the controls and processes that make sure the effectiveness, efficiency, ethics and economics of a sector. The sector might refer to the entire organization or to an organization unit, a process, or data.

Grace period(s): The time (usually 15 or 31 days): during which a policy remains in force after the premium is due but not paid. The policy lapses as of the day the premium was originally due unless the premium is paid before the end of the 15 or 31 days or the insured damage.

Grievance procedure: The required appeal process an health maintenance organization (HMO) provides for the customer to protest a decision regarding medical necessity or claim payment. Insurance companies also may have grievance procedures.

Group life insurance: This type of life insurance provides coverage to a group of people under one contract. Most group contracts are sold to businesses that want to provide life insurance for their employees. Group life insurance can also be sold to associations to cover their members and to credit institutions to cover the amounts of their debtor loans. Most group policies are for term insurance. Generally, the business will be issued a master policy and each person in the group will receive a certificate of insurance.

Group of companies (or Group): Several (insurance in this book) companies under common ownership and often common management.

Health benefit plan: In most cases, health care services provided to employees by an employer. It can be an indemnity plan or an HMO plan.

Health maintenance organization (HMO): Managed care plans that provide health care services to their members through networks of physicians, hospitals, and other health care providers. HMOs are popular alternatives to traditional health care plans offered by insurance companies because they cover a wide variety of services, usually at a lower cost.

Hijacking (in ICT security): The attacker takes control of a communication between two entities, masquerading as one of them. As with cloning, hijacking could give the hacker access to the victim's financial information.

Identity management: Managing personal identity information so that access to computer resources, applications, data, and services is properly controlled.

Incident: Any event that is not part of the standard operation of a service and that causes or may cause an interruption to, or a reduction in, the quality of that service.

Indemnity plan: A health plan that allows the customer to go to any physician or provider the customer choose, but requires that the customer pay for the services himself and file claims for reimbursement. (Also known as fee for service.)

Indexed life insurance: A whole life plan of insurance that provides for the face amount of the policy and, correspondingly, the premium rate, to automatically increase every year based on an increase in the Consumer Price Index (CPI) or another index as defined in the policy.

Inflation protection: Automatically adjusts insurance policy limits to account for increases in the costs to repair or rebuild an asset.

Information risk: The risk of incurring financial, reputational, and market share losses in relation to the use of information technology and communications. In the integrated view of the business risks for prudential purposes (ICAAP), this type of risk includes operational, reputational, and strategic risks.

Information technology and telecommunication (ICT): The combination of computers, storage, network, applications, and so on that provides integrated computer-based services also remotely (through telecommunication).

Information technology infrastructure library (ITIL): A method for the management of ICT services.

Instant messaging (IM): A protocol for communicating between two parties using text-based chat through IP-based customers.

Insured: The person or organization covered by an insurance policy.

Insurer: The insurance company.

Integration: The process of combining components or systems into an integrated entity.

Interaction design (IxD): A customer-led design method for improving the interactions between customers and systems.

Interactive voice response (systems) (IVR): The automated telephone support systems that people hear when they call a help line or customer support number, which uses menus and responses via touch-tone and/or voice interaction for navigation.

Internal economic capital requirement (IECR): The company management's internal estimate of capital need.

Internet protocol (IP): The primary protocol for transmitting data or information over the Internet.

Internet service provider (ISP): An organization that provides Internet access to customers.

Interoperability: Concerned with the ability of systems to operate in multiple environments.

iOS: It is the Apple mobile operating system for its iPhone, iPod touch, iPad, Apple television, and similar devices.

Key performance indicators (KPI): The metrics (or measures) used within corporations to measure the performance of one aspect or department or process against another with respect to revenue, sales lead conversion, costs, customer support, and so on. Sometimes they are referred also as key process indicators.

Know your customer (KyC): Applications used to know the customer better using the customer transactions. In some countries, it is mandatory for anti-money laundering or blacklisting verifications.

Lamfalussy model: Four-level approach for developing financial industry regulation which is designed to foster rapid legislation and consistent integration across all EU territories.

Lapse: The termination of an insurance policy because a renewal premium is not paid by the end of the grace period.

Lean (thinking): Lean is a method which aims to provide a new way to think about how to organize human activities to deliver more benefits to the society and value to individuals while eliminating waste.

Lean and digitize: Make the process simultaneously lean and automated. It is a method based on re-engineering the process to make it lean and at the same time to automate wherever and whenever it is necessary.

Least privilege: The principle that states that each user or system administrator is assigned the qualifications strictly necessary for the performance of assigned duties.

Liability: Responsibility to another for one's negligence or deliberate act that results in injury or damage.

Liability coverage: Covers losses that an insured is legally liable. For homeowners insurance, for example, liability coverage protects the policyholder against financial losses if they are sued and found legally responsible for someone else's injury or asset damage.

Liability insurance: An insurance coverage that pays for damages to the other party and damages to the other assets resulting from an accident the policyholder caused. It also pays if the accident was caused by someone covered by the policyholder's policy, including for example a driver operating the car with his/her previous permission.

LinkedIn: An online social network for business professionals.

Logical security: A set of processes and activities aimed at obtaining confidentiality, integrity, and availability of data and information through the adoption of measures: techniques (system for access control, antivirus, firewalls, intrusion detection/prevention systems, and so on), organizational (definition of policies, safety standards, user profiling and related ratings, and so on), procedural (such as process definition or enforcement), and behavioral (education, awareness, and so on).

Loss: The amount an insurance company pays on a claim.

Loss history: Refers to the number of insurance claims previously filed by a policyholder. A company will consider loss history when underwriting a new policy or considering a renewal of an existing policy. Companies view loss history as an indication of the likelihood that an insured will file a claim during the tenure of the policy.

Loyalty service provider: The administrator of loyalty and rewards programs.

Malicious code: The software in the form of a virus, worm, or other malware that is loaded by hackers onto the handset, the SMS gateway, or the financial institution's server to perform an unauthorized process that will have an adverse impact on the confidentiality, integrity, or availability of financial information and transactions.

Malware: A contraction for malicious software that is inserted into a system, usually covertly, with the intent of compromising the confidentiality, integrity, or availability of the victim's data, applications, or operating system, or otherwise annoying or disrupting the victim.

Managed health care: A system that organizes physicians, hospitals, and other health care providers into networks with the goal of lowering costs while still providing appropriate medical services. Many managed care systems focus on preventive care and case management to avoid treating more costly illnesses.

Man-in-the-middle attack (MIM): An attack on the authentication protocol exchange in which the attacker positions him/herself between the claimant and verifier with the intent to intercept and alter data traveling between them.

Market value: The current value of the customer insured asset, including the prices of all the insured assets.

Market value margin: When added to the best estimate of liabilities, produces a market consistent valuation of insurance liabilities.

Maximum out-of-pocket expense: The maximum amount someone covered under a health care plan must pay during a certain period for expenses covered by the plan. Until the maximum is reached, the person covered is required to pay a co-payment or a percentage on each claim.

Medical payments and personal injury protection (PIP): They are insurance coverages which pay limited medical and possibly funeral expenses if the policyholder, a family member, or a passenger in a vehicle, is injured or killed in an accident. PIP also pays lost-income benefits.

Microfinance: A range of financial tools (credit, savings, insurance, money transfers, and so on) designed for people who do not have access to the traditional financial system.

Micro-SD card: A memory card that is designed to integrate with the mobile phone and other mobile devices.

Middle office: The part of the institution's operations providing the link between the revenue-generating front office and the administrative back office. For instance, transactions executed by the front office staff (be it a telephone operator or a virtual agent in the web or similar) may be processed by the middle office before being dealt with by the back office.

Millennials (also known as the millennial generation or sometimes generation Y): The demographic group following Generation X. There are no precise dates when the generation starts and ends. Researchers and commentators use birth years ranging from the early 1980s to the early 2000s.

Minimum capital requirement (MCR): The minimum level of regulatory capital in Solvency II.

Mission: The mission is any set of important tasks that is assigned in order to move toward a vision.

Mobile device (or simply mobile): Smartphones, feature phones and tablet computers, among others. The term "mobile device" is also used interchangeably with "mobile handset" or "handset."

Mobile insurance: Platforms that enable customers to access via mobile device insurance services such as policy issuing, variations, substitutions, suspensions, claims, unit-linked policies, and so on. It also encompasses SMS (short message service or text messaging alerts), using a smartphone to access a insurance company's Web site, as well as services provided directly through a insurance company's app on a smartphone.

Mobile network operator (MNO): The provider of mobile device connectivity services. For the purposes of this book, this role is sometimes used interchangeably with the secure domain manager.

Mobile payments: A payment service that includes digital money, either transferred or placed in a mobile wallet. The transaction is performed on a mobile device. Mobile payments are defined as either proximity or remote payments.

Mobile portal: A website designed specifically for mobile phone interfaces and mobile browsers.

Mortality charge: The cost of the insurance protection element of a universal life policy. This cost is based on the net amount at risk under the policy, the insured's risk classification at the time of policy purchase, and the insured's current age.

Mortality expenses: The cost of the insurance protection based upon actuarial tables which are based upon the incidence of death, by age or activity, among given groups of people. This cost is based on the amount at risk under the policy, the insured's risk classification at the time of policy purchase, and the insured's current age or activity.

Multiple employer plans: Benefit plans that serve employees of more than one employer and are set up under terms of a collective agreement.

National Institute of Standards and Technology (NIST): A US Department of Commerce agency that, among other stated responsibilities, promotes effective and secure use of cloud computing within organizations.

Near field communication (NFC): Allows for simplified transactions, data exchange, and wireless connections between devices in close proximity to each other, usually by no more than approximately 10 centimeters. NFC transactions for mobile payments will be transmitted using ISO 14443 A/B standard.

Network: In this book, network refers to a telecommunication infrastructure for data and voice transmittal. In insurance, it is used also with other meanings, for instance to refer to all physicians, specialists, hospitals, and other providers who have agreed to provide medical care to HMO members under the terms of the contract with the HMO. Similarly, it might refer to the car repair shops providing maintenance and paid directly by the insurance companies. Insurance contracts with preferred provider benefits also use networks.

Network software: Network software is the set of specialized programs for the management of communications. Typical examples of network software are the mailers and products management and sharing of distributed resources.

Network virtualization: This form of virtualization is a method for combining the available resources in a network by splitting up the available bandwidth into channels. Each channel is virtually independent of the others. Each one can be assigned (or reassigned) to a particular server or device or organization in real time.

Non blocking failure or malfunction: System "malfunction," but the operation of the system is not substantially compromised and the services for which the system is used can continue to be used.

Non-renewal: A decision by an insurance company not to renew a policy.

Norms: Alternative to the word standards. Norms are normally compulsory while standards are recommendations.

Organization: In this book, this term indicates a private company, a public institution, either central or local, or a nonprofit organization.

Original equipment manufacturer (OEM): Produces the digital products that are used by the user. For the purposes of this document, this role is sometimes used interchangeably with the secure domain manager (SDM).

Output: The result produced by a system or process. The final output is a product or a service.

Over the counter (OTC): It refers to the physical transactions or trades done on behalf of a customer by a trader or customer representative who has access to a specific closed financial system or network.

Over-the-air (OTA): The transmission of data using a wireless network.

Over-the-top content (OTT): Describes broadband delivery of video, data, and audio without a multiple system operator being involved in the control or distribution of the content itself. The provider may be aware of the contents of the IP packets, but is not directly responsible for, nor able to control the viewing abilities, copyrights, and/or other redistribution of the content.

Own funds: Capital, as described under Solvency II. Basic Own Funds (BOF) is the excess of assets over liabilities as determined by the EBS with any qualifying subordinated debt added back. Some forms of off-balance-sheet finance may receive regulatory approval to qualify as Ancillary Own Funds (AOF). Both BOF and AOF are allocated to tiers of

Own Funds depending on prescribed criteria, and the SCR and the MCR both have rules regarding the extent to which the tiers of Own Funds can be used as coverage of these requirements.

Own risk and solvency assessment (ORSA): An assessment of an insurer's processes and procedures used to identify, assess, monitor, manage, and report the short and long-term risks it faces or may face and to determine the own funds necessary to ensure that its overall solvency needs are met at all times.

Pass(word) code: The mobile password code is entered into a device as a user authentication method.

Payment network (or the Payment Application Creator): creates the non-user facing payment application software and manages the payment network (for instance, Visa, MasterCard, CUP, and so on).

Payment service: Provider-independent organizations that develop a payment solution. It could be entrepreneurs, online payments services, or technology organizations.

Pay-per-click (PPC): A method of paying that appears in search engine results by bidding and paying for specific actions. The customer pays at the successful bid rate every time a user/visitor clicks on the link.

PCI DSS compliant: A system or a device complying with the Payment Card Industry data security standards.

Pension products: The insurance products used for saving for retirement, arranged by customers, with the goal to provide income in retirement.

Peril: A specific risk or cause of loss covered by a property insurance policy, such as a fire, windstorm, flood, or theft. A named-peril policy covers the policyholder only for the risks named in the policy. An all-risk policy covers all causes of loss except those specifically excluded.

Personal productivity software: Software used for processing works done by individuals and, more and more, by a community of individuals (for example, WinZip, Adobe, MS Office, MS Project, and so on).

Personal property: All tangible assets such as cars, furniture, jewelry, electronics, and so on.

Phishing: Tricking a victim into disclosing sensitive personal information or downloading malware through an email or a message.

Physical security: A set of processes and activities aimed to achieve confidentiality, integrity, and availability of the assets of the organization through the adoption of measures: "active" (systems that can detect and report an event, stop it, turn on an *ad hoc* intervention, and so on); "passive" (systems which detect, possibly measure, and passively resist to an attack, delaying the possible effects); and "organizational" (set of procedures for prevention and control applied by external personnel-security guards, policemen, and so on).

Plan-do-check-act (PDCA): The improvement cycle introduced by Deming. It is based on the sequence of actions: plan, do, check, and act.

Point-of-service (POS) plans: POS plans allow an HMO to contract with an insurance company to give enrollees the option of receiving services outside the HMO's network.

Policy: The contract issued by the insurance company to the insured.

Policy loan: An advance made by a life insurance company to a policy owner. The advance is secured by the cash value of the policy.

Policy owner: The person or party who owns an individual insurance policy. This person may be the insured, the beneficiary, or another person. The policy owner usually is the one who pays the premium and is the only person who may make variations to a policy.

Policy period: The period in which a policy is in force, from the beginning or effective date to the expiration date.

Portability: Portability is the ability to run applications, components, or systems running on one device or implementation and to deploy it on another device or implementation, for instance, of another vendor.

Pre-certification: A requirement that the health care plan must approve, in advance, certain medical procedures. Pre-certification means the procedure is approved as medically necessary, not yet approved for payment.

Premium: The amount paid by an insured to an insurance company to obtain or maintain an insurance policy.

Primary account number (PAN): Based on 16 digits: a six-digit Issuer Identification Number (IIN), the first digit of which is the Major Industry Identifier (MII); a variable length (up to 12 digits) individual account identifier; and a single check digit.

Problem: Defined as the cause that creates an incident or designates the incident itself. Incidents that cannot be resolved due to the lack of available solutions to the problem, as well as repeated incidents related to a known issue ("known problem/error") are communicated to the process of change management.

Process: A set of interconnected activities that transforms a set of inputs in one or more results with a precise objective. Sometimes a process is identified with a system. In fact, it would be more correct to consider it as a system component.

Process improvement: A continuous effort to learn from the causes and effects in a process, aiming at reducing the complexity, the variations, and the cycle time. It is obtained by improving and eliminating the root causes, and then by redesigning the process in order to reduce the root causes of the most common variations.

Process management: A methodology used to optimize the organization as a system, determine which processes need to be improved and/or controlled, define priorities, and encourage leadership to initiate and sustain process improvement efforts. It manages the information obtained because of these processes.

Process of continuous improvement: A structured approach that improves the overall performance of the organization by using methods appropriate to its problems. Its scope may be the quality or social responsibility of the business.

Property damage (PD): Physical damage to property.

Provider: A hospital, physician, pharmacist, registered nurse, organization, institution, or person licensed to provide health care services. The term provider is often used collectively to refer to individual or facilities who provide products or services.

Prudent person investment principles (PPIP): The PPIP requirements start from the premise that an insurance company should be free to invest in any assets it chooses, provided that it fully understands the risks involved, makes proper provision for these risks (via the SCR), and that investment decisions are made in the best interests of the policy and stake-holders. These requirements will necessitate a change in the way assets are considered, both before acquisition and during the lifetime over which they are held.

Public insurance adjuster: An individual employed by a policyholder to transact a claim with the insurance company receiving a percentage of the claim settlement. Public insurance adjusters must be licensed by the regulatory bodies.

Quality: Customer satisfaction in a way that is profitable for the organization.

Quantitative impact studies (QIS): A series of exercises to test the financial impact and suitability of proposed Solvency II requirements on firms.

Quick response code (QR): The trademark for a type of matrix barcode. It is basically a squared two-dimensional code, of which the main feature is to redirect the user to useful information about a product, an article in a magazine, or an advertisement, or any other information.

Radio frequency identification (RFID): A short-range radio communication methodology that uses "tags" or small integrated circuits connected to an antenna that, when passed within the range of a magnetic reader, is able to send and receive a signal.

Redirecting: Intercepting a communication by substituting a fraudulent address or identity, potentially by using a Man-in-the-Middle attack.

Refund: An amount of money returned to the policyholder for overpayment of premium or if the policyholder is due unearned premium.

Reinstatement: The process by which a life insurance company puts a policy back in force after it has lapsed because of nonpayment of renewal premiums or due to a policy suspension.

Reinsurance: A transaction in which one party, the "reinsurer", in consideration of a premium paid to it, agrees to indemnify another party, the "reinsured", for part or all of the liability assumed by the reinsured under a policy of insurance that it has issued. The reinsured may also be referred to as the "original" or "primary" insurance company or the "ceding company". Reinsurance can be based on treaties or facultative agreements.

Relationship manager (RM) (also denominated account manager): A dedicated customer service manager assigned to look after specific customers, usually high-net-worth customers.

Reliability: How often, or the percentage of time, the service is available.

Remote payments: The opposite of proximity payments, remote payments can be done remotely without requiring a physical contact between the actors in the payment process. It is either done between persons or to a merchant or to an organization over the wireless network or SMS.

Renewal: Continuation of a policy after its expiration date.

Report to supervisors (RTS): A report submitted to the supervisor that contains information considered necessary for the purposes of supervision.

Reporting: The supplying and updating of representative data and indicators whose degree of detail tends to vary depending on the person or organization for whom or for which they are intended. For the purposes of sustainable development, tools such as the GRI (Global Reporting Initiative) enable a standardized methodology to be agreed upon at the international level. In France, Article 225 of the NRE (New Economic Regulations) Law requires that all organizations beyond a certain size publish a Corporate Social Responsibility (or "sustainability") report.

Request for change (RFC): A request to open a change (in infrastructure or applications).

Rescission: The termination of an insurance contract by the insurance company when material misrepresentation has occurred.

Residual risk information: The information risk to which the intermediary is exposed after the application of the mitigation measures identified in the process of risk analysis.

Return premium: A portion of the premium returned to a policyholder as a result of cancellation, rate adjustment, or a calculation that an advance premium was in excess of the actual premium.

Rider: A written agreement attached to the policy expanding or limiting the benefits otherwise payable under the policy. Also called an endorsement or an appendix.

Risk based capital (RBC): An amount of capital based on an assessment of risks that a company should hold to protect customers against adverse developments.

Rule of anticipation: Similar to "Rule of 78" where the amount of unused premium takes into account the fact that more insurance coverage is required in the early months of the loan, since the payoff of the loan is greater. As the loan is paid off, less coverage is being paid for, so the refund percentage decreases.

Search engine optimization (SEO): The method of optimizing websites so that they appear in the top results for search engine inquiries.

Secure domain: A subdivision of the secure element.

Secure domain manager (SDM): Manages access to the secure element. This role is often, but not always, combined with the role of the MNO. In this book, this role is sometimes used interchangeably with MNO.

Secure element: Refers to the embedded secure area or secure area on the universal integrated circuit card (UICC) where encrypted information is stored.

Secure key: A variant of ID-based cryptography that reduces the level of trust that needs to be placed in a trusted third party by spreading the trust across multiple third parties.

Serious incident of security: A security incident that results in at least one of the following consequences: a) high economic losses or prolonged disruption to the insured or user organization, even following repeated minor incidents; b) significant disruption to customers and other stakeholders (for instance, brokers, or payment infrastructures). The assessment of the severity considers the number of customers or counterparties involved and the amount potentially at risk; c) a decline in the financial institution's ability to comply with the conditions and obligations provided by law or regulatory provisions.

Service area: The countries, or portions of countries, where an HMO or a preferred provider organization (PPO) provides coverage.

Service provider: The service provider is an organization such as a financial institution, a telecommunication organization, a merchant, and so on that provides services.

Short message service (SMS): A system of communicating by short messages over the mobile telephone network.

Siri: An application on the iPhone that lets the user use his/her voice to send messages, make calls, set reminders, and more.

Six Sigma: A philosophy and a performance objective. As a method, it is a structured approach to the continuous improvement of processes. The objective is a measure of process performance defined in terms of defects, with 3.4 defective parts per million of opportunities.

Skype: A computer and mobile application allowing web, video, and collective and individual phone chats.

Smartphonatics: People who are fanatics about mobile phones. The term was introduced by Aci and Aite.

SMiShing: A contraction of "SMS phishing." This attack uses SMSs to facilitate bogus requests for personal information.

Software development kit (SDK): It is a package provided by a mainstream software or operating system provider to the developer community to assist them with application building.

Solvency and financial condition report (SFCR): Public disclosure report required to be published annually by insurance companies and will contain detailed quantitative and qualitative elements.

Solvency capital requirement (SCR): The risk-based level of regulatory capital, as defined in Solvency II.

Solvency II: The Solvency II Directive 2009/138/EC is an EU Directive codifying and harmonizing the EU insurance regulations. Primarily

Solvency II intends to address the concerns on the amount of capital that EU insurance companies must hold to reduce the risk of insolvency.

Solvency II internal model: A model that meets Solvency II's requirements of the following six tests: statistical data quality standards, calibration standard, validation test, profit and loss attribution, use test, and documentation standards.

Solvency II pillar 1: The portion of Solvency II focused on all the quantitative capital requirements, which cover market-consistent valuations of assets and liabilities, calculation of available capital, capital requirements, and internal model validation. This pillar aims to ensure insurance companies are adequately capitalized with risk-based capital. All valuations in this pillar are to be done in a prudent and market-consistent manner. Companies may use either the Standard Formula approach or an internal model approach. The use of internal models will be subject to stringent standards and prior supervisory approval to enable a company to calculate its regulatory capital requirements using its own internal model.

Solvency II pillar 2: The qualitative requirements, which cover the principles of internal control, governance, risk management, ORSA process, and supervisory review process. The portion of Solvency II focused on imposing higher standards of risk management and governance within a insurance company's organization. This pillar also gives supervisors greater powers to challenge companies on risk management issues. It includes ORSA, which requires a company to undertake its own forward-looking self-assessment of its risks, corresponding capital requirements, and adequacy of capital resources.

Solvency II pillar 3: Market discipline, which covers disclosure requirements, both private to the supervisors and public to the marketplace. The portion of Solvency II that aims for greater levels of transparency for supervisors and the public. There is a private annual report to supervisors, and a public solvency and financial condition report that increases the level of disclosure required by insurance companies. Any current returns will be completely replaced by reports containing core information that firms will have to make to the regulator on a quarterly and annual basis. This ensures that a company's overall financial position is better represented and includes more up-to-date information.

Solvency modernization initiative (SMI): A US initiative being driven by the National Association of Insurance commissioners (NAIC) to examine and modernize the US insurance solvency regulation framework. It includes a review of international developments regarding insurance supervision, banking supervision, and international accounting standards and their potential use in US insurance regulations.

Spam: Unsolicited bulk email sent out simultaneously to thousands of email addresses to promote products, services, organizations, or individuals.

Spoofing: Sending a network packet that appears to come from a legitimate source, rather than its actual source.

Staff adjuster: Employee of the insurance company's claims department.

Stakeholder: An individual, group, or organization that is an interest or likely to be affected, directly or indirectly, by an activity, a program, or a particular arrangement of an organization. Stakeholders include all those groups that participate or are otherwise involved in its economic life (employees, customers, suppliers, shareholders, and intermediaries), those who observe the organization (unions and nongovernmental organizations), and those that it impacts either directly or indirectly (civil society, local authorities, communities, and so on).

Standard formula: A non-entity-specific, risk-based mathematical formula used by insurance companies to calculate their Solvency Capital Requirement under Solvency II.

Straight-through processing (STP): The implementation of a system that requires no human intervention for the approval or processing of a customer application or transaction.

Supervisory review process (SRP): A process that enables the supervisory authority to continuously evaluate an insurer's relevant regulatory requirements.

Surcharge: An extra charge added to a premium by an insurance company. For motor insurance, a surcharge is usually added if a policyholder has at-fault accidents history.

Surplus lines: Coverage from out-of-state companies not licensed in the state but legally eligible to sell insurance on a "surplus lines" basis. Surplus lines companies generally charge more than licensed companies and often offer less coverage.

Suspension: In some countries, it is possible to suspend for a limited period of time the policy, which becomes valid for the remaining period of time at the expiration date. This is used for instance in the case of motorbikes, whose use during the winter is difficult, and the customer might simply decide to leave them in the garage. It is also used for roulottes or caravans due to their seasonal usage.

System: According to Deming, it is a network of interacting components that cooperate to achieve the defined goals. It can also represent the organization as a set of customers, vendors, a flow of materials, and information.

Tablets: General-purpose computers contained in a single panel, with a touch screen as the input device and, normally, at most one button.

Technical provisions: The amount that an insurance company needs to hold in order to meet its expected future obligations on insurance contracts.

Technical rules: They are compulsory indications for technical standardization or compliance.

Telematics: It is a synergy of telecommunications and informatics. In this book, it is synonymous with ICT.

Third-party claim: A claim filed against another person's insurance policy.

Throughput: How quickly the service responds do to its processing demand.

Token: A cryptographic value provided by a card issuer as proof that a delegated management operation has been authorized. It is also designated as a one-time password (OTP).

Total cost of ownership (TCO): A metric that takes into account the costs all along the life cycle of the solution it refers. Typically, it includes procurement costs, installation, testing, maintenance, use, and disposal at the end of the useful life.

Touch point: Any channel or mechanism by which a customer has day-to-day interaction with a service organization, such as an insurance company, in order to transact or conduct actions.

Transaction: The action of executing a function or an application. An example of a transaction is the execution of the issuing of a proposal, a quotation, or a policy.

Transport layer security (TLS): A cryptographic protocol that is designed to provide communication security over the network. Its predecessor was Secure Sockets Layer (SSL).

Treaty: In this book, an agreement between an insurance company and a reinsurance company stating the types or classes of businesses that the reinsurance company will accept from the insurer for a period and the coverages agreed between the parties.

Trust: The ability for two parties or networks to define a trust relationship with a formal authentication of the two parties or networks.

Trusted service manager (TSM) (or Payment Application or Payment Credential Loader): A neutral broker facilitating the connection between the handset manufacturer, the MNO, the user, and the payment service provider (PSP). It controls the secure element in the phone and identifies the user and financial institution when the transaction is performed.

Twitter: A social media website that supports limited character blogging between participants in the network, sort of like an SMS broadcast system for the Web.

Underwriter: The person who reviews an application for insurance and decides if the applicant is acceptable and at what premium rate.

Underwriting: The process an insurance company uses to decide whether to accept or reject an application for a policy and the premium rate.

Unearned premium: The amount of a pre-paid premium that has not yet been used to buy coverage. For instance, if a policyholder paid in advance for a twelve-month premium, but then canceled the policy after two months, the company must refund the remaining ten months of "unearned" premium.

Universal life insurance: The key characteristic of universal life insurance is flexibility. Within limits, a policyholder can choose the amount of insurance and the premium they intend to pay. The policy will stay in force as long as the policy value is sufficient to pay the costs and expenses of the policy. The policy value can be "interest-sensitive." This means that it varies in accordance with the general financial climate. Lowering the benefits connected with a death and raising the premium will increase the growth rate of the customer policy. The opposite also is true. Raising the benefit connected with death and lowering the premium will slow the growth rate of the customer policy. If insufficient premiums are paid, the policy could lapse without value before the maturity date is reached. (The maturity date is the time the customer policy ceases and cash surrender value would be payable if the policyholder is still living.) Therefore, it is the policyholder's responsibility to consistently pay a premium that is high enough to ensure that the policy's value will be adequate to cover the monthly cost of the policy. The insurance company is required to send an annual report and also to notify the policyholder if they are in danger of losing their policy due to insufficient value.

Universal product code (UPC): The standard used to name products in a unique way.

Up-selling: A system of selling an additional service of a higher margin or total revenue within the same product or asset class to a customer, typically upgrading from one class of product to another.

Usability testing (UT): The science of testing how users interact with a system, product, or interface through observation.

User experience (UX): Encompasses all aspects of the end-user's interaction with the company, its services, its products, its processes, its organizations, and its persons.

Value: Defined by the end customer. Conceptually, it is the relationship between benefits and cost/damage of a product or service. It is expressed in terms of a product/service that can meet the customer demands at a given price and at a given moment. It is also possible to refer to value as perceived by the customer, and see all the product/service characteristics that the customer considers as necessary and valuable. Any activity that consumes resources (including time) and does not bring value to the customer or to the organization is waste (*Muda*, in Japanese).

Variable annuity: A form of annuity policy under which the amount of each benefit payment is not guaranteed and specified in the policy, but which instead fluctuates according to the earnings of a separate account fund.

Variable life insurance: A type of whole life policy in which the benefits connected with a death and the cash value fluctuate according to the investment performance of a separate account fund that the policyholder selects. The Securities and Exchange Commission, might regulate the portion of the premium paid to the intermediary and possibly to its employees by the intermediary. A variation of variable life insurance is the unit-linked policies.

Vendor: A person or organization that provides goods or services for use in a process, such as in the case of public clouds. In the case of the private cloud, the "vendor" is normally part of the organization.

Video chat: From the English word "chat," meaning to converse or discuss informally. It is a web technology facilitating long-distance discussions in real time, combining video, sound, and text.

Virtual support center (VSC): It is a call center virtually supported by customer service representatives who typically operate from home (doing home-sourcing) or distinct locations.

Vishing: A contraction of "voice and phishing," in which victims are tricked into disclosing sensitive personal information through a phone call.

Vision: An expression of what would represent success for the organization. The objective is to produce a mental image to aim at generating creative tensions between the current reality and the vision in the organization. In order to be valuable it must be shared by the whole organization. The mission is the way to proceed toward the vision.

Voice of the customer (VoC): The requirements or needs as expressed by the customer. It is called voice of the citizen, in the case of public organizations.

Voice over Internet protocol (VoIP): An Internet-based protocol that allows users to use voice communication, such as over a telephone system.

Web 2.0: The Web applications that facilitate interactive information sharing, interoperability, user-centered design, and collaboration on the World Wide Web.

Widget: A generic type of software application that is usually portable and works across different operating systems and devices.

Wireless access protocol (WAP): The original protocol for simple Internet browsing or a simple menu interaction via mobile phones.

Notes

These definitions are synthetic; therefore, they will not be necessarily precise. Please consult the text for a more complete presentation of the terms. Only some terms have been explained, according to the eventual need to find a quick reference during the reading of this book. The conceptual sources of most of the definitions are websites with definitions of insurance or Information systems terms, to which we refer for more detail, such as:

http://www.ict4lt.org/en/en_glossary.htm
http://www.irmi.com/online/insurance-glossary/terms
http://www.opm.gov/healthcare-insurance/insurance-glossary/
http://www.tdi.texas.gov/consumer/glossary.html
https://en.wikipedia.org/wiki/Main_Page

Index

GPSR Compliance
The European Union's (EU) General Product Safety Regulation (GPSR) is a set of rules that requires consumer products to be safe and our obligations to ensure this.

If you have any concerns about our products, you can contact us on

ProductSafety@springernature.com

In case Publisher is established outside the EU, the EU authorized representative is:

Springer Nature Customer Service Center GmbH
Europaplatz 3
69115 Heidelberg, Germany

www.ingramcontent.com/pod-product-compliance
Lightning Source LLC
Chambersburg PA
CBHW071917171225
36953CB00004B/210
* 9 7 8 1 1 3 7 5 5 3 2 6 3 *